GENDERED

COMPROMISES

KARIN ALEJANDRA ROSEMBLATT

GENDERED

COMPROMISES

Political

Cultures

& the State

in Chile,

1920-1950

THE UNIVERSITY OF NORTH CAROLINA PRESS

CHAPEL HILL AND LONDON

Designed by Heidi Perov
Set in Joanna
by Keystone Typesetting, Inc.

The paper in this book meets the guidelines for permanence and
durability of the Committee on Production Guidelines for Book
Longevity of the Council on Library Resources.

Library of Congress Cataloging-in-Publication Data
Rosemblatt, Karin Alejandra.
    Gendered compromises : political cultures and the state in Chile,
1920–1950 / Karin Alejandra Rosemblatt.
        p. cm.
    Includes bibliographical references and index.
    ISBN 0-8078-2567-0 (cloth: alk. paper)—
    ISBN 0-8078-4881-6 (pbk.: alk. paper)
    1. Sex role—Political aspects—Chile—History—20th century.
2. Chile—Politics and government—1920–1970.   I. Title.
HQ1075.5.C5 R67   2000
305.3'0983—dc21   00-039249

04 03 02 01 00   5 4 3 2 1

Portions of this work appear in somewhat different form in
Karin Alejandra Rosemblatt, "Domesticating Men: State Building
and Class Compromise in Popular-Front Chile," in Hidden
Histories of Gender and the State in Latin America,
edited by Elizabeth Dore and Maxine Molyneux (Durham, N.C.:
Duke University Press, 2000), 262–90.

Para Lucy y Mario

CONTENTS

ILLUSTRATIONS

PREFACE

During a July 1999 trip to Chile, I contacted some of the activist women I had interviewed for this book in 1993 and 1994. I wanted to show them what I had made of the stories they had told me. I worried: Would they remember me? Would they disagree with what I had written? Would they be bothered by the more personal information I had chosen to include? Thankfully, they welcomed me, and, displaying the subversive edge I remembered, they reaffirmed even controversial disclosures regarding birth control, sexuality, and lesbianism.

These extraordinarily unconventional women, who had all been active in political or professional circles during the popular-front years of the 1930s and 1940s, nevertheless reminded me that their stories were and are very much their own, and that this book is very much mine. It was not that I had gotten anything wrong. Several smiled to themselves as I read back to them expressions and stories that were undoubtedly and idiosyncratically theirs. I have used those stories here to weave an account of feminist, socialist, and labor politics in the construction of the popular-front state, but for them the tales have different and more personal meanings. As I read to them what I had written, they added details, retold the old anecdotes, and remembered new ones. My account has not silenced theirs.

In some cases, we disagreed. Tomy Romeo practiced the constructive criticism she had learned as a feminist activist. She hoped, she said glancing at the overstuffed box that held my manuscript, that my book would not be too long or overly detailed. And she trusted that I would not burden the text with too many of those useless, hard-to-read endnotes. I knew I would disappoint.

Elena Varela, the social worker whose story begins this book, had a deeper difference of opinion. My insistence that intellectual practices were intricately related to politics was not only misguided, she told me, but politically dangerous. The dedication of professionals like herself to the poor and to enhanced state services was, she maintained, simply humanitarian, based on technical considerations and not on politics. To portray it as linked to the Left was to bias people against it unnecessarily. I tried to convince her otherwise.

If professional practices had been so divorced from politics, I pointed out, the military and the Right would not have been so insistent on destroying state services and the universities when they took power in 1973. An hour later, Varela and I still disagreed about the meaning of the professional vocation that I had studied and she had lived. This book provides my version. There are others.

This book is mine in other ways as well: it is at least in part the attempt of a *chilena* who grew up in the United States to understand something more about what it means to be Chilean. Hence the book's focus on national identity. My questions are also an attempt to understand my participation in both the Chilean Left and Chilean feminism. For someone who grew up in the horrific aftermath of Salvador Allende's Popular Unity and among so many political refugees, it is, perhaps, inevitable that socialism was and continues to be a point of reference, a ground. The anger of the post-1973 years have fueled this work. The Chilean feminist movement provided a home, a *challenging* home, during the years I spent in Chile, first in 1987–88 and then in 1991–94. My participation in that movement allowed me to experience firsthand the difficulties of cross-class organizing among women. It also gave me a deep sense of the enduring strains between feminism and the Left and of the complex forces that still neutralize feminism's more radical demands.

In the years it has taken me to research and write this book, I have benefited from the help of numerous collaborators and co-conspirators who have shaped my views of intellectual life, political activism, and family. The men and women I interviewed in preparing this work provided not only crucial information and viewpoints but, more importantly, inspiration. I am grateful to them for the time they spent with me and, even more, for their rich, defiant lives. Friends, family, and colleagues in Chile have given me a lasting attachment to the place and remind me of the relevance of my work. For their intellectual guidance and companionship, I would like to thank Alicia Frohman, Lorena Godoy, Tomás Moulian, Julio Pinto, Isabel Torres, and Soledad Zárate. For their long-lasting friendship and complicity, Sabrina Beltrán, Isabel Cárcarmo, Mónica Gajardo, Lilian Letelier, Lorena Núñez, Verónica Oxman, Loreto Palacios, and Carola Perales. And for always making me feel welcome and providing me a warm place to stay on my numerous trips to Chile, my Chilean family: María Rosa Bono, Rebecca Katz, Natalia Mehta, Jorge Parada, Isabel Rosemblatt, Mariana Rosemblatt, Oscar Rosemblatt, María Silber, and Albertina Valderrama. I am saddened that Oscar

Rosemblatt did not live to see this book and that Rebecca Katz is unable to appreciate it.

My intellectual debt to my teachers at the University of Wisconsin-Madison is, I think, obvious. What may be less apparent is their dedication. Florencia Mallon, Francisco Scarano, and Steve J. Stern not only read and provided detailed comments on what was an excruciatingly long dissertation but also took the time to read versions of this book and provide encouragement. Florencia has also been a careful mentor and a good friend. I would never have gotten to the University of Wisconsin had it not been for Marysa Navarro and Leo Spitzer, who interested me in history while I was still an undergraduate.

For me, the best part of being an academic has been the friendships I have made along the way. At the University of Wisconsin and since, I have shared intellectual excitement, politics, and good times with Nancy Appelbaum, Sarah Chambers, Deb Coltey, Blenda Femenías, Eileen Findlay, Roger Kittleson, Patrick McNamara, Anne Macpherson, Seemin Qayum, René Reeves, Sinclair Thomson, and Susan Traverso. I have also had the luck of working with a smart and affable bunch of Chileanists, including Lisa Baldez, Patrick Barrett, Liz Hutchison, Margaret Power, and Heidi Tinsman. Corinne Pernet and I have had so many conservations about Chilean feminism that it has often been hard to tell where her ideas end and mine begin. Tom Klubock's incisive and compelling work on Chilean labor has profoundly influenced this work. Corinne and Tom have both been models of generosity. Pablo Silva amiably and competently answered my pesky questions regarding the Chilean middle class. Marisol de la Cadena helped me understand the dynamics of race.

Many readers have helped me improve this book, and I hope they will recognize where they shaped my thinking. I undoubtedly cast aside their incisive and helpful suggestions too often. Thanks to Linda Alcoff, Arlene Dávila, Katherine Masur, Deborah Pellow, Brian Selmeski, and Caroline Tauxe. The readers for the University of North Carolina Press, Ana María Alonso, Barbara Weinstein, and Peter Winn, all made generous and important comments.

For their friendship and for helping me bring balance to my life, I would like to acknowledge Eugenia Breiva, Rosalyn Burns, David Cole, José Iribarne, Norman Kutcher, Chris Lach, Frederick Douglass Opie, Margaret Pappano, and Richard Wallach. Brian, Lisa, and Steve Beutler made escaping the winters of Madison and Syracuse even more enjoyable. My parents, Lucy Klecky and Mario Rosemblatt, each graced my life in unique and necessary ways. Truly, without them, this book would never have been written.

Gracias. Héctor Parada made sacrifices great and small that improved my life and this book immeasurably. He washed my clothes and dishes, read my chapters, drew up my tables on workforce participation, and left the city that had been his home for over thirty years. Above all, he shared his smartness, humor, and overwhelming *simpatía*.

Finally, but not least of all, a host of people and institutions contributed crucial logistical support. Carola Ramírez and Andrea Valdivia cheerfully helped with the more tedious aspects of research; Quena Lorenzini and Hugo Castillo provided expert photography; the staff at the Biblioteca Nacional in Santiago made my long days of research fruitful; and the staff of the History Department at Syracuse University rescued me from seemingly endless details. The research on which this book is based was funded by a Fulbright Grant, Syracuse University, and the University of Wisconsin-Madison. At the other end of the process leading up to this book, Elaine Maisner, Mary Caviness, and the staff at UNC Press contributed much-appreciated thoughtfulness, enthusiasm, and expertise.

ABBREVIATIONS

AMS	Acción de Mujeres Socialistas (Socialist Women's Action)
CDN	Consejo de Defensa del Niño (Children's Defense Council)
CORFO	Corporación de Reconstrucción y Fomento (Reconstruction and Development Corporation)
CSO	Caja de Seguro Obligatorio (Obligatory Insurance Fund)
CTCh	Confederación de Trabajadores de Chile (Confederation of Chilean Workers)
DGAS	Dirección General de Auxilio Social (General Direction of Social Assistance)
FEChIF	Federación Chilena de Instituciones Femeninas (Federation of Chilean Women's Institutions)
FJS	Federación de la Juventud Socialista (Socialist Youth Federation)
FOCh	Federación Obrera de Chile (Chilean Federation of Workers)
MEMCh	Movimiento pro Emancipación de la Mujer Chilena (Movement for the Emancipation of Chilean Women)
POS	Partido Obrero Socialista (Socialist Workers' Party)
SNS	Servicio Nacional de Salud (National Health Service)

GENDERED

COMPROMISES

INTRODUCTION

Elena Varela grew up poor in one of Santiago's typically cramped tenements in the 1930s. From her neighbors, she learned at a young age the tribulations of poverty: through the thin cité walls and in its shared corridor she heard of the boy forced to leave school to help feed his family, of the daily humiliations of illiteracy, of the difficulties of finding a job, and of the shame of illegitimate pregnancy. Varela found the lesson of male brutality and female vulnerability particularly difficult to assimilate. It was a harrowing but inescapable reality. Weekly, Varela witnessed a drunken neighbor, knife in hand, pursue his wife down the cité walkway.[1]

When I interviewed Varela in 1993, she attempted to convey to me her understanding of poverty by telling me about her neighbor's victimization. Yet she also spoke to me about her mother, Emilia Morales, a woman who fought back and helped others fight back. With more education than her neighbors and a more stable economic position, Morales acted as a sort of indigenous social worker, marshaling the increased resources at her disposal to help her neighbors. She assured the sustenance of her battered neighbor by making sure the woman's eldest boy, one of seven children, received the kind of education that would allow him to eventually support his mother.

Seeking to continue the kind of class uplift her mother practiced, Varela entered the Alejandro del Río School of Social Work around 1946. There, Varela soon came to the disappointing realization that prevalent social work practices differed in important ways from the type of assistance provided by Morales. Because professional social workers used casework methods that individualized and pathologized the poor, they often failed to view poverty as a collective problem rooted in class dynamics. Unlike Morales, who was more socially similar to those she helped, social workers were mostly condescending upper-class women. In fact, over the years school officials had preserved this hierarchy by visiting applicants' homes and denying entrance to candidates from purportedly disreputable, impoverished families. The democratizing impulse of the popular-front period (approximately 1936–48),[2] which led to the end of this practice in social work schools, had reached the Alejandro del Río School only a year before Varela applied.

Thanks to that reform, Varela was able to study social work and acquire the professional credentials that would help her help others.

At her first job, at a public hospital for tuberculosis patients, Varela's view of poverty evolved as she came into contact with clients and progressive professionals who forced her to question further the microsocial explanations for people's misfortunes she had learned in social work school. Subsequently, she no longer thought, "What can I do for this poor woman who is here weeping because . . . her husband hit her?" Rather, she began to see these "personal" problems in a broader social context. Organizing the poor became more important than uplifting individuals, and the increased legitimacy of popular organizing that had followed the coming to power of Center-Left, reformist popular-front governments only reinforced that conviction. At the same time, as popular organizations insistently sought to democratize and reform public health, Varela practiced more horizontal relations with her clients. Still, her professional training and her position within the public health system inclined her to hierarchical and disciplinary practices. In the end and despite her best intentions, Varela restrained her clients even as she enabled them.

Elena Varela felt a personal as well as professional commitment to the poor. Although she never belonged formally to any of the political parties of the Left, she identified herself as "progressive," an advocate for social change, and she spent many weekends doing volunteer work in shantytowns and poor barrios. The search for justice, for material well-being, for education, and for belonging permeated her life and contributed to her activism. As she became an advocate for the poor, Varela drew on her sense of solidarity and her analysis of social problems—her upbringing, her professional training, and her experiences working within the public health bureaucracy. In turn, her family, her professional life, and her understanding of what it meant to be a Chilean—indeed her entire history—were filtered through her sense of social commitment. Having come of age during the popular-front period, the historical changes that took place beginning around 1936 were also central to Varela's personal and political options.

When in 1993 I asked Varela to share the story of her past with me, she prefaced her remarks by telling me that she appreciated the value of history. Given Varela's awareness of the importance of narrating the past, it was significant that she granted the tale of her battered and cowed neighbor a prominent place in her account of her impoverished upbringing. "[T]hat poor woman," Varela recalled of her neighbor, "could not have done anything alone." It was also significant that Varela returned to the figure of the battered woman in describing her practices as a professional. For Varela, however, the figure of the weak, battered woman did not represent all poor Chileans, or even all destitute women. Neither Varela herself nor her mother was defenseless, and while the assistance of Morales apparently did not rouse Varela's neighbor to action, it did provide the helpless woman's son with tools for improvement. The resourceful boy, Varela recalled, seized the opportunity provided by Morales's intervention and propelled himself into the university. The tragedy of victimization, an inescapable reality for the battered woman, was a call to arms for Morales, for Varela, and for the woman's son.

GENDER, CLASS, AND THE POPULAR FRONTS

In this book I explain why Varela recalled her battered and impoverished neighbor in responding to my questions about her professional involvement in the state and her commitment to the poor. How, I ask, did popular-front supporters—many of whom like Varela had attained a relative degree of clout—constrain and empower subalterns by using gendered terms to represent, politically and symbolically, people like Varela's neighbor? How did gender, as both a set of power-laden distinctions between women and men and a way of signifying power as sexual difference,[3] mold the power of professionals like Varela and of political activists? And when and why did women like Varela's neighbor accept, reject, or reformulate the gendered representations of others? More broadly, how did gender shape the substantial reforms enacted in Chile during the 1930s and 1940s, when popular-front coalitions controlled the government? By answering these questions, I show how gender constructed the personal and political agency of both popular classes and professional and political elites. I also demonstrate how gender conditioned the Chilean popular-front state of that era, setting it apart from both the oligarchic state that preceded it and the more authoritarian national-popular states that existed elsewhere in Latin America.

During the 1930s and 1940s, national industry and modern, rationalized forms of state power flourished in Chile. As health, welfare, social security, and labor agencies were created and enlarged, an expanding corps of state-employed experts, whom I call "welfare professionals," concentrated on educating and disciplining the poor. Those experts sought to make working-class Chileans respectable, instilling in them the value of cleanliness, temperance, hard work, sexual restraint, and, above all, love of family. This was a gendered project: elites would make men into reliable breadwinners who produced wealth and supported their families, and women into diligent housewives and mothers who bore and raised the nation's "human capital." Honorable workers and wives, they argued, would ensure the demographic health of the nation, enhance industrial productivity, and secure national progress.

Unlike the more conservative elites who had held sway previously, the professionals and politicians who came to power in the 1930s increasingly deemed exclusionary and violent forms of dealing with popular classes ineffectual. They instead sought the cooperation of individuals and of popular, leftist, and feminist organizations. The resulting patterns of alliance and conflict between elites and their presumed subordinates, detailed in this work, granted the latter important venues of influence. Though elites ran state agencies and directly determined state policies, those policies were also shaped by diverse subaltern political actors who alternately rejected, appropriated, and transformed the gendered discourses of progress, development, nationality, and citizenship developed by welfare professionals and politicians.

Beginning in 1936, the Chilean Center and Left came together in what I call the "popular fronts," political alliances that elicited significant popular support, and, by routing the Right in presidential contests, came to control the executive branch of the state. Constituted by the Radical, Socialist, and Communist Parties, the first popular-front coalition won the presidential election in 1938, promising to democratize Chile politically and modernize it economically. Making similar pledges, succeeding Center-Left combinations sporadically presented joint lists of candidates in congressional elections and triumphed in presidential contests in 1942 and 1946. Strictly speaking, then, the popular fronts were electoral coalitions of political parties. However, they were also ministerial alliances that forged and implemented state policies. And they were social movements that formally and informally incorporated labor, feminist, and neighborhood organizations.

The popular fronts brought together middle-class reformers and vast sectors of the laboring classes under the leadership of the former. As Chapter 1 explains, the patent inability of the Chilean oligarchy to solve the country's "social question" in the first decades of the century encouraged the rise to power of middle-class reformers. Especially after 1920, university-trained professionals, most of whom came from the middle class, dominated elected offices and the leadership of political parties across the political spectrum.[4] This new cadre of professionals was imbued with a concern for the well-being of the poor. In fact, even the most conservative professional elites manifested a reformist zeal. The more progressive ones saw the working class as a natural ally. Moreover, as part of a broader middle class with long-standing organizational ties to popular groups, these middle-class professionals generally shared with the working class not only a strong nationalist sentiment but also an aversion to an oligarchy they all viewed as ineffectual and antinational. Professionals, like other members of the middle class, saw themselves as superior to the popular classes in culture (if not always in wealth). But many, especially those who were more progressive, rejected paternalism and envisioned their attempts to help the poor as solidarity. The emergence into the middle class of people who, like Elena Varela, came from working-class backgrounds, only facilitated that sense of solidarity.[5]

Scholars have long studied the novel class alliances and economic transformations that characterized Chile in the 1930s and 1940s. They have not generally recognized the importance of gender.[6] According to standard scholarly accounts, the popular fronts were crucial to the installation of the Chilean "compromise state"—a form of political bargaining in which organized popular sectors and political and economic elites respected existing democratic institutions and used them to negotiate an unevenly accepted balance between economic growth and redistribution. Throughout the popular-front period (and until the military coup of 1973), the adherence of economic elites to this political bargain wavered as popular classes pressured for democratization, including economic benefits and political influence. Yet the widely held belief that national economic and political prosperity depended on a controlled incorporation of popular sectors strengthened compromise. The acceptance of the Left into mainstream politics helped ensure more restrained forms of popular influence.[7]

Along with many left-wing activists, most scholars have been disappointed by the popular fronts. According to these analysts, the wages of the middle class rose much more quickly than those of the working class during the popular-front period, and the distribution of national wealth became more regressive. Electoral restrictions continued to limit popular enfranchisement. Perhaps most important, the relation of the labor movement to the Left and the Left's engagement in political bargaining diminished the autonomy and strength of workers. As the labor movement came within the Left's sphere of influence, it had to forego strike action in favor of political lobbying. The Left, in turn, was corrupted by power and hemmed in by the more moderate Radical Party. As a result, it did not do enough to satisfy popular demands or increase popular participation.[8]

In this book, I accept the notion that popular-front politics implied trade-offs for popular classes but argue that scholars' criticisms of the popular fronts, as well as their exclusive focus on class relations, are at best incomplete and at worst misguided. To begin, past interpretations have underplayed popular classes' enthusiastic support for the popular fronts. True, the vast majority of working-class adults did not or could not vote during this period. No more than 52 percent of literate men over the age of twenty-one exercised their right to vote (see table A.1), and neither women nor illiterates could cast ballots.[9] The popular fronts did little to expand suffrage: women did not win the vote in national elections until 1949, illiterates until 1970. Popular-front presidential and congressional candidates nevertheless did especially well in areas where the organized working class was strong, areas such as Tarapacá, Antofagasta, Concepción, Arauco, and Magallanes provinces (see table A.2). In addition, many working-class men and women who could not vote for the popular fronts marched and agitated in their favor. Fifty-eight grassroots committees of the Movimiento pro Emancipación de la Mujer Chilena (MEMCh, Movement for the Emancipation of Chilean Women), a cross-class feminist organization, worked for the election of Pedro Aguirre Cerda to the presidency in 1938. In the 1946 presidential contest, MEMCh members campaigned for Gabriel González Videla. This kind of support for the popular fronts, which ebbed and flowed through the decade but was still evident as late as 1947, should not, as has been common in the past, be ignored.[10]

Nor should scholars overlook the significant material and political advantages popular classes did obtain during the popular-front period. For instance, the scholarly claim that blue-collar workers did not reap significant economic benefit may well be false, at least for a politically powerful sector of the popular classes. According to the best figures available, the real wages of formal-sector workers in manufacturing rose 65 percent between 1937 and 1949.[11] Moreover, popular-front officials supported legislative proposals for minimum wages, family allowances, and enhanced social security and maternity benefits. (Only the opposition of the Right precluded the passage of these measures in Congress.) Although these reforms would have primarily benefited formal-sector workers, who were indeed the main beneficiaries of the popular fronts, they would also have extended some benefits to other working-class Chileans.

Politically as well, popular groups may have lost out less than many scholars imply. In fact, groups that had been marginal gained indirect and direct access to spheres of political decision making and the state, without losing complete autonomy. The Confederación de Trabajadores de Chile (CTCh, Confederation of Chilean Workers), which grouped together the vast majority of the country's unions, was represented on the popular-front national and Santiago governing boards in 1938. In that same year, members of the popular-front women's campaign committee sat on the coalition's provincial executive committee in Santiago. In 1946, women's movement activists participated in the drafting of Gabriel González Videla's presidential platform.[12] Popular organizations also gained direct forms of representation within the state. CTCh leaders, for example, sat on the boards of Chile's main social security agency, the Caja de Seguro Obligatorio (CSO, Obligatory Insurance Fund), and of the Corporación de Reconstrucción y Fomento (CORFO, Reconstruction and Development Corporation), the motor of state-led industrialization. To a degree, the government also rewarded leaders of the women's movement with government posts, both paid and advisory.[13] Leftists, for their part, increasingly won national and local elections and were elected congressional and municipal representatives. Socialists, and to a lesser extent Communists, served as ministers, as governors and intendants, as heads of government services, and as labor and sanitary inspectors as well as in more menial secretarial and administrative posts. This allowed the Left to represent popular groups within state apparatuses, to mediate between dominant classes and popular sectors, and to offer patronage and brokerage. Popular groups saw leftist officials and labor representatives as particularly sympathetic to their demands and applauded the Left's expanding influence.[14]

As most scholars have recognized, the close relation of popular and feminist organizations to both socialist and popular-front leaders undoubtedly redefined popular demands and quelled popular protest. Yet it did not, as standard accounts imply, fully stifle militancy or lead to the co-optation of working-class organizations. In fact, working-class Chileans generally manifested a decidedly defiant allegiance to the popular-front coalitions. On the eve of the 1941 parliamentary elections, for instance, a young factory worker named Josefina Morales urged her comrades to struggle "so that the P.F. candidates are elected so that the Government can no longer claim that it has

not fulfilled the program because it does not have a majority in Congress."
More generally, working-class organizations grew and maintained their autonomy as the popular fronts balked at repressing popular mobilizations.
Labor organizing and work stoppages mushroomed in the years before 1947
(see table A.3). Women took to the streets to demand the vote.[15]

For popular classes the most promising moment of the popular-front era
was the period just following Aguirre Cerda's election in 1938. The most difficult moment came after 1947, when González Videla began to repress the
Communist Party and working-class activists. Yet the popular-front coalitions
did not, as standard interpretations might lead us to believe, simply co-opt
popular groups in the intervening years. In 1942–43, Communists and Radicals, along with a sector of the Socialist Party, united in the Alianza Democrática, a political alliance that spawned vibrant grassroots committees in certain
localities. Again in 1946–47, popular organizing around the popular-front
strategy rebounded as Communists and their supporters campaigned in-
tensely for González Videla. Through a Communist presence in the president's first cabinet, his leftist supporters intended to secure implementation
of those aspects of González Videla's platform that favored popular sectors.
Around the same time, labor's perception that there was a new opening for
workers encouraged a wave of major strikes that echoed the earlier labor
agitation that had accompanied Aguirre Cerda's victory.[16] When President
Gabriel González Videla ended the popular-front experience in 1947–49,
outlawing the Communist Party and repressing labor unions, he did so not
because popular and leftist organizations were quiescent and co-opted but
because they retained a bothersome combativeness and independence.

Although scholars have often overlooked this fact, the continued vitality of
popular organizations was largely due to the embattled nature of popular-
front political elites, which forced leaders to seek popular support and make
concessions. To cement their authority, the popular fronts relied on physical
force (and its correlate, fear) and economic inducements and penalties—
especially those dispensed through labor, medical, and social security agencies. Popular-front rule was irreducibly coercive: the coalitions inevitably
suppressed alternatives as they sought to secure their own position. Yet the
popular fronts were not united and powerful enough to fully command
either the economy or the state and its repressive mechanisms. Indeed they
depended on the ballot and lacked control of the military. They controlled the
executive branch but not Congress or the courts. They were often taunted, if
not besieged, by the Right. Furthermore, there was widespread contention

within the coalitions about policies and their implementation. As a result, state institutions were created, reorganized, and dissolved. State officials were hired, appointed, and fired. Agencies battled one another; state employees fought their coworkers; bureaucrats and their bosses quarreled. Party leaders objected to the actions of their elected officials. Given these widespread conflicts, which divided and weakened the popular fronts, the coalitions themselves—and each of the political parties that made up the coalitions— amassed power in the only way they could: by seeking popular support through dialogue, argument, incentive, and negotiation as well as by the continual (re)creation of unifying national myths.

Finally, and this is a crucial oversight of past studies of the popular-front era, the conflict and agreement that characterized the 1930s and 1940s involved not only male workers, the labor movement, and capitalists but also unorganized men, housewives, and women workers. More important, they were about gender as well as class. Of course gender was not the only or always the most important arena of dispute and alliance in popular-front Chile. Chileans often argued about issues unrelated to gender. Yet, as I show in this book, even negotiations that have not commonly been seen as gendered—such as discussions surrounding the political regime, industrialization, or economic development—often had a gendered component. Many Chileans believed, for instance, that political and economic changes could transform gender relations and that changes in gender relations could influence political and economic arrangements. In addition, gender often became emblematic of broader transformations, as family and sexuality framed Chileans' apprehensions of social order and social change.

Not surprisingly, then, the Chilean Right linked the popular fronts' economic failures to the coalitions' purported dissipation and belief in free love. The popular fronts responded by insisting that they would not undermine the nuclear, male-headed family. By putting in place policies that encouraged marriage, however, the popular fronts not only sought to assuage the Right. They also attempted to win the backing of those organized working-class men and women who saw the family as a mainstay of working-class solidarity and of opposition to capitalist exploitation. Organized working-class men, for their part, argued that as breadwinners and household heads they deserved increased rights as citizens. Many working-class housewives who accepted central tenets of the popular fronts' gender ideology nonetheless contested their husbands' authority within the family. Feminists in turn rejected a normative feminine identity that limited women's possibilities outside the home. Ultimately, popular-front politics was shaped by these complex, and decidedly gendered, negotiations among diverse groups.

MODERNITY AND ITS CRITICS

This book thus argues that the focus on labor and capital that has characterized past accounts of the compromise state cannot fully explain the multilayered struggles that took place in popular-front Chile. Nor, as I suggest below, can recent postcolonial and feminist theories that fail to consider conflict *within* as well as among elite and nonelite groups. This book thus questions not only past interpretations of Chile's compromise state but also social theories that present engagement between subalterns and elites, on the one hand, and subaltern autonomy, on the other, as antithetical. Much of this scholarship provides useful critiques of nationalism, the state, racism, disciplinary knowledge, and the construction of differences. I draw on these postcolonial and feminist critiques to show how elites have used purportedly universal norms to assert their power. But I also move beyond much of this literature by developing a view of political struggle as a process of mutual transformation based on alliance *and* antagonism between elites and subalterns. In so doing, I draw inspiration from a nuanced "postrevisionist" historical scholarship on elite/subaltern interactions in Latin America, which I discuss in the conclusion to this book.

In the past decade, scholars influenced by multiculturalism, poststructuralism, and gender theory have developed broad-ranging critiques of western, post-Enlightenment ideals and capitalist modernization. Their critiques have developed along several different axes: scholars have alternately objected to the epistemological privilege attributed to the modern humanist subject, the Eurocentric or masculinist nature of post-Enlightenment universals, the overpowering presence of the nation-state, the racist underpinnings of evolutionary thought and modernization schemes, the disciplinary power of professional experts, the colonial underpinnings of Europe's modernity, and the labeling of third world "others" as backward. Following Foucault, many authors have stressed the relation between power and ways of knowing and criticized the utterly self-assured, foundational claims of modern forms of knowledge and politics. Some authors have examined how modern regimes of power reinforce and reify difference and hierarchy by casting diverse groups as "others." Other authors have shown how elites have used differences to separate citizens from noncitizens.[17]

Feminists in particular have probed the political exclusion of women in western, liberal democracies. Historically, they have argued, liberal political thinkers and politicians disenfranchised women by encoding as masculine the qualities thought to be essential to the exercise of citizenship: rationality, autonomy, and individuality. Male elites also based entitlement to state services as well as suffrage rights on activities identified as male, such as soldiering and paid labor. The propagation of scientific truths deepened women's subordination by equating sex and gender, reifying dichotomous categories based on sex, and naturalizing sexual difference. In this context, feminist opposition to male dominance was trapped in what Carole Pateman has called "Wollstonecraft's dilemma": women either insisted on their specificity as women, an option that confirmed both their distinct identity and their political exclusion, or they claimed the right to a presumably universal but essentially masculine citizenship. Either they stressed difference, rejecting hegemonic norms of citizenship, or they accepted those purportedly universal norms.[18]

Postcolonial scholarship concerned with nationalism and the legacies of colonialism has presented a vision of power and popular contestation that is similar to that of feminist scholars in its questioning of universal norms. The subaltern studies school of Indian historiography, for example, has recently begun to use a Foucauldian framework (combined in some cases with deconstructionist insights culled from literary theory) to explore the detrimental legacy of colonialism. According to much of this scholarship, British colonial rulers felt they would bring to India the purportedly universal and modern values of enlightenment and reason. This project implied inculcating European gender norms as well as implanting a capitalist economy. But to preserve the distinctions that justified their dominance, Indian colonial elites simultaneously insisted on the impossibility of their civilizing mission.[19] Neither nationalists nor marxist critics of nationalism, according to subaltern studies scholars, fully extricated themselves from the fundamentally racist, patriarchal, and exclusionary yet paradoxically universal norms posited by colonial rulers. For instance, nationalists denied absolute difference, asserting their ability to achieve progress, form proper nation-states, and attain a correct family life. They nonetheless remained trapped in the normative paradigms of the west, promoting capitalist development and a modular, disciplinary, western form of the state. Once in power, the nationalists' desire to emulate the west led them to subordinate and exclude the popular masses. Marxists recognized class struggle and so repudiated the class unity presumed by nationalist elites. Yet they accepted a teleological historical narrative in which all countries were destined to achieve fundamentally European forms of modernization. In so doing, they too covered over the specificity of subaltern mobilizations and demands.[20]

Many historians of postcolonial Latin America have told a story about Latin American nationalism that parallels that of the subaltern studies school in its portrayal of elite/subaltern interactions. According to these historians, from independence forward, nationalist elites confronted the presumed racial and economic inferiority of their countries by attempting to make Latin American nation-states more like their European counterparts. A poignant chapter in this history came in the late nineteenth and early twentieth centuries, when elites sought to "whiten" their nations through immigration and miscegenation. Racial whitening, elites believed, would not only homogenize nation-states that harbored a frightening array of cultures and ethnicities but also bring economic development and capitalist modernization. Although the extent to which marxists and socialists participated in these drives to make Latin America more European has been little studied, preliminary evidence suggests that they too promoted racialized visions of progress. On the other hand, Latin America's burgeoning professional elites—physicians, anthropologists, lawyers, and economists—actively promoted racial and ethnic "improvement" as they sought to consolidate nation-states and their own authority. They also reworked gendered codes of honor that, since colonial times, had distinguished honorable Europeans from dishonorable others. Those who would not or could not conform were simply excluded from the polity, becoming national outcasts. Latin American nations thus echoed the eminently postcolonial dilemma of India; they remained trapped by their own particular discourses of difference.[21]

As this work makes evident, in Chile nationalist projects were linked to a Eurocentric and exclusionary "colonial" legacy rooted in racialized class and gender hierarchies. I thus share with both subaltern studies scholars and critics of modernization in Latin America an awareness of the ways in which racialized and gendered European ideals have been adopted to exclusionary ends. Specifically, I draw on the postcolonial sensibility to explore how both national popular-front leaders and their socialist supporters strove to make Chile part of the "civilized world" and how gender was implicated in their plans. Chilean leaders, I show, claimed that disorganized, improper family life and uncontained sexuality, both of which were associated with barbarism, undermined national vigor and relegated the nation to a second-class status. Control over sexuality and reproduction, like control over the racial composition of the nation, was therefore crucial to the nationalist platforms of popular-front leaders and their socialist supporters. It would be secured through "scientific" intervention, state planning, and widespread campaigns to discipline popular classes and to make them honorable. In important ways, Chile's national-popular state, like other disciplinary states throughout Latin America, was constituted within and through a gendered, postcolonial adherence to norms of modernity and development.

However, I argue that too narrow a focus on nationalist elites' attempts to "ground" their projects in racialized and gendered notions of progress ignores popular manipulation of those concepts for their own ends. It also downplays the ways in which nationalist elites, even as they advocated progress and civilization, engaged and transformed subaltern demands, exercising hegemony rather than simply dominating. Popular-front attempts to modernize Chile through a rational, scientific program, like the efforts of Indian nationalists, did give popular-front plans a technocratic, naturalizing, and apolitical cast and quell popular mobilization. But despite Chilean elites' totalizing pretensions and their efforts to limit reinterpretative strategies, many Chileans saw planning and even social engineering as creating eminently political venues of communication and deliberation. Others simply interpreted progress and national well-being, and the gender arrangements said to further them, in their own ways. I thus use the Chilean case to question the views of historians and social theorists who have equated modernity and disciplinary power too squarely with male, westernized elites. The heterogeneity of Chilean politics, I suggest, was perhaps unusual and extreme, but not exceptional. The Chilean case therefore prompts us to move beyond the postcolonial view of the state as a monolithic, westernized entity and to supersede generalizations drawn from the experience of the Indian state, itself undoubtedly extreme in its unity, power, and repressive force.[22]

DISCIPLINARY DISCOURSES, THE STATE, AND SUBALTERN POLITICS

An examination of Chile's national-popular regime of power leads us, then, to reconsider certain aspects of postcolonial and feminist scholarship and of analyses of disciplinary projects in Latin America as well as of past interpretations of popular-front politics. This book seeks, specifically, to revise overly unilateral views of the state, of expertise, and of subaltern politics. First, contra the perspective of certain postcolonial scholars, my examination of Chile suggests that states do not always embody a centralized, totalizing power. Nor do they always dominate. Antonio Gramsci clearly articulated this point of view, suggesting that the extent to which any given state either dominates or leads popular classes cannot be determined a priori. It is instead a historical question that can best be answered by looking at states in relation to civil society and by examining the combination of consent and coercion that characterizes relations between ruling and subaltern groups. Moreover, as Nicos Poulantzas noted in *State, Power, Socialism*, the state itself is a locus of contestation, a "*specific material condensation* of a relationship of forces" that *refracts* social struggles. Though struggle may take place beyond the reaches of state apparatuses, the state is constitutive of social relations. At the same time, the state itself is always crossed by conflict, which is present within the state apparatuses. From this perspective, the institutions of representative democracy (or those of the welfare state), which are themselves constructed through popular struggle, can generate political openings useful to popular classes.[23]

The Chilean state, I show in this work, was hegemonic rather than simply dominant. State agents and state agencies responded to diverse popular groups, as well as economic elites and the Right. For example, state-employed social workers sought to ensure that men's wages were spent on their families and that women kept immaculate homes and practiced thrift. But social work interventions in the family were not one-way processes. Housewives who allied with social workers to secure control over their husbands' wages often rejected lessons on shopping, cooking, cleaning, and child care. Men railed against social workers who sought to limit their prerogatives, arguing that they were intrusive and unhelpful. The success of any given state policy therefore depended on conflicts within families as well as social workers' ability to build alliances with family members. In this context, social workers' experiences with clients shaped state policies and the state apparatuses in which they worked.

The significant resources of the Chilean state undoubtedly gave it a particular efficacy. But the state was also composed of diverse apparatuses— ministries, Congress, the courts, welfare agencies, the police, the military, state-run clinics and schools—that participated unevenly in the construction of the popular-front project. Distinct groups and organizations sought and achieved differential access to state institutions: while the Right and dominant classes were more firmly lodged in the courts and the economic ministries, for example, socialists gained firmer control over welfare and labor agencies and the health care system. Members of the Socialist Party occupied ministerial posts, while, except for a brief period in 1947, Communists did not. The postcolonial understanding of the state occludes these kinds of cleavages and the way they shaped interactions between the state and subaltern groups.[24]

This work also challenges postcolonial critiques of centralized, totalizing forms of knowledge, including marxism. Postcolonial scholars have denounced what Foucault called "the tyranny of globalizing discourses with their hierarchy and all their privileges of a theoretical *avant-garde*." They have also drawn on Foucault's insight that the construction of marxism as a unitary, rational discourse constituted an attempt to invest marxism with "the effects of power which the West since Medieval times has attributed to science." But as Ann Stoler claims, Foucault himself understood disciplinary power more equivocally than many postcolonial scholars. Rather than ascribing a fixity to disciplinary discourses, says Stoler, Foucault insisted on how they circulated historically, their "polyvalent mobility." In fact, state efforts to discipline individuals and normalize populations derived their power precisely from their imbrication with subjugated knowledges.[25]

In addition, Foucault pointed to the need for an examination of the concrete bearers of totalizing discourses, calling for the identification of their "real agents (those who constituted the immediate social *entourage*, the family, parents, doctors etc.)." He simultaneously acknowledged that subjugated knowledges included not only the ways of knowing of the mentally ill or the prisoner but also those "of the nurse, of the doctor—parallel and marginal as they are to the knowledge of medicine."[26] While Foucault's granting of agency to "the knowledge of medicine" over doctors and nurses is disturbing—how, we might ask, is the power of knowledge constructed if not by the people who used that knowledge?—he did resist the automatic identification of disciplinary power with professional experts. He thus invited a historical account of the relation of professional experts to disciplinary power even as he implicitly privileged an analysis of expertise over an examination of the actions of experts.

In this book, I accept the Foucauldian insight that truth claims rooted in science are part of modern, disciplinary forms of power but also that, as

Stoler points out, disciplinary discourses circulate. At the same time, I draw on the insights of Antonio Gramsci to elucidate how specific political and professional elites articulated expertise and disciplinary discourses. In contrast to Foucault, who saw scientific knowledge as integral to power, Gramsci insisted that intellectual activity per se was simply part of the human condition. What mattered for Gramsci was not therefore "the intrinsic nature of intellectual activities" but how those intellectual activities functioned in a historical context: "the ensemble of the system of relations in which these activities (and therefore the intellectual groups that personify them) have their place within the general complex of social relations." For Gramsci, the function of intellectuals did not ultimately derive from their professional status or their access to education and knowledge, but instead from the alliances that they established with the major social forces.[27] In this book, I combine these Gramscian insights on the need to consider contexts, especially the specific alliances in which political leaders and professionals engage, with a Foucauldian recognition of the power of expertise grounded in truth claims, whether exercised by "experts" or not.

To underscore the varying degree and kinds of coercion exercised by distinct social actors, I also distinguish between vanguardist, hierarchical, and foundational forms of expertise and leadership on the one hand and more horizontal, articulatory forms based on dialogue on the other.[28] In popular-front Chile, there were at least four interlocking sets of leaders who at times took on the role of vanguard: national popular-front leaders, the Left, the leadership of the women's movement, and professional elites. Popular-front leaders acted as a vanguard by claiming to know and represent the interests of the nation: they purportedly knew how to make Chile follow in the footsteps of the advanced industrialized nations. Leftists too felt themselves to be part of that national vanguard; however, they based their claims to national representation on their privileged knowledge of working-class interests. If those interests were not satisfied, they asserted, the nation could not progress. Within the women's movement, vanguardism existed inasmuch as its leaders, many of them professionals imbued with the imperatives of their fields of expertise, forged an essentialized feminine identity that ignored the diversity of women's experiences. Finally, the expressions of vanguardism among welfare professionals sprang from their privileged relation to "science" itself. By producing knowledge about social reality and social problems, professionals justified their own interventions. Each of these potential vanguards, then, tended to deny the contested character of politics.

In differing ways, the ontological claims of each of these groups rested on gendered norms. Each evoked family and gender relations to fortify its leadership, and each portrayed hierarchical but binding ties modeled after gender and generational relations—ties presumed to be biologically determined and to arise from the necessity of biological reproduction—as models for political life. Using discourses that referred to *blood* ties among "relatives," they naturalized power relations, occluded their constructed nature, and generated a nondemocratic discursive field. They also encouraged paternalistic practices that became deeply embedded in political culture at every level: within families and political parties where "the weak" were protected, in the clientelism and casework of state officials who bestowed favors on clients they considered helpless or ignorant, in charitable initiatives, and in political metadiscourses that portrayed leaders as father figures. Along with ontological notions of nation and class rooted in evolutionary and positivist thought, discourses of family and gender generated a fixed, hierarchical social order.[29]

However, the irreducible presence of conflicts, of multiple interpretations, and of contradictory goals made objectivity and vanguardism impossible as anything more than a tendency. A critique of vanguardism was already present within overlapping claims to knowledge and leadership. When the interests of the nation did not reveal themselves in the same way to socialist and nonsocialist popular-front leaders, to leftists and feminists, or to professionals and leftists, any one claim to represent those purportedly transparent interests inevitably came into question. Socialists and feminists, for instance, each sought to carve out a political space for themselves within the popular fronts by stressing that class or gender allegiances could fortify loyalties to the Chilean nation. In so doing, each of them put forth a slightly different notion of what national belonging meant.

In practice, then, vanguardism always coexisted with democracy. The intermingling of vanguardist and articulatory practices surfaced even where ontological premises were most profound, in discourses of progress. Leaders portrayed industrialization, for instance, as necessary and inevitable, a process over which political and professional elites simply watched. But workers undermined this evolutionary paradigm when they insisted that progress resulted from their willful participation in production. And when state officials made deliberate economic plans that implied choices about how development should be carried out, or when they battled with capitalists over who should be in charge of industry and how it should be run, they transcended a view of industrial development as automatic and necessary. Moreover, although at times professionals used scientific-rational thought in a technocratic fashion, at other times they openly fashioned science for political purposes. As the political nature of professional interventions and the alignment of professionals along ideological lines became evident, the neutrality and positivity of science were at least partially debunked. In these cases, the hierarchical and paternalistic leadership of professionals was, to a certain extent, subverted. Thus although leaders often presented progress as transparent, political elites and ordinary Chileans also envisioned it as the constructed outcome of contestation. In sum, Chile's professional and political elites sought to normalize popular groups and naturalize their own disciplinary power. Yet their authority was tempered by the complex social relations in which those elites were enmeshed and the contradictory aims of different politicians and professionals.

Finally, in terms of how we understand subaltern politics, this book rejects the claim—present to varying degrees in the work of subaltern studies scholars and especially in their earlier work—that subaltern groups are autonomous. As Rosalind O'Hanlon has pointed out, insisting on the autonomy of the subaltern subject obscures the mutuality, understood as struggle and contestation, between subaltern and elite groups. It cannot help us understand either hegemonic struggle or the ways subordinate groups interact with the nation-state. Nor, as Fernando Coronil asserts, can it elucidate the tensions among subaltern actors. According to Coronil, subalternity must be understood as a relation that develops in historical contexts that are necessarily plural: "There are times and places where subjects appear on the social stage as subaltern actors, just as there are times or places in which they play dominant roles. Moreover, at any given time or place, an actor may be subaltern in relation to another, yet dominant in relation to a third. . . . This relational and situational view of the subaltern may help anticolonial intellectuals avoid the we/they polarity . . . and listen to subaltern voices that speak from variously marginalized places." Scholars, Coronil says, should attend to multiple, shifting axes of domination and subordination. Such attention does not inevitably lead to a nihilistic denial of subaltern agency, since agency can exist without autonomy. Instead, it compels attention to how diverse forms of subaltern identity and agency are constructed *against and within* elite projects. In this context, the affirmation that subaltern groups are autonomous can, as O'Hanlon notes, be understood as a general claim about the possibility of withstanding and opposing domination and not as a factual assertion regarding actually existing nonelite groups.[30]

Furthermore, as Joan Scott contends in her examination of French feminists, attention to engagement between elite and subordinated groups permits a less debilitating apprehension of feminist responses to women's subordination. Criticizing much of the scholarship on feminism in post-Enlightenment contexts, Scott argues that historically feminists have simultaneously rejected *and* appropriated the exclusionary ideals of individualism, social duty, and social right used to disenfranchise women. In fact, the strength of feminism has lay precisely in its ability to criticize and inhabit masculinist universal ideals and to exploit the inevitable ambiguities of philosophy, science, politics, and common sense. In forging agency, feminists have not simply chosen to stress difference or equality, autonomy or integration, but have of necessity vacillated between the two. Furthermore, because race, ethnicity, class, and sexuality have shaped sexual difference and feminist politics, Scott notes, scholars should attend to how multiple *differences* are constructed historically.[31]

In Chile, I show, the content as well as the relative salience of popular and feminist demands and identities were transformed through dialogue—albeit unequal dialogue—among subaltern groups and between subalterns and elites. Although local leadership often emerged in relative isolation from more superordinate points of political regulation, leadership from above contributed to congealing or disbanding localized initiatives. Absolute popular autonomy was never a possibility. Elites could not simply do as they wished either.[32]

National leaders were successful in mobilizing citizens in part because conflict was never simply a matter of leaders against led. While poverty might unite working-class men and women, for example, conflict over what constituted proper masculine or feminine deportment could divide them. Working-class women at times colluded with working-class men to oppose middle-class feminists who promoted class harmony. At other times, they conspired with moderate feminists to resist male abuses. Depending on the balance of power at any one moment, they chose one ally or the other. More generally, if working-class housewives, feminists, or workers allied with their social betters, it was because they believed they had something to gain.

Those who were more powerful generated conditions whereby certain choices seemed natural, or more attractive, and whereby other choices—for example portraying male offenses as undermining class solidarity and therefore as detrimental to working-class struggles—were foreclosed. National leaders made concerted efforts to define what was normal and what was deviant. They often succeeded in setting out the terms of debates and disputes. But although state officials and professional elites were especially prone to close off debate and particularly able to enforce their disciplinary demands, vanguardist as well as articulatory practices existed among subaltern groups as well as among elites. Like popular-front authorities, socialist and feminist leaders could manifest their leadership in more or less authoritarian ways. At the grassroots, too, alliances depended on both the neutralization and the recognition of conflict. When socialists presented gender differences within class as natural or feminists glossed over class differences within gender, they neutralized those conflicts they considered secondary. The neutralization of demands and identities, however, was not always possible. Since socialists continued to stress the importance of class, and feminists the importance of gender—since they maintained agency and a degree of autonomy—class and gender antagonisms could not be fully negated.[33]

This, then, was popular-front hegemony, the root of Chile's compromise state. It was not subaltern hegemony, but it generated political alignments that allowed nonelites—some more than others—to negotiate. Forged through continually shifting alliances based in both class and gender, the popular-front coalitions tried to fix allegiances. To do so, they worked from within and outside the state apparatuses and enmeshed diverse social agents in discourses of citizenship. Popular-front leaders, national and local, co-opted some groups and neutralized others. But they never fully effaced more antagonistic expressions of class, gender, and nationality.

LOCATING CONTESTS

This book scrutinizes state policy by using state publications, professional journals, and the case records of social workers. It draws on pamphlets, national and local newspapers, and fiction, as well as on the personal archives of feminist leader Elena Caffarena, for insight into socialist and feminist politics. For a more intimate view of politics and personal life, it relies on interviews with political activists and state officials.

These sources, as well as the book's concern with gender in relation to the state and socialist politics, inevitably limit this study's scope. Perhaps most important, the book is better able to uncover elite motivations than subaltern opinion. Although I have used the writings of elites to reveal the aspirations of men and women who did not leave written traces, using elite-authored

sources to uncover subaltern motivations is difficult and ultimately unsatisfactory. Oral sources better preserve the voices of working-class Chileans. But
my interviews, like the working-class press, tell us more about activists—part
of a more privileged and vocal strata of the working class, more critical and
militant, often more educated—than about average working-class men and
women. And since oral sources privilege the heroic over the mundane, they
neglect many of the everyday complicities of common citizens.

In addition, my questions and sources lead me to slight popular classes'
more hidden resistances to class and gender domination, the more direct
forms of domination that took place in the workplace and marketplace, or
events in the countryside. I do not explore police and penal institutions,
where popular-front and popular influence were feeble, and right-wing
political and economic elites appear only insofar as they constrained the
popular-front project. Finally, although this work draws on recent studies of
distinct regions, communities, and industries, it provides a national rather
than a local or regional analysis. Read in conjunction with those local and
regional case studies, however, it should illuminate how struggles at the
national level influenced local struggles and how local struggles were inte-
grated into or excluded from national projects. At the same time, it should
provide a sense of how national politics influenced the day-to-day lives of an
influential part of the working class.[34]

The book begins, in Chapter 1, by describing the foundational beliefs that
helped the popular-front coalitions cohere. This chapter argues that the
popular fronts self-consciously promoted national well-being, industrial
progress, and family life to distinguish themselves from previous oligarchic
governments, which they depicted as retrograde, repressive, chaotic, and
antinational. They thus justified their rule in evolutionary terms, sublimating
and neutralizing class antagonisms. Paradoxically, however, they also encouraged popular participation: one of the coalitions' explicit goals was democratization, the extension of citizen participation within, outside, and in relation to state apparatuses. Leftist and popular leaders in particular viewed
national well-being in more class-conscious ways, defining the working class
as the nation's core. The popular fronts responded by recognizing the citizen
rights of those working-class men who were hardworking, respectable, patriotic, civilized, and family-loving. At the same time, coalition leaders relegated those "others" who were not considered privileged agents of progress
and prosperity to a second-class citizenship.

In Chapter 2, I show how gendered definitions of citizenship were created and reinforced through a family wage system that defined the place of women and men within home and workplace. Although many male workers were single or uninterested in supporting families, they accepted a family wage system that sought to exclude women from the labor market and to provide men with wages sufficient to support dependent family members. In exchange, they extracted increased wages from capital and gained state recognition as legitimate social and political actors. They also buttressed their unity by reconciling conflicts between married and unmarried men. Familial relations were thus critical to the economic bargains struck between workers, employers, and the state. However, some feminists as well as some male and female workers rejected and destabilized family wage ideology. Developing a view of gender as socially constructed and contingent, progressive feminists in particular denounced the way the family wage system subordinated women by identifying them with the home and defining them as nonworkers. Although prevailing discourses on gender, politics, and work overshadowed feminist projects, feminists within MEMCh forged local alliances by convincing working-class men that male workers could not improve their lot if the labor market remained divided by sex.

Chapter 3 analyzes how contests between leftists and feminists shaped the nature of feminism and the political options open to working-class women. Progressive feminists within MEMCh, it shows, tried to find a place within the popular-front alliances but had to confront a lingering misogyny within the coalitions. Perhaps more important, although these feminists tried to build bridges among women from different classes, they could not overcome tensions between working- and middle-class members of the movement. Largely because of economic constraints, most organized housewives preferred to support the family wage system and identified with the Left, seeing male-headed families as a firm locus of working-class militancy and of necessary protection. Communist leaders who encouraged working-class women to view male family wages as their best alternative for survival and sought to undermine feminist autonomy only compounded the difficulties progressive feminists faced. Communists thus exploited differences among women to undermine the popularity of feminists' most radical proposals among working-class women and to disparage radical feminists by arguing that feminism was bourgeois. Yet Communists ultimately failed to marginalize all feminists. In the end, moderate feminists who were less amenable to working-class mobilization and more steeped in professional discourses challenged Communist leadership of working-class housewives. By allying with state officials, these moderate feminists ultimately wrested control of grassroots committees of housewives from Communists. Moderate feminists thus neutralized some of the more militant, class-based aspects of working-class housewives' demands even as they continued to advance a gender-emancipatory program.

Chapter 4 demonstrates how gendered definitions of citizenship and political participation shaped the professions as well as the institutional contours of the state and its welfare policies. State agencies dealing mostly with organized male workers were the most receptive to popular pressure and the most democratic, the chapter maintains. In contrast, agencies that dispensed aid to the indigent, most of whom were female or unorganized, remained less sensitive to popular demands. The gendered nature of popular organizing in turn marked those professionals who were most influential within the state: physicians and social workers. Social workers, all of them women, dealt largely with women as indigents and had trouble escaping the paternalistic orientation of charity work. Public health physicians, mostly male, looked after the nation's "human capital" and were, on the whole, more open to the popular fronts' democratizing impulse. Gender differences within the professions thus depended on and furthered gendered forms of citizen participation.

Chapters 5 and 6 explore the norms of gender and family life advocated by state officials and popular organizations, showing how each used gendered discourses to naturalize its own leadership. Both state officials and Left leaders sought to constitute male-headed, nuclear families, but each had different reasons for doing so and each used distinct methods. Welfare professionals who felt the family was the bedrock of the nation organized public health campaigns and promoted social work interventions in the home. Although their privileged access to scientific truth inclined them to hierarchical practices, they generally found it more effective to educate and cajole rather than to recriminate and punish. Left leaders, for their part, often supported these nonpunitive state efforts while simultaneously insisting on the need for specifically socialist efforts to regulate working-class family life. Leftists felt that by uniting families they could augment the cohesion of the working class and convince detractors that socialist men were manly and morally sound enough to hold positions of power. Both groups recognized and abetted the citizen participation of men, and indeed their agency, while portraying women as dependent victims.

The hierarchical practices of leadership within the women's movement are described in Chapter 7. Leaders of the women's movement, this chapter suggests, were oftentimes imbued with the paternalistic and disciplinary attitudes of both the middle class and the professions. Still, it was within the women's movement that a theory of democracy, and to a lesser extent democratic practices, developed most fully. A group of movement leaders came to recognize not only differences among women but also the differences among Chileans more generally. They also came to see that citizen rights could be defined in gender-neutral ways. This incipient effort to articulate democracy politically and theoretically failed to prosper, however, in part because the women's movement could not extricate itself from the broader conflicts that tore apart the popular-front coalitions.

Together, Chapters 2, 3, and 7 show how the identity of working-class women was doubly neutralized: by leftists who feared that women's emancipation would force men to abandon privileges and by a sector of feminists who saw housewives' class-based militancy as illegitimate. In comparison, the most radical sector among middle-class feminists, especially certain leaders of MEMCh, sought to articulate the class-based interests of housewives while generating a frontal critique of male dominance. Along with working-class women who themselves demanded a voice within their families, feminists contested the view that women's subordinate position within the family was natural and unproblematic. At the same time, they denounced the class exploitation of women. They thus incorporated many of the demands of working-class housewives without endorsing the family wage system as such. Unfortunately, the rifts between moderate feminists and leftists arrested progressive feminists, who might have rewoven and transformed conflicting projects and rearticulated a more democratic popular-front pact.

As a whole, this work argues that the popular fronts consolidated themselves by tapping into numerous interlocking local alliances. Despite the efforts of leaders to fix the popular-front project and to stabilize identities in order to solidify their leadership, the very terms in which they tried to do so undermined their attempts. Discourses of nationalism, democracy, progress, and family were powerful mobilizing tools for political elites. But while elites consolidated their power by invoking these discourses foundationally, they discovered that the practical force of those concepts derived in part from their ambiguity, from the way in which they lent themselves to continual appropriation and reformulation. The inability of the popular fronts to "found" themselves fully made the coalitions, and the national-popular politics they espoused, unstable but flexible. Instability did not doom the popular fronts to failure; in fact, it may have strengthened them. That precariousness did not necessarily generate equality for those who were subordinate. It did, however, give them the possibility of struggling against inequalities—and of finding allies along the way.

chapter one

FORGING AGREEMENTS

Respectability and Rule

When Pedro Aguirre Cerda and Gustavo Ross squared off in the 1938 presidential election, Ross suggested, in typical right-wing fashion, that what Chileans needed was "Order and Work." Pedro Aguirre Cerda, echoing the earlier motto of Chile's brief 1932 socialist republic, promised "Bread, Roof and Shelter."[1] That motto, and the program behind it, apparently roused many lower- and middle-class Chileans. When Aguirre Cerda triumphed on 25 October 1938, massive celebrations erupted in the streets of Santiago. In the days and months that followed, many popular-front supporters would seek, personally and collectively, to extract concessions from the newly established government.

The popular fronts responded to those collective and individual demands by installing forms of governance that broke with the exclusionary practices of past governments. At the same time, the coalitions promoted an economic modernization that was not inimical to the interests of economic elites. Among those who most clearly voiced the tensions between the promise of citizenship and the potentially demobilizing doctrines of development was a young Socialist physician named Salvador Allende who was appointed Aguirre Cerda's first minister of health. Reflecting on the popular-front electoral triumph, Allende observed that "Chile's laboring classes recognized their destiny and the deplorable reality in which they lived and therefore resolved to break the rhythm of history in order to establish a political regime that would allow them to conquer and enjoy the economic, social, technical and cultural progress that has been the patrimony of a minority. That is why the 25th of October is a transcendent date."[2] Stressing that the popular fronts would help the Chilean poor to progress, Allende portrayed capitalist development as the working class's "destiny." Yet in Allende's view, technical improvements and cultural reform justified and resulted from the broadening of political and economic forms of citizen participation. The increased agency of popular sectors would allow them to "conquer and enjoy" cultural and economic development. Paradoxically, then, progress could be both the automatic unfolding of history, a transcendent destiny, and a musical composition in which popular classes instituted a new rhythm.

As Allende's reflections suggested, the transformations instituted by the popular fronts were inherently contradictory. This chapter explores some of those contradictions and shows how they were gendered. First, it briefly characterizes the nature of elite responses to popular mobilization in the period of oligarchic rule before 1938 and the very different relation between ruling elites and popular classes that developed after 1938. It then analyzes the popular fronts' racialized conceptualizations of progress, showing how those representations helped the coalitions win supporters and assuage detractors. Finally, it explores how gender played into those notions of national advancement. As a whole, the chapter shows how ideals of economic and cultural progress that were inflected by gender and race facilitated the consolidation of the popular-front pact and contributed to the popular fronts' broader legitimacy.

POPULAR ORGANIZATIONS, THE STATE, AND OLIGARCHIC HEGEMONY

The coming to power of the popular fronts was preceded by several decades in which Chile's ruling elites failed to contain intense, if episodic, working-class mobilization. Beginning around 1900, worker organizing and collective actions mushroomed as militant anarchist resistance societies and protosocialist *mancomunales* eclipsed long-standing self-help mutual-aid associations. Strikes and mass demonstrations multiplied, especially in the cities of Santiago and Valparaíso and in nitrate- and coal-mining communities. Massive repression led to periods of retrenchment, but worker organizations gradually consolidated and institutionalized themselves. In 1912, Luis Emilio Recabarren and other working-class activists formed the Partido Obrero Socialista (POS, Socialist Workers' Party), which subsequently helped reinvigorate the Federación Obrera de Chile (FOCh, Chilean Federation of Workers), Chile's first national labor federation. In 1921, the FOCh joined the Red International of Labor Unions, and a year later, the POS joined the Communist International, becoming the Communist Party.[3]

During this period, elites brutally repressed working-class mobilizations and showed little interest in improving the living conditions of the poor. The oligarchy's primary tool for stabilizing the social order and mitigating capitalism's worst excesses was charity. The Beneficencia (Beneficent Aid Society), funded until 1896 solely by private donations and later by a combination of public and private funds, provided hospital care for the poor. The Patronato Nacional de la Infancia (National Foundation for Infancy), founded in 1901, provided health care and food rations for indigent infants and nursing mothers. Both explicitly sought to combat "Communism."[4] Meanwhile, state aid for the poor remained meager and social reforms haphazard. In 1907, a labor office was created under the auspices of the Ministry of Industry and Public Works, and legislation passed in 1916 and 1917 provided for worker holidays, Sunday rest, and work accident compensation. In 1917–19, public authorities' long-standing interventions in labor conflicts were given official sanction through a series of ministerial decrees that gave government officials limited power to mediate labor disputes. Moreover, in 1917, elites endeavored to stimulate breast-feeding by requiring all firms that employed more than fifty female workers to provide on-premises day care to women workers with children under two years of age. In that same year, they acknowledged a small measure of state responsibility in health care matters, when state-appointed representatives joined delegates from civil society on the Beneficencia's newly created governing board, the Consejo Superior. Yet these dispersed changes did not constitute a serious and concerted reform effort, and the state continued to respond to worker demands with violent repression.[5]

The nature of the Chilean political regime itself discouraged serious reform. After President Balmaceda's defeat in the civil war of 1891, which pitted the president against Congress, the executive branch was decidedly weakened. Congress further undermined presidential authority by using its considerable power to question ministerial appointments: between 1891 and 1925, 489 ministerial posts were filled. The constant rotation of politicians from the Liberal, Conservative, and Radical Parties through government ministries allowed the traditional political parties to benefit from state largesse. It also stimulated centralization as party members tied outlying areas to the political center through systems of clientelism and patronage. But because the executive branch was weak and because political parties were not programmatic, there was little concerted policy making.[6]

Despite political parties' reluctance to initiate reform, continued popular protest led the most visionary elites to see that they could not successfully perpetuate their power without more substantial political and economic changes. A less repressive relation between the state and popular classes, they realized, would not only help legitimate the state itself but also satisfy employers' desire for increased labor stability. These reformers advised employers to improve wages and work conditions, proposed the legal recognition of unions, and suggested that the state mediate labor disputes. In 1920, the election of the populist Liberal Party member Arturo Alessandri gave force and coherence to their reform program. Soon after taking office, Alessandri introduced legislation that mandated health, social security, and disability insurance for blue-collar workers; provided for state recognition of labor unions; and set up tripartite arbitration and conciliation boards. The roots of the compromise state lie in the incorporation of popular sectors projected by Alessandri and his allies.[7]

Alessandri's reform efforts caused considerable confusion among both workers and elites. Despite labor's initial support for Alessandri, many members of popular organizations feared the proposed laws would allow employers and the state to co-opt their organizations. Congress and proprietors were not overwhelmingly enthusiastic about Alessandri's proposals either. Some employers, including the U.S.-owned Braden Copper Company, supported legislative changes, but many others worried that reforms would give workers unwarranted leverage in labor disputes. Discrepancies erupted into violence: a bomb exploded at the door of the deputy who had authored social security legislation.[8]

Alessandri and his followers thus failed to generate the consensus necessary to pass this groundbreaking legislation. The nature of the political regime itself truncated the reform project. Congress simply refused to pass the proposed legislation, and within the parliamentary system, the executive branch could not impose transformations. For that reason, Alessandri also proposed constitutional changes that augmented executive power. But the traditional political parties had grown strong under parliamentary rule and refused to strengthen the executive branch. An impasse had been reached.

On 5 September 1924, a military intervention broke that deadlock. Within four days, a cowed Congress conceded to the military and passed laws that regulated the formation and financing of trade unions, the right to strike, and the establishment of conciliation and arbitration boards. Under the new laws, blue-collar workers in industries that employed more than twenty-five workers could form industrial plant unions. The law also permitted the formation of "professional" unions among workers from different firms who did the same kind of work or labored in the same industrial sector. In addition, the promulgation of law 4.054 created the Caja de Seguro Obligatorio—financed by workers, employers, and the state—to provide blue-collar workers with retirement pensions and health and disability insurance.[9]

Four months after the September coup, in January 1925, a young army major named Carlos Ibáñez del Campo ousted his superiors and put himself in command of the military government. Ibáñez pushed through additional reforms: he formed a Central Bank; instituted an income tax; and made the police a centralized national institution. In 1925, a new constitution that strengthened the executive, circumscribed congressional meddling in budgetary matters, and gave the president increased control over the congressional agenda was put in place.[10]

Like his Brazilian counterpart Getúlio Vargas, Ibáñez tried to garner popular support while neutralizing popular militancy, telling organized workers that they could achieve more by working peacefully within the legal system of labor relations. Many laborers, despite initial misgivings about the reforms proposed by Alessandri, seemed willing to cooperate. In fact, they came to perceive the legal recognition of unions as a tool for fighting recalcitrant employers. Likewise, they began to realize that the profit-sharing provisions of the new labor laws, which required proprietors to hand over a share of profits to industrial unions, would provide unions with significant financial resources. Thus though Ibáñez failed to stipulate mechanisms for recognizing legal unions until the end of 1928 or to set up arbitration and conciliation boards, he was relatively successful in attracting the support of the organized working class.[11]

Ibáñez attempted to win over and control popular sectors by undercutting the power of the traditional political parties and enhancing the authority of progressive middle-class reformers. He not only called for a corporate legislature that bypassed party representation but, when his functional legislature failed to materialize, supported the electoral bids of popular leaders who were loyal to him. In addition, he promoted corporate representation on state advisory boards. Just as important, he selected middle-class reformers who were sympathetic to popular demands to head key government agencies—especially agencies dealing with labor, health, and welfare matters. It was during Ibáñez's reign that members of the progressive middle class first learned to make state employment a springboard to political prominence. Popular organizations too began to realize the importance of tangible access to the state.[12]

Ibáñez thus made important changes, many of which would continue in place throughout the popular-front period. First, though he ultimately did not undercut the prerogatives of political parties through corporate arrangements, the functional representation of labor and capital on the governing boards of state agencies became an entrenched form of political representation. Second, Ibáñez formed a cadre of politician/state functionaries who would continue to influence Chile's political life during the popular-front period. Many of the middle-class men who would later help found the Socialist Party learned the mobilizing power of access to the state as functionaries of the Ibáñez government. During the popular-front governments, they would play a prominent role in the same kind of agencies they ran under Ibáñez. Third, Ibáñez modified working-class activists' perceptions of the state. Popular support for Ibáñez may not have been particularly profound; indeed less than a year after Ibáñez left power, many labor leaders who had supported him disavowed their past loyalties. Yet popular activists seemed to have recognized that, if their organizations maintained a degree of independence, neither corporate representation within the state nor state-led reform would necessarily be detrimental.[13]

In short, Ibáñez changed the political regime, introduced new forms of political mediation, transformed the labor relations system, augmented welfare services, and enhanced the power of middle-class reformers. But despite the significant reforms he enacted, Ibáñez could not perpetuate his neutralizing and authoritarian politics. In the aftermath of the 1930 depression, which caused atrocious social dislocation, massive street demonstrations brought Ibáñez down. Widespread discontent among students and the political Right, and to a lesser extent among workers, ended his attempt to mobilize popular sectors from above and to co-opt them. Ultimately, then, Ibáñez too failed to neutralize the popular challenge to oligarchic rule.[14]

THE EMERGENCE OF THE POPULAR FRONTS

In 1932, Alessandri returned to the presidency for a second term, and during the next six years, the traditional Right regrouped. Yet in the 1938 presidential election, right-wing parties failed to amass enough votes to hold on to the presidency. As a result, the Right's access to and influence within the state declined as it was forced to relinquish important instruments of political control. After Aguirre Cerda's victory, the owners of mines, haciendas, banks, and large-scale commercial enterprises would no longer rule directly. While the rich continued to exercise power—how could a group that controlled such vast resources not be powerful?—they were no longer hegemonic politically. Political parties of the Right would hold a majority in the Congress during much of the popular-front period, but in Chile's presidential regime, this was not enough to grant them political leadership.[15]

During Alessandri's second presidency, the political parties and social movements associated with the Left also reestablished themselves. The Communist Party rebuilt itself by organizing in the urban working-class neighborhoods and in the mining camps where it had traditionally maintained a presence. The Socialist Party, which launched its political career in 1933, developed a stronghold in the southernmost Magallanes province and recruited a heterogeneous, middle- and lower-class constituency throughout the rest of the country. In 1936, labor unions, which had increasingly rallied behind these two parties, united in a national labor confederation, the CTCh. As for the Radical Party, its members accepted ministerial appointments in Alessandri's second administration, but party leaders soon realized they would remain politically subordinate as long as they continued to ally with the Right. Pulled by political expediency and the growing, socially conscious left-wing of their party, in 1935 they joined with the Socialist Party in a congressional pact. Around the same time, the Communist Party responded to changes in the international Communist movement and to its own stagnation in the preceding years by inviting Radicals and Socialists to form a popular-front coalition. By May 1936, the three parties had worked out the terms of the alliance. Meanwhile, in 1935, working-class and professional women formed MEMCh, an explicitly progressive and feminist group. MEMCh, like the CTCh, quickly allied with the popular fronts.[16]

By 1936, increasing numbers of Radicals viewed themselves as progressives, champions of Chile's working people, and members of the Left. As Aguirre Cerda asserted on the eve of the 1938 election, "[B]ecause of the

Right's unyielding incomprehension, the Radical Party, which represents mainly the middle class, has openly taken a step to the Left to ally itself cordially with the working class." Yet the Radical Party did not fully renounce alliance with economic elites and the political Right. Nor did it fully embrace a popular agenda.[17]

The political parties of the Left opposed the dominant classes more directly than the Radicals and courted popular classes more openly. Still, they too sought the support of Chile's capitalist class to modernize the country. The Communist Party in particular believed that all countries had to pass through a bourgeois-democratic phase, like the popular-front period in Chile, to advance toward socialism. (To a lesser degree Communist leaders also thought that the "national" bourgeoisie was the necessary agent of that phase.) This formulation allowed them to see the popular fronts as an evolutionary step toward socialism, facilitating a purportedly short-term Communist convergence with both other ideological currents and the "national" bourgeoisie. More generally, Socialists as well as Communists sought evolutionary change and forewent revolution.[18]

Yet those on the Left did not always see concessions as necessary and inevitable, and Left political parties frequently debated whether the governing coalitions actually favored the poor and whether leftists' participation in the popular fronts was warranted. Differing positions on this question caused successive ruptures between Communists and Socialists and within the Socialist Party. The Socialist Party in particular was wracked with self-doubts that led to its intermittent participation in the popular-front alliances and intense factionalism within the party. Parties, party splinters, movements, and groups participated in and withdrew from the popular fronts often; the coalitions were never monolithic blocs. As Socialist leader César Godoy Urrutia indicated in September of 1939, the Popular Front was in many ways an inappropriate governing coalition because it held "great contradictions and the elements of its own separation in its bosom."[19]

Relations between Communists and Socialists were continually strained by their rivalry for control of popular movements as well as by ideological differences. The ties between these two parties deteriorated in late 1939 and early 1940 because of the Communist Party's aloofness following the Hitler-Stalin Pact. Discord between Socialists and Communists again erupted with the end of the Second World War, leading to serious violence and deaths. The CTCh labor federation subsequently split into rival Socialist and Communist factions. Although in the 1946 presidential contest many individual Socialist militants voted for Gabriel González Videla, a left-wing Radical backed by the Communist Party, the existing Socialist Party factions expressed their animosity toward the Communist Party by refusing to support González Videla's candidacy. In spite of this dispersion, the popular-front strategy rebounded as Socialists cautiously lent their support to González Videla once he took office.[20]

That conflict within the popular fronts was not more disabling was in large part due to the even greater disunity within the Right, which stunted the ability of Liberals and Conservatives to articulate an alternative political project. The Right did consistently attack the popular fronts. An attempted military coup in August 1939 and the rabid ranting of right-wing parliamentary representatives in January 1940 made leftist politicians fear that an armed insurrection was close at hand. In late 1940 the Right agitated unsuccessfully for the banning of the Communist Party and soon thereafter threatened to boycott the March 1941 parliamentary elections. Yet differing positions on economic and social policy made it impossible for the Right to agree on a common presidential candidate in 1942 or 1946. (In fact, they had been unable to agree on a candidate since 1931.) In 1942, portions of the Liberal Party even supported the presidential bid of popular-front candidate Juan Antonio Ríos.[21]

In part because of this lack of unity within the Right, the popular-front strategy did not begin to wane definitively until late 1947. After that date, popular-front politics exhausted themselves as the emerging cold war heightened tensions between capitalist development and democratization. In the postwar period, the United States conditioned much-needed loans on the repression of striking workers, the Communist Party, and working-class activists more generally. González Videla and the Chilean Congress complied, sending Communist and labor militants to jails and concentration camps and outlawing the Communist Party. Many activists were forced underground. But the Communist Party survived, as did labor organizations. And in the decade following 1947, Congress finally enacted important reforms that had long been championed by popular organizations: it granted women suffrage rights, clamped down on electoral fraud, set minimum wages for blue-collar workers, mandated the payment of family allowances to blue-collar workers, and created a health care system that would serve the indigent as well as workers. Thus although González Videla's cold war crackdown stifled militancy in the short run, it did not fully reverse the substantive transition from oligarchic rule that had begun in 1938. In the years leading up to 1947, the popular fronts had revitalized economic development, contained opposition to social reform, and attracted popular support. Perhaps most important, they had permanently rearticulated relations between popular sectors and the state, succeeding where previous national leaders had failed. The repressive politics of the postwar era did not, in the end, undo those vast changes.

NATIONALITY, PROGRESS, AND POLITICAL COHESION

To quell class antagonisms and dissipate resistance to their program the popular fronts promoted national identity among popular classes and elites and portrayed their project as a national endeavor. In fact, Aguirre Cerda and his followers resuscitated the concept of *chilenización* (Chileanization) to describe the process of national identification they encouraged. By rousing feelings of *chilenidad* (Chileanness), they encouraged citizens of all social classes and political orientations to view and express their demands in terms of national prerogatives. As early as his presidential campaign, Aguirre Cerda identified the fashioning of a national identity as one of the Popular Front's achievements. "The Popular Front," he said in an election manifesto, "has *formed a national political consciousness around a program.*"[22] Later, as president, he reaffirmed the importance of this collective process whose goal was the building of national consensus when he decreed measures aimed at a "defense of the race." "I understand," he proclaimed, "there are some basic ideas to which the whole collectivity agrees, or should agree. If these ideas are not realized, any political orientation will necessarily be incomplete for it will lack that uniform feeling of love of nationality that, lying above all other considerations, makes possible the fusion of a collective national sentiment that has as its basis a primordial element: a unified patriotic love that is collectively understood."[23] Characterizing patriotism as primordial, Aguirre Cerda sought to unite the Chilean "race" by invoking an organicist vision of nationality, one that alluded to mythic origins. At the same time, he undermined his own effort to ground the popular-front project in an authentic national past by acknowledging conflict. If the collectivity was not already "in agreement," he noted, it should work toward that end.

Right-wing politicians, who insistently questioned the national character of the popular-front coalitions, cast further doubt on the organic unity of the Chilean nation. As a result, there was widespread contention over who deserved to be a part of the national community, who was worthy of repre-

senting it, and what was in the national interest. For the Right, the freedom
to pursue profit was patriotic, and the openly procapitalist bent of the popular fronts did not dispel their suspicion that the coalitions represented the
uneducated rabble rather than the nation as a whole. Popular-front leaders
frequently confirmed their worst fears. When Socialist deputy Natalio Berman squared off against Liberal deputy Eduardo Moore in a heated congressional debate, Berman declared: "When I say 'the country' I mean el
pueblo that triumphed on October 25." Moore, who would not let Berman
define who was a member of the nation, retorted, "But, deputy, we are
speaking of a matter that is of interest to all citizens." A few months later
it was Moore who spoke in the name of all Chileans and Deputy Juan Bau-
tista Rossetti, a popular-front supporter, who could not contain his disgust:
"What do you mean Chileans?" he asked. Before Moore could answer, Socialist deputy Manuel Hubner mimicked his reply, shouting, "The exploiters!"[24]

Despite these virulent conflicts, or because of them, the popular fronts at
times sought to assuage conservative elites. Thus as Communists prepared
to assume cabinet positions in González Videla's government, Communist
Party secretary-general Ricardo Fonseca portrayed the popular-front program as a moderate, "patriotic and human" plan favored by "all Chileans,
regardless of their social conditions or their political or religious beliefs."
Similarly, Allende, who forcefully advocated measures to alleviate poverty,
insisted that the war against poverty would not be a war against the rich. In
1943, as the European Allies united to defeat fascism and Chileans rallied in
defense of "democracy," Allende conveniently avoided mention of the rich
when he declared, "In Chile, we are in a state of war, not against exterior
adversaries but against centenary internal enemies: we are at war with hun-
ger, with misery, with social insecurity, with the fear of living, with the
uncertainty of not having work."[25]

The promotion of economic and cultural modernization was central to
the coalitions' effort to encourage national cohesion and sublimate conflict. As references to civilization and barbarism became less frequent in the
1940s, the notion of progress—and its antitheses, stagnation or decline—
condensed much of the signification of the older dichotomy. Popular-front
leaders insisted that Chile emulate the trajectory of "more advanced" nations.
By leaving behind its inglorious past, they suggested, Chile could become a
modern, prosperous country. They thus harnessed a teleology rooted in
western models of modernity and nationhood to create consensus—even as,
paradoxically, they deployed anti-imperialist rhetoric, encouraged industrial

self-sufficiency, and promoted national folklore, theater, and literature.²⁶ Chileans were urged to leave aside their differences and cooperate to lift Chile from its second-class status.

In championing this developmental model, popular-front leaders drew on widely held beliefs about the superiority of more "advanced," industrialized countries. Indeed, Chileans on both the Left and the Right envied not only the prosperity and technological advances of the United States but also the Soviet Union's progressive social legislation, centralized state planning, and extensive industrialization. In 1936, a publication of the state social security agency printed sections of the Soviet constitution. Three years later, even right-wing professor Francisco Walker Linares was touting the advances of the Soviet Union. Tomy Romeo, who later became a Communist, studied with Walker Linares at the state-run Alejandro del Río School of Social Work. Her professor, she recalled, was "right-wing but very objective. And he said that in the Soviet Union there had been extraordinary progress, that people— [starting] from illiteracy—had advanced centuries, in a matter of years had advanced centuries."²⁷ The popular fronts appropriated and built on this widespread consensus regarding the benefits to be derived from joining the forward march of civilization. Under popular-front leadership, they said, Chile would industrialize, acquire technological sophistication, replace chaotic economic growth with planned development, improve sanitation, enhance the health of its population, achieve demographic vigor, and educate its citizenry.

Faith in progress was a profoundly racialized worldview. White Europeans, it was commonly thought, were the bearers of a superior culture that ought to supplant other ways of life. One worker publication decried the incomplete nature of Chile's modernization, which had not yet improved the living standards of the poor, mocking the "ridiculous pride of newly literate *indígenas*." "Is it surprising," the article asked, "that we are therefore called degenerate mestizos and that we are constantly threatened by invasion and extermination at the hands of more capable, virile and intelligent races, accumulators of energy, spirit and will?" Class uplift and economic advancement, this author implied, were part of a process of racial whitening that would allow Chile to leave behind its degenerate mestizo past. Likewise, writer Luis González Zenteno explained in the Socialist daily *La Crítica* that popular-front leaders would help Chile "move beyond the crisis that stagnated progress" by coming to terms with and moving beyond Alexander von

Humboldt's portrayal of the Americas as "a starving Indian sitting on a chunk of gold."[28]

More important than the popular fronts' nationalist embrace of such racialized (neo)colonial concepts, however, was how they appropriated, transformed, and deployed them. For, as Ann Stoler has argued, how racist and exclusionary discourses change as they circulate may be more significant than the continuities between nationalist and colonialist projects.[29] In Chile, the popular fronts used the notion of progress to sublimate both popular and elite demands, obfuscating differences between the popular fronts and their detractors (as well as distinctions between the "first" and "third" worlds). But in a conflict-laden political climate, the connected themes of national progress, economic development, and class uplift also signaled the popular fronts' distance from past governments and their allegiance to a political alliance that garnered its reformist strength from working-class militancy and agency.

Popular-front discourse was thus fundamentally ambivalent. While using notions of progress to sublimate conflict, coalition leaders simultaneously foregrounded the popular fronts' own particular contributions to national prosperity and denounced the barbarism of the retrograde dominant classes. "Feudal" landowners were commonly criticized for their paternalistic labor relations and traditional production techniques and faulted for Chile's economic stagnation. Writing in the publication of the state social security agency, one contemporary noted: "Chile's hacienda regime is patriarchal and primitive. More than anything else, it has opposed Chile's social and cultural development. . . . The retarding effect of the hacienda has marked Chile, stigmatizing the national soul . . . [but] Chile is one of the few countries that, if it is led well, can realize its social evolution in peace and tranquility." Likewise, Allende emphatically blamed "the oligarchy's egotistical and irresponsible governments" for the "painful spectacle" of poverty, which he said degraded the entire nation. Popular classes and the popular fronts themselves were, in comparison, patriotic and progress-loving. Allende continued by praising the popular class's "profound conquests in the area of democracy, its superior political culture."[30] When Graciela Contreras de Schnake, the Socialist mayor of Santiago, opened a hostel for bootblacks, the Socialist newspaper *La Crítica* similarly contrasted Contreras's cooperation with the "civilized" poor to the paternalistic practices of prior governments. Contreras's success, the newspaper reported, was due to "two new forces that have begun to act

in Chile. . . . One is the disciplined organization of *los de abajo* which elevates
its members to higher planes on the scale of culture. The other is the social
conscience of those who govern [and] who exercise authority with an authentic sense of human solidarity."[31]

Despite this combative rhetoric, officials contained conflict by emphasizing that progress was an inevitable, quasi-natural process. Portraying the
actions of the oligarchy as part of a shameful past that had been—or should
be—left behind, officials denied continuing right-wing opposition and left
open the possibility of a future alliance with "progressive" capitalist sectors.
In addition, they implied that their own opposition to retrograde and reactionary landowners was simply rational or inevitable—a historical necessity,
not the result of the popular fronts' alliance with popular classes. Their praise
of popular classes, moreover, at times betrayed a vanguardist attempt to
channel and contain popular mobilization. After all, the popular fronts sanctioned disciplined, organized, and civilized forms of popular agency. In
short, by encoding the popular-front project as developmental, the coalitions
stressed their historical continuity with past governments and denied the
roots of reform in specifically class-based mobilizations and demands. "Social evolution" would, after all, take place in "peace and tranquility."

The popular fronts further depoliticized popular demands by presenting
them as national imperatives that in turn flowed from required economic
changes. Allende, for instance, linked popular well-being to capitalist development and work, characterizing the working class as the nation's "human capital." If Chile's "human capital" was healthy and robust, he said,
industrialization would proceed apace. But if Chileans remained ill fed, ill
housed, and ill paid, Chile would not have the healthy and dense population
it needed to ensure its national security and its rise above second-rate status.[32] Allende thus told economic elites that social reforms benefiting the
nation's "human capital" were good for the dominant classes because they
were good for the economy and good for the nation. In the process, he
presented the working class not as opponents of capitalism or allies of the
popular fronts but as producers. Still, Allende, like Contreras, insisted that the
amelioration of poverty was a crucial element of national progress.

The popular fronts' racial discourse was similarly ambiguous. Racial categories were, without doubt, intrinsically hierarchical. Yet popular-front intellectuals did not create racial taxonomies based on either biology or fixed
cultural attributes, and popular-front supporters refrained from mobilizing

racial categories for the purposes of outright exclusion. In fact, the popular fronts generally equated race and nationality and portrayed Chile as a racially homogeneous nation. This racial formulation denied existing ethnic differences within the country and inspired criticism of foreigners and immigrants, deemed un-Chilean. Yet it also precluded rigid racial or ethnic boundaries. A Chilean was simply a Chilean, popular-front leaders implied, and if most were poor, dark skinned, or uncultured, then all the country's inhabitants were tarnished by ungainly national attributes that retarded progress in general.

In fact, the term "Chilean race" was frequently used to refer to poor Chileans, el pueblo; and in popular-front parlance to plead for the "defense of the race" was to advocate uplift from poverty: improved hygiene and housekeeping among the poor but also better housing and sanitation, more recreation, and access to libraries. Rather than promote whitening through racial engineering, elites steeped in the prevailing neo-Lamarckian eugenics sought to modify the environment, which they saw largely as the product of sociopolitical factors. Racial improvement would come about not through immigration or miscegenation but through enhanced welfare services and "modern" childrearing practices and through a more equitable distribution of wealth. Insofar as popular-front officials saw these material improvements and cultural competencies in racial terms, their program depended on and deepened racialized hierarchies. Efforts to uplift and "civilize" popular classes undoubtedly buttressed a hierarchy in which "European" customs—and the popular-front elites who embodied rationality—stood at the apex. Yet notions of progress and national uplift that were rooted in a civilizing mission also articulated popular demands for improved living conditions. This was a more democratic, if not unproblematic, mestizo ideal.[33]

In this context, leftist and popular audiences—which equated el pueblo with the nation itself and had little trouble accepting that the elimination of poverty was crucial to the progress of the nation—generally embraced the nationalist rhetoric of development. As popular-front leaders affirmed that, in contrast to past leaders, they understood popular well-being as part of the health of the nation, the laboring classes responded with patriotic rapture: "What is useless to the country is useless to socialism," a Socialist publication from Arauco asserted in 1941. "That is to say, always the nation above all other considerations, no matter what they may be." Like these Socialists, Communists made patriotic proclamations devoid of any explicit class content. In 1946 they described themselves as following in the "honorable tradition" of their "glorious ancestors who lifted the banner of national independence."[34]

As popular-front elites promoted discipline and civilized behavior among popular classes, many activists agreed. Some workers also believed that progress would benefit them—and that excessive militancy was therefore unnecessary. A "true socialist," according to the Socialist Youth newsletter *AS*, "FIGHTS constantly and with faith to produce wealth, trying to improve the means of production . . . [and] PRACTICES and makes others practice self-discipline, and discipline at work, at home, within the party, and within our country, because he knows that we are all particles of an immense social conglomerate that marches toward perfection and happiness." Flaunting the slogan "Excellence at work," the Socialist newspaper *Barricada* asked workers in both public and private industries to work toward increasing production. Anticipating resistance, *Barricada* asked rhetorically: "Will the application of this slogan only benefit the bosses?" "It doesn't matter" was the reply. "The unions will soon enough take responsibility for demanding the part that belongs to workers. In the meantime we will have advanced toward the perfecting of our workers, toward their increasing adaptation to technology, and we will have introduced the habit of taking maximum advantage of individual energies in the service of the collectivity. In sum, we will have forged workers that are worthy of that name for tomorrow's Socialist Republic." A faith in the positive nature of technical knowledge coupled with a belief that social change could be evolutionary and sequential allowed these Socialists to see collaboration with bosses as beneficial.[35]

The allure of nationalism and progress notwithstanding, popular faith in progress and popular patriotism could also take on a more restrained and class-conscious tone. From this standpoint, the task of popular-front supporters was not simply to follow in the trajectory of the "glorious ancestors" who fought in Chile's independence wars. For the independence battles of Chacabuco and Maipú, Communists asserted elsewhere, had not liberated Chileans—most of whom continued to be servile, ill housed, ill clothed, hungry, and exploited. Instead of continuing on that path, what most Chileans needed was a more substantive "Second Independence" that would give them greater material comforts. Likewise, according to workers at the El Teniente copper mine, "effective patriotism" meant "a better distribution of the benefits of [our] riches." Socialists agreed. They ostensibly wanted changes that transcended the banners of Left and Right and served the entire

Members of the Communist Youth at a monument honoring an independence war battle site, Maipú, c. 1935. Sitting in the front, center, is Ricardo Fonseca, secretary-general of the youth group, later secretary-general of the party. Photo courtesy Emperatriz Villarroel.

nation. But then they made clear the type of reform they had in mind: "The liberation of a social class that has been ferociously exploited by another that made itself powerful at the expense of the secular fatigue of el pueblo." Activists thus framed their needs in the language of national advancement championed by popular-front leaders and thereby impelled those leaders to see their specific, class-based needs as part of national progress.[36]

Other sectors of the Left rejected the twin notions of progress and national fellowship outright. In an allegorical tale titled "Resignation" and published in the Socialist magazine *Rumbo*, a hungry and tethered young calf asks her mother why she is not allowed to drink the mother's milk. The mother explains that in the days of "barbarie" cows ran free and fed their milk to their children. "But now," the mother continues, "we have progress, civilization, culture." The innocent calf replies, "Of all that progress you just listed I do not enjoy any of it, I'm always cold and hungry." The mother concedes that the cows she knows do not benefit from progress. "[B]ut," she adds, "they say [it benefits] the collectivity." With less embellishment, another Socialist publication (which represented the nonconformist faction that opposed Socialist participation in Aguirre Cerda's cabinet) stated: "[The] presumed social solidarity that exists in relation to the nation does not exist. And that is why, for us there is no other solidarity than that of our class, that of the workers. . . . [M]ost of the benefits of civilization do not reach us."[37]

At times, then, Left activists recognized the way that nationalist rhetoric stimulated popular quiescence and called for a more absolute popular autonomy. Yet only a minority held this more combative position. More frequently activists combined nationalism and progress with their own struggles for better living. The Communist Party maintained that technical improvements could make workers' lives more comfortable but that better living conditions would not materialize without popular struggle. In general, by highlighting the needs of popular classes and their willingness to struggle for a nation that was not only more prosperous but also more just, popular activists modified popular-front leaders' more teleological formulations. Nonetheless, as we shall see, left-wing popular-front supporters also accepted and built on problematic aspects of elite formulations: they used notions of progress not only to castigate "backward" economic elites but also to reproach those poor Chileans whom they considered less "civilized." Recognizing this, one unusual worker publication decried slogans such as "pride in being Chilean," "respect for hierarchy," and "veneration of work" that were, according to the newspaper, simply "racist and jingoistic sermons."[38]

FORGING SOLIDARITY: FAMILY AND NATION

As popular-front leaders attempted to neutralize elite opposition and popular demands, they found that the promotion of a nuclear family form could help them win supporters on both the Right and the Left. As later chapters demonstrate, the popular-front state implemented reforms aimed specifically at constituting male-headed nuclear families in which husbands acted as stable breadwinners and women as housewives and mothers. To fortify and stabilize nuclear families, it not only sought to assure men jobs that would allow them to support women and children. It also attempted to legalize family ties and mitigate marital disputes through health and social security apparatuses and their social work and public health interventions.

Since popular-front leaders' gender ideals drew on models of work and family that had been prevalent in the workers' movement since at least the turn of the century, they served to secure the adhesion of organized laborers.[39] But the popular-front model of gender and family not only coincided with that of organized workers but also with that of conservative elites so that it cemented upper-class, as well as popular, allegiances to the governing coalitions. Shared gender ideals thus stimulated alliance between the popular fronts and the Right and between popular-front leaders and organized workers. In fact, by rooting their political and economic innovations in family forms that connoted stability because they had been normative for so long, the popular fronts implied that the new social order would be precisely that—an *order*.

At the same time, since the popular fronts used gender to signal social reform, their model of gender also provoked conflict, especially between the coalitions and the Right. Indeed the popular fronts' gender project, like their economic project, was in a sense at odds with itself: it served to mark distinctions between the popular fronts and their opponents while simultaneously creating a common ground. During the 1938 presidential campaign, for instance, gender emerged as a powerful yet contested symbol, an emblem of both the popular fronts' (historical and contemporary) uniqueness and of the moral and political sensibilities they shared with the Right. In that campaign supporters of Ross claimed that the Popular Front would undermine mutual respect among family members and fellow citizens. While refuting his opponents, Aguirre Cerda did not question the validity of their ideals: he countered by saying that the economic modernization projected by the Popular Front would provide youths with jobs and thereby allow young people to make homes for themselves.[40] In fact, most popular-front leaders suggested that the unfavorable economic conditions associated with oligarchic rule, and not the popular-front project, undermined family life.

Popular-front supporters employed the concept of "solidarity" to connect gender to both class loyalties and national unity. According to Aguirre Cerda, for example, the solidarity and agreement within (first) class and (then) nation that would make the popular fronts successful began at home: "Why do people say that the Popular Front wants to destroy the family—that family whose regularity affects all those who worship our home—when the only desire of men of the middle class and el pueblo is to have a legitimate *compañera* who today participates heroically in the struggle against their misery? Where there are sickly beings who live in overcrowded conditions—be it in the city or the countryside—united in a common misery, we want to institute a home which will be the basis of an understanding that human solidarity also applies to the destitute of today."[41] Noting that families could unify "el pueblo," Aguirre Cerda implied that middle- and working-class men could construct solidarity in the face of misery and attempt to alter their class condition by allying with "legitimate companions" and forming a family. Aguirre Cerda also intimated that solidarity could be practiced within the national-popular bloc embodied in the Popular Front: by helping poor Chileans attain a proper family life, popular-front politicians could exercise solidarity. Through the popular fronts' occupation of the state, human cooperation and unity could be enacted on an even larger, national scale.[42]

Anti-individualism and loyalty to both family and nation were part of the Left's own tradition, and leftists, including left-wing Radicals, often understood "socialism" itself as a vocation for "solidarity," a propensity to think in "social" as opposed to "individual" terms. Indeed a Socialist publication defined "the true socialist" as someone who "sacrifices individual interests when he or she understands that his or her action will produce a social misfortune, no matter how small."[43] Chileans who thought first of the bonds that tied them to fellow citizens and kin would stimulate social harmony.

By feminizing the nation itself and suggesting that men's loyalty to nation was akin to loyalty to family, popular-front leaders presented the Chilean "race" as an ethnic national brotherhood. And insofar as they not only portrayed the family as a "natural" unit rooted in kinship and shared blood but also made family stand metonymically for nation, they naturalized the popular-front project.[44] In 1941, for example, Antofagasta workers coupled love of family with devotion to nation as they recalled a refrain by Luis Emilio

Recabarren: "To love one's family, by loving other families, is to love the *Patria*. To love oneself in order to love all others equally is to love the family. And we symbolize our love for woman, for the *compañera* of our life, through love for the *patria*. And we symbolize our love for our mother through our love for Humanity."[45]

However, the popular fronts found it difficult to depict either their project or the gender reforms they championed as solely (or even principally) the reassertion of natural proclivities. In fact, popular-front leaders and state agents often noted that progress and industrialization, which made the reconstitution of gender roles necessary, were the antitheses of an uncivilized oligarchic past rooted in nature. Indeed descriptions of the proper roles to be played by family members often invoked the ideals of productive activity and order on which the legitimacy and economic development project of the national-popular state itself rested. The teleological view that progress, and even the transcendence of capitalism, was an automatic, even natural, process undoubtedly subverted the empowering potential of elite insistence on the need to break with the past. Still, coalition leaders could not always repudiate the past without recognizing the reality of conflict and struggle.

For example, politicians and popular-front state officials often portrayed the "abnormalities" that disrupted family life as products of an unreformed nature and inheritances of the past. Marshaling eugenic concepts, they marked these afflictions with the stigma of heredity, a natural genetic process. They thus sublimated class conflict as they drew upon a eugenic science to which they had privileged access. Yet their focus on heredity did not lead to a denial of social and environmental determinants, and elites often suggested that human intervention could conquer illness and even heredity. Leftists occasionally pointed out that "abnormalities" were the products of capitalism itself. Referring to the proliferation of social diseases and in particular syphilis, which allegedly wreaked havoc within the family, the Socialist newspaper *La Crítica* castigated past governments and promised the popular fronts would end "this true social scourge, the *inheritance* and product of capitalist society." At the same time, the article downplayed conflict and buttressed the importance of professional expertise and science by lamenting Chile's lack of demographic vigor and calling for the sterilization of the insane.[46]

Vida Sana, a CSO propaganda magazine for workers, portrayed national advancement and proper home life as the antitheses of a natural order: "Each giant step taken by Nations, by Humanity, was based on an aggrandizement of the Home, of the Family, on the sweet wisdom of converting Woman into an authentic Mother. A Nation that does not hold the Home as a motto above all others is a jungle populated by men. Worse than a jungle. Nature denies the animals of the jungle the capacity for evil that man can use."[47] While portraying the past, "natural" order of the jungle as relatively devoid of evil, this manifesto insisted on the "aggrandizement" of the family as part of the nation's "giant step" forward. Though the author asserted that these changes should not undermine the family, he or she clearly saw the formation of proper families as rooted in human purpose, not animal instinct. After all, "Woman" would have to be *converted* into an "authentic Mother."

In a later issue of *Vida Sana*, a CSO social worker similarly echoed the language used to champion modernization and national solidarity to posit the advancement of the family. If each family member carried out his or her anointed role, she noted, the family would be a "society of reciprocal protection" that harbored "hope of a better future" and "prosperity." "Efficiency and harmony among the factors that constitute it," she continued, "determine the happy and prosperous march of the convoy. Similarly, when those who make it up abandon it, they produce confusion and disgrace."[48] The advancement of the family, in sum, mirrored that of the national community and reflected back on it. Under popular-front leadership, family and nation would leave behind a bestial past tainted by oligarchic rule.

In short, professionals and politicians positioned the family—and the popular-front project that rested on it—between nature and industry. Elites sometimes defined the family as a "natural" unit based on blood ties or construed deviant forms of family life as medically pathological. At other times they viewed the family as a crucial link in the popular fronts' modernizing project. In turn, the popular fronts oscillated between a more teleological and evolutionary vision of progress and family and one that acknowledged conflict.

Furthermore, popular-front leaders metaphorically represented oligarchic rule as family disintegration while using the reconsolidation of the family to connote popular-front governance. Using the watchword *abandono* (abandonment), which unambiguously evoked men's failure to provide for and protect their family members, they indicated the insufficiencies of past right-wing governments. During Alessandri's second term, for instance, the Communist newspaper *Frente Popular* disapprovingly referred to "the abandonment of this regime." Similarly, in late 1942 *La Crítica* condemned "the irresponsible negligence of reactionary governments that the country [had to] put up with."[49]

These formulations compared the political and economic elites who had ruled in the past to irresponsible men who deserted their wives and children.

This discourse depicted the popular-front state as a responsible father to the Chilean nation and popular-front leadership as strong paternal guidance.[50] Because past political elites were associated to the parliamentary regime, while the popular fronts wished and needed to prop up the executive branch, this formulation also buttressed the popular fronts' authority by asserting the need for a strong (presidential) father figure. Thus reform of family and economy was articulated to changes in the political regime.

Yet popular-front leaders did not want to seem authoritarian and therefore also characterized themselves as motherly. Borrowing a refrain originally used during the socialist republic of 1932, in 1938 Aguirre Cerda asserted, "We want the *Patria* to be a loving mother who protects all her children equally and not a stepmother who privileges those who need it least." Arguing that the correction of social problems required both sternness and understanding, in 1943 a government publication proposed acting in an "energetic and loving" manner, with "scientific valor and maternal tenderness."[51] In signaling attention to popular health and happiness as both paternal and maternal, the popular fronts distanced themselves from an oligarchy that was, at its best and most charitable moments, sternly patriarchal and at its worst moments, irresponsibly indifferent. At their most populist, the popular fronts openly condoned struggle within the nation by portraying popular-front governance as a rupture with the past that echoed conflict within the family. Just as subordinate family members questioned the prerogatives of patriarchs who were less than dutiful, they suggested, the popular fronts would challenge an oligarchy that had shirked its responsibilities to the nation. The familial rhetoric of the popular fronts thus cemented the authority of the popular fronts not simply because it promised solidarity, progress, or a return to a natural order—although it undoubtedly did all that—but also because it expressed broader conflicts over how authority could be rightfully exercised. The popular fronts offered change without relinquishing their claim to continuity.[52]

GENDER AND POLITICAL INCLUSION

Aguirre Cerda's claim that the popular-front state would act as a "loving mother" to all Chileans notwithstanding, the popular fronts were more like stepmothers to some: industrial workers and miners were like blood kin to the popular-front leaders. But rural and nonindustrial workers as well as women were like adoptive *hijas de casa*: subordinate family members who worked for their patrons in return for protection, but, having no rights, were fed only what was left over after the real family members had eaten. The popular fronts thus created a hierarchy of privileges among their constituents, their ostensible family members.

This gendered hierarchy was constructed in part by relating the kinds of productive labor said to promote progress—namely industrial and mining work—to hegemonic forms of masculinity and then by associating hegemonic masculinity with political entitlement and power. Because industry and mining were seen as crucial to Chile's economic well-being, (male) industrial workers were considered important members of the national community. Conversely, because industry and mining had long been considered critical economic activities, organized industrial workers were able to refigure progress as the outcome of their intentional activity and to demand political and economic entitlements. Thus a main reason neither women and the unemployed nor campesinos and informally employed workers attained more political or economic benefit was that popular-front governments, and the organized popular groups that supported them, continued to see "workers" as exceptionally consequential political and economic actors and to define women and nonindustrial workers as nonworkers. In this gendered political economy, women who performed industrial work were either ignored or portrayed as anomalies, thus reaffirming the association of masculinity and industrial work. Men who performed informal or "unproductive" work or who did not work were implicitly—and sometimes explicitly—seen as "dependent" and feminized. Popular-front leaders and their supporters in the labor movement therefore defined "work" in ways that subordinated not only women but also laborers who performed supposedly unproductive and retrograde work, especially campesinos. Gender not only structured relations between men and women, and between Right and Left, but also among men.[53]

The gendered political economy of the period thus simultaneously advanced and circumscribed political and economic democracy. At least in relation to rural labor the exclusionary policies of the popular-front leadership were undisguised. They apparently resulted from an explicit bargain between popular-front politicians and the Right: in return for passing legislation that created CORFO, right-wing politicians demanded that rural unionization be stopped. The exclusion of women was more subterranean. But as Chapter 7 shows, political elites denied women full political rights— and other restrictions on suffrage such as literacy requirements continued— because elites on both the Right and the Left believed universal suffrage would cause political dislocations. The popular fronts' position on the family wage system, which defined women as dependents and subordinate citizens, was negotiated even more quietly. Yet on balance the popular fronts cemented male-headed nuclear families materially and ideologically, making it more difficult for women to make political and economic claims. Male industrial workers made concrete economic gains as a result. Just as depressed rural wages benefited urban workers materially by keeping the prices of foodstuffs low, the family wage system assured men that women would not compete for the best-paying jobs.[54]

In regard to women in particular, political elites and labor activists together circumscribed women's rights by rejecting paid labor for women, downplaying the importance of informal forms of employment, and defining full-time homemaking as women's proper occupation. Throughout the popular-front period, the family wage system and the segregation of the labor market endured: few women worked for wages, and only a minority of women workers did industrial work (see tables A.4 and A.5). Of those women who were employed, most did industrial work at home, engaged in artisanal production, or participated in domestic service and laundering (see table A.6). Of 144,589 blue-collar women paying social security taxes in 1945, for example, 17.3 percent were self-employed (as opposed to 3.6 percent of men); 58.8 percent of the non-self-employed were domestic servants.[55] These informal occupations (which official tabulations never fully documented) were neither well regulated nor recognized as socially useful. Even labor leader María González, herself a domestic servant, denigrated domestic service when she characterized it as "unproductive" and "semi-feudal" because it remained untouched by any division of labor. While championing a modernization of paid domestic labor, González reaffirmed the idea that it was a secondary form of work. And since popular-front supporters defined paid work in general as unwomanly, they saw women as secondary laborers and citizens. José Vizcarra, a popular-front supporter and CSO physician, asked of the limited legislation regulating domestic service: "Have these social laws . . . made domestic servants into citizens who are incorporated into the benefits of society?" He answered himself with a rotund no. Women were thus identified with either the home or informal and intermittent work, neither of which were said to promote progress, and marked as dependent and subordinate. Women's ability to make effective claims within the prevailing politicoeconomic climate was consequently circumscribed.[56]

Furthermore, leftists embraced norms of masculinity that, at least implicitly, excluded unmanly men who did not do "productive" and therefore "real" work. Mario González and Roberto Quiroga, two textile workers who later became labor leaders, clearly believed some forms of labor did not constitute work. When interviewed in 1994, González repeatedly maintained that he had begun "to work" when he entered the El Salto textile factory at age twenty. Pressed as to whether he had worked before, he insisted that he had not. Yet in responding to a question about his education, he admitted to having left school as a teenager to help his family economically. González had in fact held several jobs before entering El Salto. Among other things, he had sold paper bags constructed by his mother in Santiago's Vega Central and served as a guide to a blind man. To González this did not constitute work. Similarly, although Quiroga made money playing music at local *quintas de recreo* (open-air taverns) near Los Andes, he claimed to have "worked" only as a mechanic at the SILA sack factory. Actually, Quiroga spent much of his time, and earned most of his money, playing the mandolin. Frequently, his musical activities forced him to stay up so late that he did not make it to the factory. On those occasions, Quiroga hired a friend to replace him at SILA. But in Quiroga's view, he worked at SILA; mandolin playing was not work. González and Quiroga had reasons for seeing their factory jobs as legitimate and therefore real work: in entering the factory workforce they joined unions and became politically active. In addition, they performed the kind of work that others clearly saw as allowing men to make proper contributions to both their families' sustenance and the progress of the nation. In all likelihood, they believed that these political and economic prerogatives and responsibilities—and not the income they earned—made a job into work. Insofar as these rights and obligations were, as I suggest below, associated with masculinity, the distinctions made by González and Quiroga were gendered.[57]

Male labor leaders tended to diminish the political and economic rights of nonindustrial workers and nonworkers by characterizing them as effeminate and therefore unworthy. In Volodia Teitelboim's fictionalized account of the life of Communist leader Elías Lafferte, for example, Lafferte, who was still "attached to his mother's skirt," felt unmanly as well as "useless and perverse," and "extremely incorrect" because he was unemployed. While the labor movement actively combated male unemployment, it usually focused on providing jobs to men who had previously been productive laborers. As Socialist deputy Carlos Alberto Martínez stated in the wake of the massive unemployment caused by the 1930 depression, the state had an obligation to provide work "except naturally for those [individuals] judged to be vagrants." For many socialist activists, migrant rural laborers may well have qualified as "vagrants." Certainly the employment agencies championed by unions did not include the kinds of work performed by women or rural folk. There was no use in trying to rescue the masculine virtue of those who, by definition, could not be manly.[58]

At the same time, Left leaders portrayed male workers who contributed to national progress and national cohesion as "proper" men and citizens worthy of rights. Socialist labor leader Roberto Pérez Núñez pointedly expressed this view in an article titled "The Working Class and Its Future." In this piece, Pérez argued that because (male) workers labored diligently to increase production and took care of their families, they deserved better wages.

> On his way to work, the joyful, happy worker marches thinking of those he left at home, the little woman surrounded by their little children, or, an aged little Mother for whom he feels immense affection and because of them he wishes to arrive soon at work so that he can assure the Bread for his home.
>
> The day goes by and the laborer works full steam to satisfy his bosses, in this manner he wishes to demonstrate that he doesn't want to be reprimanded, he cares for the machines and the tools he is in charge of as if they were his own, because he is aware of his responsibilities and has a working-class consciousness. . . .
>
> That Capitalism which inspired [to do] something noble for Society, [and which] wishes to serve the Patria should leave aside pride and self-love and help the worker who knows his responsibilities and fulfills his obligations and respond by paying Wages which lift his morale and his living conditions to a level worthy of human dignity.

In Pérez's view, capitalist intransigence, which "drove [workers] into strike movements," not only harmed workers but also harmed the nation. In contrast, because workers had "working-class consciousness" (and were patriotic family men) they obeyed their bosses and cared for capitalists' productive infrastructure.[59] In this formulation—and in others like it—it was always necessarily manly men who furthered national well-being as productivity and class conciliation.

Besides their gendered propriety, male industrial workers' rationality and moderation made them respectable members of the national community. Together, these qualities differentiated respectable workers from dirty, itinerant, and ignorant "others" who were also not family men. For example, Carmen Lazo remembered her presumably respectable family having to leave the Chuquicamata copper mine where her father worked because groups of men from the south of Chile—they were called "mauchos" because they came from the Maule region—attacked workers on payday. "At that time," Lazo recalled, "there was a lot of insecurity in the [mining] camps because a lot of people from the south who were not exactly workers [obreros] would arrive, and they would rob the workers, assault them." A Communist Youth publication described ignorance, darkness, and crime as characteristics of that "other" and cited the high rate of illiteracy among delinquents who the oligarchy "pushed into that dark destiny of ignorance and crime." While delinquents might be uplifted, until they had risen above their vices and acquired "culture," they could not be considered real workers or part of the Left. Even male industrial workers could not be fully respectable members of the national community if they were uneducated or unenlightened. Copper miners at El Teniente thus asserted that real chilenidad did not consist of adoring a flag or feeling roused by an anthem. Rather it meant "elevating the cultural level of our pueblo, helping our compañeros . . . to increase their knowledge, through advice or through books, so that they themselves recognize the errors they committed because of their ignorance." Using a similar notion of respectability, the same workers demanded the reinstatement of quintessentially respectable labor leaders who the company had laid off and prohibited from coming into the mining camp. "Are these workers bandits, assassins, or rabble?" they asked. "No! . . . [T]hey are honorable laborers who should be working for the company." Within the nationalistic discourse of progress used by these workers, the company should not fire union organizers since those organizers were rational, "honorable laborers" and not disruptive or uneducated rabble.[60]

Even as popular-front leaders used the differences between respectable male workers and dishonorable "others" to justify the incorporation of popular classes (of which the respectable male laborer was both leader and emblem), professional elites as well as right-wing politicians accepted and amplified those distinctions. For example, social worker Margarita Urquieta praised industrial workers who "produced the manufactured elements that modern civilization had made necessary" and who had morally sound, well-constituted homes. In contrast to the day laborer, whose attire was "dirty and disordered," the factory worker wore "clean and ordered clothing." Social worker María Santelices categorized workers similarly, noting that day laborers were "dependents" since they usually worked as subordinate helpers and earned lower wages.[61] Likewise, in interviewing Communist leader Elías Lafferte, right-wing author Ricardo Boizard reported favorably on the Lafferte household: "Those old Chilean portraits of static ancestors hang on the walls. Everything is clean, everything in order. There is no trace of bohemia or of revolution. Only traces of home." When an interviewer asked Rosa Markmann de González Videla, soon to be first lady of Chile, her opinion of Communists, Markmann replied, "I respect them because they are honest people who [carry on] the clean life [*limpieza de vida*] led by the members of their Party."[62]

As evinced by Markmann's reference to "*limpieza de vida*"—which echoed the term *limpieza de sangre*, used since colonial times to denote racial purity— the contrast between respectable workers and unrespectable "others" evoked racial as well as gender difference. In fact, elites often made explicit the racialized nature of those distinctions. According to Santelices, for instance, the indigenous people of Chile had only a "primitive" sense of family. The morally robust male Spaniards who invaded Chile believed in strong, united families but lost their moral bearings in the New World. Their mestizo children therefore had a "weakened sense of home" that caused poverty and moral degeneration. In her view, then, gendered propriety was part of racial whitening as well as class uplift. Only respectable workers approached the allegedly superior family life of Europeans.[63]

Male worker legitimacy was thus advanced through a set of distinctions related in complex ways: male/female, productive/unproductive, patriotic/unpatriotic, progress-loving/retrograde, cultured/ignorant, disciplined/unruly, European/Indian. Implicit in these distinctions was a notion of male worker respectability in which all the positive traits cohered. Respectable workers were not only good family men and diligent workers, they were also cultured, disciplined, law-abiding, viceless, and orderly. The popular fronts thus delineated the prerogatives of unionized male workers by contrasting those men with disorderly and illegitimate "others." But despite the exclusionary nature of popular-front worker politics, notions of respectability could also work expansively as legitimate political actors insisted that through education and moralization the disreputable could become worthy and strong. Women who participated in "productive" industrial labor could claim the privileges of citizens. This discourse did not promote nonhierarchical relations but only postponed equality, making it a future aspiration: for if the unruly had to be taught respectability then there had to be moral superiors who could do the educating. During the popular-front period this moralizing contingent was expanded to include an ambiguously defined group of working-class leaders. Yet as popular-front leaders articulated a project of nation building, constructing a more democratic vision of national development, the teleology inherent in the idea of progress partially subverted their efforts, opening the door for vanguardist forms of political leadership.

As the following chapters show, the generalized social ferment that accompanied popular-front rule facilitated local alliances that empowered unmanly "others" and forced popular-front hegemony to rearticulate itself. Socialists and Communists continued to organize rural laborers and to seek material improvements in the countryside, and some male workers refused to identify themselves as disciplined, hardworking family heads to obtain privileges. At the same time, feminists associated with the popular fronts rejected the automatic association of women with home and family, pointing out that many women did industrial work and insisting that women's work within the home contributed to national progress. They also articulated alternative models of citizen participation not based on gendered rights and responsibilities. However, these oppositional voices remained muted. Given the need to make economy and polity run in an orderly fashion, the popular fronts—and the Radical Party especially—chose not to rouse the radical expectations of campesinos or women. Yet that failure should not occlude attempts to redraw popular-front hegemony in a more democratic fashion.[64]

CONCLUSION

As this chapter has shown, the popular fronts did more than simply bring together actors by harmonizing their previously delineated interests. They worked to define and reshape those interests. The promotion of democracy and justice, progress and modernization, discipline, order, and respectability was central to that (re)definition. The articulation of those elements helped fashion a national project that drew upon and reformulated the nature of class, racial, national, and gender identities. While elites formulated a view of male respectability that made workers' place within the popular-front coalitions more palatable to the Right, workers themselves used that concept to highlight their own needs. The fact that workers rearticulated their demands in the language of progress, education, and national development did not necessarily lead workers to reject the incorporation of the "unproductive" and "uncultured" into the popular-front alliance, but it did justify vanguardist forms of working-class leadership that made exclusion, or limited forms of inclusion, more likely.

In advancing personal, social, and political moderation and order, popular-front leaders advanced a class-conciliatory stance that stressed popular discipline for the sake of national advancement and modernization. In this context, democratic practices were seen more as an instrument for creating consensus around an evolutionary—but paradoxically radical because historically novel—model of social change than as a channel for the expression of conflicts. All Chileans, but subalterns especially, were encouraged to hold back from excesses, act in an orderly manner, and forswear violent or sudden methods of provoking social change. Aguirre Cerda reassured his detractors and reminded his collaborators that "by using suffrage, a constitutional tool, we can advance democratically toward the conquest of civilization and progress for all social classes. The Popular Front's joining of forces is not the disorderly and amorphous mob of '20, with its secret hope of overturning the existing order. It is made up of organized, responsible parties that do not intend to disrupt but rather seek an orderly social and economic reconstruction that will benefit all Chileans regardless of their religious or political creed."[65] To advance their interests and move beyond the unfavorable conditions of 1920, Chileans were encouraged to act as reasonable and moderate democrats; at the same time, the success of the popular-front project and of democracy was said to rest on each citizen overcoming selfishness and acting in the interest of the national community. Yet Aguirre Cerda's reference to suffrage, which could be exercised only by literate males, also pointed to the way in which "organized, responsible"—and indeed proper, cultured—men were the main members of the popular-front alliances. In this context, it is not surprising that popular-front leaders could not hear the view of democracy advanced by some feminist leaders: citizenship as the economic, political, and cultural rights of individuals, conferred by birth. Within the prevalent discourse of gendered rights and responsibilities this formulation was simply too subversive.

chapter two

CONSTRUCTING A
FAMILY WAGE SYSTEM

Wage Work and Identities

As we saw in Chapter 1, gender helped constitute a national-popular project by facilitating the political incorporation of respectable male workers. It also helped unify the nation and restrict women's claims to citizenship. As this chapter explains, gender was part of a family wage system that delineated interlocking norms of deportment within politics, the family, and the workplace. The family wage system positioned men as breadwinners and women as housewives and mothers. By driving women out of the workforce, segregating the labor market sexually, and augmenting male wages while lowering women's, it cemented women's economic vulnerability. By denying women economic leverage and granting men power as household heads, it subordinated women within the family.[1]

The gender identities articulated through the family wage system, though widely accepted, were not monolithic. In fact, gendered models of behavior resulted from widespread negotiations between popular organizations and political and economic elites, between organized popular sectors and feminists, and within both popular sectors and feminist groups. As popular-front authorities supported the claims of labor, for instance, labor organizations unified themselves around the association of masculinity and work. Male workers gained political legitimacy, material benefits, and increased power over the "dependent" family members they supported and protected. This negotiated arrangement, which built on and intervened in more localized consensuses about what constituted proper behavior for men or women, was nevertheless fragile. Not all men were workers, and even in all-male occupations not all workers were family heads. In addition, where men and women worked alongside one another, the association of wage work with masculinity was weaker. Consequently, the unification of workers around a male identity that linked paid labor and family was never complete. Moreover, although working-class housewives accepted central tenets of family wage ideology, they rejected others. Stressing male responsibility over male prerogative, they contested male control within the family. And, much to the displeasure of employers, they resisted the elements of class collaboration inscribed in normative masculine and feminine identities. Feminists and certain wage-earning women, whose interests differed in many ways from those of housewives, forced the reorganization of the family wage system in yet another way. Insisting that they too were breadwinners, they fractured the identification of women with the home and of work with masculinity. Feminists also built a more inclusive and gender-neutral working-class identity that undermined men's privilege within the family and weakened the alliance between male workers and employers. Gender divisions within the labor market, feminists argued, created divisions within the labor movement and therefore weakened working-class organizations. These alternative interpretations of gender in relation to family and work transformed the family wage system and made family wage ideology malleable. They did not, however, replace hegemonic norms. In fact, the family wage system persisted in part because it could accommodate differing definitions of proper masculine and feminine deportment.[2]

WHAT IS A WAGE?

By 1952, when the Chilean Congress passed a law mandating the payment of family allowances for blue-collar workers, male workers generally agreed with employers and popular-front state officials on the utility of family wages. Yet twenty years of often difficult negotiation preceded that agreement. Those negotiations began in earnest when Chileans first discussed legally mandated family allowances in 1933–34. In the two decades that followed, both workers and employers would cede significant ground. Laborers would give up autonomy and independence but gain increased material benefits and a degree of control over dependent family members. Employers would exchange economic inducements for a more stable workforce.

During the first decades of the twentieth century, the meaning of wages remained ambiguous. Workers, employers, and state officials debated whether wages should reflect a worker's productivity, cover the cost of a worker's subsistence, or guarantee proper profits to capital. And how might workers' subsistence be determined? They also asked who should provide economically for children. Should wages ensure the subsistence of only workers or of workers and their families? And if wages should allow the reproduction of entire families, who might properly be a part of those families? Workers, employers, and the state each held divergent opinions on how to determine a fair wage.[3]

In the mid- to late 1930s, the labor movement began to recover from the devastation wrought by the 1930 depression and by Ibáñez's repression of existing unions and from his attempt to replace autonomous unions with state-sponsored labor organizations. Backed by fortified labor organizations, workers asserted their own views regarding how to determine just wages. Against employers who claimed insufficient profits and sought to increase their returns, workers maintained that wages should be tied to workers' needs. A typical article on wages in the labor press asked, "How much do we need to live?" and went on to detail the price of rent, bread, meat, malt liquor, noodles, potatoes, lard, sugar, heating coal, electricity, and vegetables. In 1949 a hotel workers' publication similarly invoked explicit notions of what constituted a deserved, "human," or "proper" subsistence: "No male or female worker [obrero ni obrera] fails to feel anguish at not being able to dress his or her children like humans; at not being able to give them a proper education; at not giving them the medication they deserve as children of workers who forge wealth." Where capital wished to link wage gains to increased productivity, labor asserted, and made calculations to prove, that workers already contributed to productive gains. Workers further affirmed that through their productive labor they made an important contribution to the nation's progress, sacrificing their health and happiness in the process. Didn't toil, which laborers gladly carried out for the sake of national improvement, merit a wage that enabled dignified living?[4]

Laws enacted before 1938 validated in an incipient way the notion that wages should allow workers a just living. In 1934, Congress established the legitimacy of assuring worker welfare through state intervention in wage matters when it passed legislation fixing a minimum (living) wage for nitrate workers. Three years later, intense agitation by white-collar employees led to the passage of a law calling for the payment of a living wage (salario vital) and family allowances to white-collar empleados. The salario vital was meant to cover personal expenses in housing, clothing, and nourishment; the family allowances would allow employees to support legitimate family members. Although the 1937 law excluded blue-collar workers, like the nitrate law it set a precedent by establishing the notion that wages should reflect worker needs.[5]

Congress consistently rejected minimum-wage and family allowance legislation for blue-collar workers. (It would fix a national minimum wage only in 1956.) Popular-front politicians nevertheless continued to press for a living wage for manual laborers. Given the more favorable balance of forces in Congress after 1941, they reintroduced minimum-wage and family allowance legislation. Unsuccessful in the legislative arena, popular-front leaders and state officials sought to improve worker wages in other ways. State officials employed in agencies that served workers, such as the Dirección del Trabajo (Work Inspection) or the CSO, backed the labor movement and adopted its point of view on wages. Although state officials generally continued to uphold capitalists' right to profits, they responded to intense popular lobbying by pressuring employers to recognize unions and consider worker petitions. In addition, they called more liberally on arbitration boards and mixed commissions (composed of worker, state, and employer representatives) to settle wage disputes. In turn, members of arbitration councils drew on and validated the worker's viewpoint in arguing for improved wages. Like popular-front officials and welfare professionals in general, they frequently justified wage gains by citing the rising cost of living or the need to assure the subsistence of workers. Through complicated calculations of how much workers needed for housing, clothing, and foodstuffs, they tried to determine exactly what a proper wage was. And they rebuffed the protests of employers by showing that capital, in fact, made reasonable profits.[6]

When President Aguirre Cerda sent legislation on family allowances and living wages for blue-collar workers to Congress in 1941, popular-front officials identified openly with labor's view on wages. On that occasion, the magazine of the Dirección del Trabajo editorialized that the notion of "labor-commodity had no place in the world" and insisted that an adequate salary required "compensation for work that considers the worker's basic needs." The laws of supply and demand simply did not assure just wages, the Dirección continued, but the state could and should. Similarly, a 1941 decree fixing minimum wages in the nitrate industry recognized that wages should reflect a company's ability to pay but also that "[m]inimum wages . . . are established without regard to the law of supply and demand by rating . . . the importance of the job, the physical and social needs of the worker, his family charges, the importance of his functions, work conditions, and the cost of living in the zone in which he labors."[7]

Popular-front state officials thus supported workers' efforts to wrench economic benefits from capital. They thereby secured popular cooperation with their broad-ranging projects. But state agents also modified and complemented popular demands, highlighting the need for agreements between workers and employers that would assure national integration and prosperity. Proper wages, they argued, would ensure "social tranquility," increase production, enhance employer prestige, and "strengthen harmonious and collaborative social bonds between capital and labor." In addition, they supported the idea that a just wage was not simply a minimum or living wage but a family wage, one that would allow male workers to support their dependent wives and children.[8]

BACHELORS, HUSBANDS, AND CLASS UNITY

Materially, family allowances were at the center of worker, state, and employer efforts to frame wage demands in terms of family. Before Congress passed family allowance legislation in 1952, only a small (albeit growing) number of private and public employers voluntarily paid allowances to workers for legitimate family members. Despite the small proportion of workers who received this benefit (around 17 percent of industrial workers), the largest and most economically strategic industrial establishments provided allowances. By 1948, the Caupolicán and Bellavista Tomé textile mills and the Fanaloza Penco tile factory—which employed 2,200, 960, and 1,000 workers respectively—each paid family allowances. Given the visibility of large establishments such as these, conflicts over allowances and the terms on which they were paid undoubtedly had a broad impact.[9]

Although workers, professionals, and politicians commonly referred to family allowances as family wages, the allowances were rarely, if ever, substantial enough to ensure the subsistence of workers and all their dependents. Neither employers nor the state accepted that workers supported not only their wives and children but also brothers and sisters, parents, and even nieces and nephews. Moreover, allowances never fully covered adequate housing, nourishment, and clothing—not to mention education or recreation—for even those family members recognized as legitimate dependents. Working-class families experienced great poverty even with allowances to mitigate deprivation. Often wives, children, and other household members continued to work in order to balance household budgets.[10]

That family allowances did not in fact constitute real family wages capable of supporting entire families did not undermine the notion that women and children should remain at home, away from reputedly exploitative and dangerous wage labor. Since employers in many cases denied allowances for wives who worked, allowances may in fact have discouraged women from working. And workers and state officials insisted that family wages could help men keep their dependent family members within the safe confines of the home. One worker publication noted the inadequacy of women's wages but ended by lamenting: "The salaries of family heads are never enough to cover the necessities of their homes. In the homes of blue- and white-collar workers and professionals, other family members must go to work in industry, etc., at an early age. . . . In this way, women are sacrificed to capitalist exploitation at an early age."[11]

Thus workers as well as state officials generally supported family wages as a way of keeping dependent family members out of the labor market. Yet discussions surrounding the first legally mandated family wage provisions in Chile, set in place in the all-male nitrate industry, revealed the difficulty of consolidating a male worker identity that linked wage-earning to family responsibilities. In 1933, when Chileans began to debate a projected law to put the nitrate industry back on its feet after the crises of the 1920s and 1930s, the issue of family wages came conflictually to the fore. In Congress and in the press, Socialists, Communists, Radicals, and labor leaders opposed the proposed law, labeling it unpatriotic because it granted foreign capital favorable credits. Labor leaders in the northern nitrate provinces set up meetings to discuss the proposed law and rallies to oppose it. They sent a commission to Santiago to lobby Congress and the executive branch. Nitrate companies took measures to stop this oppositional popular mobilization and to discredit labor representatives who opposed the law. In response, Communist and Socialist deputies—seeking perhaps to mollify angry workers who felt sold out or to increase the benefits laborers extracted from the projected revitalization of the industry—submitted an amendment to the law that set minimum wages in the nitrate industry. As passed, the law granted married workers with children a wage calculated to support the worker, his two children, and his wife. For 1934, the minimum wage was fixed at 15 pesos a day for married workers and 10 pesos a day for single workers.[12]

After its passage, law 5.350 continued to spark controversy among both workers and employers. Though employers did not attack the idea of family wages, they fixed quotas for married workers. According to company officials, the mining companies could not provide enough housing for all the married workers who now wanted to work in the mines, or schools for these workers' children. By 1936, the Corporación de Ventas del Salitre (Nitrate Sales Corporation) had instructed labor recruiters not to enlist any more married workers. And while the Dirección del Trabajo claimed toward the end of 1934 that the number of married workers fired in nitrate mines since the passage of the law was not disproportionate and that there was "nothing unusual" in hiring and firing, workers perceived things differently. To obtain contracts, married workers felt obliged to falsify legal documents, claim they were single, and accept the lower wage. In arguing against the wage provisions of the law, both employers and workers noted that because it encouraged workers to deny ties of kinship and to abandon their wives and children, its effect was to break up families.[13]

From the point of view of workers, the wage provisions of the 1934 law were problematic because they situated married and single workers differently vis-à-vis capital. Workers without dependents could afford to accept lower wages, union leaders recognized, undercutting the wage demands of workers with dependents. In fact, as one observer remarked, one crucial function of labor unions was to prevent workers from signing individual contracts, since in isolated negotiations single workers could accept lower wages than married workers. Since law 5.350 was implemented just as the unions reconstituted themselves—at the María Elena nitrate mine, where workers hotly debated the law, attempts to form a legal union took place only in 1936—these divisions were potentially devastating. In 1936, another observer noted of family allowances in general,

> Nevertheless, *there have been voices* that have raised up not against the family wage itself, but against the way it has been put into practice. *These workers have said* that, since the adoption of family wages, the worker element [*el elemento obrero*] tends to divide itself between those who receive family subsidies and those who are not entitled to it [*sic*], each of these groups having different, and on some occasions opposing, interests. One example of this, according to these same workers, occurs in the

case of a strike, when the right to family allowances is suspended for the strikers. It has been noted that for this reason the workers who are entitled to allowances are less likely to participate in workers' movements, breaking in this fashion the solidarity of the workers.[14]

To overcome the discrimination faced by married workers, Socialist deputy Carlos Müller introduced an amendment to the law that stipulated that at least 75 percent of future workers contracted by nitrate companies should be married or family heads. A proposed 1936 law mandating family wages for all blue- and white-collar workers was even more radical, stipulating that no more than 10 percent of employees in any industrial or agricultural activity could be single. Yet as the Dirección del Trabajo pointed out to Deputy Müller, although married workers were "worthy of protection," single workers were "no less worthy."[15]

Despite the initial reluctance of certain nitrate companies to pay family wages, other employers assented to, and even promoted, the payment of family allowances as a way of disciplining male workers by encouraging them to have families. These employers believed that family allowances could serve as a means of paternalistic control aimed at combating labor turnover and creating a stable workforce. With their all-male workforces, mining establishments in particular faced the problem summarized by a social worker for the Tarapacá and Antofagasta Nitrate Company: "On the pampa, our Chilean worker has a natural inclination to move about from one mining center to another, to look for better horizons or simply to experience new environments. This is harmful to the company: replacing workers is costly, and labor efficiency declines." Indeed miners who faced difficult working conditions and unsympathetic foremen frequently left one mining center to search for better employment opportunities in another. Workers in southern mines who remained physically close to the agricultural communities from which they came—for example, miners at the El Teniente copper mine or coal miners from the Lota-Coronel region—routinely abandoned work in the mines to spend time with their families and participate in agricultural labor. Entrepreneurs increasingly saw the transitory nature of male employment as an impediment in their race for riches.[16]

Family allowances were part of employer efforts to discipline through welfare and family values. Married workers, employers believed, would be less likely to pick up and leave if their families lived with them in mining communities—and because of the pressures of supporting a family, less likely to protest or go on strike if they were unhappy. Since work opportunities for women and young children were scarce in mining towns (and no one thought of promoting local employment opportunities for women), the only way to get workers to marry and live with their families was to pay them enough to support their wives and children.[17]

The leftist deputies who proposed the family wage provisions of law 5.350 were likely interested in their material effects. However, other legislators and state officials sympathized with employer efforts to promote stability through the family and believed that a proper family life would temper workers' rebellious and nomadic spirits. When in 1934 the Dirección del Trabajo's magazine published tables documenting why workers abandoned work in nitrate mines—reasons that included theft, absenteeism, taking unauthorized leave days, drunkenness, "bad conduct," "disorders," "disobedience," "incorrect complaints," and even "mistreating animals"—those tables detailed how many of those workers were single and how many were married. For the officials who constructed these tables, marital status explained class unrest.[18]

State officials also promoted family wages as a way of succoring children. Increased wages, they believed, would allow men to properly support their offspring and ensure the health of the nation's future "human capital." By rewarding only workers who could properly document that they lived with legitimate offspring and were married to their partners, family wages and allowances would do away with illegitimacy, paternal abandonment, and common-law marriages, all of which officials saw as threats to children. State agents would simply oversee the well-being of children by securing adequate wages for parents, and especially for fathers. Thus while direct state aid for minors remained meager, the promotion of family wages became an important state welfare policy toward children. However, state officials generally recognized men as family heads and identified women as dependents who were not economically responsible for children.[19]

The paternalism of employers and state agents who promoted family wages provoked worker disapproval. Moreover, at least in the nitrate industry a majority of workers were single,[20] and as prevalent antimarriage maxims in the labor press revealed, men were not completely convinced of the benefits of lifelong marriage:

> All that is one's own seems better than one's neighbor's, except when it comes to one's woman.
>
> [*Todo lo propio parece mejor que lo ajeno, excepto la mujer.*]

The only difference between marrying [*casarse*] and getting tired [*can-sarse*] is one letter.

[*De casarse a cansarse no hay más diferencia que una letra.*]

Not even the most tame dog would let itself be tied up for its whole life.

[*Ni el perro más dócil se dejaría atar para toda la vida.*]

In the majority of cases, a man marries a woman and a woman marries a solution.

[*En la mayoría de los casos, el hombre se casa con una mujer y la mujer con una solución.*]

"Family life" is usually the most difficult.

[*La "vida familiar" suele ser la más difícil.*]

Death leads to something agreeable: widows.

[*La muerte hace algo agradable: viudas.*]

Black is worn to one's marriage and funerals. There must be a reason.

[*Al matrimonio y a los funerales se va vestido de negro. Por algo será.*]

What that longtime bachelor thief hated most was wearing hand-cuffs. . . . [*esposas*, handcuffs and wives].

[*Lo que más sentía aquel ladrón, soltero empedernido, era que le colocaran las esposas. . . .*][21]

Despite these prevalent manifestations of men's distaste for stable married life, most men within the labor movement and the organized Left eventually united around a family wage system and a male identity that bound wage-earning to paternal and marital responsibilities. Unions came to justify petitions for increased wages and benefits by arguing that because workers were men, they needed wages that would allow them to support not only themselves but also their families.[22] But given that many workers were not married and the obvious existence of antimarriage sentiment among them, why didn't workers choose to rally around an identity that rejected stability in favor of male autonomy from work and family ties? Besides a more generous wage for some, perhaps the most important gain for workers who accepted the family wage system was state support for their wage claims. (The state, of course, was centrally interested in social peace and the welfare of children.) In addition, family wage ideology promised male workers a family life in which they would be the undisputed heads. As one observer noted, "On the part of workers, the family wage has been received with great enthusiasm. It could not be otherwise . . . because the family wage constitutes a recognition of the social value of the worker as a family head." In these negotiations, male

May Day issue of the CTCh newspaper Noticiario Sindical, *1949. Photo courtesy Biblioteca Nacional.*

workers lost a degree of freedom to familial and work responsibilities but won privileges as upstanding citizens and providers for their families.[23]

State agents, laborers, and capitalists thus converged around the association of masculinity with paid labor and the fortification of male dominance within working-class families. Each used family wage ideology in different ways and for diverse reasons, yet all drew on the prevalent idea that men should provide materially for family members. Labor leaders argued that workers needed increased wages to support their dependents, and workers with families reaped the benefits—whether they actually spent their allowances on their families or not. Workers, who recognized that it would be harder for employers to reject wage claims made in terms of strengthening the sacred family and feeding needy children, thus manipulated family wage rhetoric to procure increased benefits from capital. Socially recognized as family heads, working-class men also gained authority within the family and the privilege of claiming women and children as their dependents. For employers, a central function of family wage rhetoric was that it allowed them to grant increased wages without recognizing the importance of workers' contributions to production, progress, and profits. By focusing on the familial roles of workers, labor and capital sidestepped conflicts relative to production and were partially able to bridge their contradictory interests relative to wages. At the same time, both employers and workers helped assure the social peace and child welfare so desired by state officials. In this way, the family wage system strengthened the compromise state.

The conflicts surrounding the *ley del salitre* nevertheless revealed the difficulties inherent in positioning male workers as family heads. Although all nitrate workers were men, some of them were married and had families and others were not; some single men aspired to a family life, and many men with children wished to—or actually did—forget their responsibilities to kin. These distinctions mattered to workers, especially since the new law positioned married and single workers differently in relation to employers.

Because of these potential divisions among workers, the labor movement continued to seek reform of family allowance provisions. Though laborers did not call for the abolition of family allowances, they did reject the terms of the 1934 law. As the debate over the family wage provisions of the law continued throughout the 1930s and 1940s—as late as 1953, workers at María Elena were still demanding that the company recognize the real marital status of married workers who had been contracted as single—workers began to suggest that family allowances in the nitrate industry should be paid into a collective fund. Under this scheme, employers would contribute a fixed percentage to the fund for each worker, regardless of whether the worker was married or had children. The plan thus mitigated against the discrimination of workers with families while taking into account workers' differing needs. Insofar as the family allowance became a portion of the salary not regulated by the labor market, workers with dependents would no longer have to compete with single workers who could accept lower wages. Employers would no longer prefer single over married workers when making individual hiring decisions. The family allowance law adopted in 1952 functioned in precisely this manner.[24]

To summarize, workers' own need to forge a unified labor front converged with the state's insistence on the family as a source of societal order and of child well-being and with employers' insistence on the greater stability and discipline of married men. Yet male workers acceded to a normative masculinity in which all proper men were defined as breadwinners despite continuing, if subordinated, expressions of male distaste for married life. Although employers and the state helped persuade working-class men that a proper worker should be a proper provider, in accepting family wage ideology, laborers reinscribed the notion that wages should be gauged to their subsistence needs. Just as important, they consolidated their control of dependent family members. The family wage system thus buttressed male authority within the family while generating a compromise between labor, capital, and the state.

CONCURRING CLAIMS

Women, and housewives in particular, were not crucial partners in the initial public discussions of the family wage system. Yet most supported male family wages as a way of securing their families' subsistence. That support did not, however, imply that housewives passively accepted the views of employers, state officials, or male family members. In fact, the women who were most vocal—militant, organized, working-class women—rejected both male privilege within the family and the class conciliatory gender identities promoted by capitalists and state officials. Although many other women quietly adopted the versions of family wage ideology promoted by em-

ployers, the state, or worker organizations, those militant housewives ensured that the family wage system neither fully subordinated women nor
produced working-class quiescence.

In contrast to employers and popular-front leaders, activist working-class
housewives championed a confrontational proletarian virility and a class-
conscious femininity. For instance, a "working-class mother" from Punta
Arenas agreed that proper men were breadwinners and manifested a desire
for male family wages. But seeing family wages in markedly classist terms, as
a concession to be won from employers, Teolinda Villarroel objected to
bosses' charitable Christmas gifts to workers' children. "As a mother," she
wrote in a local Communist newspaper, "I believe that what the bourgeoisie
should do if it is so 'humane,' is to give our husbands work and improve their
salaries and in this fashion we ourselves would buy our children toys."[25]

In isolated mining centers, where employment opportunities for women
were limited, women were especially active in reproducing a militant
working-class version of family wage ideology.[26] During a 1947 coal miners'
strike, Communist Eusebia Torres, a municipal councillor from the coal-
mining community of Coronel, touted the importance of the miners' labor
and praised her women constituents for refusing to work outside the home.
Speaking in Santiago to members of the feminist organization MEMCh,
Torres characterized her own constituents as real working-class women,
"authentic *obreras*" and went on explain: "I say *obreras*, *compañeras*, not those
workers who must go to the factory to win their daily bread, but we are the
wives [*mujeres*] of the authentic workers, those workers who [endure] pain
and suffering. They are the ones that, risking their lives, because the work
they carry out is the most outrageously dangerous work, I am referring to the
miners, contribute every day to the grandeur of our *patria*." As Torres explained, loyalty to their family members pushed these authentic *obreras* to
participate in class-based movements like the miners' strike: "How painful it
was for the women to go get the flour so that their husbands could go to the
mine and they found they did not have enough money with them to buy it.
So right there the women said we've had enough, we have to make a movement, we're not going to have anything to give our *compañeros* and children to
eat. . . . The women said, we who sacrifice so much are going to make a last-
ditch effort."[27]

Women who like Torres rallied around the wage demands of their male
relatives also called into question the virility of men who failed to take part in
labor mobilizations. Fresia Gravano, who grew up in the José Francisco

Vergara nitrate-mining camp in the 1930s and 1940s, remembered the local
MEMCh committee acting as a women's auxiliary during strikes. Members of
this committee not only expressed their own identities as housewives in a
militant class-based way by organizing around subsistence but also humiliated men who were strikebreakers. As Gravano recollected:

> [In the camp] the women in MEMCh worked with the unions. And
> when workers presented their demands, they worked with the strikes.
> They worked with the strikes. And what were the activities they carried
> out? My mother had a *comadre* who was always up in arms. She was one
> of those who used to hit the men. She hit the men. They used to strip
> them naked when they "sold jobs," as the union says. That was the ac-
> tivity MEMCh carried out. It was an activity, let's say, not so much a po-
> litical activity as a social activity, in the sense of supporting the union,
> supporting the workers with women's struggle.[28]

Volodia Teitelboim's biographical novel of the life of Communist leader
Elías Lafferte similarly portrayed women's efforts to enforce a class-centered
masculinity. According to this fictional account, as a youth Lafferte worked as
a nitrate miner. During the strike that led to the 1907 massacre at the Santa
María School in Iquique, Lafferte and a friend refused to march on the city of
Iquique with their coworkers, preferring to remain in the mining camp. In
response, Lafferte's girlfriend's mother chastised Lafferte and his friend, declaring their lack of class solidarity unmanly: "I warn you great big sissies
[*maricones*] that if they [the strikers] haven't taken your pants off by noon . . . ,
we women up here are going to do it for them. For being cowards!"[29]

During quieter times, women in mining communities continued to organize as housewives around issues of subsistence. At the Vergara camp,
women protested the high price and low quality of goods available at the
company store, and their struggles spilled over into the nearby city of Antofagasta. "There was no social center more important than the company
store," Gravano remembered.

> All the women gathered there to shop, to fight with the store clerks
> who would sometimes give out rotten vegetables, or vegetables that
> had dried out after hours traveling on the trucks from Antofagasta to
> the nitrate camp. And that was the struggle that those women carried
> out. Also because of the quality of the food, [and] because the vegeta-
> bles didn't arrive, because sometimes there was no meat. All those

things. It was like MEMCh's work. They also . . . would get involved with the shops outside [the camp], in the sense of [protesting] the prices. That was also a campaign they carried out. I saw a lot of activity. I was a child, but I remember. A lot of activity.[30]

Through actions such as these, activist working-class women reinforced the gender identities contained in family wage discourse but gave them a specific working-class content. Without doubt, many other women accepted employer versions of family wage ideology, either actively or tacitly. Yet the militant version of family wage ideology articulated by these working-class women helped defeat state and employer attempts to quiet labor agitation.

Activist women ultimately augmented the authority and power of male workers not only in relation to capital but also within the family. Yet at least some of them understood family wages as their own right. In fact, they often invoked hegemonic norms of masculinity to resist male abuses within the family and to diminish their own economic vulnerability. Many housewives asserted, for example, that they should rightfully control their families' income, including their husbands' wages. It was not unusual for a wife to visit her husband's workplace on payday, taking his pay envelope before he had a chance to spend it. Virtuous men, these women insisted, handed over sealed pay envelopes to their wives. Working-class leaders drew on and reproduced this prescription for virtuous masculinity—although they did not always practice it. When Enrique Quilodrán, the adolescent protagonist of Nicomedes Guzmán's novel *La sangre y la esperanza*, receives his first pay envelope, his fellow workers say he ought to "pay his dues" and take them out drinking. Enrique's coworkers eventually let Enrique, still too young for this manly ritual, off the hook. The boy nevertheless shows his virility when he gives his mother the first 5 pesos he has earned. Less virtuous than Enrique, many men insisted on controlling their own wages. Nights out with their coworkers were fundamental to their own sense of masculine identity. Still, many wives had a different understanding of family wages and the standards they implied.[31]

Seeing family allowances as a portion of the wage that rewarded them for their childrearing and domestic labor, women sought outside intervention to ensure control over male wages. As discussed more fully in Chapter 5, they solicited the help of company social workers, who could requisition husbands' family allowances or portions of their wages and deliver the money to the workers' wives. Working-class housewives also petitioned courts to guar-

antee husbands' compliance with their legal obligation to support their
wives and children economically. And in political organizations, too, housewives worked to establish their right to the economic support of their husbands. In 1941 in El Teniente, the local affiliate of MEMCh demanded "the
prompt approval by Congress of the Family Wage Law and the disbursement
of the totality of this wage to the wife." Six years later, a commission of the
CTCh labor confederation led by two women called for the passage of similar
legal provisions. And to guarantee that fathers took responsibility for their
children, a 1951 CTCh committee called for state prosecution of men who
abandoned their children.[32]

Thus individually and in women's organizations, activist housewives challenged the privileges men possessed as heads of families. Political organizing
also gave women prestige and legitimacy within their communities and a
sense of empowerment that tempered their support for male supremacy
within the family. However, in resisting elite versions of family wage ideology activist women often undercut the protofeminist content of their struggles to mitigate their economic vulnerability. As a poetically inclined woman
from the Vergara nitrate camp put it: "What does it matter that they give her
all their wage / even if she has money / what she needs she cannot buy?"
[*¿De qué le sirve que ellos le den todo el jornal / si aunque tenga dinero / lo que ella necesita no lo
puede comprar?*][33] Struggles to increase the resources available to families should
come before contests over the distribution of resources within families, she
implied. Since struggles to increase wages were in many ways premised on
male control within families, this strategy might easily fail to improve the
condition of women.

Conflicts over what male family wages actually meant—male control
over family members or wives' control over their husbands—nonetheless
prompted a reactive reaffirmation of women's subordination within marriage. Within the worker press, a significant (but not necessarily widespread)
prescriptive literature urged wives to act as faithful helpmeets to their husbands. A woman, one publication explained, "should sweeten the life of the
compañero who after long, attentive hours of studying the problems of his class
comes home to his humble shack exhausted. . . . She should at this moment . . . be at the side of our brothers [*sic*] of sacrifice, giving him courage
and comforting him with her presence in the tenacious campaign for the
total liberation of this country's working class." Such a *compañera* should rouse
her husband to action, avoid quarreling with him, and keep a clean, attractive house. This prescriptive strand redefined women's political participation

so that it did not threaten husbands' prerogative over their wives or question the association of women with home life.[34]

Going even further, a CTCh publication extolled conventional gender differences and warned women not to adopt the domineering and daring behavior of women who commanded their families with virility. These women, the article suggested, were deviants who might even take on the physical aspects of men, driving their humiliated husbands into the hands of other women. Instead of acting like brutes, the publication counseled, "real" women would use their feminine wiles and gentle persuasion to get what they wanted from their husbands. This exaggerated call for women's submission, a call that had little to do with the explicitly class-based and activist notions of femininity expressed elsewhere, betrayed a defensive posture. It could not accommodate women's demands for greater control within the family.[35] Nor, as Chapters 5 and 6 show, did it serve popular-front efforts to domesticate and discipline men. As a result, it would remain ancillary.

WOMEN WORKERS AND THE FAMILY WAGE SYSTEM

Even in its milder formulations, however, socialist family wage ideology promoted the notion that women more properly belonged in the home, where they could be protected by male family members. This not only subordinated housewives but also had tremendous consequences for women in paid labor who—because they were not seen as breadwinners—were branded exceptional and special workers. Socialist family wage rhetoric thereby legitimated the exclusion of women from wage work, the segregation of the labor market, and lower wages for women. It also inscribed work identities for women different from those of men. In so doing, it augmented women's economic vulnerability and circumscribed their ability to reject the protection of male family members.

Despite the existence within the labor movement of alternative views on gender, discussed below, many working-class leaders suggested that wage work posed particular dangers for the female sex. A front-page article in the newspaper of the Partido Socialista de Trabajadores decried the miserable working conditions, long hours, and bad pay faced by white-collar women workers. Commercial establishments, it noted angrily, paid women salaries less than the legally stipulated living wage but forced them to sign receipts for the *salario vital*. To remedy this situation, the author of the article called on labor inspectors to do their job and trap scoundrel employers. He went on to argue, however, that prohibiting women from working would be just as effective and class-conscious a measure:

> We should immediately organize united, serious, and organic actions against these shameful abuses on the union and legislative fronts. Women's work in certain "businesses" should be prohibited, not only limited. This measure would oblige the employment of men and make an enormous contribution that would benefit workers' homes, at the same time that it would oblige those hasty financiers, who have made an enormous market of our *patria*, to curb a bit their overflowing profits. White-collar employees' union politics should be a little more dynamic and classist—not to mention revolutionary—and our legislators' actions implacable and constructive.

Believing that women took jobs away from men who really needed them and thereby destroyed the possibility of a proper home life for those men, this article called for the achievement of class unity through the exclusion of women from paid labor. In a similar but more misogynistic vein, when Socialist mayor of Santiago (and women's movement activist) Graciela Contreras de Schnake provided women employment in the municipality, a rival Socialist faction accused her of misspending on "hundreds of worthless and frivolous girls who took the bread away from many workers [*obreros*]."[36] Marking the home, and not the workplace, as the locus of solidarity between working-class men and women, these labor leaders refused to recognize a possible alliance between working men and women. Moreover, they implied that working-class families could function properly only if the male family head had adequate employment.

More subtle insinuations that women did not belong in the labor force were more prevalent in the labor press. Articles in *Vanguardia Hotelera*, the official newspaper of a hotel workers' union, displayed male workers' ambiguity toward women's workforce participation. Around 1949, *Vanguardia* began a concerted campaign to attract female hotel workers, fully 40 percent of all workers in the industry, to the union. The newspaper called on women to join the struggle for better wages and assured them that as the most poorly paid hotel workers they would benefit by participating in union struggles. Yet the newspaper also insinuated that women workers were a species apart:

Industrialists take advantage of this cheap labor to increase their profits and commit all kinds of abuses: ridiculous salaries, exhausting 1 2- or 1 4-hour workdays, the mockery of social laws, immoral propositions, etc., these are only some of the feats performed against our *compañeras* in the industry.

If the situation of our *compañeras* within the industry is bad, that of the hotel workers' *compañeras* who are housewives is no better; perhaps there is no struggle more difficult than that of the working-class housewife.

VANGUARDIA HOTELERA, understanding the enormous importance of defending our *compañeras*, will dedicate its best columns to that which is most noble and beloved to each worker: our wives, our sisters, our daughters, our mothers.

From these columns we will denounce all the exploiters who amass their fortunes at the expense of our *compañeras'* weakness.

We call on all our *compañeras* to write to or converse with VANGUARDIA HOTELERA.

Male hotel workers identified work with masculine family responsibilities and likened female workers to their own wives, sisters, daughters, and mothers. Through references to sexual harassment by male employers and supervisors, the ever-present "immoral propositions," they suggested that work posed particular hazards for the female sex and that women workers needed to be defended by men.[37] Female coworkers surely felt excluded from the virile hotel-worker identity forged by their journalistically inclined comrades.

By accepting the notion that women were frail or vulnerable, some women workers themselves reinforced gendered divisions that relegated them to the worst-paid jobs. Communist Youth leader Ruth Saldías, for example, suggested that some types of work were too strenuous for women. In Chillán, she complained, women were driven to work at the local distillery because of "the absolute lack of work more in accordance with our condition as women." She also portrayed women workers as frail and delicate, complaining of rough treatment by bosses who "don't take our female condition into account."[38]

Undoubtedly, prevalent ideas about women's "natural" abilities and inclinations influenced women's aversion to certain types of work. Yet perhaps working-class women also understood that if they entered traditionally male occupations they would not necessarily receive the same wages as men. Despite the Labor Code's promise of "equal pay for equal work," working-class women could not count on getting the same salaries as men, even when they performed the exact same functions. In fact, they routinely received one-third to one-half as much as men in the same occupations. A recognition of pay differentials led another young worker employed at the Bourjois perfume factory to complain that she and her coworkers did not "receive a penny more" for the heavy work they performed—carrying boxes to the factory storeroom.[39]

Similarly, women's self-exclusion from paid labor may have reflected their evaluation of possibilities within the labor market as well as their belief that women belonged at home. Politically and economically constrained, many women likely saw finding a constant male breadwinner as the best way to assure their own subsistence and that of their children. Women who worked faced real difficulties: not only poor pay but also the scarcity of steady and well-paid work; the rigor and discipline of work outside the home; and the limited availability of child care. A young seamstress stressed the difficulties faced by women who wanted jobs: "There are thousands and thousands of young women like me in the countryside, the mines, the cities, industries, who cannot lead correct lives because it is extremely difficult to acquire a profession, and when we obtain one we find that work in our specialty is very scarce. Every young woman of our class should earn a living, but until now we have found no help." Given these problems, which included a widespread ideological aversion to women's work, the possibility of staying home without excessive material sacrifice attracted many women. Bereft of strong allies who could help them improve work conditions—"we have found no help"—marriage seemed an attractive alternative. As another working woman told a reporter, in the towel factory where she worked wages were so low that "of the seventy *obreras* who work there, only twenty have been around for a while, all the rest have recently entered the factory because, with the starvation wages we earn, they get married and leave."[40] In this context, women's rhetoric about what constituted proper work for women may not have simply indicated their adherence to rigid, dichotomous, and naturalized gender ideals—although ultimately it reinforced those ideals and contributed to women's continued subordination within the workplace and family. Women workers' political marginalization—along with their belief in an ingrained and unchangeable womanly essence that made them unsuited to certain types of work—fed their devotion to the family wage system.

FEMINISTS, PROTECTION, AND THE FAMILY WAGE

Despite many women workers' feelings of political desolation, a group of progressive feminist intellectuals within MEMCh, the cross-class women's organization, did develop a coherent program for ending women's subordination within the family and the workplace. Given MEMCh's attempt to address the needs of single and married women, working-class housewives, wage-earning women, and salaried professionals, the organization's plans were contradictory. Some MEMCh proposals aimed at expanding the possibilities for women in the workforce. Others sought to empower women by vindicating their traditional family-based responsibilities. Yet the more radical feminist members of MEMCh—women like longtime MEMCh secretary-general Elena Caffarena and MEMCh ideologue Marta Vergara—staunchly rejected the notion that women should be dependent on men, economically or otherwise. Vergara, Caffarena, and their allies spent considerable energy opposing policies that sought to exclude women from the labor market, circumvent the "equal pay for equal work" clause of the Chilean constitution, or "protect" women workers. Like men, women supported families, they argued, and deserved family wages. Furthermore, they rejected the notion that because women were more frail than men women workers could not carry out certain kinds of work.

Although Vergara and her allies understood the allure of protection, they believed that the family wage system ultimately produced inequality. According to Vergara:

> Of the two paths available to woman to fix her position in relation to work—which are the paths of protection or equality—unfortunately, the former often seems more beneficial. Not everyone is convinced that protectorates are always fictitious creations that maintain privileges that benefit the protector, nor have they stopped to take stock of what they have paid for their weakness. The egalitarian attitude is difficult not only because it goes against ideas that have been around for centuries about the female sex's intellectual and physical capacities but also because oftentimes we have to struggle against our own workmates and because it is necessary to take on this struggle with large doses of social sense and ability in order not to harm workers in general. . . .
>
> Because of a spirit of abuse, indifference or inertia to change . . . , society notoriously maintains the idea that woman's work is accidental

[and] semiclandestine, and it is accepted with a certain smugness to
"help her meet her expenses." Society continues to see maternity and
home as the predominant social function [of women].[41]

For Vergara and her allies, by contrast, it was clear that unless family wage
ideology was overturned, women would remain secondary family members, secondary workers, and secondary citizens.

MEMCh's more radical feminists worked hard to reform protective labor
legislation in general and maternity legislation in particular, both of which
reinforced the notion that women needed special protection. Although their
rejection of maternity laws was tempered by their perception that children
needed their mothers' care, they clearly saw that maternity laws pigeonholed
women workers because of their reproductive capacities and excluded all
women, as potential mothers, from the labor market. Required to pay 50
percent of a blue-collar woman's salary during a portion of her maternity
leave—the CSO covered the other portion—employers resented having to pay
a worker who was not producing. (The law also required employers to hold
the woman's job for her while she was on maternity leave.) A law that
compelled any factory that employed more than twenty women to provide
on-premises infant care facilities—the idea was to encourage mothers to
breast-feed their children—also potentially raised the cost of hiring women
workers.[42] Because MEMCh members, like state officials, believed these laws
safeguarded children, they did not call for their repeal. In fact, MEMCh often
called for stricter enforcement of existing maternity leave provisions and
their extension to women workers who were not covered: home-workers,
domestic servants, rural workers, government employees, and (in the case of
nurseries) industrial workers in establishments that employed fewer than
twenty women. In so doing, feminists invoked mother-workers' shared experience as mothers and suggested that women in more "informal" occupations deserved the same rights as industrial workers. They also projected the
idea that women had a special responsibility for children and reinforced the
notion that women workers were different from male workers.[43]

Still, memchistas (as MEMCh members affectionately called themselves) emphasized that maternity laws were meant to protect children, not women, and
they looked for ways to provide for the well-being of children without dimin-
ishing women's employment opportunities. In 1940, the MEMCh newspaper
La Mujer Nueva defended certain protective maternity laws. Yet, paraphrasing
MEMCh member and social worker Clara Williams, who headed the state's

female work inspection, it added that "[p]artisans of equality consider maternity the only exceptional case, because there in reality, it is a matter of legislation for children, and they do not accept the idea of legislating for women in general, taking all women as potential mothers."[44] In addition, MEMCh sought to mitigate the discriminatory effects of maternity laws by promoting the payment of maternity subsidies by either the state or an insurance scheme akin to the CSO. At the First National CTCh Congress, it also suggested that all employers and workers of both sexes should be taxed to raise revenues for maternity subsidies.[45] If businesses did not have to pay maternity subsidies directly to women, MEMCh reasoned, they would no longer have economic reason to discriminate against them. Just as state payment of family allowances would remove that benefit from the labor market and do away with competition between married and single workers, state-paid maternal subsidies would end unfair competition between men and women. After much feminist lobbying, a law providing for state payment of maternity subsidies was enacted in 1952.[46]

On the issue of nurseries, MEMCh proceeded similarly, trying to balance the needs of children with those of women workers. Laws regarding nurseries were an integral part of the scientific-rational project of child welfare favored by state officials (see Chapter 5), and feminists too promoted nurseries to succor children. Yet feminists did not consistently put children's needs above women's desires for economic independence and meaningful work. Instead, they attempted to offset the discriminatory effects of the nursery law by calling for state-funded child care. At the First CTCh Congress in 1939, feminists helped push through a resolution demanding preschool programs for the children of women workers and CSO-funded local nurseries. By 1946, MEMCh was advocating state- or municipally-funded, community-based child care centers for older infants and preschool-age children (jardines infantiles). As Caffarena explained, a law setting up state-run day care centers "would not discriminate between the sexes nor go against the principle of equality that we defend, because it would not protect women, but rather children, infancy." If employers did not have to pay for nurseries, she and other MEMCh members realized, they might discriminate less against women. By calling for community-based centers, moreover, feminists completely separated the question of child care from work.[47]

Overall, then, the focus of MEMCh campaigns regarding maternity laws was on remedying the discriminatory and unfair effects of existing legislation as well as on protecting children. Moreover, where the well-being of

children was not at stake, MEMCh argued vigorously against special treatment for wage-earning women. Unlike other sectors of the Left, which
excoriated capitalists for sexual exploitation on the job (see Chapter 6), the
feminist press rarely denounced sexual harassment. Furthermore, feminists
usually refused to use gender-specific arguments to critique poor work conditions. When in 1939 and 1947 feminists supported prohibitions on night
work for women, for example, they asserted that neither men nor women
should be allowed to work at night unless it was strictly necessary. Recount-
ing the conclusions of MEMCh's Second Congress, a leader of the MEMCh
committee in the mining community of El Teniente explained that "what is
bad for women's health is bad for men's also." She further insisted that
neither men nor women should be allowed to work at night without a prior
medical examination. Indeed if women were physically weaker than men,
she asserted, the state should promote women's sports to help women overcome that liability. By 1940 even MEMCh member Clara Williams, whose
feminism was clearly tainted by a professional concern with hygienic childrearing practices, questioned the efficacy of the protective provisions of the
Chilean Labor Code. Existing legal norms were "restrictive," she noted, and
seemed to "punish more than protect."[48]

Caffarena's most impassioned repudiation of protective labor legislation
came in 1951, when Deputy Carlos Acharán Arce proposed to reward the
childbearing and childrearing activities of women in the civil service by
granting them an early retirement. In a letter to the editor of a newspaper that
had publicized Acharán's proposal, Caffarena recognized that the prospect of
retiring early might be attractive to women. But in the long run, she argued,
it was detrimental because it violated the principle of equality for which
feminists had fought for so long. Feminists simply could not demand equality and accept privilege, she maintained. If it was not feasible for all workers
to retire early, then women should not accept this entitlement. Protection,
Caffarena emphasized, always implied subordination. And in a highly significant rhetorical strategy she likened this protection/subordination to both
imperialism and marriage:

We always pay dearly for protection, whether it is granted to individuals or countries. I think . . . that it is not necessary to tell you what the
loans, so "generously" granted to help us by our protector Uncle Sam,
mean in terms of our homeland's submission, in terms of the limita-
tion of our sovereignty. Every protection has submission as its counter-

part. Article 1 3 1 of the Civil Code says, "The husband owes his wife protection," but then it adds, "and the wife [owes] obedience to her husband." The same thing occurs in relation to work, all protection signifies, at bottom, greater exploitation.

Caffarena then indicated that if women were allowed to retire early, this fact could be used to justify women's relatively lower standings on the civil service ladder. The proposed measure would thus hurt women who had been struggling for years for promotion. Finally, Caffarena implored feminists not to betray their most cherished principle, equality: "We are now faced with a situation that tests the fiber of Chilean feminism and its vision of how to defend existing victories and safeguard future achievements. To allow legislation that discriminates against women under the pretense of protecting them is equivalent to beating down the path of postponement . . . which it would be useless to lament down the road."[49]

In sum, Caffarena, like Vergara and the more militantly feminist members of MEMCh, understood that protective laws contributed to the exclusion of women from the labor market and their relegation to the worst paid jobs. Hence Caffarena and her allies argued that protective labor legislation should be abolished or (in the case of maternity benefits) implemented in a way that discouraged discrimination against women.

In addition, radical feminists within MEMCh countered the notion that women did not need to earn as much because they did not support families. Women were not dependents, they insisted; women too supported families and deserved to be paid as well as men.[50] When, based on the notion that women were not breadwinners, legislators proposed a minimum-wage law that allowed women to be paid 20 percent less, telegrams from MEMCh affiliates in Valparaíso, La Serena, and Rancagua helped defeat the proposal.[51] Properly paid employment, memchistas signaled, would not only allow women to care for their children but also help them interact with their husbands in a dignified manner.[52]

Many of MEMCh's more effective campaigns challenged government agencies that discriminated against women based on their purported status as dependents. MEMCh succeeded in convincing the CSO to do away with a provision that forced white-collar women employees of the institution to give up their jobs when they married. In addition, it lobbied and circulated petitions against a legislative project that precluded married women from working for the Postal and Telegraph Service and that stipulated that women could occupy no more than 20 percent of the positions within that service. On the day Congress debated this proposal, MEMCh members filled the congressional galleries, and the quota did not pass (though the prohibition on married women did).[53]

MEMCh also successfully fought government agencies that discriminated against women based on their supposed indisposition for certain kinds of work. In 1940, for example, MEMCh opposed the terms of a civil service competition for positions in the Dirección General del Trabajo. According to the terms of that competition, women could occupy no more than 50 percent of new positions and 10 percent of total inspector positions. In response, MEMCh asked President Aguirre Cerda to intervene. When the president contacted the head of the Dirección, the latter explained that the "dangerous" job of labor inspector was not suited to the "feminine condition" because it demanded much travel. Aguirre Cerda asked the agency head to reconsider his position, and the agency later rescinded the rule. "Thanks to this campaign and the intervention of the president," Caffarena told fellow MEMCh members later that year, "many women were able to enter the work inspection services."[54]

Julio Pistelli, who ran the Internal Revenue Service, proved a more intransigent adversary. Pistelli sought to deny women the possibility of applying for positions as accountants and inspectors by requiring prior military service of applicants. This inspired Cora Cid, a prominent Radical and MEMCh member, to respond that she would ask for the passage of a law allowing women to serve in the military. In an angry letter to Pistelli, Caffarena argued that the provision violated the constitutional right of women to work. She also noted that the director was contravening Aguirre Cerda's express orders to incorporate women into civil and political life on an equal footing with men. Anticipating Pistelli's objections based on MEMCh's previous encounters with the Dirección del Trabajo and the Postal Service, Caffarena rejected the idea that women's health and physical condition prevented them from doing the job. "Time and again experience has shown the inefficacy of that argument," Caffarena wrote with considerable irony, "unless naturally you intend to systematically post women in regions that are inadequate even for the most forbearing and brave of men."[55] Pistelli countered in a predictably offensive manner: "I think that the functions of Accountant and Internal Revenue Inspector, which have much in common and which must frequently be carried out with a lot of physical effort and on occasion even in surroundings not exempt of violence, are not compatible with female nature; and that, on the contrary, they are clearly incompatible with it."[56] Prompted by MEMCh, President Aguirre Cerda requested that Pistelli withdraw the requirement in question, and Pistelli finally acquiesced. But much to Caffarena's disgust, in subsequent announcements of openings in Internal Revenue, the requirement reappeared. Having exhausted the channels that had proved so effective in the past, Caffarena complained bitterly that Pistelli was "as reactionary as he is recalcitrant." *Memchistas* then got President Aguirre Cerda to insist that Pistelli take women applicants, and MEMCh itself publicized the openings in the press and at commercial institutes.[57]

MEMCh, in sum, opposed state policies that discriminated against women: maternity benefits, prohibitions on night work, discriminatory minimum-wage laws, and exclusionary quotas. Feminists thereby confronted a family wage system that positioned women primarily as mothers, classified them as secondary workers, and saw them as naturally weak and unsuited to work outside the home. Women's subordinate position in the labor market, radical *memchistas* realized, was based on their status as dependent members of the family—and vice versa. By suggesting ways of making work and mothering compatible, they tried to generate employment possibilities for women. At the same time, they struggled to do so without reaffirming the notion that all women workers were (potential) mothers and wives and hence dependents and secondary wage earners. At their most radical, MEMCh members rejected protection outright, suggested that responsibility for children should not influence the nature of work or wages, and proposed that the whole Chilean nation should contribute to the raising of children.[58]

Despite this sophisticated and broad-ranging feminist critique of women's coinciding subordination within marriage and the labor market, MEMCh as a whole did not consistently criticize the family wage system. When Emma Parker Lara of MEMCh Santiago made a fraternal visit to MEMCh Naltagua in 1940, she echoed experts' notion of what constituted valuable behavior for women, initiating contests for the "best-kept child" and "home decorating." And when in 1936 MEMCh launched a campaign to pass legislation providing school lunches to children, *La Mujer Nueva* proclaimed, "Let no woman—potential mother—remain deaf to our call." In a public forum, social worker and MEMCh member María Astica similarly advocated "special legislation to protect maternity not only for the [woman] who is [pregnant] but also for her as a latent mother." This group of feminists denounced the subordinate status accorded women within the family wage system and tried to elevate the standing of mothering and housework. The group nevertheless continued to associate women with home and family. Not all *memchistas*, in short, rejected the view that women needed to be protected or the dichotomous gender hierarchies inherent in the family wage system.[59]

In fact, MEMCh at times took positions that reinforced job segregation, promoting forms of work that drew on women's roles within the family. As part of efforts to provide income to women, for instance, local MEMCh committees worked hard to establish and improve schools, especially schools for girls. They also lobbied for the extension of vocational training to working-class women. Most of these efforts, however, taught women skills that allowed them to generate income at home through handicraft production— and at the same time to become better housewives and mothers. Local MEMCh committees thus helped organize courses in tailoring, knitting, cloth cutting, domestic economy, toy-making, knitting, weaving, slipper-making, first aid, and *puericultura*. That domestic-economy courses were offered alongside sewing classes exposed the way this kind of training was meant to foster family-based activities for women.[60]

Some feminists put a new twist on manual work done in the home by focusing on the ways in which it furthered national prosperity. They thus suggested that the production of handicrafts was like industrial labor and that women's labor, even when performed in the home, was an important contribution to national development. This orientation expressed itself most clearly in mid-1939 when Elena Caffarena and Aída Yávar were appointed (without pay) to set up a Division of Specialties within the Ministry of Foreign Affairs. Caffarena and Yávar intended to train women so that they might modernize home-based production techniques. They also hoped to improve the marketability of women's products by developing designs that followed prevailing styles. The division planned to use vocational schools to reach out to women, distribute raw materials, and buy finished products, which the division would then sell in Chile and abroad. In fact, the division had already consulted the U.S. ambassador regarding the possibility of exporting to the United States. From Valdivia, Lía Laffaye (who would later become the first woman elected to the Chilean Senate) applauded the exertions of Caffarena and Yávar and noted that in Europe home-based production had become the springboard for flourishing national industries.[61]

Schemes to foment home industry sought to raise both women's income and the worth of traditional kinds of female work, now equated with industrial labor. Yet they confronted labor force segregation only indirectly if at all. The promotion of home industry obfuscated the question of how work outside the home—work as performed by most men—was defined in opposition to noneconomic family responsibilities. Yet the apparent safety and appropriateness of homework attracted grassroots MEMCh members. As a result, even women as perceptive as Caffarena and Yávar promoted projects that ultimately undermined MEMCh's more radical feminist plank.

Despite these contradictions within MEMCh, an alternative view of women's contributions to family and work—and of men's as well—did develop within a sector of the organization. Writing in 1935 a piece called "War" in *La Mujer Nueva*, "Myriam" evoked a world in which both men and women "worked the earth" and raised children: "Woman who works at all hours, woman and man have given their efforts to produce the gold that is amassed by the ambitious, woman and man have worked the earth and made bread to feed their children and the children of their exploiters." In the ideal world Myriam envisioned, men and women could join together as workers and parents to provide sustenance for themselves and their children and to oppose capitalist exploitation. Similarly, a woman from Los Angeles who wrote to *La Mujer Nueva* spurned the notion that women should stay home to reduce male unemployment with a simple assertion: "Man and woman together form the social body, both need to live, and to live they need to work."[62]

POLITICS, ALLIANCE, AND THE CONTINGENCY OF FAMILY WAGES

MEMCh believed that the best way to expand the rights of working women was to augment feminist influence within mixed-sex unions, and to that end MEMCh encouraged feminist participation in the labor movement. *Memchistas* knew that women's own political inertia, as well as the double shift, precluded women's presence within the labor movement. They nonetheless chastised male labor leaders for their indifference to women's labor concerns. In addition, they suggested that if unions incorporated women and their demands, the labor movement could better defend democracy and help the nation progress. Since women's lower wages undercut wages in general, they told the male-dominated union leadership, increased attention to women's issues would augment the strength and unity of the working class.[63]

The extent to which labor leaders adopted family wage ideology therefore depended not only on negotiations among workers, the state, and capitalists—and within the labor movement, working-class families, and communities—but also on alliances between union leaders, feminists, and women workers. In part because of feminist activism in general and because of feminist penetration of the union movement in particular, the labor movement at times accepted that gender differences and the family wage system should be eliminated. "Until now, it was commonly thought that a worker's *compañera* was a machine for making children; in truth, she is not," the copper miners' publication El *Despertar Minero* declared. Similarly, a columnist in El *Obrero Municipal* wrote: "The time has passed in which it was thought that women should only attend to domestic tasks, when in truth their social responsibilities to the community lie within and outside the home." This discursive strand expanded the range of activities women might legitimately pursue to include many that had been encoded as male.[64]

Many union leaders recognized that paying women less, like paying lower wages to male single workers, made women unfair competitors in the labor market. In fact, these divisions could drive wages down generally. This predicament might be resolved through the exclusion of women from paid labor, quota barriers to women's employment, or the segregation of women in all-female occupations. Increased equality for women in the labor market and in unions might also improve the situation. The labor movement fluctuated between these positions. On some occasions, male workers rallied around a masculine work and familial identity that figured women as dependents. This tendency was most pronounced where the association of masculinity and work was strongest, in all-male occupations. On other occasions, workers dissociated work and gender, sought increased female participation in labor organizations, and advocated a more equitable insertion of women in the labor market. This tendency was especially evident in mixed-sex industries where women workers and their allies in the women's movement forcefully identified women workers as family heads. Where the success of labor organizing demanded other bases for working-class unity, in short, the labor movement abandoned the gender distinctions inherent in family wage rhetoric.[65]

The labor movement generally fought for "equal pay for equal work" and opposed wage discrimination. When in 1936 legislators proposed minimum-wage legislation that stipulated a lower minimum wage for women (and men under twenty-four years of age), male labor leaders protested along with *memchistas*. Communists in particular spoke out forcefully against the legislative proposal. Similarly, in 1941, the CTCh in Antofagasta declared during its Third Provincial Congress: "At our past Congresses our good intentions have not gone beyond literary agreements regarding our blue- and white-collar *compañeras*. . . . Consequently, this Congress must support just remunerations for women and, for their stubborn participation in industry and commerce, compensation equal to men's."[66]

Where men and women worked side by side in the same occupations and where women formed a large portion of the labor force and of labor organizations, rallying around equal pay for equal work was particularly widespread. Not surprisingly, women actively participated in unions that promoted pay equity, and organizations in which large numbers of women participated seemed effective in furthering working women's demands. In mixed-sex industries, where the ideological barriers to women's work had already been largely dismantled, men who advocated better wages for women acted as much out of self-interest as out of a sense of justice. They simply realized that employers might replace them with more poorly paid women.[67] A male leader of workers at the Beneficencia, where women made up about half of all workers, noted with distaste that "the female *practicante* plays the same role as the male *practicante* and often she does so with greater dedication and under less favorable conditions because of the quality of the patients and because she is subject to greater discipline and less professional independence. Nevertheless, she has a lower rank and inferior pay."[68]

In manufacturing, women made up a significant portion of the workforce and participated actively in union struggles for equal pay. Perhaps as a result of those struggles, the wage gap between men and women narrowed noticeably. While between 1941 and 1947 average nominal wages rose 2.5 times for men insured by the CSO, they rose 3.1 times for insured women. And although wages in the all-male mining, construction, and transportation industries rose 3, 2.6, and 2.3 times respectively, in manufacturing increases were well above average, especially for women: in 1947, men in the industrial workforce earned 3 times what they had in 1941, and women, 3.8 times.[69]

The sex segregation of the labor market diminished the effectiveness of struggles for equal pay. Much of the labor movement believed, like Communist Youth leader Ruth Saldías, that there were proper male and female employments. Where there was no equal work, seeing inequality was harder. Purportedly more skilled and predominantly male occupations were better paid, but neither men nor women workers extensively challenged gendered definitions of skill. That Beneficencia workers received wages and salaries well below those of government and semifiscal employees carrying out the same tasks in other institutions was no doubt influenced by the large number of women who worked in the institution. But while the Beneficencia union denounced pay differences among state agencies, it did not link the variations with the sex composition of the labor force. The Communist Party's call for female participation on mixed commissions charged with setting minimum wages in certain industrial sectors sought to eliminate wage inequalities caused by the gendered criteria used to evaluate skill. It was closely linked to MEMCh's 1939 proposal that the "equal pay for equal work" clause of the Labor Code be replaced by a clause mandating "equal pay for work that requires equivalent effort and capacity, without regard to sex." Yet this Communist proposal was extraordinary and exceptional, and it was not acted upon.[70]

Still, even in all-female occupations, where men had nothing material to gain from improving women's wages, male labor leaders on occasion sought to mobilize female workers, attract them to the labor cause, and improve their work conditions. Domestic service, an all-female profession; homework, primarily executed by women; or small industrial establishments, where many women labored, received scant attention from the labor movement. But when women in these activities organized, they were welcomed into labor organizations. For instance, Graciela Sánchez, a domestic servant and leader of a union of domestic servants, won a spot within the provincial leadership of the CTCh in Santiago. Sánchez subsequently succeeded in placing the demands of domestic servants within the confederation's platforms and in its publications. Similarly, strikers in the shoe and leather industry included the demands of home-workers in their petitions. Attempts to establish an industrywide pay scale in textiles sought to protect the workforce of smaller establishments, made up largely of women. The Communist press consistently encouraged women in smaller factories to unionize.[71]

At the El Teniente copper mine, labor leaders waged an extended campaign against the abuses faced by the *empleadas* who worked in the mining camp's hotels, pensions, and canteens. *El Despertar Minero*, the union newspaper, called on the *empleadas* to form a union; pressured labor inspectors to support the women in these efforts; and even scolded male workers who treated the women badly, suggesting that these men betrayed their class. More generally, the newspaper likened the *empleadas* to male workers, emphasizing the way both were exploited by capital and could be liberated through organization and struggle. Highlighting women's female vulnerability, one worker suggested that meager wages pushed these women, who could otherwise become "good housewives, good loving and affectionate daughters," into prostitution. But in the next paragraph the same man made the unusual proclamation that "[t]he Sewell and Mine Union, its leaders or workers who know the Law of Union Organization should have the moral obligation of helping you, *compañeras*, at the same time that you have the same rights as all the citizens of our *patria*, if you have yet to gain political rights, through your Organization you will obtain them." In this worker's conceptualization, women should be unionized to exercise their universal rights as citizens. Although men might support women's exertions to obtain these rights, he insisted that women's own self-organization was crucial to the success of those efforts.[72]

At times, the labor movement even suggested that the family wage itself was a universal right that did not depend upon a worker's sex. In so doing, it loosened the association of wage-earning with masculinity that was at the center of family wage ideology. Hotel workers tepidly asked for the recognition of women's right to work, arguing that "she helps support her home, supplementing the reduced income from fathers, husbands or brothers with her salary."[73] But many labor leaders went beyond the idea that women were auxiliary wage earners who did not support their families. In the worker press, exposés of women's low wages often made reference to the family members women supported. Graciela Sánchez complained that domestic servants frequently "did not have the resources to feed their children." The union at El Teniente supported the demands of workers at a laundry in Sewell, saying the laundresses put up with cruel exploitation so as to "win their daily bread, for themselves and their families, since many *obreras* who work at that establishment have dependents."[74] In this manner, certain sectors of the labor movement belied the notion that women could accept lower wages because they did not support families.

In their most lucid moments, unionists exposed the way that the family wage system served to subordinate women by identifying them as dependents. Salvador Ocampo expressed this belief when he combated the discriminatory minimum-wage law proposed in 1936, saying: "There [in the proposed law] it says that the wage earner, with the product of his labor, has the right to satisfy normal necessities in food, clothing, etc., and to make a home, have a wife, etc. There is no doubt about it. This proposed law must have been inspired by nazi labor legislation that fails to recognize women's right to independence from male tutelage."[75]

In addition, certain workers refused to frame wage demands in terms of normative gender roles. Recognizing, perhaps, that some women were family heads and that many men were not, the newspaper *Obrero Textil* called on laborers to join the union to fight for wages that would increase either their own well-being or that of their family members.[76] A recognition of workers' diverse family circumstances even allowed workers outside the nitrate industry to divorce family allowances from the ideals of masculinity and femininity they were designed to further. As a result, in these other industries the concept that only family heads should receive family wages (and that there ought only to be one family head) lost force. So did the idea that the family members of those family heads were necessarily dependents. Characterizing family allowances as just another wage gain, these workers transcended the potential divisions between workers that allowances installed. At the Compañía Manufacturera de Papeles y Cartones, where a traditional conceptualization of family allowances held sway, the company denied married male workers allowances for their wage-earning wives. In contrast, other factories that hired workers who were married to each other paid each spouse an allowance for his or her dependent children. Here, allowances were paid not only for dependents' survival but also as a worker benefit. In 1950, at the El Salto textile factory, which employed approximately 300 men and 350 women, male laborers received allowances for their wives, whether they worked or not (125 pesos if they worked in the same factory, 140 pesos if they worked elsewhere or did not work). But married women at the factory also collected allowances for husbands occupied outside El Salto. El Salto thus paid allowances for family members who were not necessarily dependents. It is easy to imagine that both the women workers at the factory and broader feminist discourses on the nature of work and family influenced El Salto. Indeed Elena Caffarena retained a clipping of a newspaper article on El Salto's welfare department, published by the Communist *Frente Popular* in 1938, for over fifty years. A social work student who interned in El Salto's welfare department, by contrast, regarded El Salto's family allowance provisions as absurd, an unacceptable deviation from the gender norms implicit in the family wage system. Wives, she knew, did not support their husbands.[77]

CONCLUSION

Few Chilean men or women ever received a real family wage, and not all workers advocated them. Even among proponents, the reasons for supporting family wage provisions varied. Using and reformulating family wage rhetoric that accepted workers' need to support families, feminists and portions of the labor movement sought to alter the gender inequality it inscribed by extending benefits to women workers. Nevertheless, struggles over family wages among actors with unequal power eventually led to the consolidation of male-breadwinner and female-housewife identities. Alternative visions never became hegemonic. They did, however, disturb the association of paid labor with masculinity and lead to limited changes in family allowance provisions. Hegemonic gender prescriptions preempted, co-opted, or ignored these alternatives, but could not banish them.

The normative gender identities propagated through family wage rhetoric and in struggles over paid labor were inscribed principally through negotiation. Negotiation did not take place between free and equal social actors, nor was it completely free of coercion. Bargains achieved locally—in certain unions or economic sectors—did not necessarily project themselves nationally. But all negotiations involved give-and-take. Wage-earning women interested in equal pay and single men who recognized the value of labor unity negotiated with male labor leaders who wished to propagate the hard-won notion that salaries should reflect the needs of workers and their families. Workers negotiated with employers and state professionals who cherished familial and labor stability. Feminists, who had fewer short-term rewards to offer their constituents, negotiated with working-class housewives and workers, and among themselves. Aware of the limits of their power (but also testing those limits), male and female workers often let certain aspirations recede. Wooed by much-needed material gains offered by employers, or by the state's power to legitimate their demands, they yielded on many counts. Yet men and women accepted ascendant norms not simply because they were less powerful than state officials and popular-front leaders but also because those norms incorporated their desires to a degree. Indeed most working-class men and women converged with popular-front leaders around the project of augmenting male wages so that men might protect dependent family members. Feminist proposals for a cross-gender worker solidarity suffered as a result.

chapter three

AUTONOMY AND ALLIANCE

Feminists, Socialists, and Citizenship

Despite progressive feminists' success in securing partial reforms of the family wage system, they could not make the popular fronts move beyond the political inclusion of respectable male workers. That failure was due in part to unreconciled class divisions within MEMCh, which made it hard for the organization to speak democratically to or for women. MEMCh leaders like Caffarena and Vergara showed a clear commitment to working-class women. Yet many of those women saw feminist criticisms of family wage ideology as a threat to class unity and their own livelihoods. That progressive feminists failed to have a broader impact was also due in part to the enduring animosity toward feminism of male leftists, who continued to view the (male) working class as a political vanguard, to fear that feminist demands threatened male privilege and working-class solidarity, and to discredit feminist leaders. This leftist response was particularly damaging to progressive feminists because they believed that fuller democratization demanded both popular-front sensitivity to women's problems and feminist concern for the rights of the disenfranchised. Progressive feminists persistently reached out to Left political parties and other popular-front leaders as well as to working-class women. But besieged and divided, they could not impose themselves more forcefully.

Progressive feminists' weakness—their divided loyalties, a consequence of the tensions between long-standing working-class gender norms and feminist projects—nevertheless forced them to develop a less teleological, more democratic theory and practice of political alliance. It also encouraged them to forge a less essentialist conceptualization of women's identity. To feminists, who faced not only differences among women but also the related difficulty of articulating their struggles within the popular-front project, the fulfillment of their goals could not seem like a preordained national destiny. Gaining support among both working-class women and other popular-front partisans was simply too difficult, and the ways in which popular-front intervention within the feminist movement complicated that project too obvious. That MEMCh's leftist interlocutors often felt they had history on their side did not make those negotiations any easier. Nor did widespread support for the family wage system. Progressive feminists' political experience thus told them that democratization would not be the automatic result of industrialization, national progress, or "history." It would instead be a painful, laborious process that often dead-ended. Progressive feminist leaders held on to the view that, to defeat the capitalist outsider, alliance with the Left was useful. At times, they articulated their demands in the language of national uplift. Still, they challenged their potential allies to rethink how a political pact should be built.

This chapter charts the feminist challenge to popular-front and leftist leaders and how those leaders responded to it. How, it asks, did feminists and leftists articulate class- and gender-based demands, and how did negotiations between the two influence shifting expressions of class and gender?[1] More specifically, this chapter explores the relation of MEMCh and the Communist Party to each other and to working-class women and examines the actual and potential forms of political alliance and autonomy that emerged from those relations. The Communist Party, while extremely suspicious of MEMCh, was the only male-dominated political organization that sustained enduring ties with the group. Because women associated with the Radical and Socialist Parties dribbled out of MEMCh during 1936–40—the Socialist Party feared Communist influence in MEMCh and demanded that Socialist women withdraw—memchistas and Communists were drawn closer together. Moreover, the internecine squabbles of the Socialist Party prevented Socialist women from constructing a strong feminist alternative to MEMCh. MEMCh became the most long-lived, independent, and militantly feminist women's organization—and the most criticized.[2]

The chapter begins by briefly examining women's organizations within the Left and leftist views on feminism in the period before MEMCh formed in 1935. It then discusses MEMCh's conceptualization of its relation to the Left and to the popular-front coalitions. The remainder of the chapter explores the conflicts between MEMCh and the Communist Party and how those conflicts interpellated working-class women. Through a series of often backhanded maneuvers and a populist anti-intellectualism, it argues, the Communist Party successfully used the class differences within MEMCh to discredit progressive feminist leaders. Although the Communist Party's criticism of MEMCh as bourgeois was largely a way of neutralizing its more radical feminist plank, Communists did tap into working-class women's support for the family wage system. They also drew on working-class women's continuing uneasiness with class differences within the women's movement. As a result, Communists succeeded in displacing radical feminist leaders from MEMCh. The Communist Party nonetheless failed to effectively rout feminists. Instead, control of MEMCh fell into the hands of more moderate feminists who were also more centrist, more steeped in disciplinary professional discourses, more suspicious of the Communist Party, and more closely tied to the state. Although these moderate feminists continued to organize working-class housewives and to promote a program of gender uplift, they clearly opposed class militancy among working-class women. After 1944, they would use their access to the state to consolidate their control over housewives' organizations and displace the Communist Party. As the political climate turned Right-ward after 1947, they would go even further: acting in conjunction with political authorities, they helped squelch Communist organizing among housewives. In the end, then, the progressive *memchistas* who attempted to reconcile class- and gender-based demands were stifled by Communists who failed to challenge women's subordinate position within family and polity and moderate feminists who failed to take into account class differences.

THE EXPANSION OF FEMININE ORGANIZING

Within the Chilean workers' movement, women's organizations began to develop in the first decades of the twentieth century—and with them contention regarding women's proper place within working-class politics. In 1905–7, wage-earning women in Santiago embraced a worker feminism (*feminismo obrero*) that sought to defend women's rights in the workplace. However, both the worker feminists and their male supporters saw improved work conditions for women as a short-run solution. They worked for an ideal future in which male laborers earned enough to keep their wives and daughters at home, away from dangerous and exploitative wage work. Working-class women, they argued, should mobilize to defend male family wages. A few years later, in 1913–18, women in the nitrate communities of the north created the protofeminist Centros Belén de Sárraga. Yet women from those communities more commonly closed ranks around their brothers in misery, rallying around the demands of the nitrate miners. And while the FOCh labor confederation admitted some all-female sections in 1919–21, in the 1920s it shifted to organizing women's auxiliaries that included the female family members of male workers as well as wage-earning women. Despite the fledgling feminisms of 1905–7 and 1913–18, then, the Left easily subsumed the demands of women within male-dominated organizations that defended the rights of male workers.[3]

In the 1930s, this slowly began to change. The resurgence of a middle-class feminism concerned primarily with women's suffrage forced the Left to reconsider women's demands. The parallel revitalization of the Left propelled attempts by political parties to mobilize women. In the Socialist Party, regional and local women's federations proliferated between 1935 and 1937, and in 1937 Socialists granted formal recognition to the Acción de Mujeres Socialistas (AMS, Socialist Women's Action), a national women's confederation affiliated with the party.[4] Within the Communist Party, separate women's departments sprang up as well; however, beginning around 1940 Communist leaders repudiated what they deemed "a women's party within the Party." In their stead, party officials championed comisiones femeninas (women's commissions) that mobilized women, and especially housewives, into party ranks. Like the AMS, the women's commissions often acted as auxiliaries that raised money, held raffles and buffets, made sandwiches for party social events, and served the coffee at meetings. Yet they also acted as spaces where women discussed their social and political needs as women.[5]

The Left now emphasized women's emancipation more than it had in the early decades of the century. Yet women's demands were still subordinated to larger struggles. In 1937, a Socialist Party newspaper made the rather typical proclamation that "[t]he Socialist Women's Brigade was born because of the S.P.'s doctrine, which considers women the social and political equals of men, in their rights and qualities. It attacks men's exploitation of women and seeks a perfect equality between men and women. Women must play an active and decisive role in life, and for that reason they must struggle with devotion to change the present, exploitative and abusive, regime. Women play a decisive role in the shaping of future citizens, and they should mold

them in accordance with socialist and revolutionary ideals." Equality between the sexes was good and necessary, according to this author, insofar as it
encouraged women to struggle for socialism, revolution, and the well-being
of children. As G. Fernández, another Socialist, commented, "We are in favor
of women becoming equal to men in every way, but not in today's society . . .
but rather in an INTEGRAL SOCIALIST SOCIETY." Until that day, this author
suggested, women, who were still fooled by capitalist propaganda, should be
denied the vote.[6]

Eschewing what they characterized as rabidly antimale feminist calls, leftist publications urged women to struggle alongside their menfolk for the
socialist cause and to avoid an overidentification with the plight of women.
"As the *compañeras* of working-class men," wrote Socialist Carmen Franck,
"working-class women should not rally under a separate banner." "Red Star,"
one of her comrades, concurred, urging female readers to "join up with your
compañero in the struggle, don't be the vile toy of those who exploit you. . . . It
is time we broke away from our exploiters, every conscious, proletarian
woman should struggle and leave aside that stupid feminism in which she
lives and realize that she has the same rights as a man." The defense of the
working class thus seemed to require a repudiation of "stupid feminism,"
which leftists identified as elitist, divisive, and secondary.[7]

However, the recognition that women's liberation and socialist revolution
were not incompatible allowed women to stress the plurality of socialist
projects. Carmen Franck suggested that women's consciousness of both their
class and sex would lead them to take up the socialist cause. Writing of the
"struggle for justice and social *equalities*," she portrayed socialism as a plural
form of liberation in which women's demands would not necessarily be
secondary. As to whether women were clearheaded enough to vote, Franck
answered comrade Fernández: "[W]e will not let ourselves be mystified."[8]

MEMCH AND THE LEFT

The creation on 11 May 1935 of MEMCh, a broad-based leftist women's
organization, further challenged the Left to reconsider its views on women's
organizing and women's gender-based demands. When Marta Vergara and
Elena Caffarena convened more than two dozen women at the University of
Chile on 11 May, they were careful to include not only professional women
and middle-class women who had a trajectory of feminist organizing but

also working-class women and party militants. In the years that followed, MEMCh would project itself as an autonomous, pluralist organization with a strong feminist bent and would continue to mobilize a heterogeneous group of women. According to Elena Caffarena, MEMCh "achieved something that, until then, seemed incredible: to see women of all social classes acting together in perfect harmony: white-collar workers alongside doctors, lawyers alongside campesinas, señoras alongside domestic servants, artists, writers, alongside women of the people." MEMCh would become the first mass women's organization.[9]

MEMCh did not displace women's organizing within political parties. As Caffarena admitted in a 1942 interview, women could and should struggle on "two fronts": in women's organizations for their rights as women and alongside their children, fellow workers, and family members for other more general demands. Indeed the advent of MEMCh seemed to spur women's organizing within party ranks and vice versa. The AMS picked up speed, for example, around the time of MEMCh's First National Congress in 1937, and some women's groups that came out of partisan politics later joined MEMCh. In La Serena, the women's branch of the Popular Front turned itself into a MEMCh affiliate in October 1936. In nitrate-mining camps, MEMCh affiliates were in many ways the direct successors of prior housewives committees linked to union organizing.[10]

MEMCh feminism combined an analysis of women's particular interests with a consideration of the broader needs of the working class and the nation. Elena Pedraza, a Communist Party militant from the 1930s forward, explained MEMCh activists' approach:

> [T]hey also became involved in the general problems: the mothers' centers, education, health, housing. They took up those social problems, but from a specific women's sphere, because they could not participate like men in political parties. After work, men go to their organizations, and after work women have to go back to tend to their homes, their families. As a result, women aren't affiliated with those parties, and they can't be either. MEMCh took all this very much into consideration. That's why it became an organization that incorporated hundreds of thousands of women from around the whole country.

Pedraza saw MEMCh as an organization that tended to the social demands of women, and especially of housewives, by organizing them in their neighborhoods.[11]

At the same time, MEMCh feminism converged with the popular-front project. As Elena Caffarena noted in 1948, "MEMCh has never advocated the limited criterion of framing its campaigns in terms of antagonism toward the masculine sector of society. The institution's point of view has always been that men and women must join forces to perform tasks in common. Faced with unjust sex discrimination, MEMCh has protested, but it has never circumscribed its work to only this kind of complaint. So at both [MEMCh National] Congresses, studies of general problems, both national and international, figured alongside the just demands of women." Applauding this stance, in late 1937, the Communist newspaper *Frente Popular* lauded MEMCh, saying that MEMCh members "clearly understood the intimate links between their specific problems and politico-social possibilities of the entire country."[12]

MEMCh involvement with "national" problems, such as the cost of living, made alliance with popular-front forces possible and attractive. Speaking in 1936 of the fight to stem the rising cost of living, one MEMCh member wrote, "If the organizations of workers, campesinos, professionals, women, and white-collar workers do not unite to struggle for demands of this type, the cost of living will spiral upward, for the exploiters' base drives [*bajos fondos*] will never be satiated. The degeneration of our pueblo will continue and we will die at the hands of fascism and foreign Imperialism."[13] MEMCh and the popular fronts were thrust closer by the expressed need to combat villainous and shared enemies such as fascism and imperialism—or just plain "exploiters."

MEMCh's clear adhesion to the progressive cause distanced it from an elite feminism that *memchistas* described as contrary to their own desire for political and economic democracy for both men and women. This point of view was especially prevalent among women with ties to political parties. For instance, a 1936 article written by Communist Leontina Fuentes for the MEMCh newspaper *La Mujer Nueva* admitted that women shared many problems but considered these shared sexual traits "minimal in comparison to the general problems that affect both sexes in the same manner."[14] Going even further, in 1940 Caffarena claimed that "[t]he struggle for democracy, to extend democracy from politics to the economy, is fundamental and must come before any feminist struggle." By distancing itself from feminism, or at least from a certain kind of feminism, MEMCh certainly sought to convince allies that it would not be divisive. The organization's avowed concern with "general problems" also reflected its members' sincere interest in a variety of political issues.[15]

Although MEMCh reached out to the Left and the popular-front coalitions and refused to restrict its political agenda to women's issues, it was fully committed to women's improvement and feminism. The organization lobbied for even controversial feminist reforms: the repeal of protective labor legislation, increased access to birth control, the reform of marriage laws that subordinated women, the legalization of divorce, and economic autonomy for women. When the moment seemed propitious, radical feminists focused on these issues rather than on other, more "general" problems. At the convention that approved Gabriel González Videla's presidential platform, for instance, Elena Caffarena performed her duty as delegate of the women's movement by leaving aside "national problems" and concentrating on women's specific concerns.[16]

Feminist leaders hoped that MEMCh's unequivocal allegiance to the popular fronts would make it difficult for leftists to brand feminism as reactionary and divorced from working-class struggles. And indeed once MEMCh began to devise and agitate a concrete political agenda for women that put forth specific social and legal reforms that might be implemented in the near future, it became harder for the Left to postpone discussion of women's expressed needs until after the revolution. The emergence of a less workerist, less messianic, and more pragmatic leftist politics also paved the way for leftist women's efforts to reform their own lot. If workers did not have to wait for the advent of a socialist society to improve their well-being, feminists could now argue, neither did women. If workers could court bourgeois allies to further their goals, so could women. MEMCh member Marta Vergara countered the idea that feminism was bourgeois and irrelevant to socialism by arguing that women's problems were not secondary. The popular-front strategy, she noted, was based precisely on reforms and an alliance with the bourgeoisie. When she and her Communist boyfriend Marcos Chamudes quarreled about the relevance of feminism and its class nature, Vergara pointed out that Communists advocated a reformist, bourgeois-democratic revolution carried out in alliance with bourgeois sectors. As Vergara recalled in her 1963 memoir, "In relation to these [women's problems], my point of view and Chamudes's did not coincide. I believed that equal rights for women were more important than the class struggle. In the end, I used to argue, the Chilean Communist Party believed at the time that the country's revolution would be bourgeois-democratic in nature. Why then exclude bourgeois women? Why not help them obtain the benefits enumerated in the platform?"[17] While male popular-front politicians concerned themselves with the economic aspects of the bourgeois-democratic alliance and framed the demands of male workers as national imperatives, women like Vergara sought to broaden the range of political actors and interests articulated into the popular-front project (and the intended beneficiaries of reforms).[18] By both attempting cross-class organizing in a sustained way and continually pushing for the formal and substantive extension of democracy, feminists were perhaps the main promoters of a bourgeois-democratic alliance.

However, leftist politicians criticized feminism precisely because it was a cross-class movement and continued to see the working class as the main protagonist of reforms. They thereby hindered the impulse to democratization and national unity that they themselves claimed to champion—and that women conscientiously tried to carry out.[19] In fact, the frequency with which leftist men and women sought to distance themselves from feminism (even when MEMCh went to great lengths to show that it practiced a socially conscious feminism) suggested that perhaps the class bias of feminism was not the only problem. That was what Marta Vergara hinted at when she told her boyfriend that, given the popular fronts' stated goals, the fact that feminism was bourgeois should not be problematic. And although an elite brand of feminism devoid of concern for the social and political rights of the poor had existed in Chile, by 1935 it was mostly defunct. It is therefore likely that feminism was considered divisive for other reasons: because men and women feared its deeply subversive elements and because men were anxious about losing sexual and political control. These anxieties did not usually surface in public. Still, the hidden dangers of feminism emerged in private when leftists maligned feminists by insinuating that they were mannish or lesbians. Elena Pedraza remembered how Isabel Díaz, an outspoken feminist and Communist, was discredited in precisely that manner by male party members:

> Isabel Díaz was an *obrera* who sewed pants and jackets, . . . and she was old, had white hair, was rather large, had lost her teeth, I think. But when she spoke she was a tremendous feminist. And because she was a feminist and since she fought with men as their equal—this is what I think, she could even have thrown a man a punch, [she was] stout—I remember that they spread the rumor that she was a dyke. But that woman, Isabel Díaz, always fought for women. . . . She was in the party, and she always said things to their face, that's the impression I have, about those things that the men, the party's policy, of always considering women, seeing women as secondary.[20]

No matter how hard MEMCh members tried to prove their allegiance to the popular fronts and no matter how often *memchistas* invoked the coalition's stated goals, they could not get around men's unexpressed fears and unspoken anxieties about the sexual ambiguity that feminism might bring. Although MEMCh members countered antifeminist sentiment on the Left by showing how women's emancipation was linked to other popular-democratic reforms, many men and women maintained a lingering skepticism toward feminism.

"LA ESCRITORA AL LADO DE LA MUJER DEL PUEBLO": NEGOTIATING CLASS AND GENDER

That male leftists expressed their uneasiness with feminism by labeling it bourgeois did not mean that the class content of feminism—as ideology and movement—was not the subject of contention among women activists. The mostly professional women who made up MEMCh's leadership saw the incorporation of working-class women as an essential part of the organization's mission and believed that feminism spoke to the needs of those women. Nonetheless, MEMCh did not achieve the "perfect harmony" Caffarena desired, for men were not the only ones who felt threatened by MEMCh's most subversive feminist proposals. Many working-class women who identified themselves as housewives and mothers and who saw male protection, especially male economic protection, as their best bet for survival also felt uncomfortable with certain elements of MEMCh's platform. For that reason, *memchistas* found it difficult to forge a cross-class feminist project and modes of citizen participation coherent with that project.

MEMCh's bids to find a political voice for women, in themselves complex, became even more complicated because of the tensions between MEMCh and the Communist Party. Throughout the popular-front period, the Communist Party would challenge MEMCh on the grounds that it was an elitist group guided by the interests of professional women. And professional women within MEMCh would question the Communist Party on the grounds that it did not respect their right to independent thinking and organizing. The conflict between MEMCh, an organization that defended its autonomy, and the Communist Party, which wanted to enlarge its own following, overlay the discrepancies between more feminist and more traditional models of social and political citizenship for women. This produced unfortunate effects: it made it hard for the mostly professional leaders of the women's movement to see the ways in which their more radically feminist proposals could be unattractive to working-class women, and it precluded a more sustained consideration of feminism on the Left. To the extent that both feminists and leftists imposed their own definitions of working-class femininity—this more unilateral stance was especially prevalent among Communist Party members who put class struggle above all else—they hampered dialogue between feminists and the Left. Institutional and ideological affiliations occluded class differences among women and (more commonly) gender inequality within class.

Collaboration between the Communist Party and MEMCh was based on convenience and principle. On a practical level, MEMCh and the Communist Party needed each other. The party needed MEMCh because it mobilized large numbers of women efficiently. In addition, female Communists legitimated themselves within the broader women's movement by participating in MEMCh. MEMCh in turn needed the Communist Party, or at least certain women Communist militants, to reach working-class women.

Through circulars and letters and *La Mujer Nueva*—a sporadic newspaper that reached a circulation of 3,000—MEMCh leaders sought to rouse women to action on behalf of a common cause, inform them of the MEMCh program, and recruit them into the organization. Still, organizing tours, many of which were undertaken by Communists, were MEMCh's most successful mobilizational tool, and MEMCh relied heavily on its Communist militants to reach out to working-class women. María Ramírez and Eulogia Román, both Communists of working-class extraction and union leaders, toured the country in 1937, and Ramírez visited the northern provinces just before MEMCh's Second National Congress in 1940. Since Communist *memchistas* who traveled outside Santiago capitalized on their political connections to build MEMCh, these tours mostly succeeded in recruiting women in places where there was a trajectory of working-class organization. As a result, many of MEMCh's grassroots affiliates came from areas where Communist organizing, and Communist organizing of women, had been strong. The northern nitrate-mining region, for example, became one of MEMCh's strongholds, and there were also MEMCh committees in the copper-mining town of Sewell and in the Lota-Coronel coal-mining region. When *El Siglo* reported in 1943 that the seventeen MEMCh committees in Tarapacá province constituted "the majority of the organized feminine population," it was probably not exaggerating. At least outside Santiago, MEMCh was more successful in recruiting working-class housewives than middle-class women.[21]

In addition, male Communist leaders often instigated the formation of MEMCh committees. When Communist senator Elías Lafferte toured the nitrate-mining region in early 1939, the women's department of the Communist Party in the mining office of Buenaventura offered a lunch in his honor. Lafferte urged the women to constitute a MEMCh committee. Elsewhere, the ties between Communist political efforts and MEMCh were also clear. The MEMCh committee in Conchalí, for instance, was affiliated with Socorro Rojo, a Communist-front organization that provided assistance to political prisoners and their families. More generally, memchistas participated in union struggles and neighborhood associations in which Communists were active. In fact, at some point after 1935, it became common for activists to refer to organizations associated with the proto-Communist POS or the Communist Party as MEMCh groups, even when those groups existed prior to the formation of MEMCh.[22]

Members of local MEMCh committees outside Santiago, and members of local committees with strong links to the Communist Party in particular, continued to struggle principally for their demands as working-class housewives and mothers: more schools, urbanization, and cheaper prices for subsistence goods.[23] These women also participated in the life of their male relatives' unions, collaborating in strike activities and, as we saw in Chapter 2, calling for the extension of family wages to men. Drawing on hegemonic notions of proper masculinity, they sought to make men more responsible toward their wives and their children. To improve the physical and material well-being of women and children within male-headed families, for instance, several local committees lobbied for dry laws in their localities, and in Corral, MEMCh members succeeded in getting a dry law set in place. In Ovalle, MEMCh undertook an antibetting crusade. In addition, memchistas from Lota, Coronel, Valdivia, and Naltagua promoted temperance through newspaper articles, talks, rallies, and social events. MEMCh Concepción was particularly active in this area: its members marched against drunkenness, sponsored an athletic contest to provide men with alternative recreational pursuits, and organized an exhibit of posters that depicted the horrendous consequences of drinking. Along with mutualist and union groups, it organized a broad-based anti-alcoholism committee.[24] It was largely thanks to MEMCh campaigns such as these, which sought to enforce male responsibility and respect for women, that the organization became a powerful institution with grassroots committees throughout the country.

While many grassroots MEMCh committees reaffirmed a more traditional feminine identity, not all local committees were uninterested in MEMCh's more explicitly feminist proposals. An article by a local MEMCh activist published in the union newspaper at El Teniente made manifest the ambiguity of working-class housewives in relation to feminist demands that questioned the family wage system. This article approvingly presented the conclusions of the 1940 MEMCh congress, focusing first on MEMCh's rejection of restrictive protective labor legislation for women. Since protective labor laws prohibited women from working underground, the effects of these laws might have been particularly obvious in a mining camp, where women would have been legally excluded from the best-paid positions. Yet after describing some of the resolutions of the MEMCh congress, the author concluded: "Those are some of the problems taken up by MEMCh in its Second National Congress. . . . In this Camp, as a consequence of the rising cost of living, nourishment has become a frightening problem."[25] In this rendition, the conclusions of the MEMCh meeting were presented as important and interesting but distinct from the concerns of the local women. At the same time, an anonymous article in another issue of the El Teniente union newspaper concluded: "Many of us women wish to go to the Union, to help in the struggle for our necessities."[26]

More than a few of MEMCh's working-class constituents, then, had previously participated in working-class politics, and they came to MEMCh with an already delineated political identity as working-class housewives and mothers. These women had already reaped important gains by rallying around a more traditional feminine identity—most notably more constant male economic support and increased concessions from capital—and as they entered MEMCh, MEMCh ideologues would find it more difficult to generate a frontal critique of male dominance and of stultifying normative gender roles.

TO NEUTRALIZE AND DIVIDE: THE COMMUNIST CHALLENGE

Communist militants within MEMCh, many (but not all) of whom showed more loyalty to their party than to feminism, aggravated the difficulties faced by feminists like Vergara and Caffarena. By continually mobilizing women around more class-based concerns and reinforcing those women's political identities as housewife-mothers, they eventually neutralized MEMCh's more radical feminist project. This outcome was not, however, inherent in MEMCh's attempts to organize working- and middle-class women as well as single women, housewives, and mothers. Instead, the derailing of MEMCh's more subversive feminist project was largely the work of Communist *memchistas* such as Micaela Troncoso and María Ramírez who acted on orders from the Communist Party hierarchy. Yet blaming the Communist Party, or Communist women, for MEMCh's increasingly accommodating stance tells only part of the story. What it fails to disclose is the way that many Communist women opposed their party's pressures. And it also obscures the ways Ramírez and Troncoso succeeded largely because they tapped into and mobilized grassroots *memchistas'* perceptions of class differences and resentment toward professionals.

While the Communist Party in some ways tried to broaden its political line during the popular-front period, it continued to advocate an anti-intellectual, worker-oriented political stance that stressed class as the center of political organizing. This tendency, which emerged forcefully after the Hitler-Stalin pact in late 1939, had always been latent within the party. As women's organizing proliferated, it was invoked specifically to discredit non-Communist feminist leaders. Communists had manifested a marked anti-intellectualism as early as 1937, when they ran a headline in *Frente Popular* that praised MEMCh's First National Congress by remarking (as if erudition were somehow inappropriate for women): "The Feminine Congress Will Not Be a Tourney of Learned Discussion."[27] Elena Pedraza, herself a Communist, recalled *memchista* María Ramírez as a prime exponent of that political line:

María Ramírez was like that, for her everything was black and white, bourgeoisie, capitalist exploitation. There was nothing to understand, not even political alliances. We were alone like the three musketeers, united against capitalism. So she conveyed that to the women, and the women in MEMCh [would say], "Well, no, we are struggling for this, for schools, for equal pay—which was the most important slogan—for equal work, protection of maternity, nurseries, to better the condition of women in the *poblaciones*, etc., etc., recreation, the problems of infants." MEMCh worked on all of that. They took it up as it pertained to women. And now that I reflect on it . . . I see things clearly. What would happen? María Ramírez would come and say, "In these times, no." Because the party said that we had to go out on strike, . . . or do

solidarity work, that we had to struggle for something that was completely foreign to what they [MEMCh leaders] were doing. And so a
rupture developed with the group of women who had a program.
That was the quid of the matter.

This workerist stance weakened feminism as a cross-class political movement. Yet some Communist women actively resisted it. According to Pedraza,
"There was also Eulogia Román who was another blue-collar worker, also in
the party. . . . María Ramírez was a terrible Bolshevik, struggling for the
takeover of power. And Eulogia Román was more balanced in her way of
seeing things. She was a lesbian who understood more, was more open,
understood the problems more. The other one was hard."[28] On the eve of the
MEMCh Second Congress in 1940, however, it had become clear that the
"Bolshevik" María Ramírez would have her way and that feminism would
suffer as a result.

It is difficult to evaluate whether MEMCh's feminist platform was attractive
to working-class women, or the extent to which working-class women felt
MEMCh leaders adequately represented them. Some clearly felt that MEMCh
leaders were too highbrow, their discussions too arcane. Communist Iris
Figueroa said she did not participate in MEMCh because "it was something
very aristocratic." Extrapolating from her own experience, she suggested,
"So a woman from the *población* felt inhibited being around people of that
standing. They were wonderful to me. I never had any problems. I worked
with Elena Caffarena. For a long time I worked with Olguita Poblete. But
women of other sectors, let's say the majority of women, didn't draw closer
because of that same thing, because it was so academic, all those ideas or the
discussions. So it didn't really take hold because the woman of our pueblo is
a fighting woman, a woman of struggle, because they have their problems."[29] The intellectuals in MEMCh, Figueroa believed, did not adequately
articulate the problems of fighting women.

Unlike Figueroa, Mercedes Fuentealba participated personally in MEMCh
and believed that the organization helped her grow personally and politically.
Yet although Fuentealba enjoyed contact with MEMCh's leaders, she clearly
understood that there were differences between herself and them. In a 1993
interview Fuentealba tempered her praise for MEMCh as a cross-class institution with a scathing depiction of class differences among women:

[In women's groups] woman finds, how shall we say, her Club de la
Unión [Santiago's most exclusive men's club], I would say. Because it's

really nice to arrive and not have differences. You who live here in this apartment can rub elbows with a woman who lives in a shack, and you two can use the *tú* form and give your opinions. And the woman also acquires culture and begins to see that she can converse with the lawyer, that she can converse with the other one, learn. And she says, well this señora, this señorita who I find so pretty—because there are pretty women—look, they can participate in this. So that gives her confidence, and she treats her like a person and that gives her confidence. She doesn't treat her like a *patrón*. She is no longer the foreman of the factory; she isn't the *patrona* who treats her with indifference. So the woman starts to acquire a personality. . . .

Let's say there's a middle-class woman. Let's say that she has someone here to do things [housework] for her, that she can find a way to pay someone, so that you can go to work at your office or wherever, at school, I don't know. Now wouldn't it be lovely if you could establish a human relationship with that person? If you no longer looked at her so much as a servant, but you saw her now as a collaborator, and you tried to straighten her out so that she understood that she is a person, that she can change, that she has the defects that she has, the quirks we could say, she can overcome them. And at home she can apply some of these things.[30]

In this testimony, Fuentealba clearly described the pervasiveness of class differences. To signify disparities based on class, she employed the trope of female beauty, available only to elite women. (Insofar as those ideals of beauty were also racial markers, Fuentealba alluded to racialized class distinctions.) And she invoked the most direct way in which elite women exercised power over other women: in their relation to domestic servants. But Fuentealba also claimed that professional women, who had built their own self-esteem through education, could show working-class women that they too had a right to be respected. Signaling the possibility of even more horizontal ties, she noted that organizations such as MEMCh allowed all women, rich or poor, to "give opinions." Women could collaborate despite class differences. And, Fuentealba made the very suggestive comment that working-class women could apply this experience at home, where they might presumably demand that their husbands and family members treat them as equals.

Elena Pedraza countered criticism of MEMCh leaders as elitist in another way. She claimed that those who criticized MEMCh's leadership were only showing resentment and an easy anti-intellectualism that dismissed "anything that smelled of books." These critics, according to Pedraza, "never understood intellectual women." Moreover, those who deprecated MEMCh leaders by suggesting that intellectuals might betray workers put class background above what really mattered: the actions taken by the intellectuals and the spirit in which they took them—in short, their participation in and creation of a progressive political project. Confronting poverty was part of that project. Caffarena and others, Pedraza recalled, went out into the streets and organized neighborhood groups, and "they did it because they were convinced." At the same time, Pedraza castigated those who overlooked the fact that "sometimes a very exploited worker who lives in misery can be a traitor."[31]

The events surrounding MEMCh's Second National Congress, which began in the last days of October 1940, brought to a head tensions that had previously existed: strains based on class differences, strains between the Communist Party and an organization that prided itself on its autonomy, and strains based on distinct visions of how to organize working-class women. In a letter explaining why she resigned as secretary-general of MEMCh, Caffarena detailed these conflicts. Conceding in this missive that a "Communist fraction" had always worked within MEMCh, Caffarena nevertheless praised Communist memchistas for their contributions to the organization. Communist women, she wrote, acted with "tact and prudence," moderation, and discipline. She herself had often turned to them to fortify weak local committees, and "without this fraction," Caffarena continued, "MEMCh would not have obtained the standing it now occupies."[32]

The controversy between MEMCh and the Communist Party was therefore not due simply to the presence of Communists within MEMCh. Rather, it flared up when Communist Party secretary-general Carlos Contreras Labarca mentioned MEMCh in a speech given at a party plenary session, implying that the party controlled MEMCh. MEMCh's Executive Committee objected to the speech, which had been reprinted in the Communist daily El Siglo, because it openly associated MEMCh with the party. The speech, they felt, would hinder their ability to reach apolitical women. The MEMCh Executive Committee asked memchista Delia de la Fuente to request that the party make a public declaration clarifying MEMCh's status as an autonomous organization. The Executive Committee's petition did not receive a response.[33]

To add insult to injury, two days before the MEMCh congress, Micaela

Troncoso, a member of the party's Central Committee, published an article in *El Siglo* in which she ratified Contreras Labarca's report to the Communist plenary session, terming it "magnificent." Troncoso, who had helped organize FOCh affiliates—and women's auxiliaries—in the coal-mining region of the south in the 1920s, clung to the model of organizing women prevalent in those mining communities. In her article, Troncoso characterized MEMCh as an organization with "great weaknesses" that was "stagnating or even moving backwards" and enjoined MEMCh to "abandon its false apoliticism" and get down to the real task of organizing women in their neighborhoods and unions. Caffarena deemed the article "petulant in tone." To her, it signaled a new modus operandi on the part of Communist women, who had always aired their points of view within MEMCh's Executive Committee, not in the press.[34]

As Caffarena herself pointed out, this dispute was not simply a matter of jurisdiction, a turf war. Troncoso, Caffarena believed, wanted to make MEMCh into an organization solely for working-class women. Such a group, the party said, would advance the kind of women's movement to which the party aspired, a movement "closely linked to popular and workers' struggles."[35] To this, Caffarena replied:

> The working-class elements have, without a doubt, a great value. But in my understanding, MEMCh's work should especially be aimed at attracting middle-class elements. This is not to underestimate the working-class woman, but responds to a practical reason, to a complete vision that looks toward the total liberation of el pueblo. In effect, the working-class woman can be channeled by unions, by renters' leagues, by multiple organizations; in contrast, the middle-class woman, prejudiced, ignorant, with elitist tendencies, is completely unorganized, in circumstances in which by attracting her and orienting her she may become a useful element that ends up joining the parties of the Left. It seems to me that this is a fundamental task for MEMCh along with attracting women intellectuals such as schoolteachers, social workers, nurses, women in liberal professions, so that they can put themselves at the service of culture and well-being for the working masses.[36]

Prodded by Communist leaders, the Communist women who attended MEMCh's Second Congress seemed to reject Caffarena's vision. They refused to attend a commission in which María Durois participated, because Durois "had undertaken specialized studies of the subject." Troncoso showed so much hostility toward Durois that *memchista* Susana Depassier, herself a Communist sympathizer, threatened to withdraw from the congress. Moreover, in a concerted attempt to overshadow the professional women in MEMCh, Communists used their massive presence at the congress to elect five working-class women, four of them Communists, to head the congress's commissions. Caffarena conceded that the Communist women were merely exercising the right to representation, which their substantial presence within the proceedings gave them. She also noted that Communists in MEMCh had never exercised that prerogative before. All the work commissions elected Communists to present the conclusions of their debates, she pointed out, while at MEMCh's First Congress, in 1937, only three of ten commissions gave that responsibility to Communists. Because of this maneuvering, Caffarena reported with some condescension, debates were ineffectually led by people who were ill prepared for that task.[37]

As a consequence of these events, Caffarena, who had actually been reelected secretary-general at the congress, resigned. Vergara, who, like Caffarena, came to the conclusion that Communists were trying to take over the organization, followed in her tracks. Other non-Communist women left the organization as well.[38] Graciela Mandujano, a feminist with no ties to the Communist Party, was later elected secretary-general. Mandujano was, according to Vergara, "an apolitical liberal with a certain interest in the working class. Also a sincere feminist." Yet the departure of MEMCh's most penetrating feminist thinkers—and in the case of Caffarena, of a profoundly efficient organizer—decidedly weakened the organization's ability to advance women's emancipation. According to Marta Vergara, the Communists had "buried" MEMCh.[39]

Ironically, the insistent challenges of working-class women and Left leaders, which ultimately drove Caffarena and Vergara from MEMCh, forced progressive feminists to problematize essentialist formulations of feminine identity. When asked in an October 1940 interview if a woman could perform properly as a professional, Elena Caffarena responded, "Of course, there is nothing in her character or in her nature that prevents it. Why shouldn't she be as good a professional as a man? In the countryside and the city, there are women who work at tasks that are harder and less suited to their nature than the tasks demanded by professional activities. Certain manual jobs exhaust her organism, but cerebral work does not." When her interviewer then asked, "What about her femininity?" Caffarena replied that femininity was something that making a woman's brain work could not alter. In making this argument, Caffarena used widely acknowledged differences between manual and intellectual labor, and between women of different classes, to show that there was no immutable core of womanhood—or at least that historically women had been forced to go against their womanly nature. Working-class women, who had always performed backbreaking work, had never conformed to norms of feminine deportment. In another interview published a little over a year later, in January 1942, Caffarena answered a similar question by saying that femininity, usually portrayed as a certain coquetry and good looks, was "something subjective, women's particular way of being." It was, she continued, "permanent, constant throughout the ages and across customs." Still, Caffarena clearly asserted that neither paid labor nor political activism could alter that subjective core: "If work influenced femininity," she explained, "then, believe me, there would not be any femininity left in the world."[40] Thus Caffarena granted women a particular subjectivity, but she pointed out that women's subjectivity did not flow from their work or political involvement. The diversity of women's political, economic, and family lives, she recognized, made it impossible to place these activities at the center of feminine identity. In this view work and politics, two endeavors intimately tied to men and women's bids for citizenship, were not gendered.

Communists, by contrast, essentialized the identity of working-class women and refused to grant them greater political autonomy. This weakened and limited not only MEMCh but also the popular fronts more generally. For despite the Left's professed interest in a broad national alliance, in its dealings with women it manifested a shallow understanding of what forging such an alliance really meant. To the extent that the male-dominated Left claimed to know what was best for working-class women and failed to consider feminist demands seriously, it missed the opportunity to develop a theory and practice of democratic collaboration. Left leaders rarely shared opinions with either feminists or working-class women activists. As a result, it remained possible for leftists to use class-based rhetoric to neutralize gender-emancipatory practice, and as we will see below, for the moderate feminists who took hold of MEMCh after 1940 to use the banner of women's emancipation to neutralize class militancy. Left leaders, in short, refused to come to terms with all the difficult transactions that a bourgeois-democratic revolution entailed. This option was not available to progressive feminists. For despite never fully reconciled class differences among memchistas, MEMCh leaders were forced to collaborate with working-class women like Mercedes Fuentealba and to negotiate the meaning of feminine identity alongside them. To avoid doing so would have doomed them to the political margins and vitiated their own aspirations.

MODERATE FEMINISTS, THE COMMUNIST PARTY, AND THE STATE

MEMCh survived the events of late 1940, and, in the end, its feminist impulse was not completely arrested. The organization endured because of the incredible perseverance, astuteness, and sensitivity of many local and national Communist leaders. And feminism (albeit a more restrained feminism) lived on within MEMCh because there were still women eager to struggle for their rights as women and to break out of constricting molds. Perhaps most important, MEMCh and its feminism persisted because they were part of a larger women's movement that became more active beginning around 1942. In that context, Caffarena later rejoined MEMCh, although in a more modest role.

The activism that flowered around 1942 was more moderate—in terms of both its feminist and its class politics—than MEMCh had been under the leadership of Vergara and Caffarena. It was also a movement in which professional women, many of whom had strong ties to both the Radical Party and the state, played a more prominent role than they had in the past. In this situation, Communist animosity toward intellectual women and autonomous women's organizations would come back to haunt them. Beginning in late 1944, moderate feminists would mobilize their ties to the state to marginalize the Communist Party, which continued to distrust professional women and to compete with feminists for leadership of working-class housewives. Even more, as anti-Communism took hold and President Gabriel González Videla moved to restrain the Communist Party, moderate feminists would cooperate with state efforts to co-opt and repress party activists. Ultimately, then, Communists' suspicion of women like Caffarena and Vergara not only devastated progressive feminists' efforts to forge a pluralist, progressive feminism but also facilitated a polarization of the political climate and anti-Communism. After 1947, working-class women would have to choose between a program of feminist uplift that explicitly sought to neutralize class militancy and a class politics that neutralized gender inequality.

This process was especially evident in the consumer movement, where Communists tussled openly with moderate feminists. Since at least the mid-1930s, feminists and leftists had competed for leadership of committees against the high cost of living. Yet until the mid-1940s there was substantial cooperation between groups associated with the feminist movement and groups associated with the Left. In 1937, for instance, the Agrupación Femenina of Concepción called on housewives and wage-earning women to rally together so that they might participate, in a "completely organized" fashion, in an upcoming gathering sponsored by the mixed-sex Comité pro Abaratamiento. Moreover, many housewives' committees, especially those in mining communities, had links to both MEMCh and the Communist Party. In Tocopilla, Communist women in the Sociedad de Protección a la Mujer Chilena (Society for the Protection of Chilean Women), a MEMCh precursor, urged women in the nitrate camps and the city of Tocopilla to form committees against the rising cost of living.[41]

However, in late 1944, as both the consumer movement and the broader women's movement entered a period of heightened mobilization, tensions between feminists and Communists surfaced. In May of that year, Caffarena had returned to MEMCh as secretary of organization, and other intellectual women who had left in 1940 also rejoined. Among them was Clara Williams, a prominent social worker and member of the Radical Party.[42] A few months later, in November of 1944, MEMCh and other more moderate organizations as well as women from various political parties founded the Federación Chilena de Instituciones Femeninas (FEChIF, Federation of Chilean Women's Institutions), an umbrella organization that grouped together women's professional, social, and political associations. Recognizing the importance of consumer organizing, FEChIF activists vowed to join the Comité Nacional pro Baja de las Subsistencias (National Committee for the Lowering of Subsistence Goods), a national consumer group created in May 1943 and made up of retail merchants, members of the social-christian Falange, representatives of trade unions, and Communists. However, FEChIF's cooperation with the Comité Nacional never began in earnest. Within a month, Mandujano and her allies in MEMCh revealed plans to bypass the Comité Nacional.[43]

MEMCh instead established a direct relation with the Comisariato de Subsistencias y Precios (Commissariat for Subsistence Goods and Prices), a state agency revitalized by the popular fronts to regulate the price of subsistence goods. *Memchistas* envisioned carrying out a joint program of consumer education with the Comisariato that would teach women how to refrain from unnecessary and superfluous purchases, budget, shop, cook, detect false advertising, avoid debts, and create consumer cooperatives. They also hoped that the Comisariato would appoint MEMCh members as unpaid inspectors and empower them to scout out violations of consumer laws. Since MEMCh secretary-general Mandujano understood that the feminist organization could not bargain effectively with the Comisariato from a position of weakness, she proposed that MEMCh immediately organize a massive rally of women consumers. Fearful of being openly identified with the more confrontational Communist Party, Mandujano also insisted that participants in the proposed rally act in the spirit of reasonableness and instruction and avoid demagogy, speeches, and attacks.[44]

In late December 1944, MEMCh, along with other women's organizations, constituted a new consumer organization: the Liga de Consumidores (Consumer League), an all-female organization with official ties to the Comisariato. The reasons behind the rapprochement between MEMCh and the Comisariato and behind women activists' decision not to participate in the Comité Nacional are unclear, although the professional inclinations and personal connections of both Clara Williams and MEMCh secretary-general Mandujano undoubtedly played a role. Both women had close ties to the Radical Party and had held posts in the state. Moreover, Roberto Yunge, second in command at the Comisariato, was Clara Williams's husband. Yunge and Williams's daughter, Gabriela Yunge, brokered MEMCh's initial contacts with the Comisariato. It also seems likely that the moderate feminists in MEMCh and the Comisariato shared concern about what they saw as excessive militancy within the consumer movement, presumably prompted by Communist influence in the Comité Nacional. They likely joined forces to divide the consumer movement, calm activist fervor, place initiative back in the hands of the Comisariato, and diminish Communist control over consumer organizing.[45]

At least that was what the Communist Party and Comité Nacional feared. In January 1945, Comité leaders lambasted the Comisariato for what they saw as its attempt to supplant the Comité by establishing consumer leagues:

> We have heard that the Departmental Comisariato has been working on the formation of Consumer Leagues that will cooperate with that organism. The Comité Nacional, by means of this editorial, affirms that this is not the Comisariato's role. . . . [If] it needs the support of

consumers, it should not hesitate to ask for that support from all the popular organizations and especially from the Comité pro Baja de las Subsistencias, which on repeated occasions has declared that it is willing to support all the good measures taken by this organism, while combating those with which it does not agree. Both the Comisariato and the Movement for Subsistence need to maintain their independence, in a climate of mutual aid and comprehension.

This editorial further enjoined feminists to associate with the Comité, telling leaders of the women's movement, "[I]t is not necessary to form new organisms, what we need is to come to an understanding among all parties." A month later, Communist Party leader Julieta Campusano repeated this message, calling on FEChIF to collaborate with the Comité.[46]

As Comité leaders suspected, the Liga's strategies indeed differed from those of the mixed-sex Comité Nacional, which had focused on organizing local committees to pressure for government enforcement of price controls. They also differed from those of prior housewives' committees. Eschewing confrontation with the Comisariato, the Consumer League focused on imparting consumer education, teaching domestic economy, and instigating consumer cooperatives to distribute foodstuffs supplied by the Comisariato. The Comisariato rewarded the Liga's cooperation with what Clara Williams referred to as "enthusiastic support" and "understanding collaboration." The local leagues continued to monitor merchants' adherence to Comisariato norms and succeeded in having women appointed as voluntary Comisariato inspectors. But, drawing attention away from the punishment of speculators, the Liga also focused on disciplining consumers. Referring to shortages caused in part by the Second World War, Williams wrote that "the scarcity of some food items has forced modest Consumers to acquire foresight and has paved the way for the League's teaching." The leagues thus drew on and reinforced a more conciliatory, less class-based, model of femininity. Simultaneously, they clearly pursued feminist goals. Williams believed participation in consumer leagues would allow women to develop leadership skills, artistic abilities, and commercial know-how and to "escape the narrow confines of the home, benefiting from social interaction." By September of 1946, a little over a year and a half after it had begun functioning, the national Consumer League had organized thirty-five groups with 3,403 members. Its domestic-economy teachers had given 596 classes in nutrition.[47]

Williams and Mandujano thus succeeded in implanting a more vertical and disciplinary model within a sector of the consumer movement. Yet the establishment of the Liga did not immediately divide the consumer movement or rout consumer militancy. In February 1945, the Comité came to its own arrangement with the Comisariato. Realizing perhaps that a closer collaboration with the Comisariato was not necessarily debilitating, the Comité agreed to distribute propaganda for the Comisariato. In return, the departmental Comisariato for Santiago would select members of the Comité as unpaid inspectors, choosing from a list proposed by the Comité's leaders. The Comisariato would also recognize "conflict secretaries" in local consumer committees, granting them the authority to gather consumer complaints and present them to the Comisariato. The Communist Party, for its part, soon found that although women in consumer leagues now had to sit through talks by social workers and domestic-economy teachers, the leagues might also carry out more confrontational activities. By November 1947, a party publication was characterizing both autonomous subsistence committees and the consumer leagues as "true and authentic popular organisms of struggle against speculation."[48]

However, the truce between feminists and Communists soon ended. As the political climate veered sharply Right-ward in late 1947, President González Videla began to repress consumer organizations linked to the Communist Party, and the Liga de Consumidores folded, perhaps because of internal disputes over Communist participation in the leagues. To replace the Liga, Williams and her allies in the state created the Asociación de Dueñas de Casa (Housewives' Association) in August 1947. With First Lady Rosa Markmann presiding and Williams as executive vice president, the Asociación constituted a vigorous and successful attempt by the state to co-opt the consumer movement. Unlike the Liga, it was a wholly top-down initiative, and it had the full weight of the state apparatus behind it. The new organization enlisted the aid of the wives of governors, intendants, and mayors, and by 1950, it had formed groups in at least 129 localities. To buttress the organization, President González Videla finally acceded to a long-standing consumer demand: in October 1947, he promulgated a decree regulating the composition and the functions of Juntas de Vigilancia (Vigilance Juntas), charged with overseeing local commerce, enforcing consumer laws, and punishing violators. The law granted the Asociación—along with municipal authorities, the police, and the Comisariato—a place on these local juntas. In an unparalleled state delegation of authority, by 1950 the state had appointed 1,330 Asociación members as unpaid Comisariato inspectors. In the last

Working- and middle-class women at a luncheon sponsored by the Asociación de Dueñas de Casa, Santiago. Photo courtesy Tomy Romeo.

six months of 1948, these inspectors fined or shut down 970 commercial establishments.[49]

The state was much less generous with other consumer groups. As the Comisariato again made women—whose leaders were less threatening—its allies, it moved to repress Communists and their consumer committees. In some cases, local authorities boycotted consumer committees headed by Communists; in other cases they jailed consumer leaders. Mandujano and Williams, who had for over a decade collaborated with Communist women, did not protest. In fact, they resigned from MEMCh, distancing themselves from the Communist women who remained in the feminist organization. They remained silent as FEChIF expelled its Communist members.[50]

The Communist Party now discovered that its long-standing rivalry with professional women deprived it of important allies at the moment it most needed them. Grassroots activists, for their part, found it harder to escape the lessons in conciliatory femininity offered by moderate feminists. Thus, in the end the incorporation of women into state-sponsored consumer activities neutralized some of the more contentious elements within popular culture. The distance between moderate feminists and sectors of the consumer movement close to the Communist Party, as well as moderate feminists' close relation to more conservative members of the Radical Party and their resulting access to the state, accelerated this process—as did the Communist Party's animosity toward women intellectuals.

Although functional to the Radical Party as it veered to the Right and to a state now less open to popular influence, the Asociación had its own proto-feminist project, which it inherited from MEMCh, FEChIF, and the consumer leagues. It explicitly sought to prepare women for civic and social participation; to encourage women to exercise their newly won right to vote; to develop women's leadership potential; to stimulate women's assertiveness; to overcome female confinement and isolation within the home; to provide a respite from routine, monotonous, and tiring household tasks; and to inspire loyalty to democratic values. But in other ways, it furthered a vision of conciliatory femininity. As smart shoppers and brilliant homemakers, women would bring harmony to family and nation. Williams and her allies did not fully ignore women's specificities, yet they clearly rejected—and worked to dissuade—working-class women's militancy. And even when it came to women's rights as women, which moderate feminists clearly wished to bolster, they were limited by their professional training and their political links to a state project that by 1947 sought to neutralize popular demands and diffuse confrontation of all sorts. The government cited the Asociación as a splendid example of national cooperation.[51]

At the grass roots, women faced these developments with ambivalence. Some women felt they had no choice but to join the Asociación. Others staunchly resisted and continued to work, wherever possible, in consumer leagues and other grassroots groups. Communist Party member and memchista Eusebia Torres bitterly criticized moderate feminists who attended the FEChIF congress in late 1947, just as the Asociación was being established. "Certain ladies," she said, "were bent on twisting the righteous thought the different delegates presented. . . . They said the best way to solve, for example, the problem of inflation, was to educate the population and teach them first of all to eat less, so that in that manner we might help the government with the famous task it has." As the country moved toward anti-Communism, the condescension of certain "ladies"—which had long been present within women's organizing—had become intolerable to women like Torres. Torres's militancy had become equally intolerable to moderate feminists in FEChIF.[52]

CONCLUSION

Regardless of the outcome of the conflicts between feminists and the Left, the friction was significant for what it revealed about the dynamics of creating female political identity and a feminist political project. Communists did not infiltrate MEMCh; progressive feminists welcomed an alliance with Communists for reasons of expediency, but also because of their own political beliefs. The Communist leadership, however, was skeptical of feminism and feared that women's emancipation might undermine its own power and its ability to satisfy its male constituents. For that reason, it failed to allow Communist women, grassroots *memchistas*, and MEMCh leaders to decide among themselves how to reconcile MEMCh's radical feminist program with the expressed needs of working-class women. Instead, it discredited feminists by mobilizing a populist anti-intellectualism that drew on women's own awareness of class difference and that mobilized working-class men against feminism. In turn, moderate feminists discredited the Communist Party and its militant, class-based politics, even as they promoted a program of gender uplift. Rather than bargaining with the Communist Party and grassroots committees, moderate feminists used their alliance with the state to further their goals. Often relying more on the disciplinary and hierarchical discourses of the professions than on an analysis of women's subordination, they insisted on teaching women how to act properly and acquire culture.

The women in the middle of these battles, who were rarely heard by moderate feminists and leftist leaders, were the real losers. For although many sought to combine participation in feminist and leftist movements, they found it increasingly difficult to do so. Communists told working-class housewives that opposing exploitation meant struggling alongside their husbands and renouncing feminism. Moderate feminists told them that domestic education would make class confrontation unnecessary. In this polarized setting, other options, including the less rigid, more tolerant model proposed by Elena Caffarena and Marta Vergara, were foreclosed. Caffarena and Vergara's program, though often inconsistent and at times elitist, constituted an earnest attempt by feminist professionals to listen to and dialogue with working-class women. Communists and moderate feminists, by contrast, had a more vanguardist approach to organizing. They nonetheless achieved a degree of success because their programs coincided, at least in part, with the needs of national popular-front leaders. After 1947, Communists would find that they could no longer cooperate with state officials. Yet the Communist Party would ultimately survive González Videla's cold war repression, and it would continue to organize among women. MEMCh would not.

chapter four

GENDER AND STATE BUILDING

Charity, Rights, and the Professions

As we saw in Chapter 3, progressive feminists attempted to develop a less vanguardist, more articulatory form of leadership that recognized the complex and sometimes contradictory needs of women. Yet progressive *memchistas* were routed by moderate feminists and Communists who were more willing and able to channel and restrict the demands of working-class housewives. As a result, the forms of collective pressure available to working-class women remained limited.

This chapter shows how gendered forms of subaltern mobilization shaped the diverse state agencies that were created, enlarged, and reformed by the popular fronts, and how those forms of activism molded the perspectives and possibilities of state-employed welfare professionals. It also reveals how state apparatuses and welfare professionals reinforced gendered patterns of popular mobilization and citizen entitlement. The chapter argues that as a result of these alignments, (male) industrial workers would receive state benefits that were seen as rights, while the indigent—a category that included disreputable men and most women—would receive forms of assistance that were akin to charity.

In 1939, the CSO, the agency charged with providing social security, disability, and health care benefits to blue-collar workers, foregrounded the distinction between charity and rights in an advertisement published in the Socialist magazine *Rumbo*. "The social security system," read the ad, "tries to replace the denomination of 'indigent' with that of 'taxpayer' [*imponente*], a switch from 'charity' to 'insurance' and from 'alms' to 'rights.'" The CSO thus courted *Rumbo* readers, who had long rejected the paternalism implicit in charitable assistance, and aligned itself with a "modern" notion of welfare as a right. By 1939, workers as well as bureaucrats and welfare professionals had come to view the extension of CSO-administered social security and health benefits as a way of suppressing patronizing forms of public and private welfare, which they characterized as "charity."[1]

The publication of a CSO advertisement in a Socialist magazine was not coincidental. During the popular-front era, members of the Socialist Party obtained influential positions within welfare agencies, most notably within the CSO and other health care apparatuses. From January 1939 to January 1943, Socialists Luciano Kulczewski, Salvador Allende, and Miguel Etchebarne headed the CSO. During those years, Allende and Etchebarne also took turns as minister of health—a position held in 1946 by Socialist physician and longtime public servant Juan Garafulic. Even in the lower reaches of the bureaucracy, Socialists—and to a lesser extent, Communists—used their political connections to gain employment and then brought their political ideals to their jobs. Responding in part to workers' own mobilizations around issues of welfare, Socialists within the CSO and the Ministry of Health defended workers' right to good health care and adequate social security benefits.[2]

Enhanced leftist and worker influence notwithstanding, paternalistic forms of state assistance flourished in popular-front Chile, and, especially outside the CSO, even state functionaries who considered themselves progressives failed to empower recipients of state aid. At the same time that Socialists first gained control of the CSO and the Ministry of Health, for example, President Aguirre Cerda reinvigorated the Servicio de Cesantía (Unemployment Service) and charged it with aiding the unemployed, vagrants, the indigent, and victims of natural disasters. The Servicio (later rebaptized as the Dirección General de Auxilio Social [DGAS, General Direction of Social Assistance]) was placed under the leadership of popular-front supporter Elena Yávar, who in alliance with feminists and progressive social workers, attempted to do away with the agency's almsgiving approach. Yet Yávar's project, which was modeled after changes within the CSO, foundered, and the nonworkers she served remained relatively disempowered.[3]

More generally, (male) workers received social security and health care benefits that were seen as a "right," while nonworkers did not. Characterized as aid given in times of temporary need, social security did not imply worker dependence on the state. And since workers themselves helped finance social security benefits, worker organizations consistently demanded—and obtained—participation in the administration of social security and health programs. Often voicing their views through labor unions and leftist parties, they insisted that welfare professionals treat them with dignity. Women, who were for the most part non—wage earners, had fewer "rights" and little, if any, say in the operation of agencies that dispensed aid to them as indigents. Their status as "dependents" was not widely questioned, and they continued to receive handouts that did not significantly alter the class and gender determinants of their poverty. Feminists, who gained only a very weak foothold within the state, could not really modify the gendered nature of citizen entitlement.[4]

Gender differences within the welfare professions contributed to the gendered nature of welfare initiatives. Physicians, most of whom were male, allied with respectable male workers. Rejecting paternalism, they adopted a social approach to medicine that recognized the relation between poverty and ill health. By entrenching themselves within the CSO, an institution financed in part by worker contributions, physicians sealed their pact with workers. Social workers, all of whom were women, found it more difficult to distance themselves from charitable approaches and empower clients. Trained in casework methods that conceived of poverty as an individual pathology, social workers often failed to win the confidence of clients. Social workers did ally with women clients, helping them contest male abuse. Yet these localized alliances between social workers and working-class women were not generally linked to a broader feminist politics. And those social workers who, like Yávar, ascribed to the democratizing precepts of the public health movement and were associated with the women's movement were circumscribed both by male leaders who saw them as potential competitors and by male workers who objected to their interventions in the family. In the end, gender distinctions within the professions intensified the gender cleavages generated by the discourses of charity and rights.

In sum, gender differences within the professions and within working-class organizations contributed to and were deepened by gendered forms of state welfare. As the state itself expanded, a newer stream of welfare, based on the recognition of rights by the state, developed alongside an older, charitable stream anchored in personal initiatives and casework. Public welfare was two-tiered: Men received benefits "rationally" distributed by scientifically trained, and usually male, technocrats who controlled agencies like the CSO. In contrast, women were the principal beneficiaries of charitably oriented institutions such as the DGAS, which were generally run by women as well.

Whereas workers, in alliance with physicians, successfully used "scientific" discourses to open up the state, neither social workers nor working-class women effectively wielded science as an activist tool. In effect, popular and leftist pressures on the state encouraged a simultaneous process of democratization and modernization that was particularly pronounced within certain state apparatuses concerned with wage earners. But while agencies like the CSO were loci of open conflict, the nature and development of agencies and programs not aimed specifically at workers were less frequently discussed in explicitly political settings. As a result, the state apparatuses in which women professionals were more influential continued to function more like charities. There, the pace of modernization was slower and the depth of democratization more shallow.

"SCIENCE DRESSED IN OVERALLS": WELFARE PROFESSIONALS AND THE EXPANSION OF THE STATE

Beginning around 1920, the Chilean state expanded and became more centralized, and public responsibility for welfare, especially for health care, grew. That process began in 1917, when the Beneficencia, an until-then wholly private institution providing hospital care for the poor, was placed under the supervision of a Consejo Superior made up of both state-appointed representatives and delegates from civil society. By 1924 the Ministry of Hygiene, Assistance, Work and Social Security had been created, centralizing disparate state agencies that had a stake in improving Chileans' living and working conditions. Furthermore, the enactment of a new sanitary code in 1931 gave the Dirección General de Sanidad (Health Administration) attributions previously reserved for the municipalities. Perhaps most important, the CSO was created in 1924 and its health services were reorganized in March 1932, when the agency recovered control of functions that had been handed over to the Beneficencia in December 1927.[5]

As state spending rose and welfare programs, CSO programs foremost among them, proliferated, the number of state-employed professionals multiplied. From 1930 to 1950 total state spending rose nominally from approximately 1.131 billion to approximately 20.637 billion pesos, and between 1929 and 1949, state employment rose from 30,147 to 68,225. Proportionally, social services absorbed the largest number of new state employees. In 1941, the social service department of the Dirección de Sanidad's Mother and Child Department went from three to five social workers; in September 1943, the Comisariato de Subsistencias y Precios contracted its first six social workers; and by 1943, the number of social workers in the DGAS had increased from one to twenty. The CSO spearheaded this growth: in the six years between 1934–35 and 1940–41, its income rose from 93.7 million to 292 million pesos, and between 1935 and 1939 the number of physicians in the CSO medical services alone grew from 396 to 926. During this same period, the number of social workers and sanitary nurses employed by the CSO medical services rose from 17 to 74. Within the CSO as a whole, there were 25 social workers in 1935 and 115 in 1945. The CSO social service division, one *visitadora* commented, was one of the most complete in the country.[6]

Medical doctors, nurses, and social workers—all of whom were educated by the state itself—learned the value of public service along with their trades. Most medical doctors were educated, for free, at the University of Chile. Most social workers studied either at the Beneficencia's Alejandro del Río School or, after 1940, at one of the three social work schools run by the Ministry of Education. Sanitary nurses initially attended classes sponsored by the Dirección de Sanidad's Department of Sanitary Education; they later studied at the University of Chile. These institutions of higher learning trained professionals to meet the needs of the state. Not surprisingly, Chile's first schools of sanitary nursing and social work—the latter the first in Latin America—began functioning in 1925, just months after the passage of laws that set up the CSO and extended state regulation of labor relations.[7]

In contrast to students of the Catholic University's Elvira Matte de Cruchaga School of Social Work, who more often worked in private industries and haciendas, graduates of state-run schools of social work overwhelmingly found employment with the state. A 1946 survey of 415 employed social workers revealed that 106 worked for the Beneficencia and 84 for the CSO. Forty-nine worked with public and semipublic agencies assisting children; and only 51 could be clearly identified as working in the private sector. In 1950, of the more than 500 social workers who had graduated from state-run schools of social work in their first twenty-five years, 223 worked at the Beneficencia; 99 at the CSO; 47 in agencies assisting children; and only 53 in the private sector. In comparison, the Catholic University's school of social work joined the Asociación de Agricultores (Agriculturalists' Association) to station social work students on haciendas.[8]

Initially, during the period of transition from oligarchic rule, members of the welfare professions saw themselves as forgers of "social peace." In 1930, a commission put together to review the social security system urged laborers and capitalists to embrace the system since it produced "a coming together and harmony between bosses and workers." Sanitary nurses, a government publication explained around the same time, were not mere caretakers of the sick, but rather social reformers who sought to allay social conflict. For them, as for medical doctors and social workers, nonconflictual reform was a professional imperative.[9]

In the 1930s, physicians articulated this conciliatory view of public service to notions of progress, scientific advancement, and national development. Doctors portrayed the provision of health services as functional to capitalist development and reworked discourses of "social peace" within a language of modernization. As a CSO medical publication explained in 1935, the protection of "human capital" would increase labor productivity. "Children," the publication proclaimed, ". . . are the only 'real value' worthy of a secure and reproductive investment. It is true that this is not a value quoted on the stock exchanges. But it is the future creator of the value of all stock." From the vantage point of these modernizing physicians, science transcended ideological orientations and bettered the nation as a whole. When, in 1938, physician and Liberal Party member Víctor Matus Benavente enjoined statesmen and professionals to listen to his analysis of the problems generated by a legal ban on abortions, his self-declared intention was to "fulfill my professional obligations and render a service to my country." Touting a similar theme, a Communist newspaper proclaimed in 1936, "In problems related to public health there are neither left- nor right-wings." And in 1944 a CSO publication noted that when it came to issues of maternal-child health, "Amidst waves of protest . . . Tiryns and Trojans suspended their attacks and even claim participation in [producing] the results."[10]

As labor and leftist organizations began to couch their demands in terms of national prerogatives and to articulate the scientific project of modernization to their own leftist venture (see Chapter 1), physicians found it increasingly difficult to claim ideological neutrality or to characterize reform as a necessity dictated by the advance of knowledge. In 1934, a local Socialist newspaper termed a conference on the causes of tuberculosis given by a physician at the University of Concepción "subversive," and commented: "It's about time that Science dressed in overalls. Science will have to start lying if it wants to stay in tune with the present regime. Otherwise, it will suffer the same hostility and persecution suffered by Socialists." Taking a more combative view of science, leftists portrayed the Right as unscientific and insisted that only the Left worked hand in hand with progress.[11]

Especially after 1938, progressive physicians articulated medical modernization not only to progress and state intervention but also to democratization, promoting a view of health care as an entitlement that could best be provided by the state. According to practitioners of "social" medicine, workers' productive contributions were an essential part of national well-being, and in recompense the state should collaborate with workers to ensure their health. CSO medical care was, a 1942 agency publication stated, "a right, which gives the contributor motive to demand efficiency from an organism created with his own contributions." Moreover, although physicians could easily have neutralized working-class protest by tying progress and science to state control, they portrayed state rationalization as a process that, because it emerged out of class conflict, could not be guided by scientific considerations alone. According to many medical analysts, environmental conditions, namely poverty, caused illness. One CSO physician who analyzed the causes of tuberculosis went so far as to claim that they escaped the domain of medicine and might be better understood from a sociological or socio-economic perspective.[12]

After 1938, leftists within and outside the state apparatuses argued that the expansion and modernization of the state would make it more sensitive to social determinants of health and disease, well-being and misery. They would also allow physicians to undertake the sort of massive preventive campaigns needed to rout infant mortality, tuberculosis, and sexually transmitted diseases. In 1942, the Socialist *La Crítica* paraphrased a 1935 article, saying, "Tuberculosis, a social disease, requires a corresponding social hygiene, a hygiene of the masses, the application of which cannot be handed over to the individual, his family, or public charity. The state must adopt new and bold criteria, going to the very origin, which in 80 percent of all cases is no other than the physiological poverty of the collectivity."[13] Leftists now saw state control as the sine qua non of effective solutions to working-class problems. Charity and private initiative could not do the job. In 1939, Allende criticized the Beneficencia, claiming that it did not exercise a "social function." According to Allende and other progressive professionals, the Beneficencia— although it received state funds and was overseen by state agents—was tainted by its palliative medical approach and its roots in private charity.[14]

Over the years, the medical intelligentsia and state officials of all political persuasions increasingly embraced a social approach to medical care. In

1944, for example, Dr. Exequiel González Cortés—author of the legislation that had created the CSO, member of the Liberal Party, former senator, and noted academic—affirmed the right of workers to a proper standard of living and lauded social medicine, recognizing its links to labor and Left politics. Speaking at a ceremony honoring him on the twentieth anniversary of the creation of the CSO, González Cortés even felt it necessary to apologize to the more conservative members of his audience, who might object to his embrace of social medicine. "We have grown up and lived," he noted, "hearing that there is no such thing as sickness, but only sick people, which is, in other words, equivalent to proclaiming the ascendancy of an individualistic medicine, which, with the pardon of those who think otherwise, it is necessary to substitute with a social medicine, employing the same steadfastness with which we sustain the concept of public order. . . . [T]he State has had to intervene so that there are no exploiters or depressed people." At a conference on medicosocial issues held as part of the CSO's anniversary commemorations, and attended by the president of the country, González Cortés spoke even more forcefully, linking public welfare explicitly to both socialism and to the extension of democracy to the working classes (which he termed "the most valuable factor"): "Today, we cannot ignore our individual and collective responsibility to improve the condition of the pueblo, an urgent precept, nor can we deny the influence of socialist doctrines, which have even shaped the agendas of governments, just as it is impossible not to notice the dignity bestowed by universal democracy, which has even led the most valuable factor down the road to victory."[15]

As the social approach to welfare services took root among state officials and professionals, workers increasingly embraced state expansion. Initially, in the 1920s, working-class organizations had been skeptical of state-controlled welfare and social security. When the law creating the CSO was first debated in Congress, popular organizations had objected to bureaucratic control of pension and health funds that were partially financed by workers themselves. Two years after the passage of the law, in 1926, they were still demanding its repeal. However, as I show below, after about 1936 worker support for the CSO mushroomed as professionals more attuned to popular demands flooded the agency. Although many workers continued to find CSO services lacking and CSO professionals overbearing and condescending, they increasingly saw agency officials as potential allies.[16]

As welfare services and health care were modernized and democratized, however, social work continued to be portrayed as unscientific, more rooted in feeling than in planning. A 1931 article titled "A New Profession for Women: The Work of Sanitary Nurses" began: "Feelings of charity have driven women of all races and at all times toward the care of the helplessly ill." More than ten years later, Minister of Health Etchebarne was still insisting on women's particular emotional aptitude for helping the poor. "No one is better suited," said Etchebarne in a speech to social workers, "to the magnificent labor of carrying out the titanic struggle against pain, suffering, misery—which man is unable to alleviate—than woman, with her treasures of ingeniousness, tenderness, and abnegation."[17]

Because alleviating the suffering of the irremediably poor (and not the "incidentally" indigent who were covered by social security benefits) was seen as a natural female activity, social workers gained responsibility for dealing with the helplessly destitute. Indeed social workers stepped in where aristocratic ladies had exercised philanthropy. For instance, in the Patronato Nacional de la Infancia, which provided free milk rations to impoverished infants, social workers replaced well-intentioned volunteers, carrying on in a similar manner. Professional training provided *visitadoras* with tools that separated them from traditional charity workers, but prevalent casework methods that emphasized the individual and familial causes of social pathologies encouraged social workers to view the poor as passive and fueled clientelism within the profession. The well-to-do young ladies who entered the profession thinking that the poor were responsible for their woes and incapable of helping themselves reinforced these teachings. Elena Varela knew that she was up against a lot when she decided to study social work. "Social workers, or *visitadoras* [as they were known] then," Varela recalled, "were supposed to be people from an acceptable socioeconomic status, upper-middle or upper [class]. First there were the charity ladies, you know, don't you? Then there were the society girls. . . . The concept, right, of working with the poor was to help the poor, to assist the poor." Social workers would soothe those who could neither uplift themselves nor struggle for their rights.[18]

Especially in its early years, then, social work constituted an attempt to neutralize popular mobilizations. Social medicine, by contrast, represented a less demobilizing response, on the part of the medical intelligentsia, to heightened popular demands. Social medicine, which public health physicians (known as "*sanitaristas*" or "*salubristas*") implemented largely as a response to worker pressures, developed as a form not simply of social engineering but also of medical democratization. Of course some physicians were just as anchored in a view of individual pathology and health as social workers, but they became increasingly marginal within their profession. Social work remained more conservative as a profession, in part because it was more loosely tied to popular organizing, in part because it did not gain an institutional foothold that would allow social workers to offer more than sporadic help, and in part because many Chileans were skeptical of its proto-feminist program.

"CAJA DE SEGURO OBRERO"

Salubristas' preferred home was the Caja de Seguro Obligatorio, and it was through their control of the CSO—known popularly as the Caja de Seguro Obrero—that politicized welfare professionals sealed an alliance with workers. By lodging themselves in the CSO, the country's largest and most innovative welfare institution, physicians assured their own access to resources. An emblem of the state's sensitivity to Chile's downtrodden and of its related transit from a charitable to a scientific orientation, the Caja de Seguro Obligatorio contributed powerfully to the framing of welfare for workers as an entitlement.

The immense resources handled by the CSO made it a prized asset, and its large budget made the agency a trendsetter in matters of welfare. While theoretically the Dirección General de Sanidad was charged with setting health policy and coordinating campaigns among private and public healthcare providers, in practice the CSO took over this task. Caja programs were far-ranging, and they often addressed problems to which other state agencies should have attended. The CSO alone provided health care to between one-fifth and two-fifths of all children under the age of two. In Santiago, between 1930 and 1933, at least 9,000 children of CSO beneficiaries received free school breakfasts. As early as 1935, a CSO publication described the agency as a "quasi-revolutionary institution," praised its own "necessary unity and cohesion," and criticized other state agencies for lagging behind. Over the years, CSO physicians would come to perceive the agency's centralization as a way of imposing a social approach.[19]

Before the consolidation of the national-popular state, landowners and capitalists, who indirectly received low interest loans from the CSO, had been principal beneficiaries of the institution's economic reserves. After 1933, however, CSO investment policies shifted as worker representatives on the agency's governing board allied with state functionaries to oppose the representatives of capital. Beginning in 1933–36, when Santiago Labarca, a progressive Radical, headed the agency, CSO functionaries worked to revamp investment policies. The Caja's funds, they asserted, should capitalize economic ventures that directly favored Chile's workers. The CSO bought the Central de Leche, a milk-pasteurizing plant, to increase the production of pasteurized milk. Through the purchase of stock in Laboratorio Chile, it sought to increase the availability of pharmaceuticals and reduce their price. In addition, the agency acquired farms and ranches that were to produce cheap and plentiful foodstuffs; bought clothing for sale to contributors; and built apartments and houses for rental to workers. Under popular-front leadership, the CSO would continue and expand the policies implemented under Labarca's leadership.[20]

The CSO tried to forestall criticism from the Right by arguing that improving the standard of living of workers would bring social harmony and benefit the country as a whole. But conservatives, faced during Labarca's administration with a CSO governing board they could not control, tried to limit the autonomy of the agency by extending congressional control of CSO investments. A campaign launched by the Right and certain members of the Radical Party early in Aguirre Cerda's term was even more vicious. Alleging Socialist misuse and mismanagement of CSO funds, opponents of the CSO's new policies succeeded in forcing the removal of the CSO's Socialist administrator, Luciano Kulczewski. On a local level, employers also boycotted the CSO. When the Caja contracted out the provision of medical services for blue-collar employees to the Tarapacá and Antofagasta Nitrate Company, medical doctors hired by the company refused to cooperate with a Caja physician carrying out a campaign against venereal disease in Tarapacá province. Even the company's own social worker suggested that she could carry out her work more freely if either the CSO or the Ministry of Work hired her.[21]

That employers sabotaged CSO initiatives was not surprising considering the agency's direct support of workers' organizations. It was not simply the Socialist Militia's purchase of low-cost shirts at a CSO store that outraged right-wingers. They also opposed the Caja's contracting of agents to "study" unionization in six provinces. In addition, the Right was surely irritated by projects such as the Centro de Reposo Valparaíso (Valparaíso Nocturnal Rest Center), a CSO boardinghouse for men deemed to be at medical risk. The center explicitly saw its role as "stimulating men's associative tendencies, in the interest of social solidarity and brotherhood [compañerismo]." The cen-

ter's social worker corresponded with a union representative, and although
boarders were not generally permitted to leave the house during the eve-
nings, an exception was made for union meetings. In fact, residents of the
center were actually encouraged to participate in union events, and the
center's social worker happily reported that many former participants, after
leaving the center, were elected to leadership positions within their unions.
This cooperation between CSO officials and unions was especially remarkable given the condescension of the center's founders, who saw workers as
"big children."[22]

While the CSO often spoke of its actions on behalf of Chile's poor, its principal mission was improving the welfare of workers. Family members of insured workers received only very limited benefits. After 1932, the wives and
orphans of those CSO beneficiaries who died before retirement could collect
pension funds. Beginning in 1936–39, the CSO provided prenatal care to
workers' wives and health care to their children aged two and younger. Wage
earners could also opt to insure their family members for a fee. Yet because
the CSO granted benefits to children and non-wage-earning women only on
the basis of their relation to insured workers, the agency reaffirmed the
dependent status of those family members who were not in their own right
entitled to CSO services. Family members who were dependents also had to
rely on the goodwill of insured workers who could and did withhold benefits. Men who failed to legally recognize their infants or refused to marry
the women they got pregnant denied those family members access to CSO
clinics. In 1945, only 2,500 CSO beneficiaries paid for the voluntary family
insurance.[23]

Wage-earning women were independently entitled to CSO benefits. But
because women's childbearing and childrearing responsibilities often forced
them to abandon work, they were especially likely to find themselves cut off
from CSO services at the precise moment they needed them most.[24] To
extend entitlements to women and other nonworkers, members of the Socialist Party proposed reforms to existing social security laws. Yet until 1952,
they were largely unsuccessful. In October 1938, for example, Socialist deputy Natalio Berman proposed a "social solidarity insurance" scheme, under
which all the country's inhabitants would have access to public health care.
Yet this initiative did not prosper, and when Minister of Health Allende
introduced legislation that would have extended health insurance to workers' families, it stalled in Congress. Even if the proposed extension of cover-
age had passed, many Chileans still would not have been insured: Allende

insisted that the popular fronts intended to provide all citizens with CSO health care, and a CSO publication argued that if such legislation passed, "only a small minority of *rentistas* and social parasites would be excluded." But in reality the proposed legislation covered only family members of the insured, and that "small minority" was likely larger than Allende and CSO officials granted. If the popular fronts' failure to recognize the rights of Chileans circumscribed their plans to enlarge the CSO, the fiscally precarious CSO was doubly limited and could assist nonworkers only occasionally. The CSO thus succeeded in extending and democratizing welfare services, but many Chileans had no right to CSO services.[25]

SOCIAL WORK, WELFARE FOR THE INDIGENT, AND FAILED ATTEMPTS AT PROFESSIONALIZATION AND REFORM

Taking up the CSO's slack, a diverse array of state-funded, state-overseen, and state-run institutions and programs provided welfare for nonworkers. These institutions included the Patronato Nacional de la Infancia, the Dirección General de Sanidad, the Beneficencia, the Consejo de Defensa del Niño (CDN, Children's Defense Council), the Caja de Habitación, the DGAS, and municipalities. Like the CSO, these agencies moved in the direction of professionalization and rationalization of services as the state increased its role in welfare provision. Especially in agencies charged with assisting children, modernization and social approaches proceeded apace as physicians argued that children were the nation's future "human capital." By 1942, the state had forged the Dirección General de Protección a la Infancia y Adolescencia to coordinate diverse public institutions that provided services for children, including the Patronato. In 1943, the Consejo de Defensa del Niño, an agency that provided preschool care to indigent children, came under the control of the Ministry of Education.[26]

Yet outside the CSO, centralization and state control did not always lead to the abandonment of casework methods that clients themselves often equated with charity. *Visitadoras* would continue to determine the "needs" of clients who had no "rights," deciding who to help and how. Many would also continue to replicate a piecemeal approach to helping the poor. For instance, Rina Schiappacasse Ferretti, a social worker at a Centro de Defensa del Niño, had little more than charitable aid to offer "M. Q.," a domestic servant whose child attended the day care center where she worked. M. Q. could not support her nine-year-old son and her six-month-old infant on her meager salary of 120 pesos per month. Yet, although Schiappacasse sympathized enough with M. Q. to find her a higher paying job as a cook, the social worker could not offer M. Q. assistance that would allow her to maintain a home for her two children. Indeed the social worker could do no more than solicit the help of a charitable former employer, who purportedly "cared deeply" for M. Q.'s son and agreed to take in the boy. M. Q., who had no "rights" in this situation, would have to content herself with the vow Schiappacasse had extracted from the former employer: the *patrón* swore to clothe and feed M. Q.'s child, "treat him like a son," see that he finished primary school, and assure that he acquired an adequate occupation.[27]

More generally, agencies like the CDN and the DGAS were poorly funded and their clients—generally single, widowed, or abandoned women and their children—were not only destitute but also politically unorganized and therefore marginal to the popular-front project. As a result, social workers employed in these agencies found it difficult to build the kind of alliances with clients that might have allowed them to improve and reform the social services they provided. The organization of mothers' centers among institutions' clients was a top-down initiative that, in this period, did little to stimulate women's collective articulation of demands.

Beginning in the mid-1940s, however, a group of social workers did attempt to democratize public and private social work, professionalize their field, and make it more socially conscious. In an effort to replace casework methods and the clientelism that went along with them, they sought to dress science in skirts. Linking the inertia of the field—its lingering similarity to charity work—to social workers' professional instruction and the placement of social workers within the state, progressives worked to change both social work training and the organization of social work within state agencies.

The issue of social work instruction first came to the fore in July of 1940 when lawyer Lucio Córdoba unveiled plans to found three new schools of social work. In response to Córdoba's proposals, the Communist daily *Frente Popular* generated an extensive debate on social work and sanitary nursing, interviewing more than twenty people on the subject. Among the physicians, social workers, sanitary nurses, and educators questioned by the newspaper, several criticized the inability of social workers to do more than document poverty and offer sporadic assistance, and others criticized their lack of technical training. A couple of the interviewees noted "aristocratic" tendencies within the profession. Physician Víctor Puelma recognized that although many workers distrusted all social workers, ineffective and charitable orientations in fact characterized graduates of the Catholic Elvira Matte school but not of the Beneficencia school. And Communist social worker Irma Sierralta rejected negative evaluations of social work that were "abstract" and that failed to take into account the specific contexts in which social workers carried out their work. Almost all agreed, however, that social workers should be trained more like sanitary nurses, who studied at the university and were well versed in the supposedly modern, social field of medicine. Leftists and progressive social workers thus insisted that dignifying social work and transforming it into an efficient tool in the fight against misery required professionalization.[28]

The Círculo de Estudios Sociales (Circle of Social Studies), formed in 1945 at the instigation of a core of Communist social workers, was crucial to progressive social workers' continuing attempts to transform their craft. From the start, it was clear that Círculo members were an ambitious lot who wished to elevate the standing of their profession. Some were likely frustrated that they had been forced, because of their sex, to acquire a purportedly second-rate profession like social work. As Círculo member Tomy Romeo recalled, in the 1930s and 1940s parents often prohibited their daughters from entering professions like medicine or law. Romeo herself had completed a semester of medical school but dropped out when her parents waged a "war" against her decision. "At that time," according to Romeo, "it was really looked down upon for women to enter the professions, because they would become old maids." Elena Yávar, who led the Círculo for many years, had similarly wished to study law but was routed by her mother's insistence that she acquire a more ladylike occupation: pharmacology. (Yávar obeyed her mother but never practiced her profession.)[29]

For women such as Romeo and Yávar, elevating the prestige of social work was undoubtedly a way of acquiring the authority they were forced to relinquish when they gave up their aspirations to become doctors or lawyers. More generally, by seeking to make social work "scientific," the Círculo sought to distance social work from approaches that, because they were purportedly rooted in maternal tenderness, were deemed unprofessional and old-fashioned. As one Círculo document explained, "Economic, social, scientific and technical evolution obliges professionals from every science or technique to concern themselves with renovating, modifying or critically analyzing their work methods. This revision allows them to progress in lockstep with the reality in which they carry out their functions. Social workers, still young technicians without the precedent of centuries of experimentation or investigation, should especially worry about critically analyzing and studying not only their work methods but above all the results of their efforts." Círculo members wished to move beyond condescension and act in conjunction with the poor. Drawing from and contributing to the parallel social approach to medicine advocated by physicians, they favored a move away from social casework—no more handouts—and toward community organizing and work in groups. And trying to replicate the kind of centralization favored by physicians, they called for state coordination of public and private welfare.[30]

The Círculo recognized that changes within the social work profession meant little without changes in the state agencies where social workers were employed. Circle members therefore studied and critiqued the performance of diverse state apparatuses—the Beneficencia, schools, the DGAS, among others—and presented the conclusions of their inquiries to heads of services, ministers, and even the president. In addition, the Círculo made the ambitious suggestion that the DGAS should become the central coordinating agency for social services within all public and private welfare institutions. According to the Círculo's plan, the Dirección would curtail inefficient and paternalistic social work interventions by overseeing and coordinating private, municipal, and other institutions that received funding from the state.[31]

Progressive social workers encountered resistance among their colleagues and government officials. When Irma Sierralta and Elena Varas first spoke of their work in community organizing at a social work conference, a fellow social worker whispered with distaste about the dust on Sierralta and Varas's shoes.[32] Not all social workers were predisposed to bicycle, like Sierralta and Varas, through the *poblaciones* of Quinta Normal. Furthermore, individual social workers who did try to move beyond casework were blocked by the inertia of state agencies with less rights-based approaches to welfare. In 1945 Tomy Romeo, a Círculo member who worked at the Consejo de Defensa del Niño, established contact with Communist women in a local consumer league. But because Romeo's superiors were unhappy about her political ties, she was forced to resign and seek employment elsewhere. Thus although progressive social workers allied with local women's groups, certain agencies imposed limitations on their ability to do so. "The Consejo de Defensa del Niño was," according to Romeo, "a very right-wing thing." Her clients, who did not have a powerful central organization akin to the CTCh, could not force more conservative state officials to accept their collaboration. And finally, the collective efforts of the Círculo were more often than not ignored.[33]

The genesis and evolution of the DGAS ran counter to that of the CSO, revealing the difficulties faced by progressive professionals in state agencies that served marginalized sectors of the popular classes. While Congress mandated the creation of the CSO after ample public discussion, the DGAS was the brainchild of Juanita Aguirre, President Aguirre Cerda's wife. Established by presidential decree, the agency began to function in 1939 under the auspices of the Servicio de Cesantía. By that time the Servicio, which had been set up in 1920 to provide emergency assistance to miners affected by the crisis of the nitrate industry, had evolved into a broader social service agency offering aid in the form of housing, clothing, and food rations. Individuals went there looking for relief, usually armed with recommendations from politicians or functionaries. When Aguirre Cerda took power, the Servicio was widely used as a source of patronage.[34]

Elena Yávar took charge of the Servicio's social service in 1939 and tried with limited success to change the bureau. According to Yávar the bureaucrats who had worked there "believed they were performing a social service, [but] were in reality far from it." Servicio employees did not appreciate her efforts to correct this mode of operation either. "[F]rom the start [they] saw Social Workers as enemies, putting a maximum of obstacles in their way." Although the Servicio was rebaptized as the Dirección de Auxilio Social in 1942 and its pool of social workers increased from one to twenty, the difficulties generated by the grafting of a social work department onto an already existing institution remained. If Socialists complained that the personnel and policies of past CSO administrations stunted them, Yávar had even more to complain about. Inertia painfully checked her attempts to rationalize the agency, especially since the Dirección carried on some of the same functions that had been performed previously, such as aid to disaster victims and the distribution of food rations. How could the Dirección face the social determinants of indigence when poverty was likened to a natural disaster? The appointment of male directors, who were intent on using the agency to provide political favors and unsympathetic to Yávar's attempted professionalization, was an additional barrier. And then the Dirección, unlike the CSO, which boasted of its wealth, was chronically underfunded. The accumulation of challenges eventually led Yávar to resign.[35]

Yávar nonetheless instituted important changes in the approximately ten years she headed the service. In an attempt to do away with an almsgiving approach that promoted dependency, the Dirección set up workshops where women, along with a few men, were taught a trade. These establishments took on the character of small industries that provided laundering services for other state agencies and marketed and sold clothing produced by the Dirección's clients and purchased by the Dirección at a piece rate. The Hogar de la Mujer (Woman's Home) and the Hogar Modelo Pedro Aguirre Cerda provided clients with child care. The Hogar de la Mujer took on female boarders and their children.

The fact that the state should assume responsibility for providing women with jobs was extraordinary. While the provision of state jobs for the unemployed was nothing new, public works projects had traditionally employed only men. In an era when female unemployment was not considered problematic—it was widely thought that unemployed women should just get married and let their husbands provide—the Dirección was one of the few state agencies that confronted the issue. Granted, the Dirección's approach did not directly challenge either the notion that women should be dependent on men or the segregation of the labor market: the workshops accepted participants only if they had children and if their (ex-)spouses, (ex-)partners, or (ex-)lovers would not or could not provide for them. And although, as workers, the Dirección's clients were insured by the CSO, they learned traditionally female occupations that left them still "unqualified" and vulnerable when they left. Of fifty clients that passed through the Hogar Modelo, eighteen ended up working as laundresses, two as domestic servants, and thirteen as housewives.[36] Yet despite the inability of the Dirección's programs to articulate a fuller analysis and responses to female poverty, the attempt to diminish their dependency by providing them with child care and work was a notable and innovative experiment. After Yávar resigned, these workshops were shut down.

In part, the failure of left-wing social workers like Yávar and of the Círculo de Estudios Sociales had to do with the timing of changes taking place in the social work field. While salubristas active in the late 1930s and early 1940s were in tune with zealous calls for reform from within and outside the state, by the time social workers began taking more radical positions, the political climate was much less tolerant. Their reform efforts did coincide with increased mobilization among women, who organized in FEChIF to win the national vote. But the repression of Communists and workers led to the dismantling of FEChIF and stunted social workers' ability to pressure the state through feminist organizations. Citing the importance of feminism, in 1946 social worker Gudelia Seguel Morales suggested that clients should become politically active.[37] Few did.

Progressive social workers' commitment to more disenfranchised Chileans, as manifested in their attempt to reform welfare for the indigent, also doomed their reform project. Social workers found that garnering attention and energy for changes within these more marginal state apparatuses was virtually impossible. Physicians' centralizing and democratizing impulses bore fruit in 1952 with the formation of the Servicio Nacional de Salud (SNS, National Health Service), a nationwide health service that would truly serve all Chileans in need. But social work would remain more private and more dispersed. The Dirección did not become the central coordinating agency the Círculo wanted it to be.

Without the ability to confront poverty, and women's poverty in particular, in a more concerted manner, social workers as a whole concentrated on doing the best they could for their individual clients. More often than not, that meant enforcing male responsibility toward women and children. As social worker Delia Arriagada Campos knew, that was the only "right" women had. Writing of her own efforts to elevate both the esteem and the economic condition of the poor single mothers she encountered at the Talcahuano Gota de Leche, a milk station for infants, Arriagada noted: "I tried to change the mistaken ideas of our woman of the pueblo, who thinks that because she is poor, her honor has no value. . . . I also taught her that having a well-constituted home is a right of every woman, no matter her social condition."[38] Ironically, in trying to enforce women's "right" to male economic support, social workers opened themselves up to the criticism that they were meddlesome caseworkers unable to see, or have an impact on, the broader social context. And, they provoked the enmity of many men. The hostility of those men was perhaps a final reason that social workers' efforts to reform their profession and welfare for the indigent did not—despite popular-front efforts to stimulate male responsibility for family members—prosper.

REFORMING THE REFORMERS

Overall, working-class Chileans faced the concurrent efforts to reform the state and the professions with ambivalence. While many individuals objected to the intrusive, restrictive, or patronizing nature of both public health and social work interventions, others came to see welfare professionals as allies. An anecdote published by the labor union at a noodle factory made manifest workers' equivocal relation to welfare professionals. The story opened with a "*rotito*"—a well-known stock character known to be ignorant, dirty, and uncouth but utterly ingenious—who had a desperate desire to urinate. As soon as the little *roto* attempted to relieve himself on the street, a police officer approached, threatened to arrest him, and urged him to move on. Routed, the *roto* searched for a new spot where he might relieve himself but was again stopped by a police officer. About to burst, the man saw a sign announcing "*Vías Urinarias*" (Urinary Tracts), and he entered an office where he was approached by a doctor. The physician asked him what was the matter, and the *roto* matter-of-factly replied, "I can't urinate." "Must be an obstruction," mused the doctor, and he went off to find a shiny metal pan that his "patient" quickly filled to the brim. Shocked, the physician asked, "Didn't you say you couldn't urinate?" "No, sir," replied the *rotito*, "not on the street, but in here, why, yes."[39]

This tale differentiated the helpful physician from the repressive policeman, indicating a nuanced popular conception of elites. The *roto* clearly viewed the physician as a collaborator, one who even undertook the degrading task of holding the receptacle into which the poor man "relieved himself." Yet the doctor's aid was based on a fundamental misconception of his "patient's" needs: the doctor instinctively made medical a problem that was, in fact, a product of restrictive hygienic conventions. The *roto* knew the difference between a medical problem and a social problem. And so did *El Fideero*'s readers.

Yet not all patients were as guileless as the man who needed to urinate and not all physicians were as kind as the one encountered by the fictitious *rotito*. Social workers and physicians were notoriously condescending toward and distrustful of their clients—and meddlesome as well. Many replicated the attitudes of the social worker at the Casa Nacional del Niño, who in the 1930s disparaged clients' parents, referring to them as "the little lady" or "the little man." Especially when their clients made demands on them, welfare professionals adopted punitive approaches. In 1936, CSO physician José Vizcarra warned his colleagues that it was necessary to weed out and punish "parasites" who were not really sick but who were driven to seek benefits by their "psycho-economic and ethical" dispositions. If Vizcarra could criticize even workers with a right to medical care for being too demanding, welfare professionals were even more critical of less entitled clients. Social worker

Zarina Espinoza, who worked for the DGAS, characterized the single mothers who entered the Hogar de la Mujer as "timid and submissive, despite the fact that they carry within themselves the firm belief that the State is obliged to attend to their case. With this temperament, after a few days, they demand rights to which they believe they are entitled such as: free support without their contribution, at the same time, [they demand] cooperation with their work. In this manner, they ignore the benefits they have received and sometimes they turn ungovernable and querulous; this happens especially when one tries to inculcate new habits of hygiene, order, and discipline and work." According to Espinoza, those women were just plain wrong to demand help from the state.[40]

Clients responded individually with indifference and defiance, leading welfare professionals to speak of the pervasive "psychological factor" that prevented patients from collaborating with physicians and social workers and ridding themselves of illnesses and social problems. A *visitadora* who worked with railway workers noted that her biggest "obstacle" was the mentality of distrustful and rebellious workers who always believed someone was trying to abuse them or make them the victims of injustices. Similarly, according to DGAS social worker Zarina Espinoza, of thirty-three women who participated in a mothers' center she organized, only ten were "useful, [and] had the desire to prosper." The rest, seemingly disagreeing with her approach, refused to cooperate.[41]

Preferring not to embroil themselves in situations they might later have trouble getting out of, clients who had the option often chose to stay away from social workers and physicians. In 1941, of 269 family heads who enrolled their children in CDN-run child care centers, 93 withdrew their children. According to the CDN, these parents simply did not want to cooperate with the CDN's efforts to help their children. And of 289 children who left programs in 1944–45, 120 withdrew because their parents "failed to cooperate." Trying to preempt resistance, *Vida Sana*, a medical propaganda magazine for workers put out by the CSO, reminded mothers: "You must tell the doctor everything. Even what does not seem interesting. Before or after the doctor finishes his or her examination, he or she will ask about the life and habits of the child, and being frank and truthful when answering such questions is indispensable."[42]

Both nonworkers and workers, in short, objected to the condescending and intrusive nature of public health and social work interventions. But welfare professionals were more likely to heed worker demands since workers, unlike the single mothers Zarina Espinoza described, made a recognized "contribution" to the nation—and a monetary contribution to the CSO. By insisting on their "rights," however, workers propped up a gendered charity/rights dichotomy that sustained differences between respectable workers and "others" and reinforced, at least to a degree, the notion that they were privileged citizens deserving special treatment. Within this widely accepted worker discourse, there was little room for the public remonstrations of the indigent.

An incident that occurred in the men's wing of the Beneficencia-run San José Sanatorium, where CSO-insured workers received treatment for tuberculosis, revealed both workers' distrust of controlling, arrogant, and even lazy welfare professionals and the efficacy of worker pressure on public officials who understood health care as a worker right. According to Sergio Llantén, a San José tuberculosis patient, the institution's social workers had no interest in helping patients and treated them "really badly" [remal]. Social workers refused to run errands for patients who needed rest and made patients wait endlessly for appointments. If anyone dared complain, the visitadoras insulted and ridiculed him. The patients organized a committee to protest, and when their leader was discharged from the sanatorium, thirty-five other San José residents staged a "patients' strike" and left the facility. The patients returned to the hospital only when the minister of health, whose intervention the patients had requested, offered them improvements. "We believed the minister," Llantén told a reporter. "We know he is not tricking us." The hospital's director was, unfortunately, less reliable. Once the patients had returned, he not only refused to meet their demands but also prohibited them from leaving San José during a period of two weeks. And, he refused to give them permission to visit the women's wing. Horrified at this retribution, the striking patients attempted to phone the minister of health and the press. Hospital staff denied them access to the phone. Llantén was then forced to travel to the Santiago offices of the Communist Frente Popular to tell his story.[43]

Workers such as these patients were particularly critical of private and "charitable" welfare institutions that, unlike the CSO, did not recognize their privileged status as male workers: hence their complaints regarding the Beneficencia-run sanatorium. The union at the El Teniente copper mine complained as well: the social worker hired by the mining company's welfare department, they said, humiliated workers and their families "with disproportionate demands and with prodigious investigations." Yet union leaders were powerless to reform the social worker or force the company to fire her. Apparently workers at the Tarapacá and Antofagasta Nitrate Company felt that their ability to pressure their bosses was limited as well. Dissatisfied with the medical care provided by the company doctor, they directed their complaints to CSO officials. The CSO, they insisted, should revoke its contract with the company and take direct charge of health care in the mining camps.[44]

Although workers recognized that CSO officials did not always treat them with respect, they believed that worker oversight of the CSO, guaranteed by the popular-front governments, would make recalcitrant officials within the agency mend their ways. On a national level, CTCh representatives on the CSO governing board worked to assure that the demands of CSO beneficiaries would be heard by agency officials. When "comrade Gardguilla" was appointed as the CTCh representative on the CSO regional board of directors in Antofagasta, for example, the leaders of the regional CTCh believed that they would henceforth "properly control this service" and "proceed to the aid of insured workers whenever necessary." "When we speak of the Caja de Seguro Obrero," they glowed, "it is appropriate to say that Mr. Luciano Kulczewski, currently its Administrator, has given its services the social character it had lost in the final years of the previous government."[45]

Because worker organizations felt they could successfully pressure the CSO, the agency's efforts to inspire their confidence largely succeeded. The Antofagasta CTCh noted that CSO medical professionals fulfilled a vital worker need and that physicians—and the medical corps more generally— were aware of "the mission of their generous and appreciated profession, in this aspect, the worker has [found] in them a teacher, a comrade, who is in the end his or her best friend." With a sense of confidence and entitlement, the confederation stated: "[A]s a way of collaborating with the Popular Front, we have the obligation of elevating its [the CSO's] prestige, development, and performance, without this meaning that we avoid criticizing the bad procedures that we discover, [procedures] carried out by the medical corps and the administration and that mortify the blue-collar *imponente*. We will scout out the bad functionaries, who are hopefully few in number."[46]

Given these attitudes—that doctors were friends, that the CSO needed gentle prodding, that paternalistic professionals were few—the vehemence with which organized workers on occasion condemned female professionals was remarkable. El Teniente miners, for example, denounced the head nurse at the Sewell hospital in typical fashion, lamenting her awful treatment of patients, patients' families, and hospital workers. A worker journalist castigated head nurse Van Horán, writing: "We are surprised that even though there is a Dr. Jefe in the hospital, there is a woman who runs roughshod over him and is more of a boss than he is." The author also referred to Van Horán as a "foreigner" who lorded over "Chilean *empleadas*." Clearly, this worker objected not only to Van Horán's arrogance and bossiness but most especially to the fact that a woman should be in a position of authority. Male workers likely objected to social workers for similar reasons, and male labor leaders' criticisms of social workers were probably fueled as well by *visitadoras'* penchant for confronting men who abused their authority. Workers discredited women welfare professionals by associating their work with unscientific and retrograde charity.[47]

Furthermore, workers and leftists often differentiated themselves from the indigent when they demanded better treatment. Although workers' organizations sometimes looked out for the interests of their more disenfranchised family members, and although the CTCh strongly supported the extension of CSO benefits to the family members of the insured, they just as often implied that for nonworkers, charitable aid would suffice. The insured complained, for instance, that the indigent and the insured received equally inadequate hospital care at Beneficencia hospitals. But instead of insisting that the Beneficencia improve services for all, *La Crítica* suggested that labor representatives on the Caja's Consejo should "struggle in particular so that the insured receive care in their own hospitals, and not, as is now the case, in public hospital rooms where workers are cared for as if this care constituted charity and not an acquired right." Workers had a right to compassionate, dignified medical treatment, which Caja employees were purportedly more adept at providing, *La Crítica* put forth, because they made "Chile great through their work." For nonworkers, respectful treatment did not seem as imperative.[48]

The Socialist Youth of Chillán took a more generous and inclusive—but less prevalent—stance. Praising the fusion of CSO and non-CSO medical services in the region between Concepción and Chillán affected by the devastating 1939 earthquake, they refuted the notion that the CSO-insured were making a disproportionate financial contribution and receiving inferior services. State agencies other than the CSO were contributing financially to medical services in the region, they pointed out. And, by studying the matter, they countered insured workers who complained that the quality of service had declined after the unification of medical services. Complaints, they found, had actually declined. Quality medical services, according to this view, could be provided by institutions other than the CSO and to Chileans who were not insured workers. These young activists thus rejected distinctions between worthy workers and undeserving "others" and between rights-based and charitylike services. Implicitly, they undermined the link between entitlement and wage work.[49]

The fusion of medical services in the area affected by the earthquake was a dress rehearsal for the establishment of the Servicio Nacional de Salud, created in 1952 to provide health care to all Chileans in need. Henceforth, women, men, and children, workers, indigents, and housewives, would all receive equivalent care in the same clinics and hospitals. Along with the Servicio de Seguridad Social (Social Security Service), the SNS replaced the CSO. By 1952, however, the popular-front experience had ended, the Communist Party had been outlawed, and popular organizations faced severe restrictions. In this context, the establishment of the SNS seemed to have had little to do with worker mobilizations. Instead, the SNS was the brainchild of medical experts who wished to further centralize health services. The dissolution of the CSO was also the work of politicians who had long objected to the CSO's financial power and wished to avoid political haggling over the investment of worker pension funds. Rather than investing pensions, the Servicio de Seguridad Social would pay retirement benefits out of a rolling fund. As a result of this reform and the creation of the SNS, struggles over entitlement would shift after 1952. Perhaps most important, although men and women would continue to make gendered claims to state services, there could be no more talk about workers' special "contributions" and how those contributions should be spent.[50]

CONCLUSION

By the time Aguirre Cerda took power in 1938, the gendered contours of the welfare state had already been established. The popular fronts transformed the legacy they had inherited by democratizing services, at least to a degree, and by expanding them greatly. But the democratization and expansion of state services promoted by the popular fronts did not touch all Chileans equally. Abetted by popular and Left organizations that encouraged democratic participation and entitlements principally for workers—characterized as reputable, manly men, who earned their rights through their contributions—the popular-front governments deepened the gendered cleavages within the state and within the professions. Physicians promoting a social approach to medicine made friends with workers, and the increased state resources they controlled made this alliance possible and attractive. Those resources also convinced workers that it was necessary and useful to struggle over *how* services would be provided.

By contrast, although social workers often aided the women clients with whom they interacted day in and day out, these women were not the kind of collaborators *visitadoras* needed to reform their professions and the state-run and state-overseen agencies in which they worked. Nor could they garner significant support among labor and leftist organizations. *Visitadoras* therefore had less incentive to abandon individualistic approaches and fewer ways to transform the forces that inscribed clientelism within their professions. Notwithstanding the efforts of progressive social workers and the remonstrations of individual clients, *visitadoras* could not extricate themselves completely from condescending casework approaches. As women with fewer venues of influence, social workers perhaps relished the authority they wielded over clients. Yet their relation to state apparatuses was just as important as their desire for authority. Progressive social workers failed to make the DGAS into an institution that could coordinate and systematize welfare for the indigent, making it less piecemeal and arbitrary. But they would later find that within the SNS, they could legitimately turn away from aiding individuals and turn toward community organizing.[51]

chapter five

STATE REGULATION, MORALITY, AND MATERIAL REFORM

Throughout the popular-front era, welfare professionals and political elites worried endlessly about the destabilizing effects of industrialization and modernization on the family. Claiming that without intervention, the family, that "nucleus of society," might perish, social worker Luz Tocornal remarked, "Modern life is antagonistic toward the family and can destroy it one day if the family is not defended with a concerted and intelligent effort." Whether or not the family was actually in danger (most Chileans married and had children with their spouses despite widespread changes in politicoeconomic organization), a belief that broader transformations undermined the family justified its constant reaffirmation. Elite efforts to vindicate the nuclear family drew upon and validated already existing gender norms, including the idea that women needed the material support and sexual protection of their male relatives. But they also revamped even long-standing notions of gender right by linking masculine and feminine identities to wage work and inscribing them in medicalized discourses of pathology and health.[1]

Hoping to mitigate gender conflict within families, which were considered the bedrock of the nation, popular-front state officials not only delineated norms of masculinity and femininity but also tried to secure conduct consistent with those norms. If husbands and wives adhered to gendered prescriptions, reformers believed, conflicting interests that destabilized families would be mitigated and relations among family members would improve. Crusaders enjoined men not to economically or physically abandon their wives and children or spend leisure time away from their families.

Gambling and drinking stimulated male irresponsibility, they argued, and squandered families' scarce resources. Women, according to reformers, should tend to their children and their homes. So that women might raise healthy and productive children and provide their husbands with clean, well-run homes, state officials instructed women in domestic economy and puericulture, the science of childrearing. Since work outside the home purportedly forced mothers to abandon their children, and since wives who were wage earners were reputedly more independent and quarrelsome, officials thought it prudent to restrict female wage-earning. Finally, reformers attempted to define proper sexual conduct for men and women. State campaigns consistently focused on the ways licentiousness undermined family life and sought to strengthen the monogamous, heterosexual family by solving the "problems" of promiscuity, prostitution, single motherhood, and illegitimacy.

By the early 1950s, state cajoling, legislating, policing, educating, punishing, and rewarding in favor of a certain model of the family had produced noticeable effects. The falling rate of illegitimacy, which dropped from 32 to 25 percent between 1930 and 1950, was one indicator of Chileans' growing acceptance of state-sanctioned forms of family life; the declining proportion of couples who legitimated children when they married (24 percent in 1933, 19 percent in 1950) was another. Furthermore, many participants in family reform efforts perceived a change. In 1949, Luz Tocornal spoke of the "complete success" of efforts to constitute the family—of efforts, that is, to encourage civil marriage, the legitimization of children, and stable, male-headed nuclear families. A year earlier social worker Blanca Urbina Moya noted that at the Caupolicán-Chiguayante textile mill where she was employed, illegitimacy had "notably diminished in relation to past years."[2]

Despite reformers' aspirations, throughout the popular-front period familial solidarity and cohesion were never fully realized. As this chapter reveals, vacillations in state policy and variations in how it was applied undermined the popular fronts' goal of creating harmonious family relations. In addition, policies could be contradictory: in succoring purportedly vulnerable illegitimate children, for example, the state might also lend support and sustenance to their unwed mothers. Social workers employed by the state understood the enforcement of sexual and familial norms as a professional mandate and a moral imperative that would save the nation. But faced with women who had abusive or irresponsible husbands or convivientes, social workers sometimes validated female independence. Even schemes unequivocally designed to strengthen the male breadwinner—female housewife model could be carried out in different ways.

Welfare professionals increasingly adopted an intentionally less repressive approach that allowed their clients to maneuver. However, as this chapter shows, professionals' efforts to constitute the family inevitably limited the autonomy of both men and women—albeit in different ways. State campaigns that encouraged men to become responsible workers and breadwinners responded to certain of men's demands and acknowledged men's responsibility to the nation and their families. At the same time, those campaigns helped rout more raucous, homosocial male behavior. Authorities also recognized the importance of women's mothering and childrearing to the nation, and social workers strengthened women's position within the family by helping them reform unreliable husbands and escape abusive situations. But by portraying women workers and single mothers as victims who needed the protection of either male family members or the state itself, they underscored and helped reproduce women's lack of sexual and economic autonomy.[3]

TO REWARD AND PERSUADE:
THE METHODS OF FAMILY REFORM

Tocornal's "concerted and intelligent effort" of rescuing the family was carried out by a concerted intelligentsia with enterprising methods. As we saw in Chapter 4, welfare professionals increasingly searched for less authoritarian ways of interacting with their clients. The blurring of lines between medical and social arenas nevertheless allowed more elitist professionals to make social problems medical and reaffirm their own expertise. The CSO thus proclaimed, "The worker, even if he is healthy, is socially ill, an inferior being in the struggle for life. The most incurable ills are at the margins of Pathology, pertain to a world of germs in which the microscope fails."[4] More generally, welfare professionals often presented both poverty and problems within the family as issues to be addressed from a medical perspective. For at least some medical practitioners, it was immaterial whether pathologies that undermined family life—such as alcoholism, prostitution, syphilis, tuberculosis, malnutrition, infant mortality, unemployment, and illiteracy—were "vices," diseases, or misfortunes. CSO social worker Luz Cañas spoke of marital breakups as health problems. Misunderstandings between husband

and wife, she explained, could lead to separations that undermined the family's financial well-being and in turn the health of family members. In a similar vein, a publication of the Ministry of Health claimed that economic, educational, marital, legal, and sanitary problems produced "a visible change in the proper functioning of domestic life. . . . [S]ooner or later well-being disappears and illnesses arise." The publication further asserted that only professionals could prevent and cure such problems.[5]

The CSO feared that the microscope might fail to register pathologies, but welfare professionals availed themselves of the survey, just as precise a diagnostic tool. *Sanitaristas*, social workers, dietitians, dentists, nurses, engineers, economists, and architects assiduously collected data. Professionals scoured the streets of Santiago, uncovering how poor Chilean families lived and worked. They asked how many family members resided, on average, in working-class households and who those family members were. In how many rooms did the family live and how much rent did it pay? Was the home clean, untidy, or filthy? Did living quarters have running water? Sewage? A toilet? How many beds did the family have? What was the family's income and how was it spent? How many calories did each family member consume? Did school-age children attend school? Were parents literate? Did they have tuberculosis? Syphilis? Cardiovascular diseases? Did they drink excessively? Survey findings were cause for excitement: "[Economics] makes graphics and statistics that rouse us with the eloquent emotion of their numbers and digits," announced *Vida Sana*, a CSO health propaganda publication.[6]

The purported scientific nature of fact collecting and the neutrality of hard data lent legitimacy to even the most dubious reasoning. Blatant "errors" in scientific reasoning belied the ideological nature of fact-finding. "The Numbers Speak," "Horrifying Statistics," blared the headlines of an article in the Socialist newspaper *La Crítica*. The article proffered the following evidence that highlighted the dangerous spread of prostitution: 52.42 percent of all prostitutes under the medical control of the Dirección General de Sanidad were infected with syphilis, and 56.96 percent of "clandestine" prostitutes suffered the same ill. In total, then, there were "more than 100% of sick women." The purported statistical precision of this analysis hid the imprecision of the language (the use of the term "women" to refer to prostitutes) as well as the faulty mathematics. Yet by availing themselves of rationality and science, these reformers bolstered norms of conduct for women and underscored their own expertise.[7]

Despite continuing elitism, however, popular-front politicians increasingly understood the state venture of familial reform as an educational project aimed at convincing Chileans of the necessity of a proper family life. Aguirre Cerda's most famous motto—cited as the epigraph to Allende's *La realidad médico-social chilena (síntesis)*—was: "To govern is to educate and give health" [*Gobernar es educar y dar salud al pueblo*]. Thus Allende and Aguirre Cerda signaled the popular fronts' project as both moral ("to educate") and material ("to give health") and indicated that material incentives would complement moral aspects of the state's reform program. They also suggested *how* the popular fronts would govern: principally through prescription and incentive, and not through punishment or repression. Concurring with this orientation, the head of the CSO's social service division saw social workers' actions as "essentially pedagogical." Similarly, the CSO health publication *Vida Sana* saw its role as "purely educational." Repressive means undoubtedly reinforced and complemented approaches aimed at convincing and building consensus, and insofar as elites controlled both economic inducements and educational efforts, state initiatives remained coercive. The national-popular state nevertheless preferred to reward and prompt.[8]

The legal and judicial systems encouraged Chileans to marry and to bear children within marriage—these children were legally classified as "legitimate." The Civil Code mandated that husbands and fathers provide economic support for their wives and legitimate children. (Wives were responsible for the economic maintenance of their children and invalid husbands.) "Natural" children, who were born outside marriage but whose parent or parents had identified them as offspring, had rights to diminished parental support, and "simply illegitimate" children, whose parents had not recognized them, had no rights at all. Likewise, legitimate children had full rights to their parents' inheritance, including social security pensions, while "natural" children had diminished prerogatives, and those who were "simply illegitimate" had none.[9]

While the legal system potentially protected the right of wives and children to marital and parental support, its regulatory power was limited. Courts were incapable of actually promoting marriage, the legitimation of children, or material support since, in contrast to welfare and social security programs, they imposed parental, and especially male, obligations without the possibility of bestowing benefits. Moreover, when fathers denied their relation to children, the legal system provided inadequate recourse for women and children: paternity was legally difficult to prove, and if husbands or fathers ran off, the courts and police rarely tracked them down. Legislation enacted in 1935 and 1952 tried to lighten the burden of proof in legal proceedings aimed at establishing paternity, but cornering recalcitrant fathers still proved difficult. One social worker complained about deficiencies and asked for more reforms: "Hopefully . . . the progress of man will make him create legislation that wakes his own responsibility for the fulfillment of his paternal duties." Without such reforms, male economic contributions to their kin rested mostly on the goodwill of individual men—and occasionally on the intervention of social service agencies.[10]

Along with legal sanctions, economic incentives encouraged popular compliance with moralizing campaigns. To encourage Chileans to marry, one physician went so far as to suggest that unmarried Chileans over the age of twenty-five should be subject to a special tax. While this radical measure did not become law, other more partial provisions granted material benefits to those who legalized ties of kinship. Laborers' marital status and the existence of legal ties to their children even conditioned their rights as workers: under the preventive medicine law passed in 1938, for example, married workers and widow(er)s with children received 75 percent of their pay as a disability subsidy; other workers received 50 percent. And this despite the fact that disability insurance was considered a replacement for lost wages. The state Caja de Habitación (Housing Fund) also conceded privileges to married couples. It prohibited partners who were not married from renting apartments in its housing complexes and favored married applicants and applicants with large families in assigning lodging. While family allowances, the most important state-enforced material incentive aimed at promoting civil marriage and the legal recognition of children, were not legally mandated for blue-collar workers until 1952, throughout the popular-front period leftist politicians, as well as representatives of other political forces, lobbied for the payment of subsidies to workers for their legally recognized children and wives. Welfare professionals within and outside the state also called consistently for the payment of family wages.[11]

The social security system was a powerful financial inducement toward stable married life. An early reform of law 4.054 granted pensions to certain relatives of the insured upon their death. Spouses and children of *imponentes* were entitled to limited CSO health care. But in order for family members to receive pensions or medical benefits, the CSO demanded that ties of kinship be legally sanctioned. Children had to have proper birth certificates to go to CSO clinics, and marital rights depended on the existence of a documented civil marriage. While illegitimate, like legitimate, children could receive medical attention as infants, they had to be recognized by the insured to be granted access. Upon the death of a parent, illegitimate children received orphans' pensions only if there were no legitimate progeny. State publications aimed at informing workers and state functionaries about social security benefits were littered with explanations of which family members were eligible for what benefits and which were not. While workers struggled for the extension of benefits to relatives, in the short run, the surest way to assure family members' access to those resources was to legally formalize family ties.[12]

Because of the difficulty of enforcing fathers' responsibility for their children through the judicial system and because material benefits were not always generous enough to entice working-class men and women, reformers found other methods. The "correct" legal constitution of families, as well as the fulfillment of fathers' legal responsibility for the economic support of their children, were encouraged largely by social workers in welfare agencies and not by the courts. Policing gave way to chiding, as social workers employed in various public agencies—and their colleagues in the private sector, as well—coaxed husbands and fathers into adequately fulfilling their obligations. In the not atypical case of one single mother abandoned by her lover, the intervention of a social worker succeeded where the courts had not. The young woman's father had sought judicial action to force his daughter's seducer to marry his daughter, legally recognize the baby, and fulfill his financial duties to mother and child. In court, the baby's supposed father denied his paternity, leaving the young woman and her father without legal recourse. Yet the social worker who later took up the case convinced the baby's father to recognize his offspring and pay a monthly sum for the child's support.[13]

In cases like this, social workers frequently acted in lieu of courts. In fact, they could often enforce familial obligations more effectively. Reflecting the proxy role they played, social workers often called themselves *judges*.[14] Social worker Tomy Romeo went even further, characterizing herself as "a real police officer." In a 1993 interview, she remembered that while working at the Casa de Socorro in Puente Alto, a settlement house and clinic on the outskirts of Santiago, she spent much of her time trying to track down fathers who abandoned their children. Her first contact with these men, she recalled, was via a polite form letter: "Mr. So-and-So, would you be so kind as to come speak with the social worker." The conversations that ensued were often less cordial. Romeo, who described herself as "unrelenting" in these cases, "a real police officer with those men," reconstructed a typical conversation between herself and a father who refused to recognize his child:

"Okay, sir, ahem, the señora so-and-so who has just had a baby says that you are the father of the baby."

"No, señorita. What hope! What a liar! Ehm, why, that woman is a public woman, señorita. She is involved with every Tom, Dick, and Harry. And, besides, she knew I was married, señorita. So why did she take up with me?"

"Ah," I would say, "she knew. But didn't you yourself know that you were married? Was she the only one who knew? Didn't you know?"

And we would cage him in like that, let me tell you. . . . In general the people had a lot of affection for us, but that little group of anonymous fathers didn't care for us at all.[15]

Attempts to educate and convince were thus sometimes less than cordial. Yet Romeo and her colleagues did not ultimately have the enforcement power of police officers, and they therefore preferred to win over potential collaborators. When the Unidad Sanitaria San Miguel was set up around 1946 to coordinate disparate health care agencies in an area of the municipality, its organizers rejected past approaches, which they saw as ineffective, and trained employees in less coercive ways of dealing with clients. They counseled inspectors, nurses, and social workers to arm themselves with patience and good manners and to discard "old work habits based on punitive-bureaucratic criteria." Collecting data on sanitary conditions in the municipality's *poblaciones* was not the same as being detectives, organizers told their team of professionals. The coercive and condescending measures used in the past, they cautioned, only estranged clients and impeded cooperation between the poor and the state. Those methods were, in their view, not only ineffective but also unnecessary. Working-class women and men, they believed, were predisposed to learn about preventive health measures. This approach apparently paid off: at least one of its doctors noted that his clients willingly answered survey questions posed by data collectors and actively participated in the educational activities sponsored by the Unidad.[16]

Welfare professionals elsewhere also deemed more democratic and horizontal relations with their clients more effective. *Vida Sana* declared itself open to collaboration with and consultation by its audience and pressed readers to share information with family and friends. Professionals promoted literacy and urged literate workers to disseminate what they had learned to coworkers who could not read: "Learn to read," a municipal workers' insurance fund publication admonished. "Ask for pamphlets so that you can instruct your *compañeros*." Acknowledging that readers might mistrust counsel dispensed by more educated and wealthy professionals, *Vida Sana* tried to reduce the social distance between state officials and clients. It often presented advice in the form of conversations among workers. A typical "Workers' Dialogue" published in one issue of *Vida Sana*, and most likely written by a physician, concluded by saying, "Let my experience be of use to you, my friend Pedro."[17]

The success of welfare professionals clearly depended on building trust. Social worker Luz Cañas responded to the reticence of the "modest classes" not with recriminations but by seeking their cooperation. Conceding that clients could sometimes be stubborn, the social worker nonetheless noted, "once one has inspired their confidence, they do not keep secrets or hide situations." "It is also necessary," she affirmed, "to possess a good amount of psychological sense to find people's 'Achilles' heel.' . . . [I]t is useful to know how to strike a sympathetic chord in the hearts of our pueblo, so that we can more easily inspire their confidence."[18] Although Cañas continued to believe in the righteousness of her probing and prescription, she recognized the need to phrase her invectives in ways that coincided with popular discourses and to make clients see how adhering to state prescription might bring them rewards that fulfilled specific needs.

A typical social worker considered errand-running, which admittedly took up most of her time, as secondary but indispensable given popular desires. Social worker Adelina Zegarra, who worked at the CSO's Santos Dumont clinic in northern Santiago, spent much of her time making sure her clients' papers were in order. This was a thankless task, made even more difficult by the lack of even rudimentary office supplies. Zegarra complained. But she knew that she could not get on with what she considered her real task without first doing the work her clients expected of her. Satisfied clients, she felt, were more likely to indulge her own passion: offering advice of a more personal nature. "[I]t is impossible," Zegarra wrote, "to deny the importance of this [palliative assistance] in the eyes of the client because its solution intrinsically holds the immediate utility he [sic] demands. For the social worker, it has a broader value. In many cases it is the first stage on the path of a preventive or constructive task." A contemporary observer concurred with Zegarra's priorities. She suggested that although a social worker might fix a CSO credential, enroll children in the Civil Registry, or show a client how to obtain welfare and social security benefits, she nevertheless had "a much more transcendent role to play for the beneficiary and for society . . . *restructuring of the mentality of the laboring classes.*"[19]

Clients of welfare agencies had their own reasons for collaborating with professionals or for heeding their advice. Women and men of the popular classes found themselves indebted to social workers who helped them steer through the social security and welfare systems. Securing pensions and other benefits entailed complicated bureaucratic operations in which the burden of proof was always in the hands of the client. For instance, insured workers who wanted to visit a clinic had to make sure that their employers had paid the requisite taxes and placed the official stamps in their CSO credentials. To be admitted to the hospital, CSO beneficiaries had to have special passes signed by agency physicians, and even with the passes, they could not always find vacancies.[20] Social workers knew how to help clients get their hands on benefits. But those clients paid a price when they visited social workers and asked for help in confronting the more impersonal and tedious facets of the state: they had to put up with often intrusive home visits, social and moral "diagnoses," and the ensuing "treatment" of social ills. They also had to listen to endless exhortations to get married and stay married.

Since not all parties in any given family group had the same interests and since not all were equally vulnerable, each family member might collaborate with state officials to different degrees. When seventeen-year-old "A. B." visited the venereal disease clinic at the San Luis Hospital and was diagnosed as having syphilis, she told the hospital social worker that she had contracted the disease from her father, who raped her after coming home drunk one day. The social worker considered A. B. herself "extremely cooperative": The young woman identified her two other sexual partners and underwent treatment. In return, the social worker found A. B. a job so that she would no longer have to live with her father. A. B.'s aunt, who lived with the family, collaborated with the social worker by corroborating A. B.'s story. In comparison, the father was uncooperative. Approached by the social worker while he himself was undergoing treatment for the disease, he vehemently denied having raped his daughter. Although one of A. B.'s partners was initially reluctant to admit he had had sexual relations with the young woman— perhaps he believed the social worker would reproach him for the sexual liaison or force him to marry A. B.—he eventually confided in the social worker.[21]

The alliances welfare professionals formed rested, in sum, on the concrete program for moral reform they put forth, on their ability to convince clients of the worthiness of their proposals, on the concrete benefits they could offer, and on their decision to forego coercion. The vast resources of the state—not only its material force but also the legitimacy it could claim as the supposed agent of the national will—gave its agents particular potency. Yet the compromise state that evolved with the popular fronts generally rejected more unilateral formulations and more repressive means of enforcing gender norms in favor of influence and bargaining, which in any case it deemed more effective. To find a client's Achilles' heel, Cañas had first to listen and understand. Since the forging of state prescriptions relied on conflict and negotiation—not only between welfare professionals and their clients but also within the family and, as we will see, within state agencies—beneficiaries found room to maneuver. Depending on circumstance, the actions and beliefs of clients thwarted, altered, or instigated state efforts, just as the actions of professional elites empowered and limited clients. Although constrained, and sometimes severely so, men and women often collaborated with professionals at least to a degree. In so doing, they not only internalized but also modified state disciplinary campaigns.

DOMESTICATING MEN

As the example of A. B. suggested, men and women tended to interact differently with welfare apparatuses. Although many women clearly resented welfare professionals, they often assented to and even actively requested the intervention of welfare professionals to gain leverage over male family members. In particular, they found social workers, many of whom were imbued with a protofeminist desire to help other women, useful allies in their efforts to curb male privilege. Since welfare professionals generally positioned women as victims of male abuse, however, they circumscribed women even as they helped them. By contrast, state officials acknowledged and even abetted the male protagonism that made their jobs so difficult. Efforts to regulate gender and family thus constructed male and female agency differently.

The foregrounding of male agency was particularly evident in one of the most famous texts in the genre of social analysis that undergirded popular-front bids to reform the family, a book titled *La realidad médico-social chilena (síntesis)*. A prototype for the political intervention of professionals, *La realidad médico-social* was written by Salvador Allende in 1939, while he was minister of health. Like most analyses of the period, the book went to great lengths to document scientifically those social problems the state needed to address. Its 216 pages contained more than ninety-five tables describing Chileans' living and work conditions and health problems. It also portrayed the actions of men as crucial to national well-being.[22]

The first page of Allende's book displayed a photograph of an impoverished youngster on a sidewalk holding an infant. Both children are barely sheltered in a doorway, asleep. In the snapshot, a man in a trench coat, only his shoes and the hemline of his coat visible, walks by, indifferent. The angle at which the photo was taken gave the impression that the man was walking upward, toward a light in the background. In this iconography the man symbolized movement and progress, in contrast to the inertness of the children. Below the photograph, the caption read:

> Chile has the highest infant mortality in the World. For each twenty births, one child is born dead. Our neonatal deaths are equivalent to 50.5% of those born alive; for each thousand born alive two hundred and fifty die. For each ten children born alive, one dies before reaching one month of age; one-fourth before the first year; and almost one-half before reaching nine years. Each year, four hundred thousand children do not attend any School, which represents 42% of the school age population. We have six hundred thousand illiterate young people. 27.9% of those born alive are illegitimate children, a figure that is among the highest in the civilized world.

The unhealthy and illegitimate children to whom the caption referred—the two qualities were seen as intimately related and equally serious—harked back to the two youngsters. In this context the indifferent male figure symbolized the twofold abandonment of Chile's "human capital," forsaken by their irresponsible fathers and by the insensitive national community embodied in the state.[23]

The prevalence of "abandoned" children put the nation at risk, Allende wrote. Along with other reformers, he characterized illegitimacy, resulting from paternal abandonment, as the *cause* of infant mortality. Infant mortality in turn impeded the development of the healthy and dense population that could make Chile part of the "civilized world." In this pronatalist logic, reducing illegitimacy was a national security imperative. But although Allende justified state intervention to rout illegitimacy by linking family reform to the well-being of the nation, he recognized the agency of working-class

CHILE tiene la más alta mortalidad infantil del Mundo.

Photo from Salvador Allende's La realidad médico-social chilena (síntesis). *Photo courtesy Biblioteca Nacional.*

men by acknowledging the importance of their choices to both their families and the country. Men who chose to cooperate with state officials, Allende suggested, could correct the interrelated problems of paternal abandonment, illegitimacy, child poverty, and demographic inferiority.[24]

Most welfare professionals believed, like Allende, that men posed the most substantial challenge to proper family life. Chilean men simply did not want to settle down and become consistent providers for their wives and children. Since at least the late nineteenth century Chilean men, accustomed to migrating in search of work or adventure, had wandered from the countryside to mining centers, from one mining center to another, from the mines to the cities, or directly from the country to the city. When living or working conditions were unsatisfactory or wages were inadequate, workers preferred to move on. Laborers' sexual and emotional ties, like their employment, were often fleeting. As one commentator put it, "With respect to adulterous unions, we can say that they are the result of . . . our pueblo's roving spirit, which drives it to look for new horizons. Neither a wife nor children pose an obstacle."[25] Moreover, welfare professionals noted that many men defined their manhood not in relation to family but in terms of how they related to other men. They proved their manliness in bars and whorehouses and by showing solidarity with coworkers.[26]

State officials objected to this masculine rebelliousness and put forward a model of masculinity that stressed abstention, restraint, and domestic ties. Hard and consistent workers, authorities put forth, were good providers; thoughtful and dependable heads of households made excellent workers. Good fathers could not be bad workers, they maintained. Nor could bad workers be patriotic citizens or good husbands and fathers. Thus work and family became two inextricable elements of the masculine identity promoted by the state. "The desire to be a good family member, a good worker, and a good citizen," the CSO's *Vida Sana* admonished, "gives life an inappreciable value."[27]

As we saw in Chapter 2, state officials as well as employers—particularly owners of mining enterprises or of industries with large workforces—increasingly linked male workers' stability on the job to marital stability. To make a highly mobile workforce more permanent, they not only rewarded workers who married by paying them family allowances but also urged male workers to be good husbands. Both state officials and employers thus reinforced the association of work and family identities that defined what it meant to be a man.

One of the state's most aggressive campaigns to domesticate men at home and at work sought to eradicate immoderate drinking. To assure the success of this campaign, the state sought the cooperation of both workers and employers. For employers, limiting the alcohol consumption of workers was a way to combat absenteeism and accidents at work. *San Lunes*, Saint Monday, was a widespread "holiday" among Chilean workers. After a weekend of bingeing, laborers often stayed home on Monday. When workers went to work still drunk, the probability of costly slipups increased. The state itself often lamented the economic losses occasioned by alcoholism. Thus employers collaborated with the state to limit the consumption of alcohol. They accorded bonuses to steadfast and abstemious workers and opened the gates of mining camps and factories to authorities preaching temperance.[28]

Because working-class leaders believed sober, disciplined men would make better activists, they embraced prohibition and applauded the setting up of dry zones in diverse localities (see Chapter 6). But not all male laborers collaborated with popular-front initiatives aimed at promoting worker stability. Unsure that they would share in the benefits of national development and fearing that only capitalists would profit, some laborers continued to act in unruly and disreputable ways: they not only drank but also visited prostitutes, bet on card games and horse races, got into fist fights, and refused to get married. Oppositional standards of masculinity existed alongside official norms. In some cases, those alternative forms of masculinity were explicitly anticapitalist, a way of expressing antagonism toward bosses who insisted that workers ought to get married, stay sober, and report dutifully to their jobs.[29]

State officials answered this continuing masculine rebelliousness with repression. Between 1938 and 1950 arrests for drunkenness were the single largest category of detentions, constituting over 40 percent of all arrests (see table A.7). However, when leftists objected to the punitive manner in which dry laws were enforced and suggested that perhaps measures aimed at improving laborers' living conditions might go further toward eradicating alcoholism, state agents responded by attempting to find less brutal methods for instilling the value of abstinence.[30] While arrests continued throughout the period, popular-front politicians—who did not care to or could not control the police—sought other methods for reducing alcohol consumption. Above all, they sought to *convince* men of the value of sobriety.

Authorities also responded to working-class organizations' rejection of punitive methods by promoting recreational activities that would keep men away from the canteen. A medical social worker noted with pride that she had convinced a young worker to give up his "incipient alcoholism" and join a sports club. Working more globally, Aguirre Cerda set up a new agency, the Departamento de Defensa de la Raza y Aprovechamiento de las Horas Libres (Department for the Defense of the Race and Enjoyment of Free Time) to provide enhanced recreational opportunities.[31]

Along with a sister program developed by the CSO, the Defensa de la Raza built soccer and basketball courts and swimming pools; set up vacation areas for workers; established libraries; worked with unions and other workers' organizations to stimulate theater and music groups; and counseled Chileans, especially Chilean men, to desist from drinking and take up sports. The CSO and the Defensa de la Raza contributed to the creation of recreational centers such as the Hogar Pedro Aguirre Cerda (Pedro Aguirre Cerda Home), located in the Santiago suburb of Conchalí, and the Centro Cívico y Cultural Valparaíso (Valparaíso Civic and Cultural Center), in the port city. In these centers, neighbors could find game rooms, Ping-Pong tables, popular restaurants, or milk bars. The centers sponsored boxing, soccer, and hockey teams; housed theater groups; taught handicrafts, domestic arts, and literacy; gave talks; and showed movies. Community, union, and women's groups held their meetings there. At the Centro Valparaíso, however, dances and alcohol were expressly forbidden, as were card games and dice.[32]

By promoting certain kinds of recreation, the popular fronts made leisure an issue of state, reinscribing recreational programs and anti-alcoholism campaigns within the discourses of national health and economic progress. According to the decree that set up the Defensa de la Raza, for instance, the objectives of the institution were: "To cultivate a consciousness of our national value and of patriotic honor; To practice physical culture as a means of obtaining the vigor and aptitude required for work; To practice hygienic habits; To worship work, peace, and human solidarity; To stimulate a feeling of individual dignity and excellence within civic and home life." Although groups promoting "healthy" amusements had existed before the state began its recreational project, according to both CSO and worker publications, prior initiatives had been inefficient and ineffective. The private sports clubs and artistic groups that had existed previously simply did not promote a vision of the sportsman-citizen. State control, in comparison, assured that recreational organizations would propagate a vision of a disciplined male citizenry.[33]

State bids to extirpate alcoholism and encourage physical fitness drew upon eugenic reasoning, thereby furthering the popular-front efforts to better the Chilean "race" and reinforcing the need for medical intervention. Experts asserted, for instance, that a heavy drinker could not be an adequate father or a biologically fit progenitor. His offspring would be weak, prone to diseases of all sorts. They might even inherit their father's addiction. In 1939, Minister of Health Allende explained, "An alcoholic inheritance, determined by the influence of the toxic substance on the sexual cells of both parents, or of one of the parents, can be recognized, from the point of view of the [resulting] physical characteristics, by diverse types of dystrophies and even monstrosities. Notable mental characteristics include: mental retardation, idiocy, moral debility, a propensity toward neurosis (hysteria, epilepsy, dipsomania, etc.)." Moreover, since alcohol debilitated men's organisms, their ability to work properly as well as their civic capacities would be diminished.

They might become criminals or lose their mental capacities. A government publication reminded workers: "Do not forget that it is indispensable that every good citizen conserve a mental lucidity and perfect control over his nervous system at every moment of his life."[34]

State agents, in sum, portrayed temperate men who heeded the advice of experts as more productive and more evolved, hence worthy and fit citizens. Overcoming an addiction to liquor and practicing sports were signs of the self-discipline that marked true manhood. Equating alcoholism with animal instinct, *Vida Sana* chided, "Who can think, then, that alcoholism makes a man more manly? On the contrary. We must proclaim this out loud. The personality looks toward evil and the instincts surface just as they were among primitive men." A didactic parable published in another issue of the magazine detailed the story of Gregorio Segundo Mesa Alarcón, "an exemplary citizen and a worker." As a child and adolescent, Mesa Alarcón had learned "to feign manhood in order to conquer his work. Manhood also meant sharing with his *compañeros*, having the same distractions, not striking a sour note. And he frequented the tavern." Suggesting that bad habits could be changed, the story detailed how this exemplary citizen "struggled with himself" until one day he visited the doctor. Heeding the physicians' words, Mesa Alarcón gave up drinking. Two years later he would proclaim eternal gratitude to the doctor who had helped him. His wife and children were also thankful. Mesa Alarcón had become a good citizen, worker, and husband: a true man.[35]

Along with eugenic rhetoric, parables such as these buttressed the authority of elites like Mesa Alarcón's doctor, who were portrayed as all-knowing and indispensable allies. Yet elites also called for men's voluntary participation in reform efforts, thereby underscoring the importance of the choices men made. And regardless of whether state agents arrested or pleaded, they clearly believed that men could change their disreputable ways and were responsible for their actions. It was the choices men made, experts recognized, that would determine the future of the family and hence of the nation. State officials thus acknowledged male agency even as they circumscribed it in a variety of ways.

Elites also addressed women's concerns as they sought to domesticate men: through anti-alcoholism campaigns welfare professionals repudiated male habits to which women objected, such as battering and improper spending. Social workers and physicians suggested that because drunk men had a propensity to beat their wives, they provoked harmful conflict that divided the family. Husbands who spent their wages in bars, like those who squandered their earnings on bets, could not be good providers either. In the view of one social worker, when wives tried to reform their alcoholic husbands, men resisted and marital disputes ensued. To avoid these perils, she suggested a measure that would have empowered women: the passage of legislation allowing wives to request that a judge legally prohibit their husbands from buying alcohol. More commonly, welfare professionals suggested that male deviance should be addressed by men themselves or directly by state officials.[36]

Women commonly conspired with social workers and other state agents to constitute families and reform men. Given the abysmally low wages women earned, their limited opportunities for employment, and the subsequent difficulties they encountered in supporting themselves and their children in the absence of a male breadwinner, women, and especially women with children, had good reason to aspire to constant marital unions. They sought social workers' interventions in their own familial disputes and cooperated in more global campaigns that sought to foster male responsibility for their families. They also allied with social workers to reform violent and economically undependable partners.[37]

However, by focusing on male alcoholism as the root of domestic and civil problems, social workers obfuscated patriarchal privilege per se and circumscribed women's ability to resist male abuse. Insofar as domestic and sexual violence, which were neither part of public debate nor directly addressed by state policies, could be presented as effects of alcoholism, social workers confronted and treated them. Yet welfare professionals did not portray wife beating or sexual abuse—as opposed to alcoholism—as an issue of national security. And because they insisted on the need to reform men, even when those men showed no sign of wanting to change, they recognized and reproduced male protagonism while limiting women's. When "C. B.," a forty-three-year-old laundress, visited the social worker at a Centro de Defensa del Niño, the social worker immediately focused on the fact that C. B.'s partner, "E. V.," was an alcoholic. According to the social worker's report, the family's problems included a faulty distribution of its income; the lack of civil marriage between C. B. and E. V.; the illegitimacy of the couple's children, who had neither been registered in the Civil Registry nor recognized by their father; the fact that the mother was ill with cancer; and most especially E. V.'s alcoholism. In her discussion of the case, the social worker also mentioned that E. V. had raped C. B.'s thirteen-year-old daughter, born of a previous union. The social worker clearly saw this sexual abuse as unacceptable and found the girl employment as a live-in servant, away from the clutches of her stepfather. However, the social worker did not name the rape as one of the family's official "problems."[38]

THE MAKING OF MODEL MOTHERS

When social worker Gudelia Seguel Morales asserted that "women's essential mission is maternity," she echoed a larger common sense. Consistent with those beliefs, welfare professionals acting within state agencies promoted a naturalized female identity with motherhood at its center. They routinely referred to women as "future mothers" and depicted women's desire to bear and raise children as a quasi-instinctual craving. Because experts presumed that women desired to raise their children within stable marriages, their vision of femininity intimately tied women, as mothers, to men.[39]

The conspicuous presence in Chilean society and in the offices of health and welfare agencies of women who bore children outside marriage, "rebel mothers," and self-sufficient women suggested that state and female models of motherhood, marriage, and, more generally, gender did not necessarily converge.[40] Class differences made it hard for experts to posit a natural, universal norm, and state officials therefore found it necessary to tend to working-class women's supposed deviations from norms of proper femininity: teaching them when and how to have sex, how to mother, how to keep house, and how to get along with their husbands. At the same time, experts often denied the transgressions—and hence the agency—of women who most openly defied gender norms: single mothers and wage-earning women. Women who had sex outside marriage or who worked outside the home were, according to many state officials, simply the victims of economically irresponsible, philandering men.

Widespread campaigns aimed at reducing infant mortality and protecting children insisted on women's patriotic cooperation with state officials and recognized the importance of women's childrearing. However, health workers who questioned mothers' ability to raise their children and sought to supervise them curbed the empowering potential of the rhetoric of republican motherhood. When the CSO demanded that women collaborate in the crusade to improve the health of Chile's future citizens, it invoked women's patriotic duty: "Mothers who form the citizens of the future! You deserve, and should expect, aid in all forms, in order to contribute to the physical, moral and intellectual development of your children. But your own responsibility is enormous!"[41] At the same time, CSO officials reaffirmed their expertise and reconstructed class hierarchies, complaining of working-class mothers' "generalized ignorance" and "rudimentary knowledge of childrearing" and demanding that pregnant women and mothers submit to the "discipline of the clinic [consultorio]." "Let us teach working-class mothers how to raise their children, let us repeat until exhaustion the rules of hygiene," proclaimed the CSO. Sanitary nurses, teachers, social workers, and physicians planned to teach young girls puericulture in schools and to give members of centros de madres lessons in proper mothering. The CSO social work code mandated the formation of mothers' centers in agency-run clinics, and Santiago's largest CSO clinics ran "mothers' schools." Participants in these groups were encouraged to knit and sew clothing for their newborns, while they received lectures on how to take care of their children.[42]

Although pregnant women did not always relish mothers' center meetings, they often attended because the state conditioned medical benefits and material aid on "future mothers'" membership in the centers or because they offered incentives to participants. At the Instituto Madre y Niño (Mother and Child Institute) in Valparaíso, for instance, members of the mothers' center received low-cost fabrics and had access to an emergency assistance fund made up of members' own quotas. Yet participants sometimes resented the paternalism of helpful young social workers and sanitary nurses who, although they were often enough not themselves mothers, felt they could instruct women in childrearing. When a social worker at a Valparaíso milk station tried to explain to one woman how to bathe her child properly, the mother invoked the usefulness of her own experiences and snapped back, "Since I am the mother of several children, I have enough practice."[43]

Surprisingly given state officials' pronatalist rhetoric, experts also championed birth control, including abortion, arguing that it would help women become better mothers. Abortion, the only widely available and practicable (albeit illegal) form of birth control, was so prevalent in Chile that a 1938 survey of 816 women found that they had had a startling 1,453 abortions, compared with 2,215 live births. A 1944 study confirmed the prevalence of this procedure—and the risks women were willing to take: during a period in which 44,584 women gave birth at Beneficencia hospitals, almost half as many (19,797 women) had been admitted for botched abortions.[44] Public health authorities, who could hardly ignore the virtual epidemic of abortions, responded by supporting voluntary motherhood and the use of other forms of birth control. Some reformers even called for the legalization of abortion, suggesting that women who were unable to support a child or who wished to assure the subsistence of already existing children should be allowed to terminate their pregnancies. Other experts invoked the horrors of clandestine abortions, which often led to the death of women—and more importantly of mothers, whose children were subsequently left motherless and abandoned.[45]

Still other welfare professionals counseled birth control and abortion in order to avoid the birth of weak, maladapted children. Birth control, they insisted, could help improve the Chilean "race." As *Vida Sana* put it, "Birth control is a means to safeguard the rights of the individual. The individual has a right to be born and also the right of being born healthy and normal." A woman's own needs, in short, might not be enough to justify an abortion, but the well-being of children and the progress of the nation might be.[46]

Authorities who drew on the social approach to medicine argued that poverty, rather than purely biological or genetic factors, limited women's ability to raise healthy children for the nation. To alleviate poverty among mothers, they pressed for laws mandating the payment of prenatal allowances to all pregnant women.[47] But welfare professionals focused above all on assisting single mothers, a category they defined to include any woman raising children without the support of a man to whom she was legally married. According to medical experts, single mothers were inordinately poor and their children disproportionately sickly.[48] To improve the health of these children, the state provided unmarried mothers important, if limited, maternal benefits. "The CSO protects single mothers," read a CSO advertisement promoting a program that placed pregnant women in the homes of supposedly respectable families. The CSO initiated and bankrolled this program, which it characterized as being "among the most transcendent measures taken by the Caja" to supply a "home" for pregnant women who could not count on either proper employment or the support of their lovers or families. To similar ends, diverse institutions, including the CSO and the Beneficencia, set up "maternal refuges." In Valparaíso and Viña del Mar, the CSO-run Instituto Madre y Niño furnished day care to mothers and taught them sewing to provide them with an income-generating skill. Taking up the slack in the Labor Code, refuges took in domestic servants—who did not have the right to maternity leaves and routinely lost their living quarters as well as their jobs when they got pregnant.[49] The CSO, like other state bureaus,

La Caja de Seguro Obligatorio proteje a la madre soltera

Entre las medidas de mayor trascendencia, tomadas por la Caja, cabe mencionarse, en primer lugar y con todo el vigor que ella merece, la actual resolución de crear en la Población Lo Franco, un servicio de colocación para aseguradas embarazadas.

El problema afecta en forma sensible a las empleadas domésticas, las obreras, etc., que van a ser madres y no cuentan con recursos ni económicos ni morales. Decimos no cuentan con recursos económicos, porque muchas veces los patrones obligan a estas empleadas a abandonar sus puestos so pretexto de no poder tenerlas por razones del embarazo. Y no

cuentan con recursos morales, porque lanzadas a la calle con la perspectiva de un hijo, se hace difícil que el padre de la futura guagua quiera reconocer su falta y ayude monetariamente a la madre.

Y en esta forma, iban por las calles golpeando de casa en casa, mendigando, podemos decir, estas empleadas completamente desamparadas que, o terminaban malamente en la sala de un hospital o tenían que trabajar diariamente hasta pocas horas antes de dar a luz.

Con un criterio social que enaltece a quienes lo han realizado, la Caja abordó este problema, y es así como se acaba de

instalar el servicio de atención a que hemos hecho referencia.

Las Visitadoras Sociales del Seguro han logrado contar con unas cuantas familias de la Población Lo Franco que están dispuestas a recibir a las futuras madres. La Caja, por su parte, ha ido más allá de su papel de mero ubicador y ha acordado pagar $ 150 mensuales por la atención de cada pensionada.

En esta forma, el Seguro Obrero ayuda no solamente a la asegurada, sino, también, a la familia que en forma tan humanitaria, presta techo a quien va a ser madre.

Las madres aseguradas y las esposas de los asegurados gozan de nuevas atenciones

La Caja de Seguro Obligatorio ha ensanchado el campo de asistencia médica a la madre y al niño, extendiendo sus servicios a la esposa de los obreros asegurados, en los casos de embarazos, y ampliando el plazo de atención a los niños.

Desde esa fecha, en todos los Consultorios de la Caja, se les proporciona los siguientes servicios:

1) Atención médica completa, desde el momento en que la interesada se presente en el Consultorio a la Oficina de la Madre. Esta atención comprende, además, como exámenes obligados en el momento de la inscripción: a) examen de Rayos X, b) examen de sangre (Wassermann y Kahn); c) examen de orina, y todos los que sean necesarios.
2) Atención del parto y puerperio.
3) Atención completa del niño hasta los dos años de edad.
4) Atención especial del niño enfermo de sífilis o tuberculosis, aun cuando tenga más de dos años.

Las esposas de los asegurados que deseen aprovechar estos servicios, deben presentar los siguientes documentos:

Libreta o certificado de matrimonio.

Libreta de asegurado, de su esposo, con las imposiciones al día.

Las madres aseguradas gozarán además de todos los beneficios que fijan la ley y los reglamentos vigentes, servicio maternal, subsidios de lactancia, hospitalizaciones, etc., etc.

"*The CSO protects single mothers.*" *CSO advertisement in* Aurora de Chile, *1939. Photo courtesy Biblioteca Nacional.*

also provided single mothers with other kinds of assistance: social workers helped women find employment—usually home work, domestic service jobs, or laundering—or helped them set up home industries.[50] The state thus validated the "rights" of even "disreputable" mothers in an incipient way. But although state protection of women undermined the monolithic character of the gendered familial norm favored by popular-front state officials and although it recognized that women could avoid poverty, it clearly did not liberate women. The state would, after all, "protect" single mothers.

Moreover, state agents felt that the best solution to the poverty of mothers and children was not state aid—or more and better employment for women—but marriage to stable male breadwinners. Although welfare professionals did help women find work, they did not champion concerted state policies aimed at providing employment for women. And they always tried to get fathers to marry their children's mothers. When men were unalterably abusive and unreliable, social workers sometimes violated the hegemonic model of family by helping wives to separate from their husbands or by providing the material assistance that made separation feasible. Yet welfare professionals more often argued that working-class men deserved wages that would allow them to support their families properly. This proposed solution to women's poverty emphasized men's economic responsibilities toward women and children and circumscribed the options available to women.[51]

To further ensure women's economic sustenance and that of their children, experts counseled women on how to keep their husbands happy. Proper housekeeping and thrift were their principal recommendations. Social worker Blanca Urbina Moya, who worked at the large Caupolicán-Chiguayante textile mill, believed that cleanliness and frugality could bring peace and harmony to even the most conflict-ridden families. When the wife of a worker visited Urbina, the woman explained that she and her husband had been married only six months, that they hated each other, and that her husband beat her. She then asked Urbina to help her convince her husband to separate. Urbina, however, did not think a separation prudent and took measures to reconcile the couple. She counseled the worker not to hit his wife and gave the woman lessons in shopping and cooking low-cost stews, a measure she believed would alleviate economic troubles and avert disputes. Urbina attributed another couple's bickering to the fact that "[t]he wife is not prepared to be a housewife," and she again instructed the woman in housekeeping.[52] Lessons in domestic economy thus were supposed to encourage harmonious relations between husbands and wives as well as—as we saw in Chapter 3—to smooth over class conflict in the name of social peace in the national community. Instead of arguing with their husbands over the distribution of household budgets or participating in protests against the high cost of living, housewives could simply learn to plan their spending more efficiently.

In discouraging female employment and supporting the family wage for men, state agents argued not so much that women should be economically dependent on their husbands but that they needed to stay at home to care for their children. Although certain state policies—such as the maternity leaves and nurseries described in Chapter 2—recognized the plight of working mothers, authorities generally presented maternity and work as incompatible.[53] Experts claimed, for instance, that neighbors or relatives who looked after the children of wage-earning women could not adequately replace the mothers. A social worker comparing fifty women workers and fifty housewives found that thirteen of the workers' children were "disobedient and lazy at school" or "out of control," compared with eleven of the housewives' offspring. She then offered the generalization that "the number of children who have good conduct is greater among the children of women who stay at home, because of greater vigilance on the mother's part." In *La realidad médico-social*, Allende correlated rising infant mortality with women's increasing workforce participation, insinuating that the latter caused the former.[54] Social worker Isabel Norambuena Lagarde railed against "rebel" wage-earning mothers who imperiled their children by not breast-feeding them.[55]

On the other hand, state agents encouraged women to take in laundering or to perform other kinds of work at home. That home work was precarious, unregulated, and hazardous and that children often helped their mothers perform it, did not matter as long as mothers were near their children. "It seems that in every woman of our pueblo, there's a potential laundress," remarked one social worker. A colleague concurred, noting of a client that she had "an aptitude for laundering."[56]

Welfare workers emphatically criticized married women workers, who could purportedly rely on the sustenance of a male breadwinner. These women allegedly left their homes "morally abandoned," and the fact that they were employed actually encouraged their husbands to act irresponsibly. Professionals who were more tolerant generally argued that married women who worked were victims, forced into the labor force by their irresponsible husbands. Married women, these reformers said, worked only when their husbands' earnings were inadequate, when their husbands squandered their families' sustenance on vices, or when their husbands abandoned them. Although these experts judged women who worked less harshly, they also denied their agency, refusing to acknowledge that women might choose to work for other reasons.[57]

Some welfare professionals argued not only that paid labor made women worse mothers but that it actually undermined women's ability to bear children, thereby contributing to the nation's demographic decline. Heavy factory work exhausted women and produced spontaneous abortions, they cautioned. More troubling was the fact that women workers might consciously limit the number of children they had. Fact-collecting social workers and physicians showed that married women had fewer children and more abortions after beginning to work. One physician even noted that protective labor legislation actually encouraged women workers not to have children.[58]

That so many working women were single only served to deepen state disapproval of female employment.[59] Analyses portrayed paid labor as a corrupting activity that stimulated women's independence and caused them to shun marriage and bear illegitimate children. To prove this association, experts surveyed single women workers and found that they had more children after they began working than before. Paid labor, they further maintained, led domestic servants, as well as factory laborers, into prostitution.[60] Working women were supposedly haughty and resisted stable relationships with men. Social worker Inés Infante found in a survey she conducted that 10 percent of women factory workers, as compared with 4 percent of housewives, declared themselves to be against marriage. Rather than emphasize that most women in both groups favored marriage, Infante chose to see this as evidence of the corrupting influence of factory work. Another social worker noted that women who worked outside the home adopted an "intolerant, extremely independent, attitudè, refusing to accept their husbands' tutelage" and that they quarreled more often with their husbands. These women were often portrayed as dangerously autonomous. The social worker at the Caupolicán-Chiguayante textile mill spoke disapprovingly of a "proud and independent" female worker who had never asked the fathers of her children for economic help. Neither pride nor independence was generally sanctioned for women, although some more progressive welfare professionals tolerated independent women if the survival of their children was at stake.[61]

Despite prevalent portrayals of women workers as sexually licentious and inadequate as mothers, social workers could sometimes be surprisingly sympathetic toward women who disregarded certain aspects of normative definitions of femininity.[62] That social workers were women did not assure that they were not patronizing or moralistic. Yet as women who themselves worked outside the home and who believed that women should not be victimized by men, they could on occasion sympathize with working-class women's efforts to work and raise their children with dignity. Social workers' sympathy for clients did not mean that public policies explicitly promoted female autonomy. Yet in some individual cases, social workers sanctioned women's independence. Social workers who broadened, in small ways, the range of choices available to women or who validated the choices women made—even when those choices violated norms of family life—made state efforts to discipline women less onerous and less unjust. But those openings were generally phrased in terms of the rights and needs of children and the nation, and they failed to question prevalent convictions regarding women's economic and sexual independence. As a consequence, they did not empower women, but only asexual mothers and congenial wives.

BETWEEN DEFIANCE AND VICTIMIZATION: SEXUAL EDUCATION AND THE REGULATION OF SEXUALITY

It was through reform efforts focused on the sexual issues of single motherhood, prostitution, and sexually transmitted diseases that elites most forcefully underscored the victimization of women and the agency of men. State agents believed that men were largely responsible for the medicosocial problems generated by improper sexual conduct. Thus even state campaigns that pinpointed women's sexual deviance concentrated on circumscribing men's most flagrant violations of sexual norms.[63]

State agents believed that sex, if conscientiously practiced, could generate familial and social harmony. According to *Vida Sana*, proper sexual conduct produced "reciprocal understanding [between men and women] that amply teaches what can, and what cannot, be licitly practiced. This allows one to act in one's own defense, and in defense of the opposite sex." If husbands or wives were unfaithful, state agents held, arguments and even violence within households could erupt. When married men took on lovers and spent money on their sexual partners, their wives and legitimate offspring suffered economically and family life was disrupted. Moreover, since male privilege was justified only so long as men were effective providers, men who did not fulfill their proper economic obligations destabilized the association of masculinity with breadwinning. On the other hand, men who acted properly—and correct sexual behavior was central to gendered expectations—earned their privileges.[64]

State officials saw all forms of sex outside marriage as equivalent and equally pernicious. They thus harnessed the stigma attached to prostitution to their efforts to solve the "problem of single motherhood." In *La realidad médico-social*, for instance, Allende noted that of 132 prostitutes registered with Sanidad, twenty-one had left their paternal home because they became pregnant. Apparently, single mothers were only a step away from prostitution.[65]

Yet according to most welfare professionals, irresponsible men were as much, or more, to blame than women for the associated problems of single motherhood, prostitution, and extramarital sex in general.[66] In a rather typical fashion, Hilda Quezada, a social worker in the Valparaíso–Viña del Mar anti–venereal disease campaign, addressed her efforts to eradicate prostitution to "a young male worker." In an article titled "¿Y qué dices ahora obrero?" she described the plight of an innocent young woman who was tricked into having sex, became pregnant, and gave birth. Repudiated by her parents, the woman began to look for employment. Turned away from factories and unable to find work even as a domestic servant, she succumbed to the invitation of a madame and took up prostitution. Quezada then confronted the young male worker with his own responsibility for the woman's "fall":

> She is only interested in money. And when in exchange for a vain pleasure you give it to her, you only sink her deeper and deeper. You deny her the possibility of lifting herself up and remaking her life. Through the money you thus give, you further the death of your race. The money of which you deprive your wife and children prepares the ground so that they themselves, hostage to misery and discouragement, follow the path that I have shown you. Would you like your daughter or sister to follow this path? With the same pride with which you respond negatively [to this question], promise yourself, before your daughter's cradle, that you will not contribute, either through your silence or with your money, to the promotion of this evil that sinks other daughters of workers like yourself into opprobrium.[67]

Removing the stigma attached to prostitution, Quezada suggested that the prostitute was like any working-class woman, similar even to the worker's own female family members.

Given women's essential innocence, many reformers advocated tolerance for women who became pregnant outside marriage: "Let us vindicate the single mothers, that is to say, to make society understand that the single mother deserves its attention, as much for the child that is going to be born as to avoid greater evils such as abortion, prostitution, etc."[68] At the same time, reformers blamed parents who failed to give their children a proper sexual education or to forgive fallen daughters and men who failed to marry the women they seduced. After all, parents who supported their "dishonored" daughters and "seducers" who married their sexual partners could prevent women who had exhibited dangerous behavior from spiraling out of social and sexual control.

By highlighting single mothers' victimization, state officials could step in where parents and lovers had failed, without sanctioning, or even recognizing, female deviance. Maternal refuges took in women shunned by lovers and parents, temporarily providing them with the support that would permit them to carry their pregnancy to full term and to assume their maternal responsibilities. Thus even as the state tried to discourage single women from having sex, state agents minimized single women's sexual transgressions and emphasized proper mothering. For them, the most odious aspect of illegitimate pregnancies was not uncontrolled female sexuality but, as we have seen, the fact that single mothers might reject their pregnancies and ultimately their children. Motherhood could wash away the dishonor of sex outside marriage.

Nonetheless, certain reformers were less forgiving. They saw single mothers as vexing and dangerous and suggested that perhaps they were not victims. These experts, who seemed more on the Right politically as well as more socially conservative, focused on the fact that unmarried mothers might actually enjoy sex outside marriage, have sexual relations with more than one man, or take up prostitution—behavior that indicated willful sexuality. They were also more likely to imply that unwed women were reluctant or inadequate mothers. Social worker María Santelices's prejudices regarding single mothers conditioned her attitude toward her eighteen-year-old client "M. P. G.," who was abandoned by her lover after giving birth to an illegitimate child. The social worker had found the mother employment as a domestic servant in a house where she could live with the baby. Yet according to the social worker, the child was not well attended to. A husbandless and promiscuous woman like M. P. G., Santelices assumed, was prone to be a bad mother, and the *visitadora* felt it necessary to "wake the girl's maternal instinct." Santelices was unsuccessful: M. P. G. had decided to give her child up for adoption, and even the courts could not convince her otherwise. Perhaps M. P. G. saw the impossibility of properly raising her child on the dismal wages of a domestic servant. But the social worker, unable to see outside her assumptions, insisted something was wrong with the woman.[69]

In general, however, welfare professionals concentrated on correcting men. In so doing, they recognized men's protagonism as well as their deviance. In contrast, the prescriptions for proper female sexual conduct inherent in their efforts to solve the problems of single motherhood and prostitution chastised women less. Yet they also presented women as more compliant, failing to concede that some women might actually seek sex outside marriage—or that they might want to avoid marriage altogether. That the "problem" of single motherhood doggedly persisted, however, signaled the limits of female compliance.

Ironically, those experts who recognized that women were not simply victims were the least willing to help them, and state agents rarely tried to reform women who willfully refused to comply with sexual norms. The failure to recognize and legitimate women's ability to make decisions regarding their sexual conduct meant that the reform of deviant women (as opposed to the protection of essentially innocent victims) was virtually unthinkable. Social workers employed by the Dirección de Sanidad, the agency charged with registering prostitutes, manifested just such an inability to deal with women's choices. In surveys, social workers documented the sexual practices of prostitutes before their initiation as sex-workers. These inquiries predictably turned up as much victimization as improper female sexual initiative. (Prostitutes who answered questionnaires either shared social workers' view of themselves as victims or knew how to answer questions in a way that satisfied their inquisitors.) Concomitant with the view that prostitutes, and especially younger prostitutes, were essentially victims, social workers assumed that these women could be easily convinced to seek alternative employment. But Sanidad social workers often found the sex-workers unwilling to abandon prostitution, principally because of their relatively high earnings. Since a woman who put her financial interests over the defense of her virtue was prone to be perverse, in these cases social workers' tolerance yielded to recrimination. And since these social workers had only limited resources at their disposal, they quickly abandoned uncooperative women, focusing instead on the reeducation of women who manifested a desire to abandon prostitution. In the eyes of state employees, a deviant woman did not deserve the same attention as a dissolute man. Indeed, state agencies that worked with these women had fewer resources. The CSO had a large budget, which allowed it to undertake massive education campaigns. However, the Caja broadcast antiprostitution propaganda principally toward male workers.[70]

Many state officials saw prostitutes as the chief agents of the spread of sexually transmitted diseases. The state therefore required prostitutes to register with Sanidad, undergo periodic medical examinations, and submit to treatment if infected.[71] Yet state officials increasingly found that sex-workers were not primarily responsible for the spread of venereal diseases. This shift in emphasis probably reflected reformed state methods of sexual regulation rather than epidemiological shifts. As bids to eradicate sexually transmitted diseases increasingly focused on modifying "incorrect" male behavior, state agents sought to convince men of the benefits to be derived from monogamous sexual relations with their wives. While prostitution was never considered acceptable, policing sex-workers did not seem as urgent or as effective.[72]

When Minister of Health Allende introduced legislation aimed at controlling sexually transmitted diseases, for instance, he characterized past efforts to prohibit prostitution as belonging to "another conceptualization, another modality."[73] Professionals who sought to curb venereal disease, especially syphilis, would henceforth rely principally on nonpunitive measures. As one CSO doctor noted regarding a proposal to require prenuptial blood tests, "The law is, in and of itself, worthless. What must be done is to form an adequate mentality."[74]

To stimulate that "adequate mentality," medical professionals availed themselves of the most varied and convincing methods. Campaigners visited mining centers, neighborhood groups, unions, and schools. They showed films and slides; distributed pamphlets, leaflets, postcards, posters, and magazines; gave talks; took blood samples; and sponsored radio shows. In Iquique alone, 4,000 copies of the CSO propaganda publication *Vida Sana*, a key element in the anti–venereal disease campaign, were distributed to labor unions, community groups, and even prostitutes who went for required medical exams. Valparaíso and Temuco had their own versions of the publication. To attract men and women to informational meetings, they were animated by variety shows. In Iquique a Social Anti-Venereal Museum, with wax figures showing the horrors of untreated venereal diseases, occupied the hallway of the local CSO clinic.[75]

Given medical doctors' limited ability to cure syphilis before penicillin was discovered, broad-ranging preventive campaigns that stimulated ample citizen cooperation were central to the success of medical efforts. Both the extremely inconvenient side effects of existing cures and their considerable length discouraged syphilitics from completing their treatments.[76] Yet working-class Chileans apparently welcomed information on how to avoid syphilis and other sexually transmitted diseases. Doctors who participated in state-run anti–venereal disease campaigns often remarked on the eagerness of their audiences. In Iquique, several community groups approached CSO officials asking for sanitary education talks; and in diverse localities, anti–venereal disease campaigns elicited the participation of large numbers of town members, who joined in "cooperation committees." When the campaign reached the southern region around Lautaro, a broad committee—made up of representatives of labor, employers, teachers, the press, cultural groups, and the state Work Inspection—collaborated with medical personnel to carry out events. Friends of the Consultorio and its female auxiliary helped in the local campaign, as did volunteer firemen, sports clubs, Friends of the Arts, and Friends of the Liceo (high school).[77]

Besides distributing information on the prevention of sexually transmitted diseases, public health authorities resorted to other, more coercive, means. Working to uncover dreaded *focos de contagio* (points of contagion), they subjected patients diagnosed with a venereal disease to extensive interrogations. After they had determined who had infected a patient and whom a patient had infected, social workers and sanitary inspectors diligently tracked down citizens potentially infected, forcing them to come in for diagnosis and treatment. If patients abandoned treatment, *citadores* (summoners) repeatedly visited their homes—or worse, their workplaces—urging them to resume treatment. The police were also called upon to scare sufferers of the disease into keeping their appointments for treatment, and patients who consistently missed appointments could be reported to Sanidad and detained.[78]

"M. P. A.," a CSO-insured, thirty-two-year-old domestic servant who sought medical help for syphilis but later abandoned treatment, learned quickly about just how invasive public health measures could be. The CSO social worker who took up M. P. A.'s case was intent on getting the woman to complete her cure, and to that end, she visited M. P. A.'s home. When she found that M. P. A. was at work, the *visitadora* left a message with a neighbor asking M. P. A. to come in for her scheduled appointment. M. P. A. failed to do so, and the social worker made a second visit to her home, speaking this

time to another neighbor and leaving a new message. On a third visit, the social worker spoke to M. P. A.'s mother, who told the social worker that M. P. A.
did not wish to continue her treatment. Undaunted, the social worker elicited the help of the mother, who agreed to convince her daughter to keep
future appointments.[79]

If M. P. A.'s mother had been unaware of her daughter's illness, she was
now in on the secret. The suspicions of M. P. A.'s neighbors had likely been
roused too. M. P. A.'s illness would now be revealed to her employer as well.
Having secured from M. P. A.'s mother the address of the house where
M. P. A. worked as a domestic servant, the social worker sought out the
woman at her place of employment. There, M. P. A. explained to the social
worker that she had failed to keep her appointments because she feared
losing her job: her boss, she knew, would not stand for a syphilitic house
servant, and she could not ask for time off for medical visits without revealing her medical problem to her employer. Apparently unmoved by M. P. A.'s
predicament, the social worker spoke to M. P. A.'s boss directly, asking the
employer to allow M. P. A. time off for medical visits. She also warned the
house servant that she would report her to Sanidad if she failed to come in for
scheduled appointments. M. P. A., now cornered, assented.[80]

Not surprisingly, patients, both male and female, resisted this sort of
invasive public health measure. When asked to supply their own addresses or
those of "contacts," they refused to answer or lied. Bewildered and angry,
social workers and citadores wasted endless hours roaming city streets looking
for addresses that patients had made up. To sidestep patient evasion, one
social worker resorted to an almost torturelike method for extracting information: she interrogated syphilitics while they were suffering the extremely
bothersome effects of the massive treatment.[81]

Both men and women engaged in illicit sexual conduct and resisted coercive state measures. Both sexes sought out information on the prevention of
sexually transmitted diseases. Yet state officials clearly felt that men were
largely responsible for the spread of sexually transmitted disease and that
their wives were their chief victims. Health care providers' analyses consistently showed that the majority of women with the disease were infected by
their husbands and the majority of men by prostitutes.[82] Given the ways in
which welfare professionals approached each sex, it is not surprising that
professionals perceived women as cooperating more fully than men in the
treatment of the disease and in the identification of sexual contacts. And yet
health care professionals insisted that men could be reformed. They por-

trayed male visits to brothels as exceptional events linked to the overconsumption of alcohol. After a visit, the husband always repented, admitting the harm he had caused his wife and children.[83] Reformers also focused on and tried to change the behavior of licentious women, but references to female promiscuity were less frequent.

CONCLUSION

During the popular-front period, public health campaigns, the social security system, and the legal system all worked to reinforce a specific type of family life and particular definitions of gender. The state increasingly intervened within the "private" familial sphere. In so doing, it expanded the reaches of the state itself and added to its "repertoire of rule."[84]

The popular fronts' "success" in implementing prescriptive gender norms depended on their ability to promote a vision of family relations that was attractive to both men and women—and to both popular-front supporters and right-wing detractors. It also depended on how the state went about generating consensus. Talks and movies, publications and pamphlets, advice columns and home visits, cooperation committees and housewives' groups effectively stimulated collaboration. These kinds of outreach had been used only sporadically by the state before 1938.

In addition, the "success" of the popular fronts depended on their ability to reconcile models of family life inherited from the past with the growth of state intervention, the rise of feminism, and women's continuing participation in wage labor. For instance, state agents effectively articulated the long-standing belief that women needed the sexual protection of male family members to newer public health discourses regarding maternal-child health in order to demonstrate the dangers of wage work for women. Professionals also deployed novel medical and demographic discourses to underscore the importance of motherhood and portray men who acted irresponsibly toward their families as barbaric, bestial, and uneugenic. They thus promoted a national project that grounded gender identities in doctrines of evolution and progress even as it naturalized those identities and intimated continuities.

Inevitably, there were inconsistencies in state policies and vacillations in how they were applied. Yet these contradictions did not necessarily imply weakness; in fact, they could be manifestations of flexibility. Given the capillary nature of so many social work and public health interventions, the implementation of policy depended in large part on the moral and political orientations of individuals and of the agencies in which they worked. Some individuals and agencies insisted more forcefully on the need to constitute families in which men asserted their authority. Others affirmed the need to protect or dignify women. Some, who were usually resented by "beneficiaries," were extremely moralistic and intolerant. Others concentrated more on proffering material rewards or on stimulating citizen cooperation. Moreover, diverse state aims contradicted and subverted each other in ways that allowed welfare workers to accommodate clients. The perceived need to protect children for the sake of the nation, for example, led experts to take measures for the moral and material protection of single mothers, measures that tended to undermine the prescribed role of men as family heads. Social workers were apt to recognize gender conflict and to support the rights of married women within marriage even as they sought to consolidate nuclear families that empowered men. In short, vacillations in state policy and how it was applied permitted a degree of flexibility and allowed dialogue between welfare professionals and clients.

State agents clearly perceived women as the main beneficiaries of campaigns to constitute the family and as the chief supporters of their campaigns to properly constitute families. The perception of these agents may in fact have reflected the views of a majority of women. Nonetheless, it seems likely that women's acceptance depended on many other factors besides their sex, such as employment possibilities, age, marital status, or whether they had children or not. Prostitutes or "deviant" single mothers—the latter were likely to be younger, have fewer children, and seek employment more readily— probably found welfare professionals more bothersome. Married women with many children, who were more vulnerable, may have been more open to state interventions. In any case, the state also *constructed* and reinforced women's complicity by ignoring certain forms of defiance. The discourse of victimization that undergirded state efforts to assist women undoubtedly acknowledged the structural limitations women faced. It also made women's efforts to resist disciplinary measures more invisible and hence less effective. The state could not react to what it did not fully register.[85]

In part because of the national-popular state's less punitive approach, in part because of the resourcefulness of social workers, in part because of state officials' ability to satisfy diverse constituencies, and in part because of the collaboration of many working-class men and women, the state's moral and material reforms of family life had an important impact on evolving gender relations within the working class. It is hard to determine how much of an impact. Statistical information tells us that both before and (in significantly greater numbers) after 1938 most Chilean children were legitimate and most adults married. But this is only a part of the picture. Data collectors who categorized Chileans as "married" or "single"—and children as "legitimate" or "illegitimate"—failed to document a variety of popular practices in relation to family. Among the workers at the Sociedad Nacional de Paños in Tomé, for example, there was one woman, separated from her husband, whose three children lived with their father. The husband of a "married" coworker lived hundreds of kilometers away in Santiago; and another married male coworker lived in a boardinghouse without his family but occasionally visited five children and his wife, with whom he continued to have sexual relations. A fourth Paños employee lived with his wife and child but also had two children, born of a previous *convivencia*, who resided with their mother and her new partner.[86] All these workers were, according to the law, "married," and most of their children were legitimate, but from the point of view of state reformers, they had clearly disordered lives. Besides hiding variations such as these, statistics on the constitution of the family said nothing of the vicissitudes of a given individual's life. Nor did statistical data reveal how many Chileans had family members, close friends, or coworkers who as single mothers, unfaithful husbands, or separated wives violated central tenets of the proposed gender order. But regardless of what the statistics said, most working-class men and women knew that many Chileans failed to live up to the standards defined by the state, by politicians, and by welfare professionals. They also knew that those who did not conform paid a price.

chapter six

SOCIALIST MORALITY, GENDER, AND CLASS UNITY

In 1943, Nicomedes Guzmán published *La sangre y la esperanza*, a novel about the Quilodráns, a working-class family that lives near Estación Central in one of Santiago's premiere proletarian neighborhoods. The adolescent Enrique Quilodrán, his father, Guillermo, his mother, Laura, and his sister, Elena, personify working-class virtue in Guzmán's novel. The hardworking Guillermo is a quintessentially responsible, if sometimes authoritarian, breadwinner and family head. Fearing the economic straits his family will confront if he does not bring home a pay envelope, Guillermo dutifully reports to work, even when ill. Guillermo also participates with fervor in trade union activities, and in contrast to other male residents of the *conventillo* (tenement), some of whom beat their wives or partners or rape their stepdaughters, he respects his wife and exercises sexual restraint. The upstanding, conciliatory, and compassionate Laura likewise avoids vice. She shows solidarity with her neighbors and helps them out economically but does not fall into the malicious, meddling gossip so common in the *conventillo*. Unlike other neighborhood women, such as the adulterous woman down the hall who likes to drink, she loves her husband and looks after her children.[1]

Although Laura's diligence assures the Quilodrán family's well-being, it is the presence of the honorable Guillermo that fully guarantees the family's economic and spiritual prosperity. As an adult, Enrique muses retrospectively about the eventual hospitalization of his seriously ill father. Although, oddly enough, the young Enrique cannot fully grasp the importance of his father's virile presence, Guzmán encouraged readers of *La sangre*, through Enrique's retrospective view, to conclude that male proximity dignifies family life. "It is true that I was not alone," Enrique later reminisces. "My mother. My brothers. All of us had a communion of heart, we were a tight pack of mutual company. But, this is the truth, my state of unconsciousness at that time grants me only today the pain of that terrible loneliness without a father."[2]

Alongside the theme of familial completeness and unity, *La sangre* explored the related issues of class and political cohesion, exemplifying the ways in which working-class organizations could enhance family ties and family bonds could magnify a sense of class belonging. When Guillermo is eventually hospitalized, for example, his union temporarily takes up his role as provider, contributing financially to the Quilodrán family. Enrique's sister and mother do not attend union gatherings or marches, and on May Day Guillermo celebrates on the streets without his wife and daughter. But the Quilodráns also commemorate the workers' holiday at home with delicious fried *empanadas* made by Laura.[3]

Through *La sangre*'s most dramatic subplot—a story line that involves Elena, a factory worker, and her love affair with the poet Abel Justiciano—Guzmán focused attention on sexuality and its relation to class unity, political alliance, and familial cohesion. Here, Guzmán sketched his view of proletarian female virtue, placing allegiance to class at the epicenter of feminine decency. In Guzmán's rendering, that Elena might lose her sexual honor in her relation with Abel mattered, but what mattered most was her loyalty to her parents and the proletarian values they had taught her. When Elena begins to date the poet, her father objects, arguing that his daughter ought to marry a worker like himself, a man of her own class: "Look, Elena, my daughter. . . . Do you see these hands? . . . This is what I wanted for you. . . . A working man. . . . A good worker is always better than a poet! Don't be romantic! . . . A woman can't live from verses, do you hear!" Elena does not shun her responsibility to marry an honorable, hardworking man, but rebuffs her father in his own terms. Although Abel is a poet, she tells her father, he too can embrace working-class values: "Many men can have the honor of being workers. . . . But not only a worker's labor is a cause for honor, father."[4] The conflict over Elena's beau heats up when her parents discover, after a tearful visit from Abel's wife to Laura, that the poet is married and has children. Elena's virtue, already tarnished by her liaison with a frivolous, unproductive poet is further tainted by her association with a married man. Guillermo, and especially Laura, are troubled.

In the end, however, Elena and Abel redeem themselves. Assassinated in a street demonstration, Abel proves his allegiance to the workers' cause. Guillermo can consequently forgive Abel and Elena's violations of sexual norms. And Abel's redemptive martyrdom allows Elena to announce proudly to her parents that she is pregnant. Shunning concern with what the neighbors might say—a concern that, Guzmán insinuates, might lead the young woman to abort—Elena refuses to assume the shame of her dishonor. In recompense for Abel's spilled blood (*la sangre*) there will be his child, a hope (*la esperanza*) for the future. By bearing and raising that child, Elena will contribute to the memory, and therefore to the projection, of Abel's heroism. Enrique, who in the final pages of *La sangre* brings home his first pay envelope, is also part of that working-class hope. Thus Elena will contribute to a better future for her class through dignified motherhood; and Enrique will do so through his hard work.

Drawing on prevalent debates, *La sangre y la esperanza* reworked the meaning of illegitimacy and sexual propriety. By speaking and writing publicly, elites who established their loyalty to workers—middle-class "poets" like Abel Justiciano (or Nicomedes Guzmán)—lifted elements of working-class morality out of *conventillos* and *cités*. Guzmán's portrayal of the emblematic Quilodrán family undoubtedly reproduced gender roles similar to those proffered by middle-class welfare professionals, and the novelist ultimately championed an alliance between the working class and the middle class, personified in the relation between Elena and Abel. But by outlining a distinctly working-class and prosocialist notion of honor, Guzmán distanced himself from those conservative politicians or state agents who failed to identify with the workers' cause. And he put class unity—albeit a class unity that could assimilate the middle class—at the center of his gender prescriptions and his definition of respectability. *La sangre* highlighted the importance of work and political involvement for men. But instead of framing these issues in terms of national prerogatives, Guzmán elaborated their importance to the construction of workers' movements and to a specifically socialist solidarity anchored in the working-class family. Similarly, Elena could be forgiven her moral breaches because she had ultimately been politically faithful in her amorous pursuits. If Abel, like other members of the middle class, contributed to the construction of a hopeful future through his allegiance to the working class, the hope for the future would still be nurtured by Elena within an upright working-class home.

As part of a larger group of proletarian novelists, Guzmán pursued a realistic portrayal of working-class life. (The epigraph to *La sangre*, part of a poem by Pablo Neruda, read: "I speak of things that exist; God save me from inventing. . . .") But as an activist interested in the political efficacy of his fiction, Guzmán, like other social realist authors, not only reflected proletarian reality but also generated a Left working-class culture, delineating appropriate gender relations within the working class.[5] Of course the extent to which working-class Chileans heeded those prescriptions depended on how readers received novelists' messages and on how much they identified with the authors' representations. At least for Elena Varela, who was fifteen years old when *La sangre* was published, the novel provided an appealing narrative of what it meant to grow up in one of Santiago's poor neighborhoods. The book, which she read and reread so often that it seemed as if she had lived it, was a permanent fixture on her night table.[6]

As this chapter shows, leftists advanced a gendered socialist morality to win working- and middle-class allies and trounce enemies, whether those antagonists were deviant leftists or immoral capitalists. Leftist moral prescriptions positioned the Left within a broader national community, facilitating dialogue with and opposition to political forces of the Center and Right. Moral prescriptions also stimulated Left cohesion and marked the boundaries of the Left, helping to make the Left a unified force for social change and, ultimately, for the exercise of power. As tools for personal advancement and for the reform of familial relations, moral prescriptions attracted men and women to the Left. As instruments of discipline, they determined the terms on which Chileans might rightly participate in leftist organizations. As yardsticks against which rectitude was measured, they played a central role in the legitimation or delegitimation of Left leaders. In this sense moral directives strengthened leftist organizations by granting them prestige within broad sectors of the working class, by creating and defining a more homogeneous Left culture, by stimulating a sense of belonging to the working class, and by justifying Left representation of popular sectors within the broader national community. Those normative mandates also marked lines of exclusion. Not all Chileans earned, by virtue of being poor, the privilege of calling themselves upstanding workers and socialists. And not all Chileans, leftists suggested, could properly call themselves defenders of the national interest.[7]

Although both Communists and Socialists linked politics to sexuality and family and sought to legitimate themselves within the broader national community by demonstrating their respectability, each political party used distinct methods for enforcing gendered prescriptions. The Communist Party had a strong and concentrated presence in distinct locales such as coal-, copper-, and nitrate-mining enclaves and in certain urban barrios and industrial centers in Santiago, Valparaíso, and Concepción. Communists consequently contributed to and even replaced localized networks of power and control. The Socialist Party was more centered on the state, more territorially dispersed, and more national, and Socialists furthered their views primarily through the press and state apparatuses. Nonetheless, the similarity of the gendered moral codes advocated by both Socialists and Communists facilitated a convergence of the disciplinary actions they took, from below and from above, in the name of national and class unity.

MORE FANATICAL THAN EVANGELICALS

Edmundo Sepúlveda grew up during the 1920s in Valparaíso. As the son of the influential POS leader Ramón Sepúlveda Leal, Edmundo was raised in a socialist world that he described in 1993 as "more fanatical than [that of] today's evangelicals." That fanaticism manifested itself in the fervor with which Edmundo and his comrades attended meetings, distributed pamphlets, went on strike, and watched over the polls on election day, throwing eggs at vote buyers. It was also apparent in the zeal with which socialists regulated the familial and social life of their community: they taught children to be mindful and respectful of their parents; made sure Sunday luncheons were alcohol free; and chaperoned dances to insure that party-goers danced with moderation—no Charleston allowed. Blanca Flores, whose father was a close political ally of Sepúlveda Leal, met Edmundo when they were both four years old, and she participated along with him in the Carlos Marx and Spartacus artistic groups. Later, she married him. For her, socialist fanaticism had its positive side: it allowed her to dream of becoming an actress. "The Partido Obrero Socialista," she commented, "produced culture."[8]

In the days before 1938, when the rich and powerful routinely repressed and humiliated socialists, Left culture was mainly oppositional. Sepúlveda woke one morning to find excrement smeared on the sidewalk in front of his house, and Flores was kicked out of elementary school for her father's political ties. The socialist press harped on the theme of capitalist immorality, exposing the exploitation of bosses and the shameful feats of dissipated and lazy bourgeois dandies who raped women and drank excessively. For workers and their families, leftist propaganda posited a proletarian honorableness. But as the Left increasingly sought participation in the national community, an emerging emphasis on the ways proletarian respectability converged with that of other social sectors facilitated the Left's alliance with other political forces and social classes. Leftists less often characterized discipline as a way of distinguishing correct proletarian behavior from incorrect capitalist conduct. In addition, socialists' rejection of spontaneous, impulsive expressions of opposition to bosses and rulers facilitated the emergence of a national-popular project that stressed dialogue over confrontation. The distinct nature of socialist morality became less pronounced. (As *La sangre* indicated, socialist values could now be practiced even by middle-class intellectuals and their hybrid progeny.) Still, socialist morality continued to mark the boundaries of a distinctly leftist working-class identity and to function as a way of critiquing the bourgeoisie.[9]

According to Left discourses on morality, the exercise of orderliness, discipline, and good habits sanctified not only paid labor, social events, and processes of political representation but also the body and the person. The search for cleanliness and fitness indicated personal, even bodily, control in the face of adversity and the rejection of a noxious passivity that ultimately benefited capitalists. The Socialist Youth bulletin *AS* advocated the practice of sports as a way of insuring personal health: "Concern yourselves with sports as well, with life outdoors, with health and the equilibrium of all our biological functions." Iris Figueroa, who later became a Communist municipal councillor for San Miguel, remembered the lessons her Communist father had taught her and her siblings when they were youngsters: "[We went] without shoes, barefoot, [but] always clean, because my old man was very clean and from a very young age he demanded, taught us, the habit of cleanliness." Working-class Chileans might not have many clothes; they might be forced into filthy work; but at least on their own terrain, at home, they could scrub themselves spotless.[10]

The useful triumph of human will and rationality over base behavior constituted a constant subtext of socialist moral injunctions. In an article titled "Habit: Precious Ally or Dangerous Enemy," *AS* differentiated good, liberating habits from bad ones that bound and reduced the will of the individual. Elsewhere, propagandists repudiated alcohol because it made men lose their reason and was a "principal factor of mental narrowness (*estrechez*)." The ultimately emancipatory development of good habits, in contrast, implied—at least initially—thought, caution, and a rejection of impulse. The worker press applauded the "habit of work" and sexual as well as political restraint. It called on Left organizations to encourage reading and establish libraries.[11]

While this working-class insistence on hygiene and health drew on and reproduced sanitary and eugenic prescriptions emanating from the state (see Chapter 5), it rebutted elite perceptions that the poor were dirty and complacent and thus unworthy. Moreover, a recognition of the need for personal action in the face of adversity did not prevent Left activists from pinpointing the material limitations faced by working-class Chileans. In signaling economic restrictions, militants reinforced an oppositional relation to the economically dominant class that impoverished them and to the conservative welfare professionals who promoted moralizing campaigns instead of granting economic benefits.

Calls to moderation and personal betterment were part of an essentially masculine code of honor: the vices leftists tried to correct were largely masculine habits, such as smoking, drinking, betting, or womanizing—all animal-like impulses that, as another publication put it, made men into sacks of vices who shunned their obligation to fortify themselves physically and morally and to care for family members and comrades. Socialist Party members warned participants in its short-lived militia of the 1930s to avoid bars and "other places" (such as, most probably, whorehouses) where "far from improving himself, the *miliciano*'s life, which should be healthy and have a strong and virile quality, might be shortened."[12]

The Left's virile orientation toward personal improvement and autonomy carried artisanal concerns with independence inherited from the past but remolded them to fit the concerns of industrial workers. In Volodia Teitelboim's biographical novel *Hijo del salitre*, for instance, the protagonist, Elías Lafferte, rejects a job offered to him by Jacinto, an independent laborer contracted by the nitrate company for which they both work. Lafferte also turns down the coca leaves Jacinto proffers. Since he is under the supervision of foremen, Lafferte explains, he can not chew coca leaves on the job. Jacinto, free to work or drug himself as he pleases, sees Lafferte as a sellout lacking in autonomy. But even when Jacinto calls Lafferte a coward and questions his manhood, Lafferte holds out his own conceptions of freedom and manliness. As Teitelboim's narrator comments, "Elías didn't want to be a man of the *lluta* and the coca. He did not want that liberty. Was there no better liberty in life?"

A gathering of the Communist Party's Joven Guardia (Young Guards), Valparaíso, c. 1938.
Photo courtesy Emperatriz Villarroel.

Countering Jacinto, Lafferte asks, "Is that your liberty, your right to that tiny heroic drug?" Teitelboim thus suggested that liberty would not be achieved simply through a reactive opposition. Freedom required engagement.[13]

Although the promotion of cleanliness, exercise, temperance, education, and hard work reinforced a sense of male protagonism and autonomy, it clearly coincided with the popular fronts' broader civilizing and modernizing missions. Widespread calls for the triumph of rationality over base, animal-like behavior were rooted in modern, Enlightenment values, nationalist ideals, and developmentalist rhetoric. In fact, leftists routinely noted how better working-class habits would improve the Chilean nation, and even capitalists could not object to the idea of making men healthy, sober, educated, and hardworking. In trying to achieve what they were often told they could not, working-class activists accepted what was also a bourgeois morality.

Yet in the end, socialist morality did not fully neutralize working-class identity and militancy. Working-class activists strengthened their oppositional stance by pointing out that elites opposed popular improvement. Workers thus exposed the hypocrisy of elites and used moral prescriptions to reject their political and economic exclusion. Going even further, workers made moral prescriptions their own, asserting that sobriety and vicelessness would not simply make the working class like the elite but would also further more intrinsically working-class interests. And they insisted on controlling disciplinary campaigns through their own organizations. Above all, in propagating good habits leftists emphasized their ability to alter and govern their own lives.

Just as important, socialist moral norms expressed women's desire to do away with forms of masculinity that distanced men from their families and made them unreliable breadwinners. Socialist morality thus responded to negotiation and conflict not only between working-class men and political and economic elites but also between men and women of the laboring classes. Given how these crosscutting perspectives informed socialist morality, the nested discourses of progress, rationality, discipline, and masculinity could be, and were, inflected differently in different situations and in different institutional locations, reflecting different balances of power. Popular classes transformed and modified a hegemonic framework they could not escape by articulating their class- and gender-based identities both within and against predominant values and norms.

TEMPERANCE, SPORTS, AND SOCIALIST POLITICS

According to leftist propaganda, betting, drinking, and visiting bars not only had detrimental effects on personal health but also weakened the Chilean "race" and nation, working-class organizations, and the family. A typical article in the worker press characterized alcohol consumption as "the principal social blemish" and stressed that the promotion of abstention would "save the race and return to the family the father who is today lost." It further noted that men who drank "lost a notion and a sense of the necessity of union organization and of the defense of their own particular interests and those of the community." Linking personal improvement, family duties, and defense of the nation in a comparable way, another issue of the same newspaper described a drunk man as being in a subhuman state that allowed the diabolical, foreign-born owner of the bar he frequented to take advantage of him. What happened after he and his friend left the bar was even worse: the man provoked a fight; his friend was stabbed while trying to defend him; the man himself ended up in jail; and "[h]is wife and older daughters cried this misfortune with grief and pain." Thus drinking harmed the man himself by reducing him to an animal state; it harmed the nation by enriching the indecent foreigner who owned the bar; it harmed his friend (and potential political ally); and it harmed his family. In formulations such as these, the civilizing project—taming the barbaric drunkard—seemed inextricable from a national project that could sometimes take on xenophobic and racist overtones. At the same time, the modernizing project was bound intimately to strengthening the working-class community and family.[14]

While employers decried the productive losses caused by alcohol-loving workers and professionals lamented the eugenic weakness of the dissipated poor, leftist organizations emphasized the detrimental effects of male vices on working-class unity. Worker publications denounced the laziness and indifference of workers who spent leisure hours in bars and worried about the politically demobilizing effects of a deadened will. Thus an "interesting letter from a *compañera*" to the union newspaper *El Obrero Municipal* deplored the political apathy of booze-lovers and chastised husbands who thought only of "satisfying deathly vices that only poison the heart and atrophy the brain." Similarly, *Obrero Textil*'s "war on alcohol" aimed to lift laborers from "the mud" in which they were submerged and "at the same time reinforce our union cadres." In another skirmish in the textile workers' "war," the union newspaper bemoaned the fact that "nothing, not even the great poverty they suffer, has been enough to make the brains of many *compañeros*, who above all adore alcohol, work." Going on to link personal care to class consciousness, the article continued, "We are no longer able to attend to our own person. I ask then, if we continue like this, will we be able tomorrow to defend our rights in the coming struggle?" While union leaders worked "night and day," sacrificing themselves for their coworkers, another union publication complained, laborers carelessly sullied the reputations of their leaders in gossiping conversations oiled by liquor. Furthermore, *Obrero Textil* noted, drunken fights undermined solidarity among coworkers.[15]

Communist Emperatriz Villarroel agreed that men with vices openly betrayed their class. Yet she articulated class solidarity to her own agenda as a working-class woman: "I never understood why a worker would declass himself," she said in an interview. "Why, for example, a party militant, being a miner would up and take the bourgeoisie's vices. . . . Taking the bourgeoisie's vices, taking another woman. Leaving his wife, his children, things like that. Well, getting drunk. Things—. Well, that I don't understand. Because, I say, a worker who is, for whom work has been difficult, I don't know, for whom things are hard, why? And we are struggling precisely to leave that behind. He up and takes up the same, does the same."[16] Villarroel equated a man's allegiance to his class to his devotion to his wife and family. Like working-class leaders, she noted the distasteful effects of male drinking on family finances and of male camaraderie on families' unity.

While agreeing with Villarroel that drinking was a bourgeois vice, other representatives of the working class chided capitalists, arguing they were the real culprits. The rich profited from the sale of wine and spirits and aspired to subdue workers' rebellious spirit by keeping their employees drunk. In response, popular organizations suggested that the state levy a tax on producers and distributors of alcoholic beverages. One physician writing in *La Crítica* even proposed that those involved in the production of alcoholic beverages be banned from holding public office. When Villarroel and her husband argued about male drinking, he similarly blamed the dominant classes. Attempting to temper his wife's criticisms of traitorous working-class men, Villarroel's husband pointed out to her that she failed to take into account the noxious effects of a bourgeois-dominated environment.[17]

To encourage national fellowship, stimulate class unity, and bring working-class men and women closer together, the Left not only encouraged temperance but also promoted healthy recreational pursuits. Previously, the Communist Party denounced, "sports had been practiced only for the sake of sports, without any practical or constructive end." But with increasing diligence beginning around 1935–36, leftists gave theater and music groups, dances, and sports a socialist intentionality and vied for control of leisure pursuits. Accenting the camaraderie of sports or social events—and not, for example, the value of competition—they incorporated these activities into a Left discursive field that stressed class solidarity.[18] Leftists also accented how sports-playing would promote harmonious class relations and improve civic life. The Socialist newspaper *La Crítica*, for example, underscored the myriad benefits Chileans would derive from the practice of sports: "For modern statesmen, it is no secret that sports have a preponderant influence on good habits [*las buenas costumbres*]. A sports-loving people is a people that can be easily channeled, directed, or oriented toward a sense of solidarity and social benefit. Sports create a morality that contributes to smoothing egotism and leveling men. And it keeps them away from the canteen." The practice of sports would not only uplift the race; it would also diminish class conflict, the newspaper suggested. Sporting and recreational events could also keep men out of bars. And it could do so without punishing or restricting them.[19]

Socialist recreational events were meant not only to keep men away from the canteen and to shore up working-class fellowship but also to induce cordial and noneroticized relations between the sexes and thereby promote male (sexual) "respect" for women. Most sports clubs organized by the Left had male soccer and female basketball teams, and in theater groups women often outnumbered men. The Left thus attempted to replace male homo-sociability with heterosociability and incorporate women into the Left.[20] The bylaws of the Socialist Militia instructed adherents to organize parties and dances where militants and family members could amuse themselves in a healthy atmosphere. Repudiating the sexual recklessness into which men might so easily fall, Communist dance organizers frowned at couples who danced too close, moved their shoulders and hips with too much abandon, or even worse, hugged and kissed on the dance floor. The absence of alcohol at these events, promoted in internal publications for party members, was also intended to encourage male sexual restraint. Clearly these were not disorderly and raucous fiestas. But even though—or perhaps because—social events instilled the value of social and sexual order, leftists believed that those events attracted adherents and especially new women supporters.[21]

The extent to which socialist morality effectively empowered working-class men and women ultimately depended not only on how moral norms were inflected but also on who controlled disciplinary efforts. Leftists did not shun the regulatory efforts of sympathetic outsiders, but they also supported personal restraint, women's oversight of their husbands, and the vigilance of their own community. The state, in their view, should campaign against alcohol consumption, pass and enforce dry laws, encourage citizen health and good habits by promoting sports, and provide resources for the building of recreational facilities. When the mayor of Valdivia prohibited the sale of liquor at union events, for example, the local Socialist newspaper applauded his decision. Valdivia's *Palabra Socialista* added that, for the measure to be truly effective, the sale of liquor in the area surrounding union halls ought to be prohibited as well. The newspaper also denounced the authorization of liquor sales on Independence Day in the otherwise dry town of Corral. Referring to the problem of alcoholism, in another publication, the Communist Party even went so far as to suggest that "in many cases the use of restrictive methods is indispensable to avoid or diminish the exacerbation of this problem."[22]

However, as diverse localities implemented prohibitionist measures, often at the insistence of worker organizations, the difficulties inherent in delegating this regulatory power to the state and its enforcement to the police became more apparent to many. At least in relation to alcohol, by the mid-1940s Left calls for state regulation became less frequent. Leftists continued to call for disciplinary state action but simultaneously affirmed their control over anti-alcoholism campaigns. The fight against alcoholism, a CTCh newspaper put forth, "is not only the job of a State agency but a privileged task of Chileans who are clean of heart and who sincerely wish a complete improvement of the nation."[23]

In addition, leftists sought to affirm their control over recreational pursuits by playing on or creating sports teams at their places of employment. They thus sought to recruit members for their organizations and supplant employer-sponsored recreational events. *AS* counseled members of the Federación de la Juventud Socialista (FJS, Socialist Youth Federation) to participate in sports clubs. "By giving these clubs a strong spirit of collegiality and sportsmanlike sobriety," *AS* suggested, "the FJS will be doubly fortified. In their bodies as a result of sport, and in its ranks by attracting new and valuable elements."[24] Cultural activities effectively helped build the Left. Roberto Quiroga, for example, began his political career in a music group organized by the Communist Youth in the rural town of Los Andes. Members of the local youth group first invited the locally renowned guitar and mandolin player to join a band they were setting up. Between rehearsals, they talked to him of the need to oppose injustice and exploitation. Attracted by the fighting spirit of his fellow musicians, Quiroga soon joined the youth organization. In addition, through their participation in cultural activities, leftists legitimated themselves as community leaders and projected themselves in their local communities. Iris Figueroa attributed her victory in the 1953 municipal elections in part to the popularity she had gained as a longtime participant in, and president of, San Miguel's Juventud Unida sports club. More generally, the creation of autonomous institutions helped leftists articulate norms of masculine deportment to their own gender-inflected, class-based project.[25]

The Left's attempts to discourage vice-inducing male homosociability and to build working-class organizations were never fully successful. Men routinely went drinking after soccer games and even after union meetings.[26] While the Left never publicly sanctioned these practices, they persisted and even contributed to a sense of class belonging and political unity among men. Noting the ways in which male socializing and politics went hand in hand, a social worker with anti-Communist intentions attributed male vices to "pernicious influences of a Communist nature that in uncultured minds

Neighborhood sports club that included members of the Communist Youth, Valparaíso, c. 1935.
Photo courtesy Emperatriz Villarroel.

produce a disorientation that has nefarious effects on an honorable and tranquil existence." Rebutting such claims, in oral testimony Communist militants frequently characterized a politically committed father or husband as "*tranquilo*" or "*de casa*," a family man who was not interested in the excesses of male get-togethers. Such characterizations effectively marginalized more rowdy forms of male class identity, facilitating socialist convergence with other members of the nation. They simultaneously constructed alternative forms of class solidarity and incorporated women's desire for loyalty and respect from men.[27]

SEXUAL CONTROL AND FEMALE VIRTUE

The contradictory impulses that shaped socialist morality expressed themselves most fully in discussions of female virtue. In those discussions, the Left appropriated a more conservative common sense, which was also part of working-class culture, and used it both to combat right-wing propaganda and to build its own constituency. By trying to tame male militants and protect female participants, leftists countered the widespread belief that public spaces, and Left politics in particular, were sexually dangerous for women. Women could be politically active, they claimed, without jeopardizing their sexual virtue. They concurrently attempted to prove to working-class parents, husbands, and Catholics that socialists could protect women. And leftists strove to show women that the Left recognized and repudiated sexual violence and exploitation. Socialist sexual morality consequently empowered women to a degree, although leftist leaders' insistence on protecting women led to a partial reassertion of men's authority over women.

Many women within the Left believed that their participation in public activities left them sexually vulnerable. They nonetheless trusted their *compañeros* to show sexual "respect." When asked in an interview how her male political allies treated her, Carmen Lazo immediately replied that they had always treated her respectfully. Although she admitted that a comrade had once tried to rape her, she dismissed the importance of this event: "I'm not going to say I never had problems. I did. Once a guy who was a Socialist tried to rape me. . . . [But] that was the only time a man disrespected me. But in general, I have traveled—. Look, I even made a trip, for example, a trip on horseback from Curacautín to Lonquimay by way of the Las Raíces tunnel. Alone. And no man has ever even so much as pinched me. . . . But I have been much respected; I have been much liked. For me that [the attempted rape] was an exception, something I don't take into consideration because maybe that guy was kind of sick, kind of maniacal." That Allende, to whom Lazo denounced her would-be rapist, threw the "maniacal" man a punch that laid him flat perhaps contributed to Lazo's sense of security—as did the blows she herself imparted to her assailant before running off. Along with her own smacks, the exemplary protection of the almost mythical Allende erased the threat posed by the other, "sick" and exceptional, comrade.[28]

Working-class organizations' sexual control of men was not the extension of a previous tradition of parental or spousal regulation. Male activists who participated in cultural or political activities traded one form of nonfamilial sociability and its rules for another form with its own regulations. They might swap a whorehouse, bar, or even the movies for a union family outing or a library.[29] In contrast, women's entrance into a mixed-sex sphere of public activity potentially distanced them from family surveillance. In Left social spaces male sexual control, and not the cloistering of women, guaranteed female safety and virtue. Still, to neutralize the sexual threat that distance from the family might pose for women, Left activists drew on and perpetuated a tradition of familial "protection" of women. Portraying the spaces of sociability they created as replicating the social and sexual norms of home life, leftists attempted to make Left artistic and dance societies, and union halls themselves, just like respectable family homes. That they were, or at least should be, second homes was a frequent theme in Left propaganda. Moreover, family control continued at Left social activities where the presence of parents or older siblings, who accompanied young adults, ensured a safe, familylike atmosphere. At dances men and boys were often expected to ask parents for permission to dance with their daughters.[30]

Although politically active women, and especially young single women, traded a degree of parental sexual control for the sexual protection of working-class organizations, parents continued to guard the virtue of their daughters. Although Carmen Lazo was only thirteen years of age when she joined the Socialist Party in 1934, her parents did not object to her political activities. Nevertheless, when Lazo went on propaganda missions to the countryside, where she read the Socialist Party newspaper out loud to local residents, her parents asked her brother to accompany her. Lazo attributed her brother's presence to the fact that her family was "very united" but also recognized that her brother was there to look after her "behind." Iris Figueroa's parents, both politically active, believed that when she was out doing political work or at Left social events, she was in good hands (and, just in case, her mother often went along). Even so, when Figueroa stayed out until two in the morning postering May Day propaganda, her father gave her a good strapping, saying that a young girl should not be out at that hour. That the "viejos," older compañeros, had accompanied her home did not appease her father.[31]

Socialist leaders thus persisted in disciplining men and making them into protectors of women's virtue while they accommodated family members who wished to continue policing female family members. At the same time, some parents of women activists trusted that, given the sexual norms their daughters had learned at home, the young women could protect themselves. When Violeta de la Cruz decided to study engineering—she was one of the first women in Chile to do so—and join the Socialist Party, her aunts insisted to her father that it was dangerous for de la Cruz to go out alone. Referring to her virginity, the women suggested that she might "lose herself." But confident that de la Cruz had learned the significance of preserving her purity, her father answered, "She won't get lost, because she doesn't want to." De la Cruz's father was right; although the young woman traveled widely, she took measures to protect herself. As the Socialist Party splintered and factional disputes intensified, often erupting into brawls, de la Cruz took on the task of convincing militants outside Santiago not to affiliate with César Godoy Urrutia's rival Socialist faction. Believing her political adversaries might use sexual violence as a weapon against her, she carried a pistol. Clara Velarde was more rebellious than de la Cruz. She objected to her mother's sexual control, putting her hands over her ears when her mother spoke of the importance of guarding her own virginity. Still, Velarde did not totally shun the value of sexual honorableness. "Don't be stupid," she answered her mother. "If I, if I want to, I'll go to bed with a man, and if I don't want to, I won't." Acquiescing, she added, "Why do you worry? I keep to myself. I don't even date."[32]

Young women looked after not only their own virtue but also that of other young women. Iris Figueroa earned the right to protect her *compañeras'* virtue by first protecting her own. "I was very popular in the *población*. Everyone thought of me as 'the young lady' [la señorita]. Parents confided in me and would give their daughters permission [to go out] if I was around. So, I would make the effort of going to pick them up, dropping them off, so that they wouldn't run off. I couldn't take on that responsibility. So—. That would have tarnished the organization, and I was from another school of thought. I was raised differently, in an old-fashioned way, in a very old-fashioned way." Similarly, Communist Clara Velarde recalled taking young girls to beach cabins owned by the party in the 1960s. "The mothers, I remember, would cry at us. They would ask us to please take care of their daughters. Because of the problem of virginity, because at that time things [restrictions] were very, were terrible. . . . So, we looked after them. We took this very seriously. So we would arrive at the beach but we would form them into a line and make sure that no one escaped into the trees, taking care of them because some would run away."[33]

Both leftists and nonleftists saw marriage as the best way of protecting women and ensuring their sexual reputation. Figueroa lost interest in marrying after her first boyfriend two-timed her, but her Communist mother pleaded with her to reconsider. According to Figueroa, her mother tried to convince her, arguing: "*Mijita*, I don't want to leave you alone. I would like you to hook up with a man, because a girl never has a good reputation. There's always someone who will make up a story, say things, and all."[34]

Figueroa's mother reflected broader societal norms in her concern for her daughter's reputation. In his fictionalized account of a coal miners' strike, novelist and Communist Diego Muñoz concerned himself with the ways in

Young women and girls from Valparaíso and Calera at a meeting convened by the Communist Party, c. 1934. Photo courtesy Emperatriz Villarroel.

which guaranteeing women's virtue through marriage fortified the working-class community. In *Carbón*, Muñoz depicted a cohesive—and indeed physically separate—coal-mining community and portrayed norms of sexual propriety as responding to the needs of that collectivity. Uniting to oppose the mining company and win their strike, *Carbón*'s protagonists abandon their homes in the company town and set up an isolated, makeshift campsite on the nearby beach. Fearing that dissent or confusion will weaken the community they have (re)founded, the strike committee and its robust Head of Order and Discipline, don Toro, enforce strict disciplinary measures within the beach camp. Thus when Farías sexually accosts the young Meche, the strike leaders take the matter into their hands. Although (for some unfortunate and unknown but ultimately fortuitous reason) Meche's father had not defended her and—as Meche's mother reminds the young woman—Meche's refusal to marry had left her vulnerable, the strike committee offers protection. Maclovio, a strike organizer and an admirer of Meche's, immediately concerns himself with the affair. At first, he considers giving Farías a good beating, but his *compañero* Reyes convinces him that as a community authority Maclovio has better methods for dealing with the treacherous Farías. Under

instructions from the strike committee, don Toro brings Farías before the
assembled committee members, Meche, and her mother. Reyes begins the
meeting by addressing Farías:

> "We are living together," he said, "in a strike that has an enormous
> significance for everyone. The simple fact that we unanimously de-
> cided to live together in an encampment means that, from the first un-
> til the last day, here, in Playa Blanca, there must be the most strict
> mutual respect."
> "I have not disrespected anyone!"
> "You have disrespected Meche."
> "I am free and so is Meche. . . ."
> Maclovio lost his cool:
> "She is not free!" he yelled. "She is going to marry me! Do you
> hear? Isn't that right, Meche?"
> That was so startling that the young woman responded almost with-
> out realizing:
> "That's right."
> The old woman stood tall, triumphant.
> "Yes sir, don Farías!" she exclaimed. "My daughter is not a loose
> woman! Besides her father and her mother, she has her master, under-
> stand that once and for all. Who do you think you are?"

In this rendering, the socialist working-class community supports male prerogatives and responsibilities and reproduces traditional notions of female
virtue, but also modifies them. Because, here, male violation of female virtue impedes class unity, class considerations guide the defense of Meche's
honor. And both the protection Meche's soon-to-be husband provides and
his power over the woman are bolstered by his political authority within the
working-class community. Moreover, as a working-class leader, Maclovio has
distinct methods for exercising his prerogatives. Reyes instructs Maclovio not
to use physical violence against Farías but grants him the possibility of
invoking the moral authority of the community and of using apparatuses of
community governance to defend Meche.[35]

Leftists further differentiated themselves from elites by stressing capitalists' violations of sexual rules and their own adherence to sexual norms.
Male leftists thus suggested that it was the capitalist "other" who victimized
women. Articles in the Left press decried wage-earning women's sexual
exploitation by bosses who were characterized as backward, bestial seducers

lacking in dignity and culture who unjustly satisfied their voracious sexual appetites with their employees. Showing the economic consequences of women's vulnerability, press accounts further emphasized that employers routinely fired women who resisted their bosses' sexual advances, leaving them penniless. One Communist publication noted that young women had "no other choice but to serve in cafés where they have only their tips for wages, to be the servants of *señoritos* or their bosses' toys, and finally, the terrible prospect of prostitution." In Baltazar Castro's novel *Sewell*, Mr. Patrick, a North American boss at the El Teniente copper mine, tries to rape the "pure" Carmela. As a result, she is forced to give up her job as a waitress in one of the mines' pensions. Luckily, Carmela's working-class beau is there to protect her, and after the attack Carmela and Filidor marry.[36]

Leftists' acceptance of hegemonic mores and their concurrent reworking of them as essentially working-class ideals, which were extensively violated by elites, were especially pronounced in relation to the most coherent expression of conservative sexual and gender norms: Catholicism. Left newspapers openly dissuaded women from associating with the church, a purportedly retrograde institution favoring the rich.[37] Drawing on a popular belief, leftists portrayed priests as sexual abusers. Tomy Romeo's mother was not herself a leftist, but she did not allow Romeo to go to church alone when the girl was young. "She distrusted the priests," Romeo remembered, "because she said the priests sometimes feel you up and such." Likewise Carmen Lazo took her son out of Catholic school fearing that the priests might sexually abuse the boy. But while leftists invoked these disparaging views of the church, their morality was not always radically different from the moral and sexual ethos of Catholicism. As a leader in the Juventud Obrera Católica (Young Catholic Worker) in the late 1940s, Clara Velarde saw "many atrocities," leading her to leave the organization and later join the Communist Party. She nonetheless continued to believe in the quintessential Catholic symbol of female purity, the Virgin Mary. "It just happened that I had to deal with priests who raped girls," Velarde remarked. "That really jarred me so I left all that, but I was still Catholic, still believed in God and the Virgin."[38]

As Figueroa and Velarde suggested, if Communists had not guarded female virtue, if they had not upheld predominant gender norms, parents would not have allowed their daughters to participate in Left events, and leftist organizing would have suffered. Their own prestige and influence rested in part on not distancing themselves fully from the social and sexual norms of nonsocialists. Since outside the Left, socialists were commonly seen as degenerates who believed in free love, unconventional behavior on the part of activists could indeed have damaged their organizations. A conservative social work student reflected an outsider's view of socialist morality when she told a Communist classmate who "couldn't wait" to marry her boyfriend that the sexually reserved woman had nothing to wait for: "You're a Communist, you don't have to wait." Also invoking sexual norms to conservative ends, the nuns at the Catholic secondary school Irma Moreno attended made their students pray a rosary for Gabriel González Videla's defeat in the 1937 parliamentary elections, saying that if he came to office, he would rape the nuns.[39]

In upholding female virtue and turning the accusations of the Right on their head, Communists dispelled accusations such as these, refusing to let conservatives lay exclusive claim to the defense of women's sexual honor. In fact, they questioned elites' essential propriety, just as they had done in relation to alcoholism, and suggested that respect for women was an essentially working-class moral attitude. Moreover, in calling for male sexual reserve they responded not only to external, elite affirmations regarding the depravity of the poor but also to competing pressures from within their own ranks: they recognized women's desire to participate without fear of being sexually accosted and parents' desire to preserve the purity of their daughters. Although the notion that working-class men needed to protect women underscored women's inability to protect themselves, individually and collectively, socialist sexual mores did not always force women into the position of powerless victims. The intention of leaders notwithstanding, they may actually have encouraged women to defend themselves.

Furthermore, leftists' sexual mores were in some ways less restrictive and more flexible, because they were more strategic and instrumental, than either previous forms of working-class control or that exercised by conservative forces such as the Catholic Church. When Carmen Lazo and her Socialist Party comrade Eudaldo Lobos preached on street corners in the 1930s, they knowingly used prevalent mores in an instrumental fashion. Lazo recalled: "When we didn't have an audience on the Alameda, we would start to talk like *canutos* [creole evangelicals]. To gather people, you see. . . . Then he would start to say, 'My brothers, I was a sinner. I lost myself in alcohol.' And the people would start to congregate. And I would say, 'I was a streetwalker.' That part was a lie, but until we had gotten an audience together we didn't spring the stuff about the party, we didn't talk about socialism. Sure, we did it with the best of intentions, but at bottom it was a lie. Because at first we made like we were evangelicals." Similarly, a Communist Youth publication saw socialist moral regulation as strategic. Lamenting parental constraint of young women, which made it difficult for those women to attend political events, the publication urged militants to make allowances. Unmarried women who earned sub-subsistence wages, the publication explained, could not leave their parents' home even if they wanted to, and one fight too many with her parents could force a would-be activist to leave the organization. Socialist morality accommodated what it could not immediately change. Prominent Communists caved in to prevalent norms too. Elena Pedraza first lived with her boyfriend, Ricardo Fonseca (later secretary-general of the Communist Party), but eventually married him, somewhat against her own belief in "free love."[40]

Mercedes Fuentealba seemed more convinced of the benefits of an austere morality. Yet in describing her own recruitment efforts for consumer organizations she too noted how socialist morality was used to specific ends: "Well, we started to spark women's interest, and well we came up against their husbands' objections too. So we had to go and talk to him and show him and say to him, 'Well, go to my house. See what I'm like. Because your wife's not going to be harmed by being around me. I'm not a libertine. I don't live on the streets. I don't drink. I live with my husband. My husband's—.' So that's how we carried out the struggle."[41]

Moreover, leftists generally preferred not to exclude those who engaged in sexually disreputable practices. Documenting the diversity of sexual norms identified with socialism, a social worker noted with horror an encounter she had with two single mothers—one a Communist militant, the other a sympathizer—who had a political conviction in the ideal of "free love." For these two women, the social worker reported, "the political party . . . seems not to have any ends other than that 'ideal' which they believe they faithfully carry out." Neither Clara Velarde nor Iris Figueroa saw the sexual norms they themselves observed as intrinsic to a socialist project. When they referred to their own beliefs as "antiquated" or "old-fashioned" they implied that as a result of historical change—progress and the greater liberty for women that progress implied—those norms would necessarily and fruitfully be abandoned. But greater sexual freedom was not only a future aspiration; it was also a long-standing popular tradition. Within the working class, leftist leaders realized, casual sex and impermanent marital unions were as prevalent as the more orderly behavior the exercise of power demanded. Reflecting their own emergence from that broader popular culture and not wanting to alienate possible adherents who did not reject purportedly libertine sexual behavior, leftists refused to vilify allegedly disreputable customs. Thus, just months before the Popular Front took power, the Socialist *Barricada* denounced the fact that single mothers were "seen by society as elements that do not deserve respect" and called for the enactment of legislation that favored them.[42]

While greater sexual latitude had the merit of recognizing that men and women might desire premarital sex or casual unions and that women could consent to sex with someone other than their husbands, in a context of class and gender domination, what seemed like liberty could actually serve to cement subordination. Violations of sexual norms implied a rejection of capillary attempts to consolidate order—and therefore governance and power—whether those attempts came from the state or from working-class political organizations. But sexual transgressions could also be disruptive of the working-class community, of socialist efforts to mobilize women, of the Left's role within the popular-front coalitions, or of the Left's opposition to capitalist privilege. Leftists did not simply accept what they could not change but went further, *appropriating* hegemonic ideals for their own ends. They did not flaunt their bourgeois virtue, but their proletarian virtue. Moreover, women were often the prime proponents of sexual control. As a maxim in the newspaper *Tribuna* put it: "Women's resistance is not always a consequence of her virtue, but more probably of her experience."[43] The sexual "protection" women who participated in the Left gained—and even promoted and enforced—may have limited them sexually as much as it freed them from sexual abuse, but that depended in large part on how much control women had over the construction and implementation of those norms—and not necessarily on the specific content of moral prescriptions. By suggesting that working-class women needed to be protected from deviant men and capitalists, leftists undoubtedly underscored the protagonism of working-class men and the victimization of defenseless women. Yet because Left organizations also controlled men sexually to open politics to women, socialist morality provided women with the possibility of participation as well. In fact, working-class women won prestige and authority within the Left, as well as within society more broadly, by policing their own sexuality and that of their female comrades. In a society marked by class and gender differences, there could be no fully autonomous or alternative expressions of sexuality. In this context, leftists' efforts to discipline their followers sexually not only served the Left as it sought to solidify itself and gain legitimacy within the broader national community but also reflected and reworked the expressed interests of working-class parents, young women, and male supporters.[44]

MARRIAGE AND FAMILY IN SOCIALIST MORALITY

As Muñoz suggested in *Carbón*, socialists prized marriage. Yet Muñoz's depiction of Maclovio as Meche's "master" notwithstanding, leftists did not promote marriage simply to confine women to the home and to grant working-class men the benefits of women's unpaid domestic and sexual services. Nor did they do so only to appease right-wing detractors. Rather, they championed marriage and stable family life primarily because they believed strong ties of kinship would strengthen working-class solidarity and identity. *El Siglo* submitted to readers as an example to be replicated the thirty-year marriage of a longtime militant, a union in which "there were never discrepancies."[45]

Despite socialists' insistence on harmony within families, there was widespread conflict between men and women over what constituted proper behavior for each family member. A maxim in the Socialist newspaper *Tribuna* pointed to a seldom disputed truth of the times: "Men like women but detest marriage; women like marriage but detest men. How is it possible for them to understand each other?" Relations between men and women were always conflict-ridden, this maxim implied, because men and women had conflicting sexual and economic necessities—and therefore divergent definitions of what constituted proper conduct for each gender.[46] Women presumably wanted sober, stable providers who did not jeopardize their families' well-being by engaging in sexual liaisons that might imply competing economic ties. Men, even when married, wanted freedom from burdensome economic obligations and unrestricted sexual access to, and control over, women.

If, as leftists proposed, each partner made concessions to the expectations of his or her husband or wife, relations between the sexes would improve. Yet socialist prescriptions regarding family life did not immediately generate harmony among family members. In fact, along with a certain expansion of what was considered proper for women, most notably the legitimation of their political involvement, restrictions on what constituted proper male deportment likely prompted women to see having a "good" husband as a right for which they should and could fight. Preliminary evidence suggests that arguments within activist families commonly revolved around male transgressions. Clara Velarde's parents argued, for instance, because of her father's interest in the races, and Fresia Gravano's parents fought because of her father's sexual infidelity. That those male breaches were publicly discussed and repudiated by the Left probably validated and perhaps even instigated, at home, leftist women's opposition to male vice and financial irresponsibility. Furthermore, by calling on the state to mandate the payment of male family allowances to wives or by abetting court action against fugitive fathers, the Left attempted to provide all women with more effective means for enforcing male adherence to gender norms.[47]

By accusing capitalists of destroying the family, leftists ignored the roots of both family conflict and family instability in gender inequality. Replicating an often repeated formula, the Communist magazine *Principios* noted that because nitrate miners earned miserly wages they could not even dream of forming a home. Capitalists were to blame. Elsewhere, Communists overlooked economic inequality within the family, proclaiming: "We struggle for genuine peace and unity in the family, to build it on solid granite foundations of economic well-being for both spouses and of understanding and amorous camaraderie." Allegorical tales about the lives of prominent male Left leaders, many of whom had grown up fatherless and in poverty, also laid an all too easy blame on capitalism. In biographies and memoirs, prominent leftists who grew up in female-headed households advocated a reversal of their own experiences—which meant not only the abolition of poverty but, significantly, the eradication of female-headed households. Like the welfare professionals described in Chapter 5, these men and their biographers saw male desertion, not inequality between the sexes more broadly, as the cause of single mothers' impoverishment. Conveniently, they characterized stable family life under the economic protection of a male family head as a reversal of capitalist norms. They thereby absolved working-class males, laying the blame elsewhere.[48] This discursive strategy tended to make male dominance (as opposed to male transgression, which was ultimately attributable to a bourgeois environment) invisible, and women's resistance to it even more so. Leftists thus neutralized women's opposition to male dominance and reencoded patriarchy as capitalism.

Consequently, the Left never openly addressed domestic and sexual violence, prime ways in which men exerted control over women and enforced their own views of what was proper for each sex. Although leftists apparently did not condone physical and sexual aggression—even as a child Fresia Gravano felt she had the right to intercede when her father lifted his hand to hit her mother—they did not openly discuss male brutality. In contrast to alcoholism and male financial irresponsibility, topics openly discussed by the Left, sexual violence within the family was mentioned only very obliquely. In those veiled discussions, domestic and sexual violence was usually attributed to impoverished families' "promiscuous" living and sleeping arrangements—again, the fault of capitalists.[49]

Familial harmony, leftists thought, generated the working-class fellowship that was necessary in the struggle against capitalism. Graciela Trujillo, whose father was a Communist and who later became one herself, identified the unity of her family as crucial to her class-conscious political commitment: "Well you saw politics right at home and at work, right? Because they [her parents] acted as a very tight-knit marriage, so we were raised in that atmosphere of unity, of conviviality." Conversely, a letter from a María Teresa to El Obrero Municipal suggested that class cohesion demanded strong family bonds: "[W]e and they, proletarian men and women, should constitute a single family, always willing to fight for another piece of stale bread." In Castro's Sewell, Carmela decides to leave the mining camp after the sexual attack inflicted on her by the perfidious gringo, and her admirer, Filidor, vows to go with her. Thus the capitalist's abuse of Carmela allows the couple "better to reveal to each other their own sentiments." Combating capitalist immorality, Castro suggested, brought men and women of the laboring classes closer together.[50]

Since ideological agreement facilitated family cohesion, in an ideal socialist family everyone was politically active. What could be better than ties of kinship sealed by a shared political commitment? For unmarried militants, whose lives centered around their party affiliations, dating and marrying within party ranks seemed natural. As Irma Moreno, a Socialist, explained, "You fell in love with the compañeros. Everything took place there [in the party]. Falling in love, getting married, dying, being bo[rn], everything. It was like a great big family." As Moreno hinted, political affinities generated amorous ties and, conversely, family ties could strengthen the party, itself a "great big family." Advice columns in the leftist press abetted courtship among comrades.[51]

Following party directives, married militants whose partners, usually their wives, were not politically active tried to turn their apolitical spouses to the cause. Mercedes Fuentealba's husband began his proselytizing while they were still dating by taking his fiancée to popular-front rallies. He found it difficult, however, to interest the young woman in Left politics. Heeding the calls of his political party, he nonetheless persisted. Fuentealba continued to resist, even after they married, but she ultimately gave in. The sense of belonging to a community that generated a cohesive worldview ended up attracting Fuentealba. Once she and her beau were married, Fuentealba recalled, "I started reading. I read a lot. My husband had good books, and we started to look them over. So in truth, he convinced me. . . . We started to talk from the time we started eating until we fell asleep in bed, talking of simple things, about what had happened, what was to come. Since he was political and understood, well, one day I did too. He never pressured me to join the party."[52]

Leftist families served not only as loci of socialist ideological indoctrination but also as crucial instances for the reproduction of Left culture and morality more broadly, and of its gender norms. Correct working-class behavior was promulgated not only in the Left press but also in the homes of socialist militants who taught their children through example. Trujillo remembered her father as displaying male economic responsibility and good habits and teaching the value of those good habits to her brothers:

> My father was a man who, when he got paid, came home and gave it to her [his wife]. "Herminia knows, Herminia is the housewife, Herminia knows," and he would give it to her. He kept just what he needed for transportation, to clothe himself. And when my brothers started to work too, he started, "You, this much for the house, this much you hand over to me to dress you." He had them—. He had the men right here, under control. . . . [Because] men start to acquire vices, right? Well, so that the men wouldn't acquire vices, my father put the brakes on them. Because he himself didn't have any vices. The only thing my father did was smoke. He never drank, he didn't drink, he didn't—. . . . So he tried to make sure that his children didn't do it either.[53]

The prime benefit of such proper masculine behavior, which was conceived of as a socialist code of honor, was the resulting familial harmony.

Notwithstanding prevalent suggestions that differing political views among spouses tore marriages apart, some families remained united despite ideological and cultural differences, and others were conflict-ridden despite political affinities. Press exhortations aimed at women may have exposed the evils of Catholicism, for example, but atheist male militants did not always try to convince their wives or daughters to give up the church.[54] Perhaps more important, although leftist leaders preached at men to get their wives involved, only some complied. Fearing that a politically active wife might be sexually unfaithful or lose interest in housekeeping and childrearing, others preferred to keep their wives at home.[55] And in families where both spouses were active politically, husbands and wives continued to have unequal power and therefore to fight. Despite leftist leaders' wishes, gender conflict did not dissolve into the struggle against capitalism. In fact, insofar as socialist morality drew on and reinforced women's own views on what constituted proper male conduct within marriage, it may even have bolstered wives' efforts to curtail their husbands' privileges. It is likely support for women's own views on what constituted proper male deportment, rather than vague notions of harmony within the family and promises of protection, that attracted women to the Left.

MASCULINE AND FEMININE FAILINGS:
THE CONTRADICTIONS OF ACTIVISM

Regardless of the Left's insistence on harmony within working-class families, activism was often incompatible with family obligations. For women who continued to be held responsible for the day-to-day comfort of family members the contradictions between political involvement and family duties were particularly acute. The intense political involvement of two associates, Tomy Romeo recalled, provoked rumors that they would lose their husbands. "Many others did lose husbands," Romeo commented. That these middle-class professional women probably had access to domestic service freed them to participate in politics but did not relieve them fully of domestic concerns—or of guilt. Working-class women activists who could not afford domestic help often relied on female family members to help with domestic chores. Others took time out from politics while their children were young. But whether they were working-class or professional, women had to confront the often competing commitments of family and politics. Husbands who were themselves activists often put up with less-than-doting wives and sometimes even helped out with housework. But some husbands were not very accommodating at all, and even those who were had their limits. Pedro Medina, for example, helped with housework—but only when there were no visitors around to see him. Children were often less cooperative and more demanding. And in the 1930s and 1940s, when antibiotics were not widely available and many poor Chileans did not have toilets or running water, a young child not properly cared for could easily die as the result of pneumonia or diarrhea. Iris Figueroa lost three children and bore three more before she began to think that it might be better not to have sex.[56]

Given the difficulties women, and especially those in leadership positions, experienced in balancing politics and family duties, they often chose to have fewer children, and the children they did have were carefully planned. Despite very limited access to effective birth control techniques and only very rudimentary information, these women scrupulously controlled their fertility. "I had them every four years, very carefully planned although at the time there were none of those things, except condoms," Elena Pedraza explained. For most women, however, condoms were a seldom-used alternative. They employed other methods, often without their partners' knowledge or cooperation: the calendar, suppositories made of laundering soap, aspirin placed in the vagina to "cut the sperm." When these precarious methods failed—and they often did—there was still the option of "going to the butcher": although abortion was illegal, certain militants aborted repeatedly. For those who staunchly wished to avoid more children and wanted to avoid a trip to the abortionist, the only remaining option was not to engage in sexual intercourse, a decision some women took. Fortunately for Left women interested in limiting the number of children they bore, neither birth control nor abortion was stigmatized in Left circles. While in many barrios and factories coworkers and neighbors suspected women who aborted of having been unfaithful to their husbands, this controlling gossip seems not to have permeated the socialist community. To leftist activists, it seemed fitting that to serve the cause better both men and women should limit the number of children they had. Women's control over their fertility, like male abstinence from alcohol, was validated as the assertion of personal will. That women might use birth control to better dedicate themselves to the political community further legitimated that decision.[57]

Politics also hindered men's ability to fulfill obligations to family. Participation in union activities, for example, often meant losing a job or missing work, making it difficult for men to act as responsible breadwinners. Just as important, politics often removed men from the home. In the anti-Communist repression of the 1920s, and again after 1948, Communists and labor leaders suffered internal exile and were therefore unable to respond to the needs of their families. And then there was the more mundane, and probably more common, problem of male militants who gave up time with their wives and girlfriends to attend political events.[58]

The failure of leftist men to measure up to gendered expectations led leaders to insist even more forcefully on proper behavior. A militant, the Communist organ *Principios* warned, should not use his political commitment to justify the shirking of gendered responsibilities to family. Such irresponsibility only bred discontent within families and ultimately undermined political goals. "All too often, under the pretext of fulfilling party obligations, *compañeros* ignore their children and *compañeras*," *Principios* explained. "In these cases, the *compañera* becomes an obstacle to the militant's work and to his development and formation as a Communist." To remedy situations such as these, *Principios* suggested that the party leadership not make excessive demands on male militants and that it teach them how to reconcile politics and family life. Likewise the party's secretary-general, Galo González, instructed leaders to make sure local party functionaries had enough money to live on, so that they did not experience economic hardships that could generate conflict with their wives. A man whose wife was happy and who did not have to worry about his family's economic situation, González added, would be an efficient cadre.[59]

Many politically committed women who understood that there were good reasons for their husbands' lapses felt they had to put up with these failings. Many other women did not. Mercedes Fuentealba recalled fights with her boyfriend over his devotion to politics: "Since I wasn't political and having a sort of, I would say, a repulsion toward Communism . . . in our youth, as boyfriend and girlfriend, we had fights that weren't the typical fights, but because he would stand me up for politics. So, uh, we killed ourselves fighting about that." Years later, when Fuentealba had taken up politics herself and become more tolerant, she and her husband laughed about these fights. Advocating a similar patience, a journalist noted regretfully, but also with a certain pride, that the Socialist Arturo Velásquez had "postponed the tranquility of his home" for the party. (And just in case a reader might then doubt the man's merits, the journalist assured readers that "few home-loving men know how to fulfill their fatherly duties so well.")[60]

In return for male sexual fidelity, which Left leaders advocated to ensure male allegiance to their families, the wives and partners of male Left activists were expected to accept their husbands' absences from the home. Politically conscious women who could trust that their husbands were at meetings and not out flirting with other women would purportedly avoid the jealous outbreaks of apolitical women who objected to their husbands' autonomy, sexual or otherwise. Blanca Flores's mother, a woman who "wasn't partisan," believed that a man should spend time at home after work and opposed her husband's comings and goings. That her husband couldn't hold down a stable job and was unfaithful only made matters worse. But Carlos Flores had different expectations of how an activist's wife should respond to his absences. Tired of his wife's jealous recriminations, he left her and took up with a "fighting woman" who would, ironically, accept his unstable lifestyle without struggle.[61]

CORRECTION AND COMMUNITY

Socialist and Communist Party leaders thus preached the values of accommodating politics and family life, and Communist Party leaders advocated making political allowances so that militants might properly fulfill their gendered duties to family. Yet, men and women often did not measure up. In her youth, the then-idealistic Clara Velarde saw her *compañeros* as "something really special." But as she grew older Velarde became disillusioned as she began to realize that they were "human beings with defects and weaknesses." Likewise Irma Moreno noted that ultimately among Socialists, as among ordinary Chileans, there were "girls with babies, problems everywhere, marriages that fell apart, just the same. In that aspect, all human beings are the same."[62]

While militants often failed to live up to socialist standards, socialist morality lived on as a utopian aspiration. Even when Clara Velarde discovered her comrades' lapses, she retained the idea that at least her friends and allies aspired to something different. "After all, the principles were the best," Velarde concluded. Like Velarde, Elena Pedraza realized that Communist militants could act immorally, but she believed they behaved improperly despite, and not because of, the Communist code of honor: "They become corrupt. In the Communist Party, the labor leaders. . . . A woman would arrive, and she had to end up in bed with them. And they led double lives, so they have no right to talk. Because I'm not against a man falling in love, but to have another woman who has to stay home making beans and to have a different life with the other one. No, that is a bourgeois morality."[63]

Since they were commonly hushed up, leaders' excesses did not serve either to reinforce the shared standards of the Left community or to force a rearticulation of socialist norms. The vanguard remained the vanguard, no matter what. But rank-and-file members of the Communist Party occasionally had to face a disciplinary apparatus that controlled and corrected them if they strayed from the tenets of socialist morality. Their errors were recognized and paraded as examples to be avoided. Going beyond prescription, the Communist Party used disciplinary measures to define standards of proper conduct. And perhaps because men were more frequently in the public eye or because male prerogatives were not effectively circumscribed by family members and neighbors, leftists focused most consistently on male violations of gender norms.

Communist Party members could be called into the party's disciplinary control commissions and subjected to sanction for drinking, marital infidelities, or failing to support their families properly. Militants were also submitted to correction for political "errors," for the improper use of party or union funds, or for supposedly unwarranted criticisms of party leaders. As a Communist Party document put it around 1940, "It is necessary to establish among ourselves rigid criteria in relation to what constitutes revolutionary morality and to carry out a severe vigilance of the private lives of party militants, regardless of what positions they hold, above all when it comes to questions of revolutionary resoluteness when confronting the police and bourgeois justice, of the purity of family relations, of habits in general, proceeding without vacillation to separate corrupt elements and to apply sanctions to those who have taken responsibility for errors."[64] Sexual impropriety was one reason male militants were summoned before the infamous *comisión de control de cuadros* (cadre control commission). The name led militants to summon the double meaning of "cuadros"—it meant "underwear" as well as cadre—and refer to the disciplinary tribunal as the "*comisión de cuadros y marruecuos*" (underwear and fly commission).

Communist control and correction began when a militant entered the party and agreed to follow its principles. "The first duty of a militant," read the party's statutes, "is to make the acts of his or her public and private life fit the principles and program of the party." Habitual drunkards or those who showed "degeneration or immorality," the statutes warned, could be disciplined. And disciplined they were. Leaders expelled Juan Rojas Serrano, former president of the union at the Mapocho nitrate office, "for his corroborated lack of discipline, degeneration in drink and for divulging party resolutions to provocateur elements." The "licentious" life of the Communist mayor of Iquique brought party leader Luis Corvalán to the city to investigate accusations and bring the man into line.[65] The party identification card, granted to potential members only if their personal and political life was in order, was another instrument of control. When members were expelled, their cards were taken away to ensure that they did not pose as party members. Local leaders were instructed to give members who moved from one locality to another passes so that party members in their new homes would know that the newcomers had not left their previous residences because of political or moral problems.[66] While clearly these methods of control were not applied as consistently as leaders might have liked, as instruments of discipline that functioned principally through the power of example, their efficacy did not necessarily rely on how widely they were exercised. Disciplinary and control measures allowed Communist leadership to indicate clearly who belonged and who did not, but more important, these measures signaled acceptable and unacceptable behavior.

At the top of the disciplinary apparatus was the national control commission, which attended to the most serious or important offenders. Below the national commission, regional and sometimes local control commissions received complaints regarding members from individual militants, from party activists' family members, or from cell leaders who denounced their comrades. In cases of sexual infidelity, a militant's wife could go to a local or regional commission. There, she generally found a sympathetic audience and favorable results, for committee members frequently told errant husbands to give up their lovers or leave the party. Often enough, the men decided to stick with the party and their wives. At the base of the disciplinary machine were the cells, where militants were urged to look after the public and private, moral and ideological rectitude of their *compañeros*. In Luis Enrique Délano's 1958 novel *La base*, which described the life of a Communist Party cell, cell members' principal tasks (besides going to street demonstrations) are straightening out the marital problems of a *compañera* in an ailing marriage and dealing with another militant's struggles with his bourgeois father. In Délano's account of cell life, socialist vigilance took on the characteristics of much-appreciated neighborly concern. Certainly, many actual cell members also saw it that way; discipline and control did not work only through fear and intimidation.[67]

Thus although one of the aims of party discipline was to enforce among party members a utopian cultural and ideological homogeneity, the contents of which were determined by the upper echelons of the party, its success depended in part on militants' consent to what did not always seem like external impositions. At least in terms of its regulation of family life, Communist correction depended on ordinary men, and especially on ordinary women, who chose to let the party enter into their personal business. In many cases, party discipline was beneficial to militants, especially women party members, or to male militants' wives. And because the party was a voluntary association, militants could always choose to leave it if they disagreed with disciplinary norms and their application. Ultimately the cultural force of the party's worldview was harder to avoid than its disciplinary apparatus per se.

Because Socialists were not as immersed in distinct working-class locales, they could not and did not regulate comrades' sexual and familial conduct in the same way as Communists. Yet they were no less diligent in their preaching, and they were particularly effective in articulating the importance of working-class norms to the legitimacy of the Left within the broader national community. In differing ways and to varying extents, then, both parties advanced the consolidation of local communities, class, or nation-state through social and sexual prescription. Together, they articulated gendered disciplinary norms within family and community to a broader national consensus on gender. Their moral interest fortified leftist organizations, generated a collective working-class identity, and ultimately solidified the state, dispersing potential contradictions among each of those regulatory instances. Women, who bargained as they could to augment their economic and sexual power within families, often reinforced mechanisms of governance at each of these levels. Nevertheless, socialist morality was not simply an externally imposed bourgeois ethos, functional to capitalist modernization. Nor was it just a means for reinforcing the vanguardist power of leftist leaders. It was also an attempt to negotiate the contradictions of working-class culture and activism.

THE INS AND OUTS OF SOCIALIST MORALITY

The ample, if partial, convergence of Socialist factions, Communists, and even right-wing forces on a gendered code of honor did not then automatically guarantee gender, class, or national unity. As differences and rivalries within the Left and between Left and Right proliferated in the 1940s, many men (and even some women) harnessed agreed-upon norms, which continued to mark lines of legitimacy and illegitimacy, to contending projects. Men drew upon moral prescriptions to defend their own honor publicly, to discredit their rivals, and to determine who would, politically and symbolically, represent their class and nation. Where national or class unity faltered, invocations of respectability were crucial to each group's attempt to legitimate itself and denounce competitors, whether those opponents were bosses, scabs, or group members' own enemies within the Left. In sum, men used moral norms to restrictive ends, as ways of cementing their own authority and discrediting immoral "others." Gendered moral precepts became manly battering rams for diverse political factions that disputed the leadership of the working class and ultimately of the nation-state.[68]

In a quite typical fashion, the melodramatic pamphlet titled "The Truth about the Regional Leaders of the Iquique Socialist Party of Chile" used gendered moral precepts to establish the political ascendancy of one man, and his followers, over another man. Written and published by the local Socialist leader Mario Mallol Pemjean, this pamphlet employed potent moral arguments to defame and dishonor Mallol's political adversary, Héctor Portillo, also a member of the Socialist Party of Chile. By exposing the despicable manner in which the traitor Portillo had treated his wife, Mallol—who had himself been removed from his position as regional secretary of the party as a result of Portillo's maneuvering—set out to tarnish the reputation of the man who had overthrown him. "His terrible egotism," Mallol wrote of Portillo,

> led him to commit the worst crime a "responsible" man can commit. He abandoned his sick wife for another woman. That *compañera* whom we all knew as loyal, patient, devoted, and intelligent. Untiring *compañera* of his disastrous days. His spiritual director who alone brought him to the seat of honor he once occupied. Magnificent example of a proletarian woman.
>
> I do not question Portillo's right to have or not another woman: but it is not possible to think that he might have her so as to abandon her [his wife] when she most needed him. Her illness was the product of her struggle alongside her husband, and it would have been logical at the start, when there was still time, for her husband to provide her with the small comforts that his salary as an employee of the Caja de Seguro Obrero in Valdivia allowed, but not only did he did not provide her with them, but he also denied her any economic aid.[69]

Not only had Portillo taken a lover and denied his wife economic sustenance, Mallol asserted in the pamphlet, but he had done so at the precise moment in which his wife, María, who suffered from tuberculosis, most needed his help. Mallol further noted that the "evil" Portillo had advertised María's ills at party meetings to extract economic assistance from party members. Mallol himself had bought medicines for Portillo's wife, and other comrades had found Portillo a job in the state Institute of Mining Development (Instituto de Fomento Minero), offered him their homes, and lent him the considerable sum of 4,000 pesos. But, Mallol stated with incredulity, Portillo refused to make the trip to a tuberculosis sanatorium in Vicuña, claiming that Mallol only wanted to distance him from local politics by sending him there. Instead, Portillo used the loan offered by his comrades to buy himself clothes, fix up his house, and have a good time, failing to take his wife to Vicuña, where she might profit from the beneficial air, or to place his daughters in a boarding school, where they would be spared the possibility of being infected with tuberculosis. Finally, Mallol lamented, despite the objections of Mallol and María, Portillo had compelled his wife to make a trip with him to a political event in the pampa and forced her to ride in an open truck, thereby causing her eventual death.

In Mallol's rendering, Portillo had betrayed the working class through his disloyalty to his upstanding "proletarian" wife and therefore could not lay legitimate claim to power. That Portillo had misspent funds disbursed by the Radical Party for an electoral campaign, or engaged in futile skirmishes with the police, also merited Mallol's disapproval, but it was precisely the way Portillo's political mistakes coincided with his personal errors that allowed Mallol to reveal Portillo's essential villainy. In his attempts to regain political credibility, Mallol tried to prove his own moral rectitude and Portillo's degeneration as a husband and family head. In turn, Portillo questioned Mallol's intentions by saying that Mallol's political ambitions, and not his concern for María, led him to arrange to send the couple to Vicuña.

As squabbles between Socialists and Communists and within each of these parties escalated after 1946, leading to fist fights and several deaths, leftists frequently used moral accusations metaphorically in disputes that, on the surface, had little to do with sexual honorableness or duty to family. The Left's regulation of gender and sexuality within working-class family and community, described above, involved negotiation among numerous participants and therefore depended on and reinforced more polysemous definitions of gender. When leftists used gender metaphorically, however, they insisted on rigid, dualistic definitions. Gender classifications rooted in heterosexual norms and Manichaean moral categories (good/bad, honorable/disreputable) thus served to validate opposing positions in contexts in which negotiation seemed impossible. The dual nature of the categories employed—neither gender nor moral categories seemed ambiguous—validated the notion that finding a middle ground was impossible.

Already in 1935 the Communist Youth organ *Tribuna Juvenil* had found no better way to discredit the Chilean fascist leader Jorge González von Marees than to call him a homosexual.[70] But with increasing frequency in the 1940s leftists saw their *compañeros* and coworkers as the immoral "others." Bernardo Ibáñez's Socialists invoked their own propriety against hysterical and therefore womanly Communist traitors who tried to undermine the unity of the working class by dividing the union movement: "[W]orking men who consciously produce for the good of their homes and the nation well know that their [Communist traitors'] preaching is just the same old story, that they are *vendepatrias*, international spies, who care more about the future of men who come from other lands than about that of Chilean workers and who, as a consequence, emit hysterical cries that are worthy of repulsion."[71] This womanly behavior, Ibáñez suggested, was a breach of class loyalty and an act of treason to the nation. Similarly, Herminio Tamoya, a leader of railway workers in San Bernardo and a former Communist, left the party, he said, because of the Communists' "political and moral impotence and cowardliness." Communists were not real men, he implied. Communists in turn accused Tamoya of "humiliating" himself before the bosses, summoning a veiled reference to homosexuality to cast doubt on his manly stature.[72] Using a similar rhetorical strategy, the Communist *Principios* repudiated vice to debunk the internal faction of Luis Reinoso. Relying on the fact that readers would clearly identify drinking and marital infidelities as immoral and unmanly, the magazine told readers that Reinoso's followers had attempted to create decomposition within the party by plying leaders with alcohol and having "their women" seduce militants to generate problems within Communists' families.[73]

In moral disputes such as these, sexual and political legitimacy seemed inextricable. Thus Socialist Party members who held positions within the state during the popular-front period were frequently attacked by rivals who disclosed their sexually dishonorable acts in order to question their legitimacy. Power corrupted, adversaries proclaimed, by provoking the political and sexual cravings of those who exercised it. An article in *Combate* referred, for example, to the "uncontrolled appetites" of Socialists who accepted ministerial posts in Aguirre Cerda's government. Another article in the same newspaper censured a Socialist who had punched his wife when she discovered him in a restaurant with his lover. After the incident, the article informed readers, the poor wife had tried to kill herself. But for the article's author, who began by noting that the man in question was a high government functionary, the lesson of this escapade was that those in power were sexually corrupt. "How much longer will we have to tolerate functionaries like this?" he asked. Similarly invoking notions of sexual legitimacy to buttress its bids for representation, the Ibáñez CTCh defined itself as legitimate because it defended the working class without "bastard capitulations." And claiming that capacity and moral austerity were the "essential ingredients of socialism," Socialist faction leader César Godoy Urrutia called on his followers to extirpate "bourgeois sensuality" and "bastard utilitarianism" from their ranks and to select members who had a public and private "moral rigidity."[74]

Moral disputes thus became manly duels in which many men might participate but not all could win. Diverse Left groups rooted their own legitimacy in a gendered honorableness, and branded their opponents as disreputable. While these duels of virility were openly used to discredit purportedly unmanly men, they also underscored the fact that, in struggles for power, women's honorableness did not matter. Irma Moreno, the first woman to be elected to the Central Committee of the Socialist Party, acutely understood the ways a masculine code of morality signaled leadership as male and denied women positions of political importance. If she had identified herself as a wife and mother, Moreno believed, she would not have attained power. Only by acting like a man in politics, at work, and at home— and for Moreno that meant not marrying, not having children, being "independent"—could she gain leadership positions. "Look," she explained, "I think I have been very independent, *hija*. I could never have put up with someone asking me where I was going. I would have thrown a fit. I was always the man in the house. [I supported] my mother, my sisters. Later, I was a leader [*dirigente*]." As in politics, at work Moreno was often the only woman around, and she had to assert herself. During the Popular Unity years (1970–73), she was head of the personnel department of the national railway and she had several men under her direction: "I had to insult them, or they would have mopped the floor with me. So all that makes you develop a personality, *hija*, that won't accept being bossed around, won't even accept being asked where you're going or what you're going to do with your money. Well, that's a marriage that won't last longer than a month, at least in my case. That's why I never married."[75] While Moreno did not openly challenge the association of leadership with the traits of a good family man, she did exert her own right to be manly. Like Socialist and Communist infighters, she insulted her adversaries.

Political disputes that were enacted as battles over masculinity and waged by men opened the possibility of encoding consensus and agreement as feminine. Applying just such a strategy, women labor leaders suggested that women activists had a special role to play in reconciling warring factions of the labor movement: "Unionized women, leaders and followers, have an extremely important role to play in setting the definitive course of [labor] movements, because it is in their hands to form a more human consciousness among their fathers, brothers, children, etc., who might then consider their *compañeros* at work, regardless of their political or social ideologies, as individuals of the human species and not hurl themselves at them like wolves hungry for blood."[76] Similarly, a call to unity among municipal blue-collar workers suggested that the union should act as a loving mother who shelters and brings together all her children, "without caring whether they are good or bad, if they are 'Moors' or 'Christians.' " "Let us elevate our organization," the article urged union members, "dislodging from her breast hatreds that should not exist."[77] These cries for tolerance notwithstanding, the unity and cohesion of the Left was often depicted as the result of masculine discipline, not feminine comprehension. Despite the Left's ability to incorporate and reconcile competing pressures, at times a vanguardist, masculine rigidity prevailed.

MORAL VANGUARDS AND THE
QUESTION OF REPRESENTATION

A central aim of Left morality was to form socialist militants into a moral vanguard, a group of enlightened representatives of the working class. The moral purity of leftists would augment the prestige of the Left and attract members to Left organizations, socialist leaders asserted. And as members of that vanguard, each Socialist or Communist militant would irradiate socialist precepts, teaching the masses through his or her example. While honesty, transparency, sensitivity to constituents, and loyalty to class over political ambition were also vaunted traits of upstanding socialists, a moral correctness based in sexual and familial norms was a paramount characteristic of the vanguard. As control commission secretary Galo González explained in 1938, Communist militants had the obligation to win "a solid moral prestige for our party among the laboring masses. The actions and the life of each Communist should convincingly demonstrate that the Communist Party is in reality the vanguard of the working class and the people. Disorderly lives, dissolute habits, immorality and alcoholism are far from the order, sobriety and honesty that are the habit of the vanguard."[78] If Communist militants in fact proved to be morally superior to ordinary Chileans, González suggested, Communist influence would swell and Communist leadership of the working class would be legitimated.

Although the Socialist Party did not strictly enforce adherence to moral norms among its members, it did ascribe to the notion that the party should be a moral vanguard. "To outsiders, you are the Socialist Party," a local party newspaper told militants. "If they see that you have bad habits [malas costumbres], lack sobriety or honorableness in your ideas or in your actions, they will say: 'See? Those are Socialists!' And the dishonor falls on all the members of the party. A Socialist therefore not only has the obligation of having good habits [buenas costumbres], but also of demanding that others show them."[79] Socialist Party members also used morality to establish their primacy.

Communist propaganda dealt with dissent of all kinds by claiming that bourgeois or imperialist outsiders infiltrated the Communist community and fomented immorality within it. In response to provocations such as these, Communist publications suggested, the vanguard should close ranks, expel intruders, and insure its own virile "purity": "Faced with the increased penetration of the corrupting propaganda of imperialist forces, the Communist Youth must maintain an active vigilance within its ranks, against the infiltration of foreign influences and elements of all types, whether these be vice-ridden individuals, 'Don Juans,' or the bearers of enemy ideological slogans, conscious that we thus defend the purity of our political line and the Communists' tasks."[80] As the tone of this pronouncement indicated, there was little, if anything, to negotiate. Communist militants might learn to act correctly but had no role to play in determining what was correct.

To guarantee unity, adherents were expected to follow the dictates of morally upstanding leaders who knew what was good and true. References to leaders as father figures underlined the vanguard's superiority and reinforced hierarchy. Thus the CTCh lauded its secretary-general Bernardo Ibáñez as the working class's "first moral authority and the best teacher [maestro] and director of its destiny." Similarly, a publication of the union at Cristalerías Chile told union delegates that as organized workers their duty was to "show a greater culture and morality to the personnel of your section; to be educated and reserved when you express yourself." The publication of a Socialist Party splinter group attributed the Socialist Party's lack of "cohesion and conscious discipline," its disintegration and demoralization, to the fact that its leaders had "lost ascendancy and moral authority." To avoid similar problems, jefes of the Socialist militia were instructed not to allow their underlings to sow discord.[81]

Elsewhere, leaders maintained that the imperatives of class unity demanded that those who were not yet enlightened avoid questioning their superiors. Branding dissent as gossip—*copucheo* or *pelambre*—other leaders vilified as immoral those who did not agree with their dictates. In *El Despertar Minero*, a union leader wrote that "*compañeros* should not—if they are honorable and sincere with themselves—annihilate the morality of those who defend and represent them; that is behavior worthy only of perverts and moral criminals."[82] A Left newspaper from the small town of Illapel concurred: "Gossip is a stain both here and there, a bitter characteristic of ours like drunkenness, syphilis or irresponsibility. . . . Gossip is all-powerful: it creates and destroys friendships, sullies reputations, rolls in the dice at canteens, disguises itself as sweet interest, enters into even the most Christian bedrooms, claims victories, in short, dominates, binds, reigns."[83] In this view, dissent as gossip became immoral tyranny.

Grassroots activists who acted independently of leaders often demonstrated their class belonging in less orderly and legitimate ways, provoking discomfort among male leaders who labeled them spontaneous or undisciplined. Perhaps because women were furthest from the manly virtue demanded of leaders they were not infrequently at the head of unruly gestures. Women in the textile industry, for instance, showed an exuberant militancy in strike movements, leading anxious male leaders to tag them as "terrible." And when, in 1943, male leaders boasted about the "discipline" that they had maintained as "responsible leaders" of a Beneficencia workers' strike, the possibility and threat of a disorderly throng made up of the largely female workforce loomed in the background. Although male leaders did not disown these oftentimes combative actions, the manifestations clearly made them uneasy. Nevertheless, unlike the rival male leaders discussed above who disputed leadership of the working class on the same terms and in the same language as vanguard leaders, the raucous masses who broke from regular routes of representation were not expelled from Left organizations or branded immoral. Rather, leaders tried to tame them. Less legitimate expressions of class identity continued to surface in an unresolved tension with more honorable venues.[84]

Leaders who urged activists not to break ranks and to follow orders nevertheless insisted that followers should consent to norms: "We obey because those orders are in line with our revolutionary postulates, with our revolutionary consciousness," Juan Godoy maintained.[85] However, the double character—both symbolic and political—of representation and leadership made calls to consent tautological. The same leaders who asked for freely given adherence, arguing that there was a shared "revolutionary consciousness," in fact largely defined the content of that "consciousness." The notion that those who were not members of the vanguard should consent to moral standards did imply an opening, a recognition that the legitimation of leaders demanded at least a degree of dialogue between representatives and represented. However, that search for consent did not necessarily lead to the construction of more democratic forms of representation. The dualistic nature of gendered moral precepts helped make finding a middle, negotiated, ground more difficult.

CONCLUSION

By laying claim to moral propriety, Left political parties and unions, and their leaders, commanded both symbolic and political aspects of representation.[86] Because of their moral refinement, leftists argued, they could properly define the contents of working-class identity and communicate the interests of the working class within the public political arena. According to Socialists and Communists, it was not simply their ability to adequately reflect or transmit the already delineated interests or demands of a predetermined constituency that sanctioned their mandate to represent the working class. Nor did they theorize their legitimacy as emanating only from a process of dialogue and conversation with those they represented. Rather, they suggested that the moral propriety they embodied and irradiated vindicated their representation of working-class interests. Although the moral bases of bids for representation did not make that process itself inherently less democratic or open to contestation, by building and reproducing very ingrained and widely shared beliefs regarding gendered propriety, leftists solidified their leadership. The invocation of a gendered morality that emanated from purportedly natural differences between the sexes and natural sexual practices tended to make socialist leadership also seem natural. Just as important, the Left presented moral standards as reflecting the imperatives of rationality and control and harnessed gendered elements of the discourse of progress to cement their authority.[87]

Left political parties' appropriation of morality limited other autonomous efforts to generate leadership and to define the class community and its moral norms. But grassroots participants nevertheless could and did question—or at least disturb—the legitimacy of leaders and of their postulates. Leaders' attempts to avoid challenges from below revealed their belief that dissent was a real possibility. And in unruly street demonstrations and strikes, grassroots activists continued to act defiantly despite the particular dictates of class unity and organization. Moreover, the Left's desire to win allies made it indulge the needs and desires of grassroots activists on occasion, and ultimately forced it to articulate sometimes divergent norms in order to consolidate and expand the class community, which it also tried to define and limit. Its acceptance of both more conservative and more libertarian sexual and familial norms, described at the beginning of this chapter, testified to the possibility of articulating a hegemonic bloc that was more plural and less restrictive.[88] Crosscutting alliances, which at times threatened to snatch working-class men and women away from leftist organizations or to create other venues of representation, also forced leftists to accommodate. And, ultimately, if many working-class men and women agreed to participate in the leftist organizations despite their continuing if unvoiced disagreement and despite the sometimes authoritarian tendencies of Left leadership, it was also because they recognized that Left leaders were more democratic than the capitalist outsiders, who indeed had a much greater ability to silence them. Those who "consented" by participating were not victims fooled by an all-powerful vanguard. Nor were those who hushed criticism simply intimidated. Participants calculated, weighing the possibility of alternative alliances. And, along with their sometimes bothersome political "superiors," they dreamed.[89]

Vanguardist conceptions of politics implied that an enlightened elite that was in many senses exterior to or distinct from common men and women could impose its norms on the masses. While some leftists clearly ascribed to such a view, at the same time they worked hegemonically, incorporating elements of popular "common sense." Vanguardism was never absolute. In such a political context, determining what norms were imposed from the "outside" and which were felt as internal by any given group is nearly impossible, and perhaps futile. Popular culture, in its multiple manifestations, was not the same as socialist culture. Nor were the moral norms of leftists exactly the same as those advocated from within the state by political elites. However, these were not separate spheres of cultural production and reproduction either, and the circuits through which normative prescriptions passed from one instance to the other were complex. It was not simply a matter of whether grassroots activists consented or not to the precepts of their leaders, but rather a question of who most forcefully determined symbolic aspects of representation and how. For each act of communication, no matter how authoritarian, implied a transformation and renewal of gendered moral precepts. With fewer and less effective instruments of repression and discipline, leftist institutions had to rely on more gentle means of insinuation and persuasion, means that opened the door to negotiation. Yet insofar as Left leaders often had greater power than those they tried to cajole and influence—and most men had more power than most women—acts of consent were never fully noncoercive. Even if a social actor might modify or choose, his or her ability to transform was always circumscribed, his or her options limited. When leftists invoked gendered ideals and associated notions of progress and national well-being foundationally, they restricted more democratic forms of participation. When they refigured male abuse as bourgeois vice and depicted men as defenders of helpless women, they reinforced the protagonism of men and undermined that of women.

Working-class women and men did not always see interventions in apparently personal matters as intrusions. To be sure, *compañeros*, like social workers and public health physicians, could be meddling and bothersome, their recommendations like sermons. Yet despite an often tedious and brutal outside world of power and exploitation, the home was not simply a comforting and tranquil refuge from daily confrontations with unscrupulous merchants and demanding bosses. Ties of kinship and acquaintance were marked too by economic and sexual conflict. Prevalent strife between husbands and wives, neighbors, parents and children, or sexual partners could not always be resolved to the satisfaction of all, or any, of those involved. Consequently, one or another party might welcome or seek the help of a more powerful outsider. Given the limited nature of local community intervention in family matters in Chile in the period under consideration—neither literary texts, nor press accounts, nor oral testimony, nor social workers' reports recorded much neighborly help—the state and political parties, which represented community as nation or class, played a preponderant regulatory role. Unfortunately, those who were in subordinate positions often lost control of how regulatory mediations were carried out.

Still, the interventions of state agents and political parties in matters of family and sexuality were not simply totalitarian impulses of the powerful—although some leaders may have dreamed of such total control. Rather, these intercessions were negotiated alliances among unequal associates who argued over the gendered coordinates of class and nation. What happened day to day in the intimacy of friendships, families, and sexual liaisons mattered to those who exercised great power. It also mattered to those who wished to exercise more of it.

chapter seven

IN THE INTERSTICES

Democracy, Representation, and the Women's Movement

As previous chapters have argued, welfare professionals played a crucial role within state apparatuses and political movements and powerfully shaped gendered notions of citizenship. Gendered forms of popular mobilization in turn influenced professional and political elites. The forms of citizenship and representation available to working-class men and women therefore depended on the normative gender identities proposed by socialist and nonsocialist elites, on those elites' use of scientific discourses, on the pressure nonelites exerted on professionals, and on the degree of elite susceptibility to subaltern influences. Chapter 4 showed that popular-front leaders and physicians allied with respectable male workers and staked a claim to science, positioning it in opposition to prior forms of charitable and clientelistic assistance. Women professionals and feminist leaders also attempted to marshal discourses of science and professionalization to augment their own influence and better women's social, political, and economic standing. But progressive feminist intellectuals failed to implement their reform program, in large part because they threatened the authority of male popular-front leaders and challenged male prerogative within the family. As a result, welfare for the indigent remained more individualized and charity-oriented. Social workers continued to intervene in families to help women and to proffer aid to mothers who could not rely on the economic support of a male breadwinner. But because these forms of welfare were never considered entitlements, they depended on the goodwill of professionals who resented excessive demands and needed to be charmed or wheedled into providing aid. Under these circumstances, women in need could not easily press for more horizontal relations with their potential allies in the professions.

Leadership of the broad, cross-class women's movement that is the subject of this chapter was for the most part in the hands of ambitious professionals. Like other members of the middle class, these feminist professionals saw themselves as more cultured than women of the popular classes. Like most welfare professionals, they wielded their access to knowledge and their personal connections as state agents to establish hierarchy between themselves and their working-class allies. The professional training of feminist leaders as well as their class position therefore encouraged clientelistic relations within the women's movement. In particular, the social welfare activities of women's organizations, which are examined in the first section of this chapter, bred paternalistic relations that tended to neutralize working-class women's agency and demands.

Progressive feminist leaders within MEMCh attempted to establish more horizontal relations within the women's movement (see Chapter 3). As this chapter shows, they also eschewed clientelism. But the MEMCh project foundered, and MEMCh eventually succumbed to both external pressures and its own internal contradictions. Within the broader women's movement of which MEMCh was a part, the contradictions between progressive and moderate feminists and between women of different classes were even more acute. The struggle for women's suffrage did momentarily generate a more democratic discourse of representation within the women's movement. That discourse, which is discussed in the second half of this chapter, built on the long-standing efforts of progressive memchistas. It valued dialogue and sought to account for differences among women, among men, and between men and women. However, as the political climate became more polarized and MEMCh itself fragmented and dissolved, the feminist attempt to articulate a theory and practice of democratic participation failed.

"OBRA SOCIAL EN BIEN DE LAS CLASES TRABAJADORAS": WELFARE, CLIENTELISM, AND THE WOMEN'S MOVEMENT

Political connections allowed a small number of feminist activists to secure important positions within the state. Besides naming Elena Yávar to head the DGAS's social service division, popular-front governments appointed Clara Williams as head of the Asociación de Dueñas de Casa, Cora Cid as editor of the CSO publication *Acción Social*, Graciela Contreras de Schnake as mayor of Santiago, and María Marchant as intendant of Santiago. These prominent women acknowledged their emergence from the women's movement and used their influence to implement policies favorable to women. Contreras, for instance, set up a communal laundry where laundresses and housewives could have access to hot water and automatic dryers. She also inaugurated a boardinghouse for women university students, launched a farmer's market to provide cheaper foodstuffs to shoppers, and took on the problem of prostitution. MEMCh hailed Marchant's appointment as a recognition of women's achievements and expressed the belief that she would use her position to "solve problems with feminine criteria." However, despite these activists' commitment to women, their rise to power depended mostly on their loyalties to popular-front parties: Yávar and Williams had personal and family ties to the Radical Party, and Cid headed both the Radical Women's Assembly and Aguirre Cerda's women's campaign committee. Socialist Party member Contreras had held a leadership position on that committee as well. Marchant had close ties to the Communist Party.[1]

Higher education provided feminist activists a more reliable avenue of influence, one that did not depend on their showing allegiance to male-dominated political parties. Professional training augmented political and employment opportunities—often the two went together—and in particular it increased women's possibility of finding positions within an expanding state bureaucracy. It also gave them a platform from which to assist other women. As social workers, health professionals, and educators, middle-class women found employment within the state and used their positions to help other women. In fact, the overlap between women's professional organizations and the women's movement was perhaps more significant than the overlap between political parties and feminist groups. Within FEChIF, the umbrella organization established in 1944, women's professional guilds were an overwhelming presence. Some of the professional organizations affiliated with FEChIF, such as the Association of University Women, broadly grouped women together. Others organized women in all-female occupations such as nursing, midwifery, or social work. Still others were made up of female professionals in areas such as law, dentistry, education, or medicine.[2]

Beyond this organizational convergence between professional groups and the women's movement, the concerns of FEChIF resonated with those of the welfare professions. On the one hand, professionals explicitly sought to augment their jurisdiction through their participation in groups like FEChIF.

Social workers and midwives who attended FEChIF's 1947 congress pushed through several resolutions aimed at increasing their professional authority. On the other hand, welfare professionals, and social workers in particular, sought, like women's organizations, to assist women and elevate their standing within the family. Acknowledging the expertise of social workers and nurses and their interest in helping other women, the head of FEChIF's standing committee on "the defense of women," Communist Julieta Campusano, solicited social workers' participation in that commission. Similarly, Graciela Lacoste, a participant in the 1947 FEChIF congress, noted the usefulness of the contributions of social workers who took part in the proceedings. Selva Saavedra, who directed a technical school for girls, likewise told delegates to the congress that she had come to selflessly "gather your gracious petitions."[3] Women's organizations thus reaffirmed the expertise and leadership of professional women and, consequently, reproduced class hierarchies.

To extend their own influence and assist working-class women, professionals within the women's movement sought to expand state welfare. A 1939 project for state welfare presented to MEMCh by memchista Pina Venegas was representative of the kind of state assistance promoted by women's organizations. Pina Venegas, who worked in the cultural secretariat of the Ministry of Finance, suggested that the state set up an agency for "social assistance and defense of the race with its own funds, ample powers, a well-informed technical board, and an efficient team of social workers." This agency's principal goal would be aiding impoverished mothers and children. Drawing on prevalent notions of racial and class uplift and popular-front beliefs about state intervention, Pina Venegas suggested that aid to the indigent should not be "abandoned to private charity." Recognizing that men often shirked their responsibilities to children, she recommended that the agency be partially financed by a progressive tax on men above the age of eighteen who did not have children.[4]

At its Second National Congress, MEMCh set out its position on social welfare, proposing the rationalization of state services and advocating a strong state role in executing and overseeing welfare programs. In this, MEMCh repeated the state-centered view of professionalization that was prevalent among physicians and that would later became the banner of the Círculo de Estudios Sociales. "Social assistance is different from charity and philanthropy because of its scientific and methodical character," read the convocation to the congress. "MEMCh believes that social assistance is a preferential obligation of the State and that the State should broach the Study and solution of social problems, accepting the contributions of private social assistance if they fall within the outlines of the integral planning that the State sets out."[5] In making such pronouncements, MEMCh echoed broader discourses about charity and state intervention and tried to inscribe the relations between women professionals and clients within broader notions of rights and state provision of welfare. In 1940, when efforts to reform social work as a field and social work practices within the state had not begun in earnest, memchistas had already outlined a program of professionalization and state reform.

More generally, to provoke advantageous state intervention, activists in MEMCh and FEChIF lobbied, marched, wrote letters, and drew up plans. MEMCh claimed at least partial credit for the passage of school lunch legislation, for the Comisariato decree that named baby formula a subsistence good, for the unification of services to children under the umbrella of the Dirección General de Protección a la Infancia y Adolescencia, and for the work-related reforms described in Chapter 2. MEMCh also promoted state-run collective homes for single and widowed mothers and summer camps for vagrant children. In addition, it called for a nonpunitive state effort to reduce prostitution, rejecting sanitary and police measures. FEChIF proposed similar measures, calling for laws in favor of mothers and children.[6]

At the local level, professional women worked together with grassroots activists to expand state services, lobbying municipal governments and national agencies on behalf of local women. For instance in Lota, a traditional stronghold of working-class organizations and the Communist Party, members of the local FEChIF-affiliated Committee for the Defense of Women and Children participated in the Comité de Subsistencias, an organization that capitalized on women's long-standing struggles around subsistence issues in the coal-mining region. The Committee for the Defense of Women succeeded in getting a health post in the city and medical instruments needed by local midwives for emergencies. It also forced the local municipality to fund a midwife to serve indigent women. As a member of Lota's comité de adelanto, the committee's president traveled to Santiago to secure money for public works: a building for the artisans' school; work on area streets; water distribution; and the construction of a slaughterhouse.[7]

Although aiming to provide women and children with material assistance dispensed by the state and, in some cases, to rationalize welfare, feminist lobbying for these state services did not constitute a concerted reform effort. Indeed many proposed measures replicated the piecemeal approach of charity work. Some reflected the paternalism of their sponsors. Few advanced notions of entitlement. And though most women reformers understood how women's needs reflected their subordinate position within family and workplace, the legal reforms they proposed did not consistently seek to democratize family relations. Even FEChIF had to concede that most initiatives did not get at the heart of women's problems: "There are laws that protect Mothers and Children," a FEChIF publication noted, "but there are no laws that stop men from exploiting women."[8]

Caffarena and her more radical allies in MEMCh, by contrast, not only proposed reforms that confronted women's subordination within the family and workplace but also advocated more horizontal relations among women. With a deeper, more political commitment to working-class women and feminism, they rejected clientelism, casework, and influence peddling, all of which they believed vitiated the democratic system. In a 1992 interview, Caffarena reported that because she had worked on Aguirre Cerda's campaign, many people assumed she might help them get government positions. "I didn't like that," Caffarena reported. "That is the truth, and I became sort of allergic." In fact, unlike party militants like Contreras and Cid, Caffarena and other progressive feminists declined political appointments to preserve their autonomy. MEMCh leaders did serve in advisory roles within state agencies. Besides working free of charge in the ill-fated Division of Specialities, which attempted to stimulate home industry among women, Caffarena and memchista Aída Yávar (sister of Elena Yávar and prominent member of the Radical Party) served on the board of the Consejo de Defensa del Niño. But despite a limited participation in the administration of government programs and MEMCh's professed adherence to the popular-front project, memchistas fought for their independence. Although MEMCh's autonomy from the state, avidly pursued by Caffarena and her allies, stimulated more horizontal ties between middle-class professionals and working-class women and allowed the organization to pursue its feminist platform, the search for political independence in many ways contradicted the social welfare objectives of the broader women's movement and even of MEMCh as a whole. Caffarena would later regret that because of her reputation as an extremist she was denied opportunities in government service. "In reality," she lamented in 1992, "my own capacities were wasted somewhat, because at that time I was very studious and hardworking." Indeed, by refusing to engage in grubby politics, Caffarena may have opened the door to moderate feminists such as Mandujano and Williams, who approached the project of organizing women with a more professionally inclined, paternalistic bent and who eagerly sought state support for their projects. MEMCh delineated a political style that ran contrary to prevalent practices, without having the political clout to significantly alter those patterns. Personally and politically, progressive feminists may have lost as much as they gained.[9]

Given that the approach of progressive feminists within MEMCh failed to take hold and that—at least prior to the formation of the Asociación de Dueñas de Casa—other activists achieved only very limited access to the state, women's organizations spent a good deal of time providing direct aid to women in need. Many of these private welfare activities closely resembled traditional casework or charity. MEMCh Valparaíso, for example, took upon itself the task of visiting sick children and the indigent and providing them financial assistance. One of its members gave the considerable sum of 2,500 pesos to a sick cancer patient. FEChIF projected setting up its own maternal refuge, and its Santiago provincial committee made up twenty baskets of goods for babies at the San Ignacio Mothers' Home. The FEChIF branch in La Serena collected money for the children's sanatorium in nearby Vicuña and for unemployed road construction workers. In addition, it sponsored talks by doctors on eugenics and tuberculosis.[10] Beneficiaries wrung maximum advantage from professional women's casework and charitable undertakings. But localized social assistance did not provide working-class women with a sense of entitlement. Nor did it confront and challenge their subordination as women.

Some social assistance efforts were nonetheless more empowering to beneficiaries. In Santiago, for example, MEMCh and FEChIF set up free legal, health, and social service clinics. To the extent that these clinics provided education regarding legal and health privileges and assisted clients in claiming state benefits, they were part of larger campaigns to extend rights and not simply palliative aid to women. Similarly, in La Serena, FEChIF planned to set up a nursery for women workers, and MEMCh Santiago supported a plan to do the same in Santiago's Vega Central. Taken within the broader context of feminist campaigns around day care, these centers were not simply isolated efforts. In addition, literacy campaigns carried out by MEMCh and FEChIF gave women a personal and political tool and helped them qualify to vote in municipal elections.[11]

In Santiago, MEMCh Providencia's plan to build housing for area residents from a makeshift shantytown marked a novel attempt to help the community organize itself. MEMCh members Eliana Bronfman, a law student, María

Astica, a social worker, and Victoria Miranda helped 115 families from the area overcome the legal and bureaucratic obstacles involved in setting up a cooperative, buying land, building their own houses, setting up schools, and securing pavement, water, and electricity. Yet the MEMCh members clearly wanted the members of the Cooperativa MEMCh to become active participants in the process. Bronfman in particular repudiated personalistic and paternalistic relations between MEMCh leaders and the *pobladores* and criticized the working- and the middle-class women who participated in clientelistic relations. Bronfman complained that many members of the MEMCh cooperative simply believed that a few well-intentioned ladies were helping them out, that they had no idea that MEMCh was behind the project, and that they were just out to get a piece of land. Certain of her fellow *memchistas*, she protested, encouraged this attitude. "Leaders," she retorted, "should orient, direct and challenge the group, but never replicate the errors and vices of the masses, since the pernicious effects on the organization of a social group of personalistic attitudes is overwhelmingly recognized." Bronfman's approach apparently took hold. Once the *pobladores* had moved onto their newly acquired land, they developed structures of community governance, and *memchistas* continued managing only the legal and financial aspects of the project that required specific expertise.[12]

In short, certain welfare activities arranged by women's organizations, especially those that emphasized self-help, allowed working-class women (and in the case of MEMCh Providencia, men as well) to gain knowledge that allowed them to intervene on their own behalf. Demands for state intervention also enabled working-class women to begin to conceive of state aid as a right. By 1948, for example, members of MEMCh Ricaventura manifested an ample knowledge of their "rights" as consumers, a knowledge they gained in part by participating first in autonomous consumer organizing and then in the Asociación de Dueñas de Casa. When local authorities refused to give proper identification cards to MEMCh members who had been appointed as Comisariato inspectors, *memchistas* complained to fellow MEMCh members in Santiago saying, "[The shopkeepers] provoke us and send us to the Union to lodge complaints, they know that we don't have anyone to defend us, they cheat us on the weight, and we don't achieve anything by talking to them, we suffer the most horrible humiliation but we can take a lot. We have faith that this will stop one day and Justice will arrive, then we will have a Free and Truly Democratic Chile and a Home for our children and mothers who today roam without Peace or a roof over their heads."[13] While suggesting that the women's movement should defend them, these women saw their political activities as part of a broader struggle for democracy. They portrayed popular-front promises of "shelter" and assistance to mothers and children as part of the construction of a free and democratic nation. They were not simply calling for charitable assistance.

However, as the above example suggests, working-class activists in the women's movement did not shun help from their more well connected associates. When Elvira Reyes retired as secretary-general of MEMCh Providencia, for example, she expressed gratitude to the professional women in the group. "So once again," she wrote, "I sincerely thank that Great Institution, the Central MEMCh, an altruistic Institution involved in working for the Social Good [*Obra Social*] of the laboring classes." *Memchistas* from the nitrate mining office of Ricaventura—including Gobinda Villalobos, who had personally met members of MEMCh Santiago when she traveled to FEChIF's 1947 congress—wrote frequently to MEMCh Santiago asking for favors. In early 1948, Villalobos asked Santiago MEMCh leaders to help secure a pension for an acquaintance whose son had had an accident, and around the same time Villalobos's fellow MEMCh members wrote to MEMCh Santiago about a local eleventh grade teacher who had married one of his students. Could MEMCh Santiago help them get a woman teacher to replace him, they asked? Besides asking for intervention in these kinds of matters, the Ricaventura committee also used MEMCh Santiago as a source of information about their rights. "*Compañeras*," they wrote, "we would be grateful if you could send us some propaganda pamphlets so that the new members can see what Organized women [have obtained] and what we are about to lose, such as maternity care for the wives of Insured Workers, and Infant Care through the age of two."[14]

At times, working-class activists who sought the assistance of professional elites were distrustful and took measures to ensure that political mediators properly represented their interests. The members of MEMCh Ricaventura who asked MEMCh Santiago to send them propaganda pamphlets in 1948 also sent along newspaper clippings that described local conditions. And they insisted that MEMCh Santiago send them the written resolutions of the FEChIF congress Villalobos had attended. With a certain suspicion, they wrote, "*Compañeras*, in closing we say that we await the resolutions of the Congress because we are going on four months and we hope this delay does not put in jeopardy the conclusions that were honestly approved. We expect them without modifications that might disavow the great sacrifice we made to arrive at that great tourney [congress], of such importance to Chilean Women."[15]

These women, who indeed made great sacrifices to attend a congress in which they hoped not only to learn but also to be heard, needed organizations like MEMCh and FEChIF and their middle-class, professional leaders. Many middle-class women could not escape the lure of becoming protectors or transcend charitable or casework approaches. The reticence of Caffarena, Bronfman, and other *memchistas* who chafed under insistent demands for "favors" was exceptional. Yet working-class women, who could extract real benefits from clientelistic and paternalistic practices, did not always escape the lure of protection either—whether that protection was provided by male political elites, by their husbands or fathers, or by middle-class feminists. Although the utilitarian needs of working-class women made them accept paternalistic relations, those needs did not necessarily lead them to a complete abrogation of their right to autonomy and vigilance. Nor did their identification with the broader projects of "Chilean Women" make them quiet followers. Like professional women, they both shared in and attempted to alter paternalistic patterns of aid.[16]

For a number of reasons, those patterns should not simply be considered "maternalist." Undoubtedly, there was an element of shared maternal identity among women, and professionals mobilized that identity to augment their own political power. Had they not shared that identity, the visit of movement members to a maternity would not make sense, nor would proposals for maternal refuges, for school lunches, and for the recognition of baby formula as a subsistence good. Yet MEMCh leaders such as Caffarena usually combined calls to help mothers and children with a recognition of women's right to work in order to support their offspring. Frequently, women reformers also framed efforts to help children as national campaigns in which men should collaborate. Perhaps most important, women's claims to leadership rested more on professional qualifications than on a maternal identity. Aída Yávar interpellated women, saying: "No one knows your suffering, no one knows more closely than I do, for professional reasons, your misery."[17]

Feminism, in short, was a diverse movement that utilized many distinct practices. Caffarena and the more radical *memchistas* insisted on developing more horizontal ties with working-class women. They bristled under the calls for material help of MEMCh's working-class members and used their personal contacts sparingly. Wanting their influence to come from a vibrant movement, they refused political appointments that bestowed authority from above. But by the late 1940s, these progressive feminists had lost out to a less principled, more practical group of middle-class professionals. Those moderate feminists had long used their access to the state and to the private assistance bestowed by women's groups to enhance their authority. In the repressive days following González Videla's crackdown on the Communist Party and labor leaders, they wielded their control over private welfare and state services to gain control not only of the consumer movement but also of FEChIF and the women's movement more broadly. Moderate feminists expelled Communists from FEChIF and moved to neutralize class militancy. Working-class activists responded by attempting to hold leaders of the women's movement accountable and by openly repudiating the now heightened clientelism and paternalism of women's organizations. But although many grassroots activists now staunchly opposed class hierarchies, in the preceding years they had often accepted favors offered by middle-class feminists. At times, they even asked for them. In so doing, they in the end contributed—albeit unwittingly—to the marginalization of progressive feminists and the ascendance of moderate feminists.

DEMOCRATIC RIGHTS

For at least a brief period, however, women's efforts to obtain the vote moved all feminists away from clientelism, patronage, and charitable and casework approaches and toward rights-based conceptualizations that stressed equality, transparency, and dialogue. In its suffrage campaigns, the women's movement articulated a broad view of democratic citizenship that broke with assistance-based practices. Of course, campaigns around suffrage did not automatically propel feminists away from paternalism, since the vote itself was part of a political system based, at least partially, on clientelism and casework. Traditionally, political parties not only promised that they would expand the rights of working people but also dispensed frequent favors to constituents to win support and votes. Yet women activists framed suffrage not simply as a means to an end but as an integral aspect of the exercise of democracy.[18]

Because electoral law consecrated political parties' monopoly over electoral representation, nonparty groups like the women's movement could not effectively present candidates. Some women party militants who were also active in the women's movement ran for municipal office, and some were elected. But parties had ultimate control over the selection of candidates. Faced with this reality, the women's movement supported candidates chosen by parties and suggested programs of action to those candidates, but was largely forced to abdicate the existing municipal electoral venue and focus its reform efforts elsewhere.[19] Partly because feminists could not field their own candidates, they were able to disengage from the electoral pragmatism that drove parties across the political spectrum to use the vote within a system of patronage.

As we saw in Chapter 1, throughout the popular-front period, suffrage remained circumscribed. While literacy requirements and a voting age of twenty-one lowered the pool of potential voters, the prevalence of abstentionism belied a degree of apathy toward the ballot. Abstention, however, did not necessarily indicate political indifference or even a disinterest in electoral politics. Many men and women simply found other forms of citizen involvement. Iris Figueroa, who herself held elected office in the municipality of San Miguel beginning in 1953, clearly valued other forms of citizen participation. When asked, in 1993, when she had first voted, she replied that she had cast a vote for Gabriel González Videla in 1946. In fact, Figueroa could not have voted in that election, since women did not win the national vote until two years later. Yet Figueroa's faulty recollection revealed another truth: for many men and women the vote was not the only or most important form of political and electoral engagement. Figueroa had worked on González Videla's campaign, and almost fifty years later it was easy for her to think that she had "voted" for him.[20]

Despite the fact that many men and women saw voting as only one, perhaps secondary, aspect of citizenship, the importance of suffrage could not be overlooked by popular-front supporters. After all, the popular fronts' control of the executive branch and their ability to carry out reforms depended on their winning elections, and popular-front supporters generally saw voting rights as a valuable aspect of citizenship. Thus in 1993 interviews, many popular-front activists could remember the exact day they had registered to vote, for whom they had cast their first ballot, or who they had supported in subsequent elections. Many even remembered for whom their relatives had voted. Mercedes Fuentealba, who marched down to the electoral registry on the very same day she turned twenty-one, was not exceptional in the importance she attributed to suffrage.[21]

Suffrage activists made a variety of arguments regarding the relation between gender and citizenship. Frequently, feminists argued that the vote would allow women to publicly assert their rights and responsibilities as mothers. In addition, they proposed more "masculine" forms of citizen participation for women. At their most creative, they articulated notions of democracy and citizenship that did not rest upon gender-specific rights and responsibilities. Depending, then, on the political moment and on their political affiliations, employment histories, and class position, feminists drew upon, subverted, and/or reformulated the feminine, family-based citizen identity favored by state officials and by the male union leaders and party activists described in previous chapters. Women both used and subverted gender-specific understandings of citizenship.

At times, feminists—and especially feminists in the labor movement—openly appropriated the masculinist rhetoric of nationalism, progress, and class uplift. Since women made the exact same contributions to the nation as men, they affirmed, women deserved the right to vote. In 1939, women in the CTCh portrayed this as a positive, evolutionary change away from family wage norms. Women had not initially chosen to sell their labor power, they explained. They had gone off to work in factories and fields, as domestic laborers and home-workers, because of economic need—perhaps even because they were never adequately protected by a male provider. Woman, Saray Cortés and Leonilda Barrancos wrote in a position paper presented to the First CTCh Congress, had first entered paid labor "more because of capitalist avarice than because of a recognition of her rights and because she was obliged to by men's meager wages." But making a virtue of necessity, she molded socioeconomic changes to her benefit. "[T]oday," Cortés and Barrancos explained, "she demands as a right what she saw yesterday as a sacrifice." With a slightly more sanguine view of what capitalism meant for the Chilean nation, a woman metal worker boasted that women, alongside their male coworkers in the metal industry, had "demonstrated great technical capacity and contributed to a greater yield for our national economy." In return for these contributions, women repeatedly claimed full equality.[22]

At other times, feminists argued that women should be granted the vote because of the specific contribution they could make, as women, to politics. Invoking women's unique contributions as mothers during a suffrage rally in front of the Congress building, MEMCh members painted the sidewalk with the slogan, "Give rights to those who give life." Echoing the same theme, during the 1948 women's suffrage week sponsored by FEChIF, feminists visited the maternity ward at the San Borja Hospital to pay homage "to the

woman who fulfills the sacred mission of giving new lives to the world."
Likewise, a MEMCh document drafted just before the 1947 municipal election maintained that women's experiences within the family should be harnessed for the public good: women could contribute to public life "the
valuable experience they have gained within the home, in the spiritual and
material formation and maintenance of the family. . . . Women will contribute to a better future . . . by helping to reestablish the natural equilibrium of a
society in which the work of men and women should be complementary
and in harmony."[23] As Victoria García, FEChIF member and president of the
Women's Medical Association succinctly put it: "We want woman to vote not
because she is like man, but because she is different."[24]

The existence of these two different feminist models of citizenship within
struggles for women's suffrage precluded either one of them from becoming
reified. Despite the fact that the state and political elites, as well as feminists,
proposed a citizen identity for women as mothers, the existence of a competing discourse on women's citizenship prevented the citizen-mother from
becoming a fully achieved identity. FEChIF president and Radical Amanda
Labarca frequently argued from both positions but ultimately proposed a
blurring of gender divisions. "Not all men have an aptitude for abstract ideas
or a vocation for the political struggle," she wrote. "It is the same with
women. Modern science has demonstrated that there are no fundamental
psychic differences between the two; but rather an immense variety of types
among one and the other, happily. Certain characteristics prevail in the female sex; others in the opposite sex; they exist more or less frequently, but
they exist. Better to let each bird sing its own song. The world enjoys and
benefits from that very sapient variety."[25]

Yet family-based identities that rested not only on women's social role
within the family but also implicitly on their biological role tended to become naturalized and therefore to seem immutable. This was particularly
evident when feminists construed femininity as a set of physical characteristics and argued that the vote would not make women lose feminine qualities.
Thus even when feminists did not relate women's purported contributions as
citizen-mothers to biological traits—for example, when feminists argued
that women contributed sensitivity, a love of peace, or a scrupulousness—
they never suggested that men could or should acquire those characteristics.
Nor did they suggest that women could cast off their womanly essence. In
contrast, as has already been noted, many of women's attempts to claim
masculine venues of citizen participation actually ended up dissociating pur-

ported masculine qualities from men. While this dissociation did not imply a permanent loosening of gender codes—masculinity or femininity could be redefined in new ways—it provided an opening through which renegotiations could take place. Most significantly, it allowed the elaboration of a notion of democracy and democratic process that was not founded on essentialist notions of gender.

Through that opening feminists articulated a third model of citizenship, a model based on a gender-neutral concept of individual rights. All Chileans should have the right to deliberate and to form and express opinions, they said. Voting, and citizen participation more broadly, a FEChIF publication remarked, was a "human right," which citizens would use as their "sacred and respectable convictions" dictated. At the same time, feminists proposed that individual responsibility could contribute to collective purposes. Women's full citizen participation, they put forth, would truly strengthen Chile and "augment Chile's prestige as a democratic nation."[26] In a January 1941 letter to President Aguirre Cerda, MEMCh expounded on its conceptualization of individual participation within a democratic polity:

> For MEMCh, the vote is not simply the right to participate in an electoral act, the right to elect and to be elected, but rather a valuable instrument that permits individuals in a democracy to contribute to the solution of problems, to deploy constructive criticism, to express their desires and necessities, and to broaden the foundations of government. In both [MEMCh] Congresses there was an orderly framing of fundamental questions of the kind citizens should ask daily if they understand their role within a democracy. To MEMCh, the exercise of citizenship means preparing women completely so that they can understand the problems of social life, take an interest in their solution, leave behind a limiting individualism and project their actions in terms of collective well-being and progress.[27]

MEMCh believed that political space should be granted not only to women but also to other excluded groups such as illiterates or campesinos, and it rallied to extend voting rights and educational opportunities to them as well as to women.[28]

In this discursive strand, democratic process—voting, but also education as the transmission of information, and political activity more generally— was as important as outcome. Because of their long-standing defense of political transparency and the expansion of political rights, women on the

Party representatives monitoring the ballot box during a municipal election, Valparaíso, 1944.
Photo courtesy Emperatriz Villarroel.

Left were particularly well positioned to highlight the value of democratic procedures. Since at least the 1920s, women had organized to oppose electoral fraud. In the countryside, women had denounced political patronage, which led men to forfeit their political independence. In the city and the country they had set up women's groups to patrol polling places on election days. Women's groups had also worked to get women to register to vote in municipal elections—a bureaucratic nightmare of a process—and to cast their ballots. In arguing for the importance of democratic procedures, the women's movement drew on this trajectory.[29]

Highlighting the importance of democratic process became particularly important to women because uncertainty regarding how women would vote was the principal stated reason political parties postponed passage of suffrage legislation. As Socialist Aniceto Rodríguez explained in 1947, women's suffrage could "lead to results that are not very easy to predict and that may radically change the fortunes of the [social] forces in the next electoral contest." Amanda Labarca and others countered by saying that limited voting made it possible to call the popular fronts' sovereignty into question. If extending suffrage rights made political parties redouble their efforts to convince the population of the value of their programs, if it forced them to seek and gain allies through dialogue and persuasion, then the extension of citizen rights would fortify them.[30]

In arguing for universal rights as a foundation for political contestation, negotiation, and alliance, feminists tried to show how democracy as a formal system of representation could be used to further substantive democracy. In other words, they suggested that the substantive aspects of the popular-front program—increased social, economic, and cultural rights—would be furthered by extending the methods of formal democracy. This postulate emerged forcefully in one of the more remarkable political deliberations of the popular-front period: when FEChIF's Commission on the Defense of Democracy and International Peace convened during FEChIF's 1947 congress, the commission's members set for themselves the ambitious goal of establishing the proper relations between political democracy and social, cultural, and economic rights.

Amanda Labarca began this extraordinary discussion by pointing out that political and economic democracy were often at odds with each other. In the United States, there was ample freedom of speech but much poverty. In the Soviet Union, citizens had economic security but not political freedom. Although Labarca, one of the few Radicals in a room filled with Communists, manifested an undying loyalty to political democracy proper, she held forth the possibility of reconciling the two. What might be the proper kind of democracy for Chile, she asked.[31]

Communists María Ramírez and Luisa Vicentini, who spoke next, emphasized the economic aspects of democracy, with Vicentini claiming that freedom from misery was as important as freedom of expression and religious freedom. Democracy, Vicentini added, meant respect for the human personality, for culture, and for work. Aída Parada contributed to the discussion by noting that democracy was not a permanent state but a social ideal that would never be fully realized. Democracy, a social act of faith, would evolve along with humanity and its problems. At bottom, she said, democracy meant that the simple act of being born would confer broad rights of citizenship, the opportunity to engage in dialogue and contestation. By the end of the commission's sessions, despite differences in emphasis, the women in attendance had agreed on a statement drafted by Olga Poblete. "Only by attending to the ample development and expression of human capacities and necessities," the statement read, "can the process of social life [convivencia social] function harmoniously. . . . This dynamic concept of democracy thus contemplates not only the individual's right to express his or her free will in the functions of government, but also the right to live in economic and moral security, the right to have his or her intellectual development and creative capacity attended to, the right to enjoy all the material as well as spiritual benefits of culture."[32] This vision of democracy allowed feminists to sidestep gender-based claims to democratic rights and to reconcile political democracy with class-based claims.

But even as these deliberations were being carried out, the broader political climate was pushing feminists in a different direction. Heightened class conflict and pressure from the United States led President González Videla to persecute Communists, union leaders, and other grassroots activists. The tensions that in late 1948 led to the promulgation of the so-called *ley de defensa de la democracia* (law for the defense of democracy), which outlawed the Communist Party, reverberated within FEChIF. As early as the 1947 FEChIF congress, an annoyed president responded to criticisms regarding the Rightward drift of his government by declaring, in a speech at the closing ceremony, that he would, if necessary, "sharpen the democratic sword to govern." Caffarena, outraged by the president's threat of force, stormed out of the proceedings with other MEMCh members following her. (And this despite the fact that prior to the start of the ceremony MEMCh secretary-general Poblete had asked MEMCh members to keep their composure.) As Caffarena rose to leave, González Videla told his audience, "Let the Communists go, we do not need them." MEMCh members turned back shouting. Much to the disgust of Caffarena and her followers, Labarca then ordered the playing of the national anthem.[33]

After this incident, relations among movement activists grew more strained. By April 1948, FEChIF had expelled members of the Communist Party. Elena Caffarena, who had been elected vice president of FEChIF, resigned in response, and MEMCh withdrew from FEChIF. MEMCh specifically accused FEChIF leaders of failing to stick by their declarations in relation to democracy, and it denounced FEChIF's failure to keep the promises it made to the working-class women who attended the 1947 congress: FEChIF had done nothing to help the women and children affected by the anti-Communist persecution that was rocking the country.[34]

In this context, the passage of women's suffrage on 14 January 1949 was hardly a cause for rejoicing. Some leaders of the women's movement gathered with González Videla and other political leaders in a posh Santiago theater to celebrate the new law, but Elena Caffarena, who had herself helped draft the suffrage legislation, was not invited to the event. She sat home and listened to the ceremony on the radio. Moreover, as a purported Communist, Caffarena was among the first women to fall victim to the electoral prohibitions enacted by Congress. She was stripped of her right to vote only a few days after the women's suffrage law passed. It was a difficult moment for Caffarena.[35]

When she appealed her electoral proscription, Caffarena invoked the promise of the popular fronts for both feminists and the entire nation and signaled recent events as a bitter defeat. In characterizing her own role, she summarized the achievements and failures of the leftist women's movement in general:

> I have struggled for the vote for women not because I am a feminist *autrance* nor because I think that women are better than men or because women's vote is in and of itself a panacea for national problems but simply out of democratic conviction. I believe in government of the people, by the people and for the people. I think that all the inhabitants of a country, whatever their color or race, their culture or sex, their political or religious creed, have a right to influence the destiny of their country.
>
> For someone who has had a long civic performance without ever obtaining monetary or honorific personal benefit; for someone who has concerned herself, to the detriment of her own interests, with the solution of national problems, for someone who has done everything within her reach to perfect the democratic regime, broadening its electoral foundations and aspiring to extend it from the political arena to the economic and social, there is no doubt that the application of the sentence that deprives me of my citizen rights . . . constitutes more than an affront or a stigma, the failure of my ideals and of my entire life.[36]

Although Caffarena's voting rights were eventually restored, the broader feminist project of which she was a principal spokesperson, had, like the popular-front project itself, in a sense failed, had torn apart at its ideological and class seams.

That apparent failure should not occlude important if partial successes. That certain movement activists were able to develop a consistent critique of protection for women, and to implement it partially, despite the opposing view of political and professional elites and many women was a remarkable accomplishment. That the women at FEChIF's 1947 congress could spend two days deliberating the meaning of democracy—and that those discussions drew on, and were the culmination of, years of difficult but instructive cross-class organizing—was another remarkable success. It was an achievement for the entire country. And that feminists were able to arrive, through their experiences in organizing middle- and working-class women, at an analysis of gender as a fluid category was a triumph. As Amanda Labarca had said in 1945, "Better to let each bird sing its own song." Six years later Caffarena, who was still fighting in her less lyrical and more cerebral way, reiterated the same message: "We know that man and woman are different and we could say humans even so. They come with differing intelligences, characters, ideologies, but it is a just, democratic aspiration to do away with advantages that favor one and discriminate against the other."[37]

CONCLUSION

Women activists focused considerable attention on suffrage as a tangible expression of democracy, but they did not see the vote as an end unto itself. Rather, they saw the vote as a means of improving women's social and economic condition, reshaping state institutions, and modifying state policy. Yet voting was only one venue of representation and delegated voice, and the fight for suffrage was only part of broader struggles to gain not only social and political rights but also voice and influence. Although feminists went to great pains to extend electoral venues of representation, their struggles to overcome exclusions based on gender went further.

Denied the vote and formal parliamentary forms of representation within the state, women relied on nonelectoral forms of representation. Through more informal political activities, movement leaders also sought influence and exercised a representative role: they used personal and political connections to lobby, and as state employees they exercised prerogatives. The women's movement applauded and encouraged those efforts, and grassroots activists who participated in women's groups assented—to a greater or lesser degree depending on who was involved and when—to being represented by the leaders of women's organizations. Yet these more informal forms of political representation bred tense class dynamics that, although often excruciatingly transparent, proved intractable. In short, the women's movement's theory and practice of democracy left certain kinds of power unexamined. Specifically, the movement did not fully or adequately dissect its own internal dynamics or the effects of its use of more informal venues of representation and influence. Progressive feminists within MEMCh made a valiant effort to bring these issues into the political spotlight, but the pressures against them were multiple, and ultimately overwhelming.

However, the women's movement, despite lingering hierarchies within it, made important contributions to the political culture of the nation. By fighting to redefine and extend democratic rights, it challenged prevailing notions of who belonged to the nation and of how Chileans might exercise their citizenship: it debunked the popular fronts' gendered teleology. And because women organized in a cross-class movement, they generated—despite contestation over the relation between political and economic democracy and despite the incipient nature of a discourse of rights that extended to working-class women—an understanding of the theory and practice of democracy that attended to both its gender and class dynamics. Indeed by addressing and trying to overcome differences among women, a topic grassroots memchistas stubbornly placed on the agenda of the women's movement, and by noting the restrictive nature of binary models of gender, sectors of the movement began to reject vanguardist forms of leadership. Questioning the exclusionary norms that existed both within women's groups and within popular-front politics more generally, the women's movement challenged the popular fronts to become more open and inclusive.

CONCLUSION

Gender constructed the popular-front project. It intensified the political efficacy of respectable male workers while limiting that of women and disreputable or unmanly men. It stratified welfare policies, welfare apparatuses, and welfare professions. It structured popular organizations and working-class communities, determining their political positions within the nation. And gendered discourses legitimated the popular fronts' social order in the making by shaping a familylike image of both the popular-front pact and of the compromise state it erected. At the same time, the popular-front project reshaped gender. Through public health campaigns and welfare benefits, the popular-front state promoted and enforced a model of gender relations based in the male-headed nuclear family and the family wage system. Moreover, by articulating certain working-class gender norms within the national arena and ignoring others, it recast gender-specific meanings of citizenship and of class.

The popular fronts attempted to create consensus by tying gender and family relations to economic and political changes within the nation. Respectable men, according to popular-front politicians, should contribute to national prosperity by working diligently, expressing grievances in a controlled manner, and providing for their families. In return, they would receive family wages and enhanced political participation through unions and political parties. Women would contribute to national aggrandizement by assuring the health and productivity of their children and husbands and by promoting harmony within the home. But because women's service to the nation was presumably indirect, their rewards were also more modest. Although state officials granted women a degree of protection as they enforced male responsibility to kin, they circumscribed women's political and economic participation.

The popular-front project rested on an essentially positivist and evolutionary view of consensus and of the identities and relations that engendered national advancement. It thereby reinscribed hierarchical norms of masculinity and femininity by linking gender to progress, portrayed as an automatic, evolutionary process. Just as important, popular-front leaders naturalized their project by connecting it to a model of family relations that had long been accepted not only by the popular fronts' working-class supporters but also by their conservative detractors. But even though the articulation of gender within discourses of national progress produced a sensation of political inevitability, antagonistic class- and gender-based claims persistently destabilized the popular-front project, preventing it from becoming a closed hegemonic order. In fact, popular-front leaders created spaces for oppositional voices by explicitly promoting democratization and tolerating alternative views. As a consequence, male workers were able to assert a more class-conscious view of proper masculine deportment. Many refused to act as proper family men and, by striking and migrating, reminded capitalists and government leaders that their compliance was voluntary and might be withdrawn. Feminists too disrupted the popular-front project, dissociating work and family identities from each other and from citizenship. In addition, despite the popular front's efforts to tame the single mother (cum wage earner, cum potential prostitute) by portraying her as a victim, rebellious unwed mothers who were on the political margins intimated that marriage was neither as appealing nor as available as politicians might have liked. These alternative discourses revealed the contingent nature of the identities on which the political and economic participation of popular classes relied, and forced the renegotiation of both those identities and political pacts.

At the same time, contrasting models of class and gender buttressed the popular-front project, or at least aspects of it. Although working-class women who organized in and around male-dominated organizations rejected the class-conciliatory masculine and feminine identities advocated by state officials and social workers, they colluded with them to reform unreliable men. Similarly, moderate feminists repudiated the subordinate stature of women that was inscribed within plans for bettering the race, but they championed a harmonious program of class uplift. And organized male workers viewed kinship ties as the basis of an oppositional class identity, yet they asserted their prerogatives within the family. Although working-class men and women as well as feminists thus departed in some ways from the consensual, evolutionary model developed by political elites, in seeking to advance claims that coincided with the popular-front program they often marshaled disciplinary discourses of progress. In attempting to rout or neutralize fellow popular-front supporters with competing points of view, they used elite popular-front formulations to affirm a vanguardist leadership.

THE POPULAR-FRONT COALITIONS AND
ORGANIZED MALE WORKERS

Among the various crosscutting alliances that underlay the popular-front pact, the one between national popular-front leaders and organized male workers was the most enduring and successful.[1] On a concrete level, it was useful to popular-front leaders, socialists foremost among them, who gained leverage within the national political arena by consolidating and mobilizing the support of male-dominated labor unions. It was immediately useful to male workers as well, for they gained increased wages and state benefits, political recognition as family heads, and perhaps most important, increased venues of participation. Along with these tangible results, the pact redrew subaltern identities in mutually beneficial ways. It helped worker organizations rebuild a masculine identity that solidified working-class cohesion and discipline, thereby propping up Left leadership within the working class and facilitating effective leftist participation in national politics. It also solidified a view of working-class women as dependents who relied on the economic and sexual protection of male kin. This served working-class organizations by attracting men who wished to act as protectors (with all the privilege that position implied) and women who gambled on protection as the best bet for survival and safety. But while consolidating the family as a locus of class solidarity, these gender norms also served popular-front leaders by restricting the direct citizen claims of women and subtly redefining those of men.

To understand why male industrial workers became the core popular-front constituency, it is necessary to look beyond the aggregate economic data and restricted view of politics that have led past scholars to conclude that workers did not on balance benefit from popular-front reforms. As prior scholarly investigations have pointed out, wage gains for the working class as a whole and improvements in the distribution of national income were meager during the popular-front period. Yet certain classes of workers—especially those that were the popular fronts' most faithful supporters—may have seen marked wage increases.[2] Furthermore, regardless of whether wages actually rose, workers received other material benefits, many of which were not part of those aspects of the labor relations system on which past scholarly studies have focused: they gained health insurance for themselves, their children under the age of two, and their pregnant wives; old age pensions; and disability insurance. In 1952, Congress finally mandated the payment of family allowances to all blue-collar workers for their dependents.

Perhaps more important than these economic benefits, workers recognized their social and political *rights*. As the worker press endlessly reminded its readers, CSO benefits were not handouts that could simply be withdrawn by political elites. They were a deserved privilege, won and maintained through struggle. Indeed throughout the popular-front period, workers rallied for better treatment by welfare professionals: unions and political parties denounced inefficient and corrupt bureaucrats at every level of the welfare apparatuses and emphasized the crucial democratizing role played by worker representatives within state agencies.

The granting of entitlements to workers, most of whom were men, reinforced the association of citizenship and masculinity on which the popular-front pact rested. In addition, both worker organizations and popular-front officials explicitly linked worker rights to masculine family identities, ignoring the substantial minority of workers who were women. Workers deserved benefits, they argued, not simply because they diligently contributed to national prosperity but also because they were wholesome family men. It was largely the way in which references to family, progress, and nation redrew male workers' class-based demands that made them more palatable to capitalists and the political Right, and to the state officials who were squeezed between workers and proprietors.

While organized male workers generally accepted the norms of respectability that coincided with those of political elites and expressed them in terms of national necessity, the gender codes adopted by popular organizations drew on prior working-class discourses on gender and family. Specifically, male leftists reinvigorated the idea that women's sexual or economic independence made them vulnerable to exploitation by capital. Wage-earning women, they suggested, faced gender-specific problems—not only low wages but also sexual harassment at the hands of perfidious bosses—which made it advisable for women to find men who would support them. Leftists thus figured the associated "problems" of single motherhood and women's wage work, which were purportedly caused by men's pitiful wages, as anticapitalist battles. Shifting blame away from working-class men, who they portrayed as protectors and not as victimizers, leftists attributed inappropriate male behavior to the noxious influence of bourgeois morality. So as to augment class solidarity, they proclaimed that class-conscious women should aid in the struggle of their male relatives and make them comfortable at home.

Although women who supported leftist gender prescriptions cemented the leadership of socialists, those women did not necessarily accept that their subordination within family and workplace was the consequence of capitalism. Having experienced capitalist (as well as male) exploitation, and adding their own knowledge of the tiresome double shift, many were enticed by the possibility of securing a constant breadwinner with a good wage, a protector. Organized housewives were especially apt to invoke socialist family wage ideology, for many working-class housewives realized that regardless of whether working-class leaders blamed capitalists for male irresponsibility or not, those leaders enforced male compliance, at least to a degree. Wage-earning women's adherence to socialist family wage precepts was more uneven. Yet insofar as they too sought defenders, they not only relegated themselves to the status of dependent victims and second-class citizens but also reinscribed Manichaean moral categories and rigid definitions of gender, thereby propping up socialist vanguardism.

However, to the extent that women, and younger women in particular, rejected rigid socialist gender ideals, they forced a slight loosening of gendered vanguardism. Consequently, leftists could not consistently insist on male jurisdiction, and they addressed the situation of young women—who wrung less benefit from familial protection and, because they were often economically independent, demanded it less often—with remarkable flexibility. While leftists secured male sexual control by recognizing the need to protect the virtue of young single women who became politically active, for example, they saw this more as a concession to parents than anything else, a necessary albeit "old-fashioned" custom that might rightfully disappear. Moreover, progressive politicians and welfare professionals manifested a more tolerant attitude when they advocated a less punitive approach to disreputable women: material aid for single mothers, education for prostitutes.

As workers' organizations became more enmeshed in popular-front politics, they distanced themselves from deviant manifestations of masculinity such as the raucous, macho, class fighter. Yet they did not fully marginalize dishonorable men. Male leftist leaders used moral precepts to discredit their male adversaries, but they also insisted on the possibility of educating them. Without condoning disreputable behavior, leftists tolerated much of it. Consequently, the popular-front project did not suppress more spontaneous kinds of rebellion, and those oppositional norms continued to be identified with socialism, especially by the Right. Nevertheless, the Left was less apt to articulate oppositional and popular "common sense" models of masculinity and femininity than it was to incorporate the more conservative common sense that it shared with national popular-front leaders. Its tolerance therefore failed to significantly broaden hegemonic gender norms or the popular-front project more generally.

LEFTISTS, FEMINISTS, AND THE LIMITS OF DEMOCRACY

The opposing model of gender relations proposed by moderate feminists and women in the welfare professions—the overlap between the two groups was significant—circumscribed Left efforts to represent working-class women by challenging socialist analyses of male abuse. Claiming that it was male irresponsibility, not capitalism, that made women vulnerable, these middle-class women marshaled professional and political resources to assure that men acted honorably. Social workers in particular coaxed men into legally recognizing their children, supporting those children and their wives, and giving up bad habits such as drinking. In addition, moderate feminists developed a discourse of republican motherhood that exposed women's direct contributions to national well-being, using that discourse to argue that women could and should represent themselves politically. Yet these initiatives were themselves problematic insofar as they avoided dealing with women's class-based concerns and allegiances. Invocations of republican motherhood, for instance, could easily fade into an essentialist view of the rights and responsibilities of "future mothers," a view that covered up not only the specificity of raising children in poverty but also differences among working-class women (some of whom would never become mothers). Perhaps most important, moderate feminists undercut women's protagonism by augmenting the authority of the welfare professionals, who would enforce male responsibility and train women to be good citizen-mothers. Like socialists, they figured women as victims even as they paradoxically sought their support.

The actions of feminist leaders, like those of socialists and other popular-front leaders, reverberated within working-class families and the political arena proper. Within their families, working-class women likely contested male domination more as they found allies in their struggles to enforce male responsibility.[3] Certainly women continued to demand control of their husbands' pay. Now they found that they could count on social workers—and if they were associated with the Communist Party, on party leaders—to enforce their claims. Although many men resisted, their resistance was certainly quieter than before. Others were shamed or badgered into complying. And given that both popular-front leaders and feminists portrayed men as culprits, workers likely found it harder to blame capitalists for male drinking (and subsequent male violence) and harder to convince working-class women that men were not responsible for their lapses. Family reform programs thus converged with the needs of working-class housewives. Yet by defining men's concessions to women as a duty to nation, popular-front leaders persuaded men that they would benefit from a masculine discipline and buried the ways in which men's adherence to gendered standards was a concession to their womenfolk. Women's alliances with welfare professionals, which ultimately restricted as much as they empowered, also concealed women's day-to-day struggles to overcome male abuse. Women might avoid problems at home, social workers and domestic-economy teachers suggested, simply by cooking low-cost stews. The inscription of gendered norms within discourses of nation thus stimulated male protagonism and covered up that of women.

Undoubtedly, many women and men knew that women did not just acquiesce to the reconstruction of gender norms. Still, when family reform was portrayed as a national or class imperative, women's own reasons for demanding the reform of family relations could not take center stage. In large part, this was a consequence of working-class women's relative political debility, itself a product of the way both leftists and feminists figured women as victims, whether of capital or of men. Women's complicity was constructed. This recognition should not, however, lead us to underestimate the importance of the choices women made: the women who saw protection as immediately useful, especially when material incentives were involved, were not simply blind followers.

The more strictly political consequences of competition between socialists and feminists manifested themselves most clearly within the consumer movement, where moderate feminists co-opted and neutralized one sector of consumers by granting them state recognition and access to cheap foodstuffs. In return, feminist leaders Graciela Mandujano and Clara Williams asked that housewives heed the advice of domestic-economy teachers and give up their class-based demands. Women who refused to make these concessions and remained outside the state-sponsored Asociación de Dueñas de Casa were not much freer to set their own agenda: their alliance with the male-dominated Left entailed their acceptance of a working-class solidarity that helped wrench concessions from capital but subordinated women. In comparison to male workers, working-class women could not express their full range of needs, in part because they were more materially vulnerable. In addition, women had fewer bargaining chips: unlike men, they could not trade concessions at work for increased power at home.

Because worker leaders as well as feminists wished to validate themselves among the upper echelons of popular-front leadership, they privileged those identities and alliances that seemed most functional to the popular fronts' broader projects. There was consequently significant agreement between them despite competing analyses. Feminists who criticized male abuse nonetheless agreed that the consolidation of the male-headed nuclear family was a desired goal. All affirmed that women's preferred place was at home and that family life should be peaceful. This convergence did not lead to a significant broadening of the popular-front alliance, however, in part because both moderate feminists and leftists were more likely to concern themselves with exposing and developing the similarities between their own projects and those of popular-front leaders than with understanding and representing the demands of their ostensible constituents. By mobilizing certain elements of the nested discourses of nation, progress, and family and using them to neutralize either class- or gender-based demands, each legitimated itself politically and discredited its competitors. Neither came to terms with what a deeper compromise might entail. Leftists, and Communists in particular, used a populist anti-intellectualism to discredit women in influential positions: their reticence vis-à-vis efforts to reform social work brought to light a mistrust of women with intellectual and political resources at their disposal. Moreover, they refused to recognize that men did not necessarily share their wages, ignoring inequality within families. Likewise, moderate feminists failed to take into account working-class deprivation. More generally, neither socialists nor feminists questioned the popular fronts' overarching conceptualization of how national consensus would be achieved and how the family would play into that consensus.

Perched between leftists and moderate feminists, progressive feminists proposed an alternative. They rejected protection, combating both protective labor legislation and women's legal subordination within the family. Stressing the ways in which women's disadvantages within the workplace hurt male workers, they held forth the possibility of concurrently furthering the demands of men and women workers. And by struggling to assemble a cross-class organization, they sought ways to represent both working-class housewives and middle-class women. They tried, in other words, to articulate a project that neither subordinated women in the name of class unity nor neutralized class militancy in the name of women's improvement. More than socialists, welfare professionals, or moderate feminists, progressive feminists gave space to the multiplicity of women's political demands and tried to articulate those demands into an expanded popular-front project. More than their allies, they came to grips with the difficult transactions a bourgeois-democratic revolution might entail.

Theirs was a formidable enterprise, and, not surprisingly, progressive feminists within MEMCh were besieged almost from the start. Hemmed in by leftists and moderate feminists who were uncomfortable with aspects of the MEMCh project, *memchistas* found it difficult to express themselves effectively. Elena Caffarena could not get MEMCh, much less FEChIF, to consistently extricate itself from clientelistic relations, because certain feminist welfare professionals could not separate their own desire for professional recognition from the needs of their clients. Grassroots *memchistas* who were more interested in satisfying immediate needs than in developing a program only compounded this problem. MEMCh's association with the Communist Party further limited the organization, as *memchistas* found it hard to reconcile a critique of the family wage system and a rejection of protection with a sensitivity to the Left's class agenda. That the radical critique of protection enunciated by women like Marta Vergara and Elena Caffarena threatened not only male leftist leaders but also the working-class housewives who MEMCh mobilized in alliance with Communists further stunted MEMCh's ability to carry forth its program. In the postwar period, these difficulties were compounded by an anti-Communist barrage that drew strength from the Left's continued distrust of "bourgeois" feminism. By 1949, along with the broader women's movement of which it was a part, MEMCh had dissipated—and with it the possibility of an expanded national-popular alliance.

Though MEMCh did not succeed in redrawing the gender contours of the popular-front project, or even in consistently contesting family wage ideology, it made notable achievements and left an important legacy. First, it challenged the association of masculine work and family identities with political, professional, and economic entitlement. Second, progressive feminists pressed for greater democracy within the family and increased recognition of childrearing and housekeeping without either consistently promoting an essential feminine identity or implying that professionals should police families. They also successfully refuted the idea that women were secondary wage earners by lobbying against the passage of discriminatory labor legislation and by helping to open state employment to middle-class women.

Moreover, the more radical *memchistas* proposed a transgender identity for wage earners, and on that basis forged momentary, localized alliances within the union movement that refigured working-class unity. These MEMCh members envisioned a class solidarity that did not depend on family ties that subordinated women.

Perhaps most important, along with other women activists, *memchistas* developed a discourse on democracy, as both method and goal. At one level, in pressing for democratization feminists simply demanded the extension of citizen rights to women—and this is how feminists themselves mostly understood it. Often enough they asserted that women did the same things as men, or comparable things, and thus deserved full citizen rights. Yet within the context of broader struggles, feminist discussions of democracy revealed a radical critique of popular-front politics. At the 1947 FEChIF conference, for example, feminists implied that democracy was contingent and specific when they asked what democracy meant for Chileans and suggested that Chile could not and should not follow the example of other countries. And perhaps because feminists realized that the ever-present call to solidarity was frequently used to marginalize women, they developed a concept of democratic participation as an individual right. They thus questioned group claims even as they insisted that there could be no democracy without the satisfaction of collective class- and gender-based demands. And whether she was thinking or not about how gender contributed to a foundational politics, Amanda Labarca acknowledged men's anxiety that women's suffrage would destabilize the political order and responded by insisting that an expanded dialogue could only create a stronger, because more widely and deeply accepted, unity and purpose.

Feminists, in short, suggested a more expansive view of democracy and alliance. They did so not because they consciously repudiated the popular fronts' unifying myths but because they repeatedly came up against the impossibility of developing a fuller feminist project, or more effective alliances, from within popular-front discourse. For Caffarena and her allies in particular, the limitations imposed by a project that tied gender not only to work, family, and recreation but also to progress and the nation itself may have become increasingly clear. Their answer to this dilemma, as they worked it out in practice, was a mix of autonomy and dialogue, of reference to specificity and to solidarity, that reworked the meaning of political compromise and democratic engagement.

POPULAR-FRONT POLITICS AND THE STATE

Demands for citizenship—for voting rights, for material entitlements, and for political and economic participation more broadly—were defined in relation to state practices, and the state intervened powerfully in restructuring gendered alliances and identities. The gendered interventions of welfare professionals as well as gendered nationalist discourses and gendered forms of subaltern organization in turn conditioned the implementation of state policies. Yet because of the multiplicity of political practices within civil society and the diverse ways in which they were articulated into the popular-front project, state actions reflected not only the popular fronts' political program but also its heterogeneity. Ultimately, state formation was a process, albeit a process through which political elites tried to structure a social order.

Novel patterns of interaction between popular sectors and the state first emerged in 1924–25, when Carlos Ibáñez del Campo forced reforms that made the Chilean state more centralized and the executive branch more powerful. After 1938, officials sympathetic to popular sectors increasingly ran agencies concerned with the issues that mattered most to wage earners. In this context, organized male workers came to understand that powerful central state agencies controlled by the executive branch would allow the popular fronts to bypass obstructionist courts and Congress. Given, too, the Right's pronounced opposition to the popular fronts and state officials' need for allies, worker organizations came to realize that they could sway state officials and state policy. This was especially true in relation to the CSO, where Socialist jurisdiction was strong and right-wing criticism virulent, allowing workers to demand increased entitlements from state officials in desperate need of support. Workers came to see CSO benefits, which they had initially rejected, as a right.

Institutional changes within the state were tightly linked to the unification of working-class organizations. This dynamic was clearest within the labor movement, where the formation of the CTCh dovetailed with the creation of the Popular Front in 1936 and rode on the coattails of corporatist labor legislation that gave the executive branch a strong mediatory role. Increased state regulation of the labor relations system gave labor a firmer and more legitimate voice; quelled internal dissent within the labor movement; and led to moments of labor quiescence. Changes in the labor relations system did not, however, silence labor unions or lead them to a full renunciation of militancy. Nor did they lead organized workers to relinquish their autonomy. The CTCh, although propped up by the state, did not depend on it. State intervention and centralization undoubtedly eased efforts to control and integrate workers, but it did not lead to a frontal state co-optation of labor groups.

However, within the heterogeneous consumer movement, state attempts to neutralize and co-opt grassroots organizing were more successful. As the popular-front era drew to a close, state officials exploited unreconciled differences between the moderate feminists and leftists who vied to lead the consumer movement. By allying with moderate feminists to create the state-sponsored Asociación de Dueñas de Casa, they successfully marginalized autonomous consumer organizations. These developments were particularly important because consumer organizations provided the main point of contact between *organized* women and the state. Although women would continue to engage welfare professionals, these contacts were more individualized and paternalistic and less rooted in rights-based discourses.

In contrast to workers, who consistently combated welfare professionals' paternalism and charitable approaches, nonworkers, many of them women, found no consistently effective way to counter condescending *sanitaristas* and social workers. This did not mean that indigent clients always cooperated. As social workers frequently noted, they could be hostile or evasive. Yet because nonworkers did not face these bureaucrats in an organized fashion, they had fewer tools with which to modify arrangements. They could choose to accept benevolent assistance or not, but they could not transform "charitable" assistance into a recognized *right* to benefits distributed by the state. Not surprisingly, then, in those agencies that dealt with the indigent, a quintessentially unmanly group composed largely of women, the twin processes of modernization and democratization of state services came slowly and were more partial. Within the Dirección General de Auxilio Social, where head social worker Elena Yávar attempted such reforms, the obstacles inherent in empowering the indigent became painfully evident. The CSO, which won the constructive criticism of organized workers, evolved in a very different manner.

These alignments projected themselves onto the professions, helping to create gendered distinctions among them. Since the expanding cadre of welfare professionals played such a critical role in the expansion and reform of the state, gendered professional differences in turn fed back into the process of state formation, helping to structure it. On balance, as physicians built alliances with male workers, they adopted a class-conscious, social approach to medicine and inscribed that approach in the state apparatuses where they worked. Social workers, especially those who did not deal with workers, found it harder to reform their workplaces and their profession or empower clients. In part social work was tainted by its origins: the first social workers, who graduated in the late 1920s, were aristocratic ladies who entered the field to smooth over the evils of capitalism and combat "Communism." The entrance into the field of progressive women, who attempted to overcome casework methods and paternalism, could not erase those origins in part because many of their middle-class colleagues were as intent as their aristocratic precursors on maintaining class distinctions between themselves and their clients. That difficulty was compounded by social workers' responsibility for the unorganized and indigent, which made it difficult for progressive social workers to create effective alliances with clients. Their efforts to professionalize social work, making it more like medicine, were met by suggestions that social workers should simply be replaced by sanitary nurses. When the Círculo de Estudios Sociales later attempted to reform state aid for the indigent and improve the standing of social workers, it succeeded only very partially.

The overlap between gender cleavages in the professions, in subaltern organizing, and within the state was not perfect. Increased stature for women professionals would not necessarily have led to either state reforms or forms of subaltern mobilization more beneficial to women. Nor would increased organization and a raised sense of entitlement among women have immediately empowered women professionals and obliterated state paternalism. Yet the gender distinctions and inequalities within each of these arenas did influence the others, and they tied professionals to subalterns, and both to the state, in ways that recreated hegemonic gender alignments. Within this context, the straitjacketing of organized women and of MEMCh, which occurred as socialists and moderate feminists solidified their leadership, was a particularly dramatic failure.

CONSENSUS, STRUGGLE, AND NATIONAL-POPULAR POLITICS

The popular-front pacts, the pact between centrist national leaders and leftist and labor movements and to a lesser extent the pact between the former and feminists, allowed the popular fronts to govern for almost fifteen years. That was a remarkable achievement, especially given the depth of economic and political transformation that took place—and right-wing opposition to that change. But what was most extraordinary about the popular fronts was not they could consolidate themselves and carry out sweeping changes but rather that they could do so in an atmosphere of continued social conflict. Union militancy ebbed and flowed during the popular-front period but was never stifled. Conflicts within families proliferated and were debated publicly. Feminists marched and rallied for suffrage. Leftists and feminists exchanged harsh as well as conciliatory words. Without a doubt, popular-front leaders attempted transformist maneuvers that smoothed out conflicts. But in the absence of strong state cohesion, more conflictual modes of expression not only surfaced but in some cases actually succeeded in transforming broader projects. While articulatory logics were more prevalent at the political margins and national leaders were more capable of neutralization, both democratic and vanguardist practices were prevalent at both the grass roots and the political center.

Compared to national-popular governments elsewhere in Latin America, the popular fronts were unusual in their extreme heterogeneity. Crossed by differences, Chile's political and professional elites were hardly unflinching bearers of a ruling-class hegemony—or even effective enforcers. And though the Chilean state was highly centralized, the political Center was particularly factious, especially when compared to that of other Latin American countries. In Chile, there was no single party, as there was in Mexico. Nor did Chileans have a charismatic leader like Vargas or Perón to rally support. The popular fronts were instead composed of multiple political parties, each with its own ideology and trajectory, and by feminist and labor movements. The lack of a firm political center in Chile—coupled with the obdurate opposition of the political Right, which seemed more unwilling to compromise than its Brazilian or Argentine counterparts—forced popular-front leaders to court popular support and to grant popular movements an unusual degree of access to the state. Subaltern groups thus gained influence even as they retained significant autonomy. The labor and feminist movements shaped popular-front policy directly through their presence within state agencies and indirectly through their pressure on state officials. MEMCh and FEChIF participated in the drafting of the popular-front programs; the CSO remained permeable to the demands of labor; moderate feminists allied with the Comisariato to extend their program of uplift for women. It was most likely the fragile nature of the popular-front alliance—and not simply, as is

commonly thought, Chilean popular sectors' long-standing tradition of autonomous popular organizing, dating back to the nineteenth century—that
allowed popular movements to flourish during the popular-front period. By
contrast, it is doubtful (and it would be exceedingly difficult to prove) that
popular classes in Chile were historically more militant than in Mexico or
more organized than in Argentina or Brazil.[4]

Despite these particularities, the Chilean popular fronts were not unique.
Elsewhere in Latin America national-popular coalitions fostered forms of
alliance that permitted popular groups to maintain a degree of autonomy,
militancy, and influence. Like the Chilean popular fronts, midcentury populist regimes in Argentina, Brazil, and Mexico incorporated and subdued
popular groups and improved material conditions for subaltern classes and
gave them tools for demanding participation and rights. In each of these
countries, professional elites—physicians, social workers, and teachers—
emerged as significant political actors and mediators, particularly after 1930,
when states expanded rapidly.

"Postrevisionist" scholarship on national-popular politics in these countries emphasizes, as I do in this book, that the control of states, parties, and
charismatic leaders was always partial. This scholarship has shifted focus
away from national leaders and corporatist arrangements and emphasized
cultural bargaining and the application of policy. Rejecting the revisionist
argument that popular classes were controlled and co-opted by populist
leaders, it has foregrounded popular appropriation of elite projects. The
success and resiliency of populist pacts, according to many postrevisionist
authors, depended on heterogeneous, locally specific negotiations between
elites and subalterns.[5]

For instance, studies of Brazil, Mexico, and Argentina have demonstrated
that urban labor movements in those countries were not simply dependent
on, or co-opted by, national leaders. Instead, Vargas, the Mexican leaders of
1920–40, and Perón gave unions crucial breathing room. Thus John D.
French argues that Vargas repressed labor in São Paulo but only at certain
moments. At other times, the Brazilian leader saw labor legislation as an
attractive alternative to repression. As both French and Kevin Middlebrook
suggest, corporatist labor laws circumscribed Brazilian and Mexican labor
unions and tied them to national leaders. Labor leaders nonetheless used
labor laws to their own benefit, trying to ensure that they were enforced in
beneficial ways. Because workers had limited power at the point of production, moreover, they needed laws to launch organizing drives and to solidify

their organizations. Middlebrook and Daniel James further note that in Mexico and Argentina workers and populist leaders were drawn together by a shared economic nationalism and anti-oligarchic sentiment—as well as by populist leaders' professed desire for social reform. Perón, according to James, linked industrialization and economic nationalism to social justice. And Peronist discourses of social citizenship actually helped consolidate working-class unity and identity, empowering a working class that saw itself as having been emasculated by past governments.[6]

These authors thus demonstrate, as I do for Chile, that labor's incorporation into the polity solidified working-class identity and augmented workers' ability to bargain with elites. Laborers in each of these countries gained a sense of their strength and worth. I build on these insights by revealing how the partial convergence of elites and laborers around a project of gender reform facilitated cooperation between them: the Chilean popular fronts granted concrete benefits to labor by enhancing the authority of reputable male workers as family heads. I also emphasize how the very terms in which the popular fronts empowered workers limited the rights of women and "disreputable," unmanly men. Finally, I show that popular mobilization shaped the application of health and welfare as well as labor policies and disclose how gender patterned those popular mobilizations. The influence of popular classes in Chile was, I maintain, due in part to the dual role of Left political parties, which participated in both the labor movement and state agencies.[7] It was also due to gendered forms of individual and collective pressure on welfare professionals.

In attempting to understand how subaltern/elite relations were gendered, this book echoes the concerns of Mary Kay Vaughan in her study of schoolteachers and local power brokers in rural Mexico. In that book, Vaughan demonstrates that while the indigenous communities she studied resisted state attempts to modernize gender relations and to involve women in civic life, the mestizo communities allowed women to participate more actively and publicly. Vaughan thus attends, as I do, to how gender influenced subaltern interaction with state officials. For Chile, I make manifest how class (rather than ethnicity) swayed both the efforts of elites to reform gender relations and the subaltern responses to those efforts. And I complement Vaughan's local approach by attending to gendered contests between diverse actors on the national level, including nonstate and elite actors.[8]

My study, in short, deepens postrevisionist approaches by exposing how our understanding of the relation between populist leaders and popular politics can be enhanced by looking at the gendered practices of the state and of professionals. It also suggests that working-class and leftist organizations shaped populist pacts through their adoption and reformulation of gendered disciplinary projects. Moreover, I argue that gendered cleavages within the state, the professions, popular movements, and the family did not simply fragment the polity. In fact, they often facilitated alliances between certain groups and strengthened Chile's national-popular pact.

Future studies of populist politics will undoubtedly continue exploring the issues that have until now guided postrevisionist studies: union and popular leaders' relation to their constituencies; the relation of state apparatuses to popular organizing; how political parties mediated relations between states and popular classes; the relative strength of dominant classes; and the diversity of interactions between localities and regions on the one hand and the political center on the other. Future studies will also need to account, as I begin to do in this book, for how gender functioned at each of these levels. We still know very little about the relation of feminism to state building, and even less about the gender projects of national-popular states. Nor do we have a good idea about how populist pacts reshaped gender and feminism or about how feminism—directly as a movement and indirectly through its influence in the professions—shaped populist pacts.

Existing studies of gender in early-twentieth-century Latin America have focused on how feminists, professional elites, and state officials sought to revamp and modernize patriarchy. In her study of gender in Brazil, for instance, Susan Besse argues that social reformers responded to class conflict, the low rate of marriage among working-class Brazilians, women's participation in the industrial workforce, a crisis of infant mortality, and middle-class women's increasing assertiveness within marriage and public life by attempting to strengthen the patriarchal family. Reformers assumed that harmony within the family would guarantee social order in an era of rapid economic changes, and they counseled women on how to be good wives and housekeepers. They also sought to curb patriarchal excesses, promoting companionate marriage as an ideal, at least for the middle class. Experts used science and rationality to legitimate their actions, and especially after Vargas's rise to power in 1930, the state took an increasingly active role in the regulation of gender.[9]

In Brazil, mainstream feminists in the Brazilian Federation for the Advancement of Women (Federação Brasileira pelo Progresso Feminino) believed strongly that women should participate in both paid labor and political life. They nevertheless emphasized the way in which feminist principles converged with and complemented those of modernizing reformers. This was, as Asunción Lavrin asserts, a general characteristic of the "compensatory" feminism that characterized the Southern Cone. Although feminists sought legal equality for women, they did not challenge the notion that differences between the sexes were "natural," and they generally sought special treatment—protection—for women. Middle-class feminists used the association of women with maternity and the domestic sphere to their advantage, justifying women's political and professional involvement on the basis on their roles within the family. Yet Lavrin concludes that ultimately "the reaffirmation of the biological destiny of the sexes, which feminists never truly disavowed and actually endorsed on most occasions, gave the state the power to define what models of motherhood and childhood were most desirable." Feminists may have desired social change, but modernizing male elites interested principally in the progress of their nations appropriated and reformulated feminist demands. Besse reaches a similar, if more pessimistic, conclusion: "Brazil's feminists contributed to the modernization of gender relations without fundamentally upsetting the organization of social and political equality. . . . Accepting the values and norms of bourgeois capitalist society, they helped to integrate women more fully into it."[10]

As I have shown in this work, to characterize the changes in gender that took place in the first half of the twentieth century as a "modernization" is helpful, but only to a degree. The characterization is useful insofar as it highlights, as I have for popular-front Chile, the intrinsic links between the reform of gender and broader economic and political projects. In Chile, as in Brazil and other Southern Cone countries, gender reform contributed to and ensued from these broader transformations. Middle-class feminists did not reject racialized discourses of progress that naturalized gender, and they were prone to use the rhetoric of reproduction provided by eugenic thought. The term "modernization" is useful, moreover, insofar as it evokes the modular, civilizing mission that animated so many reformers, feminist and nonfeminist. Desiring to make their nations more like the modernized, industrial west, those elites sought to uplift the degenerate workers and housewives of their nations. As Mary Kay Vaughan has noted for Mexico, though state officials and professionals did not simply consume knowledge and technologies imported from the north, their professional training undoubtedly instilled in them models of progress not wholly of their own making. The striking similarities among elite disciplinary projects throughout Latin America, and throughout much of the world, were clearly a result of professionals' exposure to those purportedly universal models, and the term "modernization" foregrounds the homogenizing, (neo)colonial nature of elite projects.[11]

Yet, as this work has revealed, describing gender reform as "modernization" also conceals certain dynamics. The term "modernization" cannot adequately capture, for instance, the eerie echoes, in the twentieth century, of long-standing notions of "gender right." Steve J. Stern has described these older patterns of contestation within the family in his book on gender in colonial, "old regime" Mexico. In that book, he notes that women in late colonial Mexico did not so much reject "patriarchal first principles" that bound husband and wife as contest whether and how each spouse would carry out his or her anointed duties. In enforcing male responsibility toward their families, women of the laboring classes often sought the help of more powerful outsiders. Stern acknowledges that the rise of both feminism and women's wage work in twentieth-century Mexico clearly destabilized these patterns, yet he observes that "vast changes may reconstitute old dynamics within new contexts."[12] As my study makes evident, this observation regarding historical continuity and historical change seems as true for Chile as for Mexico. In twentieth-century Chile, the constant reaffirmation of the family as well as the demonization of working women, single mothers, prostitutes, and mannish feminists must be understood as a response to the threat posed by women's potential sexual, economic, and political autonomy. Ironically, in Chile, professional and political elites who sought to make gender relations congruent with a modern social order ended up bolstering aspects of a more traditional patriarchal pact: enforcing male economic responsibilities for their families and women's domestic obligations. In fact, both the popular fronts and intellectuals played on themes of continuity and change, claiming they would reinstate a "natural" gender order even as they sought to make the family a vehicle of efficiency and progress.

Even feminism, I suggest in this book, was conditioned as much by enduring forms of gender contestation as by a radical critique of patriarchal privilege. Some feminists did, of course, question patriarchal first principles: they insisted that women had the right to support themselves and their children, sought to overturn women's subordination within marriage, and demanded that women participate as equals in public life. But much of the energy of feminists within MEMCh and FEChIF, and even more of the energy of feminist welfare professionals, went toward fortifying women's position within the patriarchal family—and helping women enforce men's adherence to patriarchal norms. This aspect of feminist practice, evident in many first-wave feminist movements, may, as Besse and Lavrin suggest, have limited the transformative potential of feminism. But, in Chile, it also helped make feminism a more broad-based movement. And, it allowed protofeminist welfare professionals to reach out to women who could not or would not reject the economic and sexual protection of male relatives. Feminism, in short, was conditioned not only by the relations between middle-class feminists and male reformers but also by the relations between middle-class feminist intellectuals and working-class women.

Finally, and most important, to characterize gender reform as a "modernization" does not adequately render the contingent pacts that under-girded elite efforts to remake gender relations. As I have argued in this work, popular-front efforts to constitute the family and shape gender were successful not only because they were functional to capitalist modernization but also because they converged in important ways with the expressed needs of diverse constituencies. Even more, both the shape of gender policies and the manner in which they were applied depended on the relative influence of diverse actors. Acknowledging this is important, for it allows us to see how a unique constellation of social forces led to the formulation of a modernizing program that was specific to a time and place.

For instance, Chile's professional and political classes seemed at once particularly intent on domesticating and disciplining men and particularly convinced of men's educability. As a result, they were less willing to chastise women and more willing to enter disputes on their side. By contrast, Barbara Weinstein notes that in São Paulo educators commissioned by the region's industrialists made women responsible for working-class "cultural respectability and good health." These educators saw syphilis as primarily the concern of working-class women while Chilean reformers focused on routing deviant male sexuality. In Brazil, elites enlisted women in their crusade to deter alcoholism among men, counseling women to provide an environment conducive to temperance. This kind of moralizing was not absent in Chile, but elites seemed much more willing to confront men directly.[13]

The reasons for these apparent differences are unclear. The fact that the Left, and the Communist Party in particular, had long seen women as essentially innocent victims in need of protection and that it directed its moralizing at men likely facilitated elites' focus on male deviance, even as it contributed to eradicating elites' more coercive practices. At the same time, social work, which developed earlier and more rapidly in Chile than in Brazil, was also more secular in outlook, more firmly tied to the state, and more closely linked to the feminist movement. Without the influence and persistence of social workers it is unlikely that so much effort would have been spent on routing male vice. Finally, the strength of the feminist movement itself likely encouraged state officials to correct men. Although, as I have pointed out, Chilean feminists had only very limited power, feminist leaders in Chile developed extensive ties to both national leaders and working-class women and they clearly sought to limit the prerogatives of men. The specific shape of the state's efforts to regulate masculine deportment emerged out of the conflicts and convergences of the Left, social workers, feminists, popular-front leaders, and working-class women and men. Portraying elite efforts to discipline popular classes as the simple consequence of a modernizing imperative occludes complex negotiations.

In concluding, it seems appropriate to reflect briefly on the diverse mechanisms through which identities and alliances became fixed or were challenged and on what these tell us about the popular-front project. Throughout this work I have noted how vanguards disciplined followers and discredited competitors by invoking foundational discourses of progress, rationality, centralization, education, and even physical well-being. Gender, which was centrally implicated in these discourses, not only ordered relations between men and women and among men but also helped potential vanguards naturalize their ascendancy. Going even further, popular-front leaders proposed that the consolidation of family and nation were inseparable tasks and that consensus within families would help forge agreements on a national level. The popular fronts could not found a new social order, they said, without ordering families. Hence the persistent calls to solidarity. Hence too the ease with which popular-front leaders used metaphors of family to refer to political pacts, especially the pact enshrined within and in relation to the state. Consensus within the family was not predicated on equality, however, nor were the agreements hammered out by the popular fronts.[14] Chile's compromises were compromised.

Yet along with a vision of alliances as familylike, there was also the view that consensus emerged through conversation and contestation. More powerful participants might easily listen selectively, with their own interests in mind. Authorities might talk at their audiences. But because weaker participants challenged the interpretations of those with greater political and intellectual resources, there was always the possibility of an outcome that was more satisfying to the former. When prostitutes sat down for CSO sanitary education talks, when unions distributed *Vida Sana*, or when women marched for temperance, they incurred costs and accrued benefits. Although political pacts were coercive, because they were restrictive, the coercive force of those pacts derived mainly from leaders' ability to reformulate alternatives. In this context, choices, even if circumscribed, remained available and dialogue was possible. As a result, foundational discourses did not always succeed in neutralizing, for they could be redrawn.

By looking at gender in popular-front Chile, this study has shown how autonomy and alliance, both of which manifested themselves organizationally and rhetorically, empowered and circumscribed elite projects and practices. Political openings emerged in Chile despite, and even *within*, the foundational discourses that Chile shared with many of its Latin American neighbors and "the civilized world." Because the persistently multilayered level of conflict created possibilities for crosscutting alliances that undermined national leaders, the control of Chile's popular-front leaders was particularly tenuous. It was undoubtedly the plurality of the popular-front alliance, compounded by the partial nature of its rule, that permitted a less debilitating form of popular incorporation in Chile. In this context popular sectors achieved political openings through a delicate combination of collusion and withdrawal, destabilizing and redrawing elite hegemony in the process. Rather than viewing Chile's lack of a firm political center as a failure, we should view it as a particularly resilient form of politics, one in which actors were quite often forced, out of necessity and weakness, to listen to each other.

APPENDIX

TABLE A.1. Electoral participation in presidential elections, 1932–1946

Voters	1932	1938	1942	1946
% of adult population	15.7	18.4	18.8	17.1
% of those eligible to vote	43.9	51.6	49.8	45.9

Source: Borón, "La evolución del régimen electoral," 428–29.

TABLE A.2. Vote for popular-front presidential candidates in selected provinces, 1938–1946

Province	Aguirre Cerda (1938)	Ríos (1942)	González Videla (1946)
Tarapacá	59.7%	67.9%	57.9%
Antofagasta	69.5	77.9	68.8
Santiago	55.8	51.1	39.6
Concepción	64.1	69.6	55.2
Arauco	51.7	95.5	55.3
Magallanes	88.9	77.8	54.5
All provinces	50.2	55.7	40.1

Source: Adapted from Urzúa Valenzuela, *Historia política de Chile*, 501–2, 531–32, 541–42.
Note: The 1938 and 1942 elections were essentially two-way races; the 1946 election was basically a three-way race.

TABLE A.3. Rates of unionization and mobilization, 1932–1941

Year	Industrial and professional unions	Members	Collective conflicts and strikes	Participants
1932	421	54,801	51	7,736
1933	619	75,050	172	24,648
1934	680	81,285	125	17,800
1935	669	83,262	135	15,549
1936	670	84,699	187	37,366
1937	812	116,378	235	38,504
1938	932	125,978	248	48,078
1939	1,687	173,438	652	128,452
1940	1,888	171,279	1,131	148,596
1941	1,985	208,775	892	116,911

Source: *Revista del Trabajo* 12, nos. 7–8 (July–August 1942): 37–38.
Note: This data includes only legally constituted unions and legally sanctioned conflicts.

TABLE A.4. Women's workforce participation, 1930–1952

Year	Men	Women	Total	% women
		Workers		
1930	1,116,513	290,961	1,460,474	20
1940	1,362,275	432,903	1,795,178	24
1952	1,616,152	539,141	2,155,243	25

Sources: Chile, Dirección General de Estadística, X Censo [1930], vol. 3, xviii, 17–18; Chile, "Censo de población, 1940," in Estadística Chilena 19, no. 9 (September 1946): 564; Chile, Servicio Nacional de Estadística y Censos, XII Censo [1952], 205–7.
Note: Economically active population has been adjusted to include the unemployed and domestic servants and to exclude students, prisoners, hospital residents, and persons living on fixed incomes.

TABLE A.5. Women in the manufacturing workforce, 1930–1952

Year	Number	% of women workers
1930	90,756	31
1940	93,904	22
1952	131,850	24

Sources: Chile, Dirección General de Estadística, X Censo [1930], vol. 3, xviii, xxviii, 17–18; Chile, "Censo de población, 1940," in Estadística Chilena 19, no. 9 (September 1946): 549–58, 564; Chile, Servicio Nacional de Estadística y Censos, XII Censo [1952], 205–7, 269.

TABLE A.6. Women in domestic service, 1930–1952

Year	Number	% of women workers
1930	114,782	40
1940	172,975	40
1952	171,330	32

Sources: Chile, Dirección General de Estadística, X Censo [1930], vol. 3, xvii–xviii, 17–18; Chile, "Censo de población, 1940," in Estadística Chilena 19, no. 9 (September 1946): 546, 564; Chile, Servicio Nacional de Estadística y Censos, XII Censo [1952], 205–7, 269.
Note: For 1930 and 1940 domestic service includes classified and unclassified domestic servants, laundresses, and cooks. Figures for 1952 include only domestic servants classified as such.

TABLE A.7. Individuals apprehended by the police for inebriation, 1938–1949

Year	% of total arrests	Year	% of total arrests
1938	44.3	1944	44.8
1939	43.3	1945	49.5
1940	41.6	1946	46.0
1941	41.7	1947	42.2
1942	44.9	1948	43.8
1943	45.0	1949	42.1

Sources: Estadística Chilena 18, no. 12 (December 1945), and 23, no. 12 (December 1950): 720–21.

NOTES

INTRODUCTION

1. Interviews with Elena Varela, 27 July 1993, 30 July 1993, and 27 July 1999. Unless otherwise noted, all translations are my own.

2. The coalition that formed in 1936, elected Pedro Aguirre Cerda to the presidency in 1938, and persisted until 1940 referred to itself as the "Popular Front." I use the term "popular fronts" and the adjective "popular-front" (which I do not capitalize) to designate the Popular Front and subsequent governing coalitions that included sectors of the Center, the Left, and eventually the Right. I take this usage from Moulian, "Violencia, gradualismo y reformas." I use the terms "leftist" and "socialist" interchangeably to refer to those who advocated socialism. I use the term "Socialist" (with a capital "S") to denote members of the Socialist Party.

3. See Scott, *Gender and the Politics of History*, esp. 42–50, and Yanagisako and Collier, "Toward a Unified Analysis."

4. Only the Communist Party, which remained more solidly working class, was a partial exception. On the social composition of political leadership see Drake, *Socialism and Populism*, 108–13, 127–30, 136–38, 151–64, 168–75, 192–94, 235, 247–52.

5. José Pablo Silva, personal communication, 8 February 1999 and 26 May 1999. Compare Parker, *Idea of the Middle Class*, and Owensby, *Intimate Ironies*, on Peru and Brazil. The Chilean middle class appears to have been more powerful than its Peruvian or Brazilian counterpart and more open to alliance with the working class.

6. Standard accounts of the popular-front period include Drake, *Socialism and Populism*, and Stevenson, *Chilean Popular Front*. The period is also examined in Moulian, "Violencia, gradualismo y reformas"; Borón, "Movilización política y crisis política"; Faúndez, *Marxism and Democracy*; Furci, *Chilean Communist Party*; Collier and Collier, *Shaping the Political Arena*; Espinoza, *Para una historia*; and Pizarro, *La huelga obrera en Chile*. For pioneer works on gender during this period see Klubock, *Contested Communities*; Lavrin, *Women, Feminism, and Social Change*; and Gaviola et al., *Queremos votar*.

7. On compromise politics see Valenzuela, *Breakdown of Democratic Regimes*; Angell, *Politics and the Labour Movement in Chile*; Moulian, "Violencia, gradualismo y reformas"; Borón, "Movilización política y crisis política"; Faúndez, *Marxism and Democracy*; and Collier and Collier, *Shaping the Political Arena*.

8. For the 1931–52 period as an aborted experience in "coalitional populism" that failed to satisfy popular needs see Collier and Collier, *Shaping the Political Arena*, 355. Although more nuanced, Drake's *Socialism and Populism* stresses the ways in which the popular fronts tended to demobilize and co-opt popular sectors. Chilean authors have tended to see the period in a more positive light. See Illanes, "En el nombre," and Moulian

"Violencia, gradualismo y reformas." On the Left's attitude toward compromise politics in the period after 1950 see Moulian, "Violencia, gradualismo y reformas"; Daire, "La política del Partido Comunista"; Furci, *Chilean Communist Party*; Faúndez, *Marxism and Democracy*; and Casanueva and Fernández, *El Partido Socialista y la lucha de clases*.

9. According to the 1952 census, 11 percent of men and 15 percent of women sixteen years of age and older were illiterate. In rural areas, however, literacy was only 63 percent (Chile, Servicio Nacional de Estadística y Censos, *XII Censo* [1952], vol. 1, 159, 162).

10. For additional information on working-class voting patterns see Drake, *Socialism and Populism*, 203–5, 257–65, 275–77, 293–96. On the electoral activity of MEMCh see "¡Ud. quiere que su hijo sea un hombre honrado. . . !" Archivo Personal Elena Caffarena (hereafter APEC); "¡¡Toda mujer es responsable de la honradez de su marido. . . !!" APEC; Memoria presentada al Segundo Congreso Nacional del MEMCh, [1940], APEC A1 4; Secretaría general a los comités MEMCh de distintas localidades, 29 July 1946, APEC A1 7; *Libertad* (Curicó), third week August 1938, 4; fourth week August 1938, 3–4; and second week September 1938, 3; *Frente Popular* (Valparaíso), 2 September 1937, n.p.; and *El Popular* (Antofagasta), 7 October 1938, 2.

11. Standard accounts stress an increasingly regressive wage structure and a modest 7 percent increase in blue-collar wages between 1940 and 1953. See Drake, *Socialism and Populism*, 229, and Collier and Collier, *Shaping the Political Arena*, 394–95, both of which seem to rely on Aníbal Pinto Santa Cruz, *Chile: Un caso de desarrollo frustrado*. However, one index of real wages in selected manufacturing industries (which likely included only workers with social security insurance) rose from 100 in 1937 to 165 in 1949, documenting a very substantial increase. Another index of daily wages paid rose from 89.8 in 1935 to 155.6 in 1949 (1927–29=100) (Chile, Dirección General de Estadística, *Anuario estadístico año 1950: Finanzas, bancos y cajas sociales*, 74; *Estadística Chilena* 23, no. 12 [December 1950]: 709). I calculated the former index by deflecting the "index of real wages" by the "index of worker-days." The "index of real wages" was derived, I believe, from total wage bills, as estimated by employer contributions to the Caja de Seguro Obligatorio. The index included the following industrial sectors: sugar; cement; beer; electricity; match-making; gas, coke, and tar; cotton cloth; cloths and woolens; paper and cardboard; and tobacco.

12. On women's participation see *Unidad Gráfica*, 9 October 1938, 1; Lenka Franulic's article in *Hoy* (n.d., c. 1938), APEC; and Comité Femenino pro Candidatura Gabriel González Videla, "Proyecto de gobierno de los partidos democráticos" (Santiago, c. 1946), in APEC.

13. On popular representation on advisory boards see *Chispa* (Iquique), February 1939, 7; *La Crítica*, 6 November 1939, 10; *Combate*, first fortnight February 1943, 2; *Noticiario Sindical*, 31 January 1949, 10; *Boletín Médico-Social de la Caja de Seguro Obligatorio* 11, nos. 117–19 (July–September 1944): 205; Aqueveque Castro, "Experiencias obtenidas," 6; Mora Campos, "Protección a la familia obrera," 135; Meneses Zúñiga, "La ley 4.054," 17; Barrera, "Desarrollo económico y sindicalismo," 6; and CTCh, 10 September 1943, 2, and 1 May 1946, 13. On feminist representation see Memoria

presentada al Segundo Congreso Nacional del MEMCh, [1940], APEC A1 4, and MEMCh, *Circular*, no. 8, April 1948, APEC A1 21.

14. The Socialist Party garnered 11.2, 16.8, and 12.8 percent of the vote in the 1937, 1941, and 1945 congressional elections, respectively; Communists won 4.2, 11.8, and 10.3 percent of the vote in those same elections (Cruz-Coke, *Historia electoral*, 81). On the Socialist Party's electoral trajectory see also Drake, *Socialism and Populism*, 203–5, 257–65, 275–77, 293–96. References to Socialists and Communists who served as governors, intendants, and heads of government services can be found in Drake, *Socialism and Populism*, 239; *Chispa* (Iquique), second fortnight March 1939, 5; *El Surco* (La Ligua), 28 December 1940, n.p., and 4 January 1941, 2; *El Progreso* (Arauco), 27 February 1941, n.p., and 6 March 1941, 3; and interview with Irma Moreno, 14 June 1993.

15. Quotation from *Mundo Nuevo*, 22 February 1941, 6. See also *La Voz del Gremio*, April–May 1948, 3, and *Principios*, no. 44 (February 1945): 15. On labor mobilization see table A.3.

16. On local Alianza Democrática committees see Figueroa Ortiz and Sandoval Ambiado, *Carbón*, 232–40; *El Progreso* (Curicó), first fortnight January 1945, 4; *Socialismo*, second fortnight October 1943, n.p.; and *Crónica* (Valdivia), 29 January 1944, 3.

17. The convergences among these disparate critiques are evident in McClintock et al., eds., *Dangerous Liaisons*. Differences and similarities among feminist, postcolonial, antiracist, and antihumanist critics are explored in Prakash, "Writing Post-Orientalist Histories," 376–83.

18. Pateman, *Disorder of Women*, esp. 195–97. For a discussion of similar issues as they relate to Latin America see Jelin, ed., *Women and Social Change in Latin America*, 1–11, 184–207. For critiques of liberalism see also Landes, *Women and the Public Sphere*; Dietz, "Context Is All"; Mouffe, *Return of the Political*, 74–89; Phillips, *Democracy and Difference*; Benhabib, ed., *Democracy and Difference*; Scott, *Gender and the Politics of History*, 93–112; and Fraser, *Unruly Practices*, 113–83.

19. On the tension between Gramsci and Foucault in subaltern studies and the differences between older and more recent work see Mallon, "Promise and Dilemma." The more recent work includes Chatterjee, *Nation and Its Fragments*, esp. 10, 16–22, and Guha, *Dominance without Hegemony*. See also Chakrabarty, "Postcoloniality and the Artifice of History."

20. In addition to the works cited in the previous note see Prakash, "Writing Post-Orientalist Histories," and Chatterjee, *Nationalist Thought and the Colonial World*. Although much of the subaltern studies' critique focuses on nationalist and marxist historiographies, a rejection of nationalist and marxist politics is implicit. The connection is made explicit in Guha, ed., *Subaltern Studies Reader*, ix–xxii. Gender is explored in Sangari and Vaid, eds., *Recasting Women*; Chatterjee, *Nation and Its Fragments*, chs. 6 and 7; Sinha, "Gender in the Critiques of Colonialism and Nationalism"; and Chakrabarty, "Difference-Deferral."

21. On the early national era see Safford, "Race, Integration, and Progress." On immigration and whitening see Helg, "Race in Argentina and Cuba," and Brading,

"Manuel Gamio." Compare Knight, "Racism, Revolution, and *Indigenismo*"; Borges, " 'Puffy, Ugly, Slothful and Inert' "; and Stepan, "*Hour of Eugenics.*" Socialist practice is examined in Helg, "Race in Argentina and Cuba"; Stepan, "*Hour of Eugenics,*" 200–201; Zimmerman, "Racial Ideas and Social Reform"; Guy, *Sex and Danger,* 28–29, 91–94, 98–99, 106–11, 131, 183–84; and de la Cadena, "Silent Racism."

22. On hegemony as leadership see Gramsci, *Selections from the Prison Notebooks,* and Roseberry, "Hegemony and the Language of Contention." For works that develop the perspective outlined here see Gilroy, *Black Atlantic;* Mallon, *Peasant and Nation;* and Joseph and Nugent, eds., *Everyday Forms of State Formation.* On the specificity of the Indian case see Mallon, "Promise and Dilemma," and Guha, ed., *Subaltern Studies Reader,* ix–xxii.

23. Gramsci, *Selections from the Prison Notebooks,* esp. 52–120. Poulantzas, *State, Power, Socialism,* esp. 11–14, 129–31, 257–63; quotation on 129. My views of the state also draw from Corrigan and Sayer, *Great Arch,* and Joseph and Nugent, eds., *Everyday Forms of State Formation.*

24. Contreras Labarca, "Por la paz," 19–21.

25. Foucault, *Power/Knowledge,* 78–108; quotations on 83, 85; Stoler, *Race and the Education of Desire,* esp. 62–94, 197–200. See also Cooper, "Conflict and Connection."

26. Foucault, *Power/Knowledge,* 101, 82.

27. Gramsci, *Selections from the Prison Notebooks,* 5–23; quotation on 8.

28. Laclau and Mouffe, *Hegemony and Socialist Strategy,* esp. 55–65, 122–34, ch. 4. See also Laclau, *New Reflections,* 17–27, 35–41, 171–73, and Norval, "Letter to Ernesto." The distinction between vanguardist and articulatory practices echoes the Gramscian distinction between war of maneuver and war of position. On Foucault's failure to note "the critical differences between state formations that discursively threaten expulsion and extermination as opposed to those that carry it out," see Stoler, *Race and the Education of Desire,* 88.

29. On gender and "nature" see Yanagisako and Delaney, "Naturalizing Power."

30. O'Hanlon, "Recovering the Subject." Coronil, "Listening to the Subaltern"; quotation on 649.

31. Scott, *Only Paradoxes to Offer,* 12–17; Scott, *Gender and the Politics of History,* 172–77. In insisting on multiple differences, Scott of course draws on the work of feminists of color.

32. As Laclau, *New Reflections,* 171–72, explains:

Let us consider the case . . . of transformism. It is usually considered to be a form of neutralization of the potential antagonism of the group. . . . If the decision between accepting the co-optation and continuing the confrontation were algorithmic, and if the correct decision were the latter, the first solution could only be a phenomenon of false consciousness. That is to say, the identity of the agent would not be affected by the decision-making process. But if the decision is not algorithmic, it constitutes a radically new identity. In this case, the identity of the co-opted agents changes and (given the contingent character of the decision) this can only occur on the basis of *repressing,* of exerting *coercion,* on other possibilities.

33. Laclau and Mouffe, *Hegemony and Socialist Strategy*, esp. 127–34.

34. Local and regional approximations to the popular-front era can be found in Klubock, *Contested Communities*; Winn, *Weavers of Revolution*, chs. 2 and 3; and Antezana-Pernet, "El MEMCh en provincia." For case studies of gender, labor, and working-class life that cover other time periods see Tinsman, "Los patrones del hogar"; Hutchison, "Working Women of Santiago"; Pinto, *Trabajos y rebeldías*; González Miranda, *Hombres y mujeres de la pampa*; Illanes, "El proyecto comunal"; Figueroa Ortiz and Sandoval Ambiado, *Carbón*; Romero, "Condiciones de vida"; Romero, "Rotos y gañanes"; J. Rojas Flores et al., *Historia de los obreros de la construcción*; and Frías et al., *Organización sindical*.

CHAPTER ONE

1. Drake, *Socialism and Populism*, 76, 180, 199.

2. Allende, *La realidad médico-social*, 8.

3. Barría Serón, *Los movimientos sociales*; DeShazo, *Urban Workers*, esp. 131–32; Ramírez Necochea, *Origen y formación*, esp. 51–62.

4. Illanes, "En el nombre," 99; *Acción Social*, no. 27 (June 1934): 30–33.

5. For chronologies that include much of Chile's social legislation see Pimstein, "Algunas referencias históricas," and *Revista del Trabajo* 6, no. 1 (January–February 1936): 21–29. On conciliation boards and the Oficina del Trabajo see DeShazo, *Urban Workers*, 51, 142, and Rojas Flores, *La dictadura de Ibáñez*, 62. On government intervention in labor disputes prior to 1920 see Figueroa Ortiz and Sandoval Ambiado, *Carbón*, 89–135, and Pizarro, *La huelga obrera en Chile*, 42–52. On the nursery law see *Revista del Trabajo* 3, no. 4 (April 1932): 45.

6. Zeitlin, *Civil Wars*; Góngora, *Ensayo histórico*; Remmer, "Timing, Pace and Sequence"; Valenzuela and Wilde, "Presidential Politics," esp. 192–96, data on ministerial instability on 195; Heise González, *Ciento cincuenta años*. Compare Scully, *Rethinking the Center*.

7. Morris, *Elites, Intellectuals, and Consensus*.

8. DeShazo, *Urban Workers*, 186–87. More general descriptions of opposition to Alessandri's legislative proposals can be found in Morris, *Elites, Intellectuals, and Consensus*, 206, 243–47, and Illanes, "En el nombre," 187–91. On the Braden Copper Company see Klubock, *Contested Communities*, 70. *Revista de Asistencia Social* 13 (1944): 436, 438, 440.

9. For a summary description of the new laws see DeShazo, *Urban Workers*, 219–21, and Rojas Flores, *La dictadura de Ibáñez*, 61–70.

10. A detailed examination of the Ibáñez years can be found in Nunn, *Chilean Politics*. On constitutional changes see Valenzuela and Wilde, "Presidential Politics," 195–96. On the reorganization of the repressive apparatus see Rojas Flores, *La dictadura de Ibáñez*, esp. 27, 59.

11. On union relations with Ibáñez see Rojas Flores, *La dictadura de Ibáñez*, esp. chs. 4 and 5.

12. Góngora, *Ensayo histórico*, 171–72; Rojas Flores, *La dictadura de Ibáñez*, 51–53, 82; Illanes, "En el nombre," 215–23; Nunn, *Chilean Politics*, 98, 104–5.

13. On Ibáñez's achievements see Rojas Flores, *La dictadura de Ibáñez*. On the roots of the Socialist Party see Jobet, *El Partido Socialista*, 30–81.

14. Rojas Flores, *La dictadura de Ibáñez*, 14–18, ch. 7; Nunn, *Chilean Politics*, 160–65.

15. On the Right during 1932–38 see Drake, *Socialism and Populism*, 113–27, 165–67. On the failures of Chile's dominant class see Moulian and Torres Dujisin, *Discusiones*, 21–39, and Cavarozzi, "Government and the Industrial Bourgeoisie."

16. Stevenson, *Chilean Popular Front*, ch. 5; Drake, *Socialism and Populism*, chs. 4 and 6; Moulian and Torres Dujisin, *Discusiones*, 56–64, 113–15. On changes in the Communist Party's line see Gómez, "Factores nacionales e internacionales," esp. 65–75.

17. Aguirre Cerda in *Unidad Gráfica*, 9 October 1938, 1. Reyes Alvarez, "Los presidentes radicales."

18. Furci, *Chilean Communist Party*; Varas, comp., *El Partido Comunista*; Gómez, "Factores nacionales e internacionales," 68–75; Millas, *En los tiempos*, 85. The Socialist Party, which had been born under the umbrella of the state, was from the start more of a reformist party.

19. *Combate*, 30 September 1939, n.p. Godoy Urrutia continued by saying, "Two things result from this; struggles for hegemony and lethargy in the government's functioning."

20. Drake, *Socialism and Populism*, 279–83; Moulian and Torres Dujisin, *Discusiones*.

21. On right-wing obstructionism see Drake, *Socialism and Populism*, 232–34, and Stevenson, *Chilean Popular Front*, 94–112 (the anti-Communist bill is mentioned on 103). On the fears of popular-front congressmen in 1940 see Chile, Cámara de Diputados, 18 January 1940, 48a. sesión (sesiones extraordinarias, 1939–40, IV, 2675–96). On the Right's lack of unity and direction see Moulian and Torres Dujisin, *Discusiones*, 153–299.

22. *Unidad Gráfica*, 9 October 1938, 1, my emphasis.

23. *Acción Social*, no. 81 (September 1939): 1. In the same vein see ibid., 4.

24. On right-wing defense of profit see, for example, Chile, Cámara de Diputados, 18 January 1940, 48a. sesión (sesiones extraordinarias, 1939–40, IV). For the debates in the Chamber of Deputies see *Rumbo* (December 1939): 84, and Cámara de Diputados, 18 January 1940, 48a. sesión (sesiones extraordinarias, 1939–40, IV, 2675). See also Teitelboim, *Hijo del salitre*, 446.

25. Fonseca, "Plan inmediato," 8. Allende, "El Partido Socialista proclama," 2.

26. For anti-imperialist rhetoric see *Juventud en Marcha* (Concepción), 12 May 1937, 4, and Allende, *La realidad médico-social*, 5. For comparisons of Chile to other industrialized countries see, for example, Allende, *La realidad médico-social*, 41–42, 51–52, 89–90.

27. The Soviet constitution was reprinted in *Acción Social*, no. 53 (September 1936): 34–42. Interview with Tomy Romeo, 4 June 1993. See also *Boletín de la Sociedad Chilena de Obstetricia y Ginecología* 3, no. 3 (April 1938): 199–200.

28. *El Obrero Municipal*, May–June 1944, 6. *La Crítica*, 13 June 1942, 3.

29. Stoler, *Race and the Education of Desire*, esp. 196–203.

30. *Acción Social*, no. 76 (February 1939): 98–99. Allende, "La contradicción de

Chile," 30–31. On "feudal" landowners see also *El Siglo*, 6 January 1943, 3, and 20 January 1943, 3.

31. *La Crítica*, 4 November 1939, 8.

32. Allende, *La realidad médico-social*, esp. 5–8, 195–98; quotation on 5.

33. *Acción Social*, no. 76 (February 1939): 97, claimed that there were two Chilean races or nations, the aristocracy and the people, and pleaded for a democratization that would abolish these differences. On the connections between discourses of race and progress see Borges, " 'Puffy, Ugly, Slothful and Inert' "; Zimmerman, "Racial Ideas and Social Reform"; Stepan, *"Hour of Eugenics"*; Knight, "Racism, Revolution, and Indigenismo," esp. 86–95; Helg, "Race in Argentina and Cuba"; and de la Cadena, "Political Tensions." On race and nationalism see Gilroy, *"There Ain't No Black in the Union Jack."* The term "cultural competencies" comes from Stoler, *Race and the Education of Desire*.

34. *El Progreso* (Arauco), 24 April 1941, 1. Partido Comunista, "Estatutos," 37.

35. *AS*, no. 4, n.d., 3. *Barricada*, second fortnight May 1940, 5. See also *Noticiario Sindical*, 31 January 1949, 2, which asked the employer of striking workers to concede "logical raises" in pay. Moulian and Torres Dujisin, "Concepción de la política," esp. 21–25, found similar conceptualizations in the worker press in the period around 1919. On workers' support of progress in São Paulo see Weinstein, *For Social Peace*, 4. On faith in technological advancement in the United States see Hughes, *American Genesis*, esp. ch. 6.

36. *Bandera Roja*, fourth week September 1936, 1. *El Despertar Minero* (Sewell), 1 August 1939, 2. *La Crítica*, 4 November 1939, 13. See also *Juventud en Marcha* (Concepción), 10 April 1937, 1, and *Noticiario Sindical*, 1 May 1949, 8.

37. *Rumbo* (June 1940): 88. *Combate*, 9 September 1939, n.p. See also Millas, *En los tiempos*, 145–46; Teitelboim, *Hijo del salitre*, 49; and *Tribuna Juvenil*, first fortnight April 1935, 8.

38. Partido Comunista, "Estatutos," 33. *Combate*, 9 September 1939, n.p.

39. Hutchison, "Working Women of Santiago"; Moulian and Torres Dujisin, "Concepción de la política."

40. *Vanguardia Socialista* (Yungay), 16 October 1938, 1; *La Crítica*, 8 November 1939, 3; *Unidad Gráfica*, 9 October 1938, 1. See also Partido Comunista, "¡Adelante!" 43–44.

41. *Pedro Aguirre Cerda*, 27 April 1938, 2. See also the CSO magazine *Acción Social*, no. 83 (November 1939): 1.

42. This discourse resembled French "solidarism" and had similar gendered effects on welfare policy. See Jensen, "Representations of Gender," 162.

43. *AS*, no. 4, n.d., 3. See also Partido Socialista, "Congreso Extraordinario del Partido Socialista, Santiago, 7, 8, 9 de agosto de 1944," and *Principios*, nos. 56–57 (February–March 1946): 16.

44. On how links between family and nation deny hierarchy and promote solidarity see Anderson, *Imagined Communities*, and Parker et al., eds., *Nationalisms and Sexualities*, esp. 5–7. The way nationalisms employ a symbolism of blood is explored in Yanagisako and Delaney, "Naturalizing Power," and Delaney, "Father State, Motherland."

45. *Ceteche* (Antofagasta), 1 May 1941, 5.

46. *La Crítica*, 20 November 1939, 7, my emphasis. On the tension between biology and environment in Latin American scientific thought see Nancy Stepan, "Hour of Eugenics." For works that explore more primordial and essentialist visions of gender and nation, legitimated through reference to a shared past, see Alonso, "Politics of Space, Time and Substance," esp. 387–90; Chatterjee, *Nation and Its Fragments*, esp. 116–57; and Chakrabarty, "Difference-Deferral."

47. *Vida Sana* (Valparaíso) 1, no. 3 (July 1942): 3. Compare the more biologically inspired explanations in *Revista Chilena de Higiene y Medicina Preventiva* 1, nos. 2–3 (January–March 1937): 150–56. On the dual, cultural and natural, aspects of gender see Alonso, *Thread of Blood*, 79–90.

48. *Vida Sana* (Valparaíso) 2, nos. 20–21 (January–February 1944): 7.

49. The quotations are from *Frente Popular*, 17 November 1937, 7, and *La Crítica*, 5 September 1942, 3. See also *La Palabra* (Valdivia), 1 February 1935, and 21 December 1935, n.p.; *Vida Sana* (Temuco) 1, no. 1 (November 1938), 1; and *La Crítica*, 20 November 1939, 7, and 5 November 1942, 3.

50. See, for example, Allende, *La realidad médico-social*.

51. Aguirre Cerda in *Unidad Gráfica*, 9 October 1938, 1. This metaphor is attributed to the socialist republic by Carlos Sáez Morales, *Recuerdos de un soldado*, vol. 3 (Santiago, 1934), 7–8, cited in Drake, *Socialism and Populism*, 74–75. *Vida Sana* (Valparaíso) 2, no. 9 (January 1943): 3.

52. On the link between political authority and conflicts over gender see Stern, *Secret History of Gender*.

53. For scholarly works that, in two very different national contexts, posit the existence of two masculine genders, one for respectable married men who earn privileges and the other for less privileged men see White, "Separating the Men from the Boys," and Rose, "Respectable Men, Disorderly Others." Both authors stress, as I do below, the ways in which the state conditioned dialogue on masculine respectability. See also Connell, *Gender and Power*, esp. 183–88.

54. On the exclusion of rural laborers see Muñoz Gomá, *Chile y su industrialización*, 92, and Loveman, "Political Participation and Rural Labor in Chile," esp. 186–87. Compare Carrière, "Landowners and the Rural Unionization Question."

55. Figures cited in Weitzman Fliman, "La Caja de Seguro Obligatorio," table 5, n.p.

56. *Vanguardia Hotelera*, 6 January 1934, 2. *Boletín Médico-Social de la Caja de Seguro Obligatorio* 9, nos. 98–99 (August–September 1942): 446–55; quotation on 450. Compare *El Obrero Gastronómico* (Valparaíso), 15 April 1939, 4. I am grateful to Rosita Bravo, Thelma Gálvez, Lorena Godoy, and Elizabeth Hutchison for help deciphering census data.

57. Interview with Mario González, 23 August 1994; interview with Roberto Quiroga, 24 August 1994.

58. Teitelboim, *Hijo del salitre*, 106. Chile, Cámara de Diputados, 24 July 1933, 32a. sesión (sesiones ordinarias, 1933, II, 1623). Compare *Bandera Roja*, first week August 1936, 3. On the Left's efforts to aid the unemployed see Partido Socialista, "La juventud en el Frente del Pueblo," 46.

59. *Noticiario Sindical*, 1 May 1949, 16. See also CTCh, August 1946, 3, which praised workers "who want tranquility in order to assure production, which means bread and smiles within the home, and is a revitalizing tonic for the *patria*."

60. Interviews with Carmen Lazo, 21 April 1993 and 15 July 1999; *Mundo Nuevo*, second week October 1938, n.p. *El Despertar Minero* (Sewell), 1 August 1941, 2, and 11 May 1939, 2. On the need for worker education see also *Principios*, no. 59 (May 1946): 13. On the historical roots of this discourse see Moulian and Torres Dujisin, "Concepción de la política," 1–15.

61. Urquieta Tognarelli, "Problemas psico-sociales," 3–4, 33. *Servicio Social* 12, no. 4 (October 1938): 164–65.

62. Boizard, *Cuatro retratos. Avance* (Magallanes), 4 September 1946, 2.

63. *Servicio Social* 12, no. 4 (October 1938): esp. 168–69.

64. For state publications that advocated increased economic and political benefits for rural workers or domestic servants see, for example, *Boletín Médico-Social de la Caja de Seguro Obligatorio* 9, nos. 98–99 (August–September 1942): 446–55; and *Acción Social*, no. 78 (May 1939): 10–11, and no. 79 (June 1939): 1–3. For leftist publications see *El Grito del Obrero Agrícola*, August 1940, 2; *Mujeres Chilenas*, December 1947, 9; and CTCh, 11 November 1943, 7.

65. *Unidad Gráfica*, 9 October 1938, 1.

CHAPTER TWO

1. On the family wage system see Pateman, *Disorder of Women*; Gordon, "New Feminist Scholarship," 19–28; and Joan Scott, *Gender and the Politics of History*, esp. ch. 7. Compare Elshtain, *Power Trips*, 62–72.

2. Robert Connell calls these widely accepted norms "hegemonic masculinity" and "emphasized femininity" and underscores women's compliance with and resistance to these gender norms (*Gender and Power*, 183–87).

3. On the notion of a just wage and its relevance to women's subordination in the workplace see Kessler-Harris, "Just Price."

4. For arguments used by employers see *Revista del Trabajo* 4, no. 12 (December 1934): 9–12, and 4, no. 5 (May 1934): 3–5. On workers' positions see *Frente Popular*, 19 July 1940, 4; *Mundo Nuevo*, third period, December 1946, 7; Fonseca, "Plan inmediato," 4; Sindicato Industrial Obrero Andes Copper Mining Co., "Pliego de peticiones"; and *Obrero Textil*, 4 October 1936, 3. The quotations are from *La Palabra* (Valdivia), 25 January 1936, 1, and *Vanguardia Hotelera*, 22 October 1949, 3.

5. On labor legislation see Mallet Simonetti, "Asignaciones familiares"; Valderrama, "El salario"; Chávez Guzmán, "La mujer ante el derecho"; Mellado, "Las asignaciones familiares"; and *Acción Social*, no. 75 (September 1938–January 1939): 38–41. For the minimum-wage provisions of the Labor Code see Chile, *Código del trabajo*, libro I, título II, párrafo iv, art. 44.

6. For legislative proposals on family allowances and minimum wages see Chile,

Cámara de Diputados, 1 June 1936, 5a. sesión (sesiones ordinarias, 1936, I, 244–49); 18 July 1939, 23a. sesión (sesiones ordinarias, 1939, II, 1245–47); and 11 May 1948, 5a. sesión (sesiones extraordinarias, 1948, II, 113–22). On popular pressure toward labor inspectors and the Work Inspection see Pizarro, *La huelga obrera en Chile*, esp. 116–17, 126; *Frente Popular*, 17 November 1937, 9; and *El Despertar Minero* (Sewell), 25 April 1939, n.p. For state officials' discourse on wages see *Revista del Trabajo* 4, no. 12 (December 1934): 9–12, and 5, no. 3 (March 1935): 87–93; and *Acción Social*, no. 75 (December 1938–January 1939): 11–41.

7. *Revista del Trabajo* 11, no. 9 (September 1941): 1. Decreto 381 (13 January 1941) cited in Valderrama, "El salario," 42–43.

8. Chile, Cámara de Diputados, 18 July 1939, 23a. sesión (sesiones ordinarias, 1939, II, 1245); *Revista del Trabajo* 14, nos. 9–10 (September–October 1944): 94–96.

9. In 1933, 19,157 workers received family allowances. By 1946, according to the Dirección del Trabajo, 421 industrial establishments employing a total of 105,562 workers paid allowances to 44,756 family heads. Since the 1930 census recorded 699,049 blue-collar workers (excluding the self-employed and including rural workers) and 252,682 *obreros* in mining and industry, an estimated 2.7 percent of all blue-collar workers and 7.6 percent of industrial workers collected allowances. The 1940 census registered 1,071,108 blue-collar workers, 269,972 of whom worked in industry and mining. The percentage of blue-collar workers who received family allowances in the early- to mid-1940s was thus around 4.2 percent, while the percentage of industrial workers was approximately 17 percent. (Since data collection was much more comprehensive for the censuses than for investigations of family allowances, I believe my calculations underestimate the prevalence of allowances.) Figures on allowances cited in Mallet Simonetti, "Asignaciones familiares," 10, and Chile, Cámara de Diputados, 11 May 1948, 5a. sesión (sesiones extraordinarias, 1948, II, 119). Census figures come from Chile, Dirección General de Estadística, *X Censo* [1930], vol. III, vi–vii, and Chile, "Censo de población, 1940," in *Estadística Chilena* 18, no. 2 (June 1945): 120. Figures on factories paying allowances come from Urbina Moya, "Proyecciones del servicio social," 55–58. For an account of family allowances in France see Pedersen, "Catholicism, Feminism," 264–69.

10. For a reference to family allowances as family wages see, for example, Allende, *La realidad médico-social*, 200.

11. On the withholding of family allowances for working wives see *Revista del Trabajo* 8, no. 12 (December 1938): 43–54. The quotation is from *La Voz del Metalúrgico*, 1 May 1953, 5.

12. Chile, Cámara de Diputados, 31 July 1933, 35a. sesión (sesiones ordinarias, 1933, II, 1817–21); 7 August 1933, 39a. sesión (sesiones ordinarias, 1933, II, 1992–93); 4 October 1933, 3a. sesión (sesiones extraordinarias, 1933–34, I, 83–94); 24 October 1933, 12a. sesión (sesiones extraordinarias, 1933–34, I, 444); and 25 October 1933, 14a. sesión (sesiones extraordinarias, 1933–34, 513); *Revista del Trabajo* 5, no. 1 (January 1935): 16–17.

13. *Revista del Trabajo* 5, no. 1 (January 1935): 17, and 6, no. 7 (July 1936): 87;

Bandera Roja, 2 July 1935, 6; *Rumbo* (Tocopilla), first fortnight 1937, n.p.; *Machete* (Tocopilla), first fortnight April 1937, 3.

14. The observation on contract negotiations is from Mallet Simonetti, "Asignaciones familiares," 17. On María Elena see *Bandera Roja*, 4 June 1936, 4, and Chile, Cámara de Diputados, 1 June 1936, 5a. sesión (sesiones ordinarias, 1936, I, 231–34). The quotation is from Villarroel Rojas, "Aspectos fundamentales," 32.

15. *Frente Popular* (Valparaíso), 2 September 1937, n.p. Chile, Cámara de Diputados, 1 June 1936, 5a. sesión (sesiones ordinarias, 1936, I, 247). *Revista del Trabajo* 5, no. 1 (January 1934): 17.

16. According to Mallet Simonetti, "Asignaciones familiares," 50, in 1933, before the passage of the nitrate law, a total of 11,983 workers in the nitrate industry received family allowances. The quotation is from *Servicio Social* 11, no. 4 (October 1937): 243. Klubock, *Contested Communities*; Ortega, "La industria del carbón," 69.

17. On the role of company welfare departments see Klubock, "Sexualidad y proletarización," 66–67; *Revista del Trabajo* 5, no. 10 (October 1935): 52–53, and 7, nos. 5–6 (June 1937): 129–32; *Servicio Social* 9, no. 3 (July–September 1935): 177; 9, no. 4 (October–December 1935): 305–7; 11, no. 4 (October 1937): 224–53; 18, no. 2 (April–August 1944): 6–9; 20, nos. 2–3 (May–December 1946): 31–39; and 29, no. 3 (September–December 1955): 17–29; *Pampa* (January 1949): 7; and Cárcamo Lastra, "Servicio social en la manufactura de metales 'MADEMSA,'" 9–11. On employers and family allowances in France see Pedersen, "Catholicism, Feminism," 253–60.

18. *Revista del Trabajo* 4, no. 12 (December 1934): n.p., 30–31.

19. See, for example, *Frente Popular*, 16 September 1936, 2. As Linda Gordon points out, the absence of concerted state action should not be misconstrued as the absence of a policy ("New Feminist Scholarship," 10–11). On family allowances and the French state see Pedersen, "Catholicism, Feminism," 256–60.

20. In April of 1935, the Dirección del Trabajo tallied 3,814 married blue-collar workers working in the nitrate industry in Tarapacá province and 5,606 unmarried workers, and in August of that year the totals were 3,863 and 5,842, respectively. In September 1936 the agency reported 7,631 married *obreros* in Tarapacá and Antofagasta provinces, and 11,976 unmarried workers (*Revista del Trabajo* 5, no. 5 [May 1935]: 30; 5, no. 9 [September 1935]: 66; and 6, nos. 11–12 [November 1936]: 27).

21. *Vanguardia Hotelera*, March 1948, 4, and October 1947, 4; *Juventud en Marcha* (Concepción), 5 June 1937, 2.

22. See, for example, CTCh, June 1946, 14.

23. Villarroel Rojas, "Aspectos fundamentales," 32. Workers who reaped a patriarchal dividend without having to mount a militant defense of male privilege manifested what Robert Connell calls "complicit" masculinity. The labor movement as a whole, however, tended toward a corporate display of "hegemonic" masculinity and a rejection of "marginalized" masculinities (*Masculinities*, 76–81, 181, 210). Unlike Connell, I use the term hegemony to refer to norms that were ascendant rather than dominant and stress that family wage ideology was "hegemonic" precisely because it could reconcile as well as "marginalize" alternative masculinities.

24. On the continued presence of married workers who had declared themselves single see *Unidad* (María Elena), c. July 1953, 1. For arguments in favor of funds for family allowances see *Revista del Trabajo* 4, no. 5 (May 1934): 4, and Chile, Cámara de Diputados, 11 May 1948, 5a. sesión (sesiones extraordinarias, 1948, II, 118). The 1952 law gave the executive the power to decree family allowances. Under Decree-Law 245 (23 July 1953), workers as well as employers made contributions to family allowance funds administered by either the state or industrywide *cajas de compensación*. This implied a small subsidy by workers without dependents of workers with families, but the workers' contributions were small, only 2 percent of their wages. Employers paid 13 percent of each worker's salary. The decree is reprinted in *La Voz del Metalúrgico*, 1 October 1953, 4, 6.

25. *Avance* (Magallanes), 26 December 1943, 5.

26. *El Despertar Minero* (Sewell), second fortnight December 1942, 3; Klubock, "Sexualidad y proletarización."

27. Palabra de la compañera Eusebia Torres de Coronel, 1947, APEC A2 3.

28. Interview with Fresia Gravano, 4 April 1993.

29. Teitelboim, *Hijo del salitre*, 194.

30. Interview with Fresia Gravano, 4 April 1993. See also *El Siglo*, 6 May 1943, 1. On women's assertion of political identities based on traditional roles see Molyneux, "Mobilization without Emancipation?" and Kaplan, "Female Consciousness and Collective Action."

31. Interview with Graciela Trujillo, 20 April 1993; interview with Fresia Gravano, 4 April 1993; interview with Clara Velarde, 25 March 1993. For a campesina's assertion, in 1962, that women should control family allowances see Valdés et al., *Historias testimoniales*, 82. Guzmán, *La sangre y la esperanza*. By insisting on the enforcement of male responsibility, women—and certain working-class leaders—manifested a more "contingent" view of male prerogative, while certain men insisted on a more "absolute" patriarchal privilege. See Stern, *Secret History of Gender*, esp. 78–85.

32. Social worker Lucía Ponce Ponce called for the payment of the family allowance to the wife in "Desavenencias conyugales," 87. On the use of courts see Klubock, "Hombres y mujeres en El Teniente." On MEMCh El Teniente see *El Despertar Minero* (Sewell), 15 March 1941, 3. For CTCh resolutions see CTCh, second period, 28 January 1947, 3, and *Noticiario Sindical*, August 1951, 12. On feminist attempts to portray the payment of family allowances to wives as a social validation of mothering as work in France and Britain see Pedersen, "Catholicism, Feminism," 261–67, and Thane, "Women in the British Labour Party," esp. 348–57.

33. *La Voz de la Mujer*, December 1947, 8.

34. The quotation is from *Obrero Textil*, 4 December 1936, 2. See also *El Despertar Minero*, first fortnight August 1943, 7. My characterization of this discourse echoes the suggestion of Stern, *Secret History of Gender*, 329–31, that the reaffirmation of male privilege became more defensive after the rise of feminism.

35. CTCh, June 1946, 14.

36. *Tribuna* (Puerto Natales), 6 March 1941, 1, originally published in *Combate*. *Combate*, 12 October 1941, 4. Compare *Tribuna Textil*, December 1947, 3.

37. *Vanguardia Hotelera*, 22 October 1949, 1. See also *Mundo Nuevo*, fourth week October 1938, 2; *Noticiario Sindical*, 20 November 1948, 7, and August 1951, 12; and *Juventud en Marcha* (Concepción), 5 June 1937, 3.

38. For Saldías's testimony see *Mundo Nuevo*, third period, November 1946, 7. See also *CTCh*, June 1946, 14. On an earlier period see Hutchison, "El feminismo del movimiento obrero," 58–61.

39. *Tribuna Juvenil*, first fortnight April 1935, 4. See also *La Voz del Metalúrgico*, 6 November 1948, 7; *El Chiflón*, December 1947, n.p.; and *Mundo Nuevo*, third period, fourth week October 1938, 2, and December 1946, 7. On pay differentials in general see *CTCh*, second fortnight July 1939, 2; *La Mujer Nueva*, 8 November 1935, 1; and Chile, Caja de Seguro Obligatorio, *Anuario estadístico año 1946*, 15; *Anuario estadístico año 1947*, 13; and *Anuario estadístico año 1949*, 12. For the "equal pay" provision of the Labor Code see Chile, *Código del trabajo*, libro I, título II, párrafo iv, art. 3.

40. *Mundo Nuevo*, second period, second week November 1941, 2, and third period, 28 January 1947, 5.

41. *La Mujer Nueva* cited in *MEMCh antología*, 20. Pateman, *Disorder of Women*, 195–204, identifies these two opposing positions—equality for women who act like men and difference leading to subordination—as "Wollstonecraft's dilemma." As I suggest below, however, feminists who argued for women's access to paid labor implicitly questioned the association of work with masculinity. On feminists' paradoxical treatment of the question of equality versus difference see Scott, *Only Paradoxes to Offer*.

42. On legislation regulating maternity leaves and nurseries see *Revista del Trabajo* 3, no. 4 (April 1932): 45–46, and 6, no. 1 (January–February 1936): 28; Chile, *Código del trabajo*, libro II, título III; Meneses Zúñiga, "La ley 4.054"; and Weitzman Fliman, "La Caja de Seguro Obligatorio." In reality, maternity legislation posed only minimal economic hardship on employers, who frequently failed to set up nurseries or to pay maternity leaves. In 1943, state inspectors found that among more than 35,000 blue-collar women workers who worked in 2,061 different commercial and industrial establishments only 1,517 had taken maternity leave during the year, and only 840 infants attended the 205 nurseries set up by employers. Even if employers had complied with legal norms, women would still have constituted cheap labor because of their relatively low wages (*Revista del Trabajo* [14, nos. 9–10 (September–October 1944)?]: 35–36).

43. *La Mujer Nueva*, January 1936, 1; February 1936, 4; and 8 November 1935, 1; *Memoria presentada al Segundo Congreso Nacional del MEMCh*, [1940], APEC A1 4; *CTCh*, second fortnight July 1939, 2; *Conclusiones aprobadas en los foros verificados en celebración del día internacional de la mujer, 9–10 March* [1949], APEC A11 5.

44. *La Mujer Nueva*, September 1940, 5. See also *Documento referente al proyecto presentado por el Diputado Carlos Acharán Arce sobre jubilación de la mujer de la administración pública a los 25 años de servicio*, August 1951, APEC A16 4.

45. CTCh, second fortnight July 1939, 2, and 26 August 1939, 4.

46. On MEMCh lobbying around this issue see *La Mujer Nueva*, January 1936, 1–4, and February 1936, 4; Memoria presentada al Segundo Congreso Nacional del MEMCh, [1940], APEC A1 4; and Boletín extraordinario del Movimiento pro Emancipación de las Mujeres de Chile, 1946, APEC A1 8. On a 1941 proposed reform of maternity provisions see *El Progreso* (Arauco), 3 April 1941, 1.

47. *Revista del Trabajo* 3, no. 10 (October 1933): 76, and 3, no. 1 (January 1933): 45. CTCh, 26 August 1939, 4; MEMCh Boletina, November–December 1946, APEC A1 9; Posición del MEMCh frente a las elecciones municipales, c. April 1947, APEC A1 11. The quotation comes from Elena Caffarena to the editor of the newspaper *Democracia*, August 1951, APEC A10 6. MEMCh's 1940 congress proposed the creation of child care centers as a way of reducing infant mortality. See *MEMCh antología*, 37.

48. For denunciations of poor work conditions see *La Mujer Nueva*, 8 December 1935, 2; February 1936, 2; and March 1936, 4. Other rejections of protection can be found in CTCh, second fortnight July 1939, 2, and 26 August 1939, 4; and Comisión de problemas jurídicos [Segundo Congreso Nacional de Mujeres], 1947, APEC A10 4. For legal prohibitions of night work and underground work for women see Chile, *Código del trabajo*, libro I, título II, párrafo v, art. 48. For the quotation from MEMCh El Teniente see *El Despertar Minero* (Sewell), 15 March 1941, 3. For the quotation from Williams see *La Mujer Nueva*, September 1940, 5.

49. Elena Caffarena to the editor of the newspaper *Democracia*, August 1951, APEC A10 6.

50. *La Mujer Nueva*, March 1936, 2.

51. Ibid., June 1936, 4; *MEMCh antología*, 27–28; Memoria presentada al Segundo Congreso Nacional del MEMCh, [1940], APEC A1 4. On local MEMCh committees' participation in the protest see *La Mujer Nueva*, December 1936, 5, 7.

52. For MEMCh's analysis of women's subordination in marriage see *Frente Popular* (Valparaíso), 31 August 1937, n.p.; 20 August 1937, n.p.; and 23 August 1937, n.p.; *Frente Popular*, 28 September 1937, n.p.; and Comisión de problemas jurídicos [Segundo Congreso Nacional de Mujeres], 1947, APEC A10 4.

53. "El Movimiento pro Emancipación de las Mujeres de Chile en el décimo aniversario de su fundación," in *MEMCh antología*, 41–42.

54. Memoria presentada al Segundo Congreso Nacional del MEMCh, [1940], APEC A1 4; Pedro Aguirre Cerda to Elena Caffarena, 2 April 1940, in *MEMCh antología*, 25; *Frente Popular*, 26 July 1940, n.p.

55. "El Movimiento pro Emancipación de las Mujeres de Chile en el décimo aniversario de su fundación," in *MEMCh antología*, 41–42; Memoria presentada al Segundo Congreso Nacional del MEMCh, [1940], APEC A1 4; *Frente Popular*, 26 July 1940, n.p.

56. Director del Servicio de Impuestos Internos to Elena Caffarena de Jiles, Santiago, 5 July 1940, APEC A1 3.

57. Quotation from Memoria presentada al Segundo Congreso Nacional del MEMCh, [1940], APEC A1 4. Vergara, *Memorias de una mujer irreverente*, 207–8; *Frente Popular*, 8 August 1940, 5.

58. On the need for a feminist redefinition of the relation of work to family see Sassoon, ed., *Women and the State*, 158–88.

59. *La Mujer Nueva*, September 1940, 7. Ibid., July 1936, 2. Conclusiones aprobadas en los foros verificados en celebración del día internacional de la mujer, 9–10 March [1949], APEC A11 5.

60. Memoria presentada al Segundo Congreso Nacional del MEMCh, [1940], APEC A1 4; El Corraleño (Corral), 8 June 1946, 6; Servanda de Liberona, Elsa Orrego, Ana Liberona, and Custodia Moreno to Olga P. de Espinoza, Oficina Ricaventura, 6 February 1948, APEC A1 21. On state and employer training efforts that also equated work and homemaking skills see Weinstein, "Unskilled Worker, Skilled Housewife."

61. Interview with Elena Caffarena, in *Familia* (c. 1939), APEC A12 15. *El Correo de Valdivia* (Valdivia), 19 June 1939, 3.

62. *La Mujer Nueva*, 8 December 1935, 1, 4. Ibid., 25 April 1939, 3.

63. On women and feminists in the union movement see *La Mujer Nueva*, July 1936, 4; 8 December 1935, 2–3; and January 1936, 4; MEMCh Boletina, November–December 1946, APEC A1 9; CTCh, second fortnight July 1939, 2; 26 August 1939, 4; and second period, 28 January 1947, 3; and *Informativo* CTCh, 9 October 1947, 2.

64. *El Despertar Minero* (Sewell), 25 April 1939, 3. *El Obrero Municipal*, June–July 1944, 3. See also CTCh, July 1946, 6.

65. Milkman, "Gender and Trade Unionism," also emphasizes the mixed record of unions. Compare Hartmann, "Capitalism, Patriarchy"; Rose, "Respectable Men, Disorderly Others"; and Baron, "Masculinization of Production." Detailed analyses of occupations or industrial sectors would be necessary to more definitively establish if and how Chilean women were excluded from paid labor. Although census data shows a decline in women's workforce participation beginning in 1920, this decrease probably reflects the changing categories with which census takers recorded workforce participation. On women's labor force participation and changing census definitions of work see Gálvez and Bravo, "Siete décadas," and Hutchison, "Working Women of Santiago," ch. 2.

66. The legislative proposal can be found in Chile, Cámara de Diputados, 1 June 1936, 5a. sesión (sesiones ordinarias, 1936, I, 247). Objections to the law are in *Bandera Roja*, 30 May 1936, 1, and 2 July 1936, 4. On MEMCh opposition to this law see the discussion earlier in this chapter. *Ceteche* (Antofagasta), 1 May 1941, 4.

67. *Vanguardia Hotelera*, 15 November 1933, 3; *La Voz del Metalúrgico*, 1 May 1935, 5. On the nature of women's trade union participation in the textile industry see 20 April 1993 interview with Graciela Trujillo, leader of the Textile Federation formed in the 1950s.

68. CTCh, 22 June 1944, 5.

69. Chile, Caja de Seguro Obligatorio, *Anuario estadístico año 1947*, 13–15.

70. On the Beneficencia see *Noticiario Sindical*, 31 January 1949, 1. On Saldías see *Mundo Nuevo*, third period, November 1946, 7; compare *La Aguja* (Valparaíso), third period, 22 July 1937, 3, which argued that male tailors and female seamstresses should unite in a single union because they had "the same or similar trades." On

the MEMCh proposal for what we would today call "comparable worth" see CTCh, 26 August 1939, 4, and second fortnight July 1939, 2. On the inclusion of women on mixed commissions see Partido Comunista, "¡Adelante!" 44.

71. Three domestic servants' unions participated in the 1946 CTCh congress. On domestic servants' demands see CTCh, June 1946, 14, and January 1947, 4. For the demands of home-workers see La Aguja, July 1943, 1; and CTCh, 24 March 1943, 7, and 1 May 1945, 5. On a uniform pay scale in the textile industry see interview with Graciela Trujillo, 20 April 1993; interview with Mario González, 23 August 1994; Obrero Textil, 3 April 1937, 4; and La Aguja, third period, July 1942, 4. On unionization of smaller factories see the Communist Youth newspaper Mundo Nuevo, fourth week October 1938, 2; third period, 22 March 1941, n.p.; and third period, 5 April 1941, n.p.

72. The newspaper also took up the cause of women hospital workers and laundresses. See El Despertar Minero (Sewell), 25 April 1939, n.p.; 1 May 1939, n.p.; 20 June 1939, 1; 31 August 1939, 4; 5 December 1940, 4; 30 January 1941, n.p.; 15 March 1941, n.p.; and first fortnight June 1943, 6. The quotation is from ibid., 5 December 1940, 4. I am grateful to Tom Klubock for pointing out to me the sources related to the empleadas. For a different reading of male worker involvement with the empleadas see Klubock, "Hombres y mujeres en El Teniente."

73. Vanguardia Hotelera, 15 November 1933, 3.

74. CTCh, June 1946, 14. El Despertar Minero (Sewell), 16 January 1941, 3. See also Mundo Nuevo, third period, 8 February 1941, 6, and third period, 15 February 1941, 6; Tribuna Juvenil, first fortnight May 1935, 5; Obrero Textil, 5 May 1937, 2, and 3 April 1937, 3; Frente Popular, 8 August 1940, 5; Juventud en Marcha (Concepción), 15 May 1937, 4; and La Voz del Cristalero, 14 April 1944, 2.

75. Bandera Roja, 30 May 1936, 1.

76. Obrero Textil, 4 October 1936, 3. Other articles that recognized women and men's need to guarantee their own individual subsistence can be found in Tribuna Juvenil, first fortnight May 1935, 4, and Unificación (Tomé), 10 October 1936, 3.

77. Revista del Trabajo 8, no. 12 (December 1938): 54; Torres Romero, "Condiciones de vida y de trabajo," 16.

CHAPTER THREE

1. For a pioneering work on feminism and the Left see Kirkwood, Ser política en Chile. For studies charting the influence of broader social, political, and ideological forces on feminism in Latin America see Hutchison, "Working Women of Santiago"; Lavrin, Women, Feminism, and Social Change; Levenson-Estrada, "Loneliness of Working-Class Feminism"; Lancaster, Life Is Hard; and Molyneux, "Mobilization without Emancipation?" Compare works more focused on the internal dynamics of women's movements: Stoner, From the House to the Streets; Hahner, Emancipating the Female Sex; and Macías, Against All Odds.

2. On Socialists' withdrawal from MEMCh see Corinne Antezana-Pernet, personal communication, 4 August 1995. On the difficulties of maintaining women's organizations in a factional party see *Rumbo* (June 1940): 65–66; *La Crítica*, 24 May 1942, 6, and 27 May 1942, 5; *El Siglo*, 17 January 1943, 7; *Combate*, first fortnight February 1943, 2, and second fortnight March 1943, 4; Partido Socialista, "IV Congreso Extraordinario," 15; Partido Socialista, "Una etapa de clarificación socialista," 23; *Brecha*, 16 September 1944, 6; and Federación de la Juventud Socialista, "Reglamentos," 28.

3. On worker feminism see Hutchison, "Working Women of Santiago," chs. 4 and 5. On women's participation in the FOCh and POS see ibid., 245–53; DeShazo, *Urban Workers*, 153; Figueroa Ortiz and Sandoval Ambiado, *Carbón*, 122, 176; Lavrin, "Women, Labor, and the Left"; and interview with Blanca Flores, 4 June 1993. On the Centros Belén de Sárraga see Gaviola et al., *Queremos votar*, 21–37, and Hutchison, "Working Women of Santiago," 230–45.

4. For a summary of the range of feminist activity see Antezana-Pernet, "Mobilizing Women," 52–63. On regional and local Socialist groups see *El Socialista* (Puerto Natales), 22 March 1935, n.p.; *Consigna*, 13 July 1935, 4; *Julio Barrenechea* (Temuco), 27 March 1937, 4; *Frente Popular* (Valparaíso), 15 June 1937, n.p.; and *Barricada*, first fortnight November 1937, 4, and second fortnight October 1938, 2. The earliest contemporary references I found to the AMS were in *Claridad*, 19 December 1937, 2; 20 December 1937, 2; and 21 December 1937, 4.

5. On the local women's departments see *El Popular* (Antofagasta), 6 October 1938, 2; *El Mensaje Obrero* (Rancagua), 1 May 1939, n.p., 4; *Juventud en Marcha* (Concepción), 17 April 1937, 1; *Frente Popular* (Valparaíso), 21 August 1937, n.p.; and *Alianza Libertadora de la Juventud* (Antofagasta), December 1936, 1, 4. The quotation is from *El Organizador*, 1 June 1940. On the Comisión Nacional Femenina see interviews with Elena Pedraza, 23 April 1993 and 28 May 1993. On women's "service" activities see *Liberación* (Tomé), 3 June 1939, 1. For a critique of this practice see Guerrero, "Por una Juventud Comunista," 17.

6. *Julio Barrenechea* (Temuco), 27 March 1937, 4. *Acción Socialista*, 7 July 1934, 8.

7. *Acción Socialista*, 6 April 1934, 6. *El Socialista* (Puerto Natales), 13 June 1935, n.p. See also *Acción Socialista*, 13 May 1934, 2. Compare the appraisal of similar rhetoric in French, "Women and Working-Class Mobilization."

8. *Consigna*, 19 March 1934, 2, my emphasis.

9. *La Nación*, 25 January 1943, 3. Information on MEMCh founders can also be found in Durand, *Mis entrevistas*, 199; Antezana-Pernet, "Mobilizing Women," ch. 2; Vergara, *Memorias de una mujer irreverente*, 168–72; and interview with Pércival Heredia, 7 May 1993.

10. The Caffarena quotation comes from Durand, *Mis entrevistas*, 20. On MEMCh La Serena and another group in Tocopilla that joined MEMCh see *La Mujer Nueva*, November 1936, 8.

11. Interview with Elena Pedraza, 28 May 1993.

12. "El MEMCh y el voto político" (Santiago, 1948), APEC A3 10. *Frente Popular*, 2 November 1937, 2. See also *La Mujer Nueva*, June 1936, 3, and 8 November 1935, 2.

13. *La Mujer Nueva*, February 1936, 4.

14. Ibid., June 1936, 4. For other sources that reflect an antagonism between upper-class women and women on the Left see ibid., 8 December 1935, n.p., and *Claridad*, 21 December 1937, 2. On the upper-class feminism of the 1910s and 1920s see Verba, "Círculo de Lectura."

15. Memoria presentada al Segundo Congreso Nacional del MEMCh, [1940], APEC A1 4.

16. On the more radical aspects of the MEMCh platform see "Programa del Movimiento pro Emancipación de las Mujeres," *La Mujer Nueva*, 8 November 1935, n.p. Boletín extraordinario del Movimiento pro Emancipación de las Mujeres de Chile, 1946, APEC A1 8.

17. Vergara, *Memorias de una mujer irreverente*, 117.

18. Although the popular-front economic project implied winning over progressive members of the industrial bourgeoisie, politicians could count on state investment and economic intervention to mend industrialists' lapses.

19. For an exploration of the *potential* for democratization inherent in Communist Parties' adoption of the bourgeois-democratic revolution strategy and of the ways continuing vanguardism stunted the more open, articulatory practices inherent in that strategy see Laclau and Mouffe, *Hegemony and Socialist Strategy*, 55–58.

20. Interview with Elena Pedraza, 28 May 1993.

21. For circulation figures see *La Mujer Nueva*, November 1936, 2. On Ramírez's activities see ibid., September 1940; and *El Siglo*, 22 October 1940, 9, and 12 November 1944, 12. On Román's activities see *Frente Popular*, 25 October 1937, 9, and Elena Caffarena, Por qué renuncié a la secretaría general del MEMCh, APEC A1 5. Information on Román and Ramírez was also provided by Elena Pedraza (interview, 28 May 1993). On Communist recruiting for MEMCh see also *La Mujer Nueva*, December 1936, 7, and *El Siglo*, 18 July 1943, 8. On *memchistas* at the Second National Congress see Lista de memchistas que asistieron al Segundo Congreso Nacional de Mujeres de Santiago, APEC A1 13, and *El Siglo*, 6 May 1943, 4. On MEMCh's early mobilizational drives see also Antezana-Pernet, "El MEMCh en provincia," and Poblete, *Una mujer*.

22. *Chispa* (Iquique), fourth week February 1939, 2. *La Defensa*, June 1936, 9. For references to prior women's groups as MEMCh affiliates see interview with Iris Figueroa, 5 April 1993, and interview with Fresia Gravano, 4 April 1993.

23. Antezana-Pernet, "El MEMCh en provincia."

24. *La Mujer Nueva*, 8 December 1935, n.p.; Memoria presentada al Segundo Congreso Nacional del MEMCh, [1940], APEC A1 4; Posición del MEMCh frente a las elecciones municipales, c. April 1947, APEC A1 11.

25. *El Despertar Minero* (Sewell), 15 March 1941, 3. On the limited employment opportunities for women in El Teniente see also Klubock, "Hombres y mujeres en El Teniente."

26. *El Despertar Minero* (Sewell), 18 June 1941, n.p.

27. *Frente Popular*, 9 October 1937, 7.

28. Interview with Elena Pedraza, 28 May 1993. Vergara, *Memorias de una mujer irreverente*, 219, also pointed to differences among Communist women.

29. Interview with Iris Figueroa, 5 April 1993.

30. Interview with Mercedes Fuentealba, 28 April 1993. Fuentealba's very direct critique of class relations implicated herself and me in these relations. The "you" in her narrative referred specifically to me, to my apartment (where the interview took place), to the domestic help she presumed I had, and to my presumed responsibilities as a middle-class professional woman.

31. Interview with Elena Pedraza, 28 May 1993.

32. Elena Caffarena, Por qué renuncié a la secretaría general del MEMCh, APEC A1 5.

33. Ibid. Partido Comunista, "¡Adelante!" esp. 24–25. For the ways in which association with the Communist Party hurt MEMCh see Antezana-Pernet, "El MEMCh en provincia," and Elena Caffarena to Lytta Weinstein de Binimelis, [c. 1938?], APEC A7.

34. Elena Caffarena, Por qué renuncié a la secretaría general del MEMCh, APEC A1 5. *El Siglo*, 25 October 1940, 4. See also *El Siglo*, 13 October, 1940, 7.

35. Partido Comunista, "¡Adelante!" 24–25.

36. Elena Caffarena, Por qué renuncié a la secretaría general del MEMCh, APEC A1 5.

37. Ibid.

38. Ibid. On Vergara's withdrawal see Vergara, *Memorias de una mujer irreverente*, 219–23. On the withdrawal of other non-Communists see Antezana-Pernet, "Mobilizing Women," 336–37.

39. Vergara, *Memorias de una mujer irreverente*, 219–21.

40. *El Siglo*, 27 October 1940, 4. *La Nación*, 25 January 1942, 3. See also *La Mujer Nueva*, 8 November 1935, 2, n.p., and January 1936, 2, 4.

41. *Juventud en Marcha* (Concepción), 17 April 1934, 1. *Machete* (Tocopilla), second fortnight May 1937, 3, 7. Antezana-Pernet, "Mobilizing Women," 328–29, 340.

42. Antezana-Pernet, "Mobilizing Women," 342.

43. Amanda Labarca and Victoria Aguila, Informe de la presidente ante la asamblea de dirigentes, 3 November 1945, in FEChIF, *Boletín*, no. 4, September 1947, APEC A4 5; *El Toro*, first fortnight June 1944, 3, 6; *Principios*, no. 24 (April 1943): 15–16, and no. 27 (September 1943): 9–10; MEMCh, Actas de sesión, 27 November 1944, 1 December 1944, 11 December 1944, APEC. On Communist organizing around consumer issues in Brazil see French, "Women and Working-Class Mobilization," 185–87.

44. MEMCh, Actas de sesión, 27 November 1944, 1 December 1944, 11 December 1944, APEC. I am grateful to Corinne Pernet for sources on MEMCh and the consumer leagues.

45. On Williams and Mandujano see *Diccionario biográfico de Chile*, 7th ed. (1948–49), and 10th ed. (1956–58); and Antezana-Pernet, "Mobilizing Women," 94–98. MEMCh, Acta de sesión, 27 November 1944, APEC.

46. *Boletín Oficial del Comité Nacional pro Baja de las Subsistencias*, January 1945, 3, 4. *Principios*, no. 44 (February 1945): 36.

47. Clara Williams in *Tribuna Social* (September 1946): 13–15; *La Voz de Conchalí*, first

fortnight July 1947, 5; Yanulaque Garrido, "La Asociación Nacional de Dueñas de Casa," 7–9. On employer efforts to discipline consumers in Brazil see Weinstein, "Unskilled Worker, Skilled Housewife," 87, 92, and Weinstein, For Social Peace, 145–47.

48. Boletín Oficial del Comité Nacional pro Baja de las Subsistencias, March 1945, 4. La Voz de la Mujer, December 1947, 6; quotation from Mujeres Chilenas, November 1947, 12.

49. Mujeres Chilenas, November 1947, 7; La Voz de la Mujer, December 1947, 6; Yanulaque Garrido, "La Asociación Nacional de Dueñas de Casa," 29–30, 62–67, 71; Servicio Social 21, nos. 1–3 (January–December 1947): 70–72.

50. On Comisariato attempts to disband consumer committees see El Pueblo (Talca), 19 January 1947, 4, and Antezana-Pernet, "Mobilizing Women," 367–69. On Mandujano and Williams see Antezana-Pernet, "Mobilizing Women," 360–61.

51. Yanulaque Garrido, "La Asociación Nacional de Dueñas de Casa," 91–123. For government opinion see "Juntas de vigilancia."

52. On grassroots groups' relation to the Asociación see Mujeres Chilenas, October 1947, 12; MEMCh, Circular, no. 5, October 1947, APEC A1 15; La Voz de la Mujer, December 1947, 6; and Servanda de Liberona, Elsa Orrego, Ana Liberona, and Custodia Moreno to Olga P. de Espinoza, Oficina Ricaventura, 6 February 1948, APEC A1 21; quotation from Palabra de la compañera Eusebia Torres de Coronel, 1947, APEC A2 3. The Asociación became a model for the state-run mothers' centers institutionalized by the government of Eduardo Frei in 1965. As Communist organizing resurfaced in 1958, party members continued to organize women within but also against the state-run centros de madres. Valdés et al. ("Centros de madres 1973–1989," 7–10, 90–91) posit the Asociación as the direct precursor of mothers' centers. I agree with this assertion in terms of the state's role. However, the roots of these centers also lie in women's consumer organizing and other grassroots women's organizations that existed long before 1947.

CHAPTER FOUR

1. Rumbo (September 1939): 89. For a Left rejection of almsgiving approaches (especially among charities that received state funds) see La Crítica, 1 December 1939, 16, and Barricada, second fortnight December 1938, 6. Social workers Elena Varas and María Zúñiga saw the movement from charity or beneficence to social assistance and then on to social security as stages in an evolutionary process (Boletín Médico-Social de la Caja de Seguro Obligatorio 12, nos. 125–27 [March–May 1945]: 179).

2. My data on Socialist employment in the state comes from the biographical catalogue on congressional representatives in the Biblioteca del Congreso and from the second through the tenth editions of the Diccionario biográfico de Chile. For an indication of other Socialists who held high-ranking positions in the CSO see Tribuna (Puerto Natales), 6 March 1941, 2.

3. Yávar and the DGAS are discussed later in this chapter.

4. My hypotheses regarding the gendered nature of the welfare state have been

influenced by Pateman, *Disorder of Women*, and the articles in Gordon, ed., *Women, the State, and Welfare*. Linda Gordon powerfully demonstrates popular manipulation of welfare provision in *Heroes of Their Own Lives*.

5. On the welfare "super-ministry" see Illanes, *"En el nombre,"* 207. *Revista del Trabajo* 1, no. 2 (August 1931): n.p. On the need for Dirección General de Sanidad centralization see *Revista del Trabajo* 1, no. 1 (July 1931): n.p. On the CSO see *Acción Social*, no. 113 (June 1942): 4.

6. On state expenditures see Chile, Dirección General de Estadística, *Anuario estadístico año 1935*, 2–5, and *Estadística Chilena* 23, no. 12 (December 1950): 703. On state employment see Urzúa Valenzuela and García Barzelatto, *Diagnóstico de la burocracia*, 74. On the Comisariato see *Servicio Social* 18, no. 2 (May–August 1944): 33. On Sanidad see *Servicio Social* 16, nos. 1–2 (January–June 1942): 73–76. On the DGAS see *Servicio Social* 17, no. 2 (May–August 1943): 31–32. On CSO expenditures see *Acción Social*, no. 113 (June 1942): 17. On social workers and physicians in the CSO see Allende, *La realidad médico-social*, 144. On CSO social workers see *Servicio Social* 20, no. 1 (January–April 1940): 44, and 16, nos., 1–2 (January–June 1942): 73, 76; Norambuena Lagarde, "El servicio social en la Caja de Seguro Obligatorio," 2, 11–12; and *Boletín Médico-Social de la Caja de Seguro Obligatorio* 12, nos. 125–27 (March–May 1945): 178.

7. On the origins of social work and sanitary nursing see *Revista del Trabajo* 1, no. 1 (July 1931): n.p., and 1, no. 2 (August 1931): n.p.; and interview with Amalia Chaigneau, 25 June 1993. On the development of social work and state employment in Brazil see Besse, *Restructuring Patriarchy*, 84–85, and Owensby, *Intimate Ironies*, ch. 9.

8. On the employment of social workers see Fuentealba Sepúlveda, "El servicio social ante las ciencias penales," 34; *Servicio Social* 24, no. 3 (September–December 1950): 3; and *Frente Popular*, 5 July 1940, 4. On the Elvira Matte School see *Frente Popular*, 15 July 1940, 4, and 1 August 1940, 4.

9. *Acción Social*, no. 4 (November 1930): 47. *Revista del Trabajo* 1, no. 1 (July 1931): n.p.

10. The quotations are from *Boletín Médico-Social de la Caja de Seguro Obligatorio* 1, no. 9 (February 1935): n.p.; *Boletín de la Sociedad Chilena de Obstetricia y Ginecología* 3, no. 3 (April 1938): 184; and *Frente Popular*, 10 September 1936, 10. *Boletín Médico-Social de la Caja de Seguro Obligatorio* 2, no. 14 (July 1935): esp. 3, 7. See also *Boletín Médico-Social de la Caja de Seguro Obligatorio* 1, no. 4 (September 1934): 2, and 11, nos. 117–19 (July–September 1944): 317; and Cárcamo Lastra, "Servicio social en la manufactura de metales 'MADEMSA,'" 17. The term "human capital" was widely used during the popular-front years. See, for example, Allende, *La realidad médico-social*, and *Boletín del Ministerio de Salubridad* (February 1936): 13–16.

11. El Socialista (Concepción), second fortnight November 1934, 4. See also *Frente Popular*, 10 September 1936, 10.

12. *Vida Sana* (Temuco), second period, 1, no. 5 (May 1941): 4; *Boletín Médico-Social de la Caja de Seguro Obligatorio* 1, no. 11 (April 1935): 1–2, and 2, no. 17 (October 1935): 3–4; Fuentealba Sepúlveda, "El servicio social ante las ciencias penales," 140. The quotation is from *Acción Social*, no. 113 (June 1942): 4. For a comparative look at public

health ideology see Borges, " 'Puffy, Ugly, Slothful and Inert' "; Zimmerman, "Racial Ideas and Social Reform"; Guy, *Sex and Danger*; and Stepan, *"Hour of Eugenics."*

13. *La Crítica*, 5 September 1942, 3. The original article is quoted in Allende, *La realidad médico-social*, 87.

14. Allende, *La realidad médico-social*, 135.

15. *Revista de Asistencia Social* 13 (1944): 443, 446.

16. *Acción Social*, no. 113 (June 1942): 5–7; *Revista de Asistencia Social* 13 (1944): 435, 438, 440; *Boletín Médico-Social de la Caja de Seguro Obligatorio* 11, nos. 117–19 (July–September 1944): 205–13; Morris, *Elites, Intellectuals, and Consensus*, 206, 243–47; Illanes, *"En el nombre,"* 187–91, 224–29.

17. *Revista del Trabajo* 1, no. 1 (August 1931): n.p.; *Servicio Social* 16, nos. 3–4 (July–December 1942): 100.

18. Illanes, *"En el nombre,"* 98–99, 129–31; *Acción Social*, no. 27 (June 1934): 30–33; *Boletín del Ministerio de Salubridad* (July 1939): 51, and (June 1939): 43–44; Pinto Ureta, "Estudio de las condiciones," 1–8, 16. Interview with Amalia Chaigneau, 25 June 1993; *Revista del Trabajo* 1, no. 1 (July 1931): n.p. Interview with Elena Varela, 30 July 1993.

19. Illanes, *"En el nombre,"* 303. On the breadth of CSO services and its leadership role see Norambuena Lagarde, "El servicio social en la Caja de Seguro Obligatorio," 2; *Boletín Médico-Social de la Caja de Seguro Obligatorio* [8, nos. 79–82 (January–April 1941)?]: 245–54, 261–65; and Chávez Guzmán, "La mujer ante el derecho," 90. On CSO infant care see *Revista Chilena de Higiene y Medicina Preventiva* 8, no. 3 (September 1946): esp. 149, and 5, no. 1 (June 1942): 103; Peralta, "La atención materno-infantil," esp. 32; and *Revista de Asistencia Social* 13 (1944): 437. The quotation is from *Boletín Médico-Social de la Caja de Seguro Obligatorio* 2, no. 19 (December 1935): 4.

20. *Acción Social*, no. 113 (June 1942): 9–14; no. 12 (January 1933): 7; and no. 51 (July 1936): 3–5; *Boletín Médico-Social de la Caja de Seguro Obligatorio* 11, nos. 117–19 (July–September 1944): 205.

21. On CSO efforts to court elites see *Acción Social*, no. 31 (October 1934): 3–4, and *Boletín Médico-Social de la Caja de Seguro Obligatorio* 9, nos. 93–95 (March–May 1942): n.p. On congressional attempts to control the CSO see *Acción Social*, no. 51 (July 1936): 3–5. For a right-wing criticism of state agencies favorable to popular sectors, including the CSO, see *La Voz de la Provincia* (Valdivia), 1944. On the Right's accusation of Luciano Kulczewski see *Rumbo* (December 1939): 85, and Chile, Cámara de Diputados, 14 November 1939, 4a. sesión (sesiones extraordinarias, 1939, I, 292–307). Caja de Seguro Obligatorio, "Campaña venérea y defensa de la madre y el niño en la provincia de Tarapacá: Segunda memoria anual, enero a diciembre 1938, presentada por el Dr. Nicolás Taborga M., médico jefe provincial" (Iquique, 1939) in *Boletín Médico-Social de la Caja de Seguro Obligatorio* 6, nos. 60–61 (May–June 1939): 71; *Servicio Social* 18, no. 2 (April–August 1944): 9.

22. Chile, Cámara de Diputados, 14 November 1939, 4a. sesión (sesiones extraordinarias, 1939, I, 301–2). *Servicio Social* 16, nos. 3–4 (August–December 1942): 195–202; *Vida Sana* (Valparaíso) 1, no. 2 (June 1942): 6.

23. On family insurance see *Estadística Chilena* 18, no. 12 (December 1945): 688.

24. Alvarez Pacheco, "El servicio social ante el problema de la madre soltera," 132–33.

25. On Berman's plan see *Boletín de la Confederación Regional de Aspirantes a Colonos de la Zona Devastada* (Concepción), October 1939, 2. For other plans to reform the CSO see "Reforma de la ley número 4.054," Mensaje, Cámara de Diputados, 10 June 1941, cited in *Boletín Médico-Social de la Caja de Seguro Obligatorio* [8, nos. 79–82 (January–April 1941)?]: 327–71; *Noticiario Sindical*, August 1951, 6–9; and Chile, Cámara de Diputados, 23 November 1950, 8a. sesión (sesiones extraordinarias, 1950–51, I, esp. 515–30). See also CTCh, 22 August 1945, 7. The quotation is from *Vida Sana* (Temuco), second period, 1, no. 5 (May 1941): 5.

26. *Servicio Social* 20, nos. 2–3 (May–December 1946): 86–94.

27. Schiappacasse Ferretti, "El problema económico de la madre soltera," 58–61.

28. See Illanes, "*En el nombre*," 337–45; and *Frente Popular*, 2 July 1940, 4; 4 July 1940, 4; 5 July 1940, 4; 7 July 1940, 4; 8 July 1940, 4; 9 July 1940, 4; 10 July 1940, 4; 11 July 1940, 4; 15 July 1940, 4; 18 July 1940, 4; 19 July 1940, 4; 21 July 1940, 4; 22 July 1940, 4; 23 July 1940, 4; 25 July 1940, 4; and 1 August 1940, 4.

29. Interview with Tomy Romeo, 4 June 1993. Interview with Elena Yávar, 13 September 1993.

30. Interviews with Tomy Romeo, 4 June 1993, 15 June 1993, and 15 July 1993; interview with Amalia Chaigneau, Olivia Piña, and Ester Atlagic, 12 July 1993; interview with Elena Yávar, 13 September 1993. The quotation is from *Servicio Social* 21, nos. 1–3 (January–December 1947): 39.

31. On the Círculo see *Servicio Social* 21, nos. 1–3 (January–December 1947): 39–41; 24, no. 1 (January–April 1950): 18–24; 25, no. 3 (September–December 1951): 34–37; 26, no. 1 (January–April 1952): 28–32; and 27, no. 1 (January–April 1953): 39–40. There was also a Círculo in Iquique.

32. Interview with Elena Varela, 27 July 1993.

33. Interviews with Tomy Romeo, 4 June 1993 and 28 July 1999; for one social worker's call for impartial competition for civil service jobs see *Servicio Social* 25, no. 3 (September–December 1951): 38.

34. My discussion of the Dirección de Auxilio Social is based on the following sources: interview with Elena Yávar, 13 September 1993; *Servicio Social* 14, no. 3 (July–September 1940): 161–65; 22, no. 2–3 (June–December 1948): 69–77; 17, no. 2 (May–August 1943): 31–35; and 24, no. 2 (May–August 1950): 41–44; *Revista del Trabajo* 12, no. 10 (October 1942): 81–85; Espinoza Muñoz, "La Dirección de Auxilio Social"; and Lillo Hermosilla, "Hogar Modelo."

35. See the sources cited in note 34, above. The quotations are from *Servicio Social* 24, no. 2 (May–August 1950): 42. For Socialist complaints regarding inertia within the CSO see the congressional debate cited in *Rumbo* (December 1939): esp. 85.

36. Lillo Hermosilla, "Hogar Modelo," 65–69.

37. Seguel Morales, "Madre soltera," 3–8.

38. Arriagada Campos, "Acción del servicio social," 32–33.

39. El *Fideero*, September 1943, 8.

40. Interview with Aída Quiñones, 19 May 1993. *Acción Social*, no. 48 (March–April 1936): 6–7. Espinoza Muñoz, "La Dirección de Auxilio Social," 23. For the argument that recipients of charity saw it as a right see the essays in Mandler, ed., *Uses of Charity*.

41. *Servicio Social* 9, no. 4 (October–December 1935): 305. Espinoza Muñoz, "La Dirección de Auxilio Social," 58. For a reference to the "psychological factor" see *Boletín Médico-Social de la Caja de Seguro Obligatorio* 9, nos. 93–95 (March–May 1942): 144–48.

42. Consejo de Defensa del Niño, *Memoria correspondiente al año 1941*, 111, and *Memoria correspondiente al bienio 1944–1945*, n.p. *Vida Sana* (Valparaíso) 3, nos. 38–39 (July–August [1945]): 8.

43. *Frente Popular*, 5 May 1940, 2.

44. El *Despertar Minero* (Sewell), 5 June 1941, 1–2. Partido Socialista, "I Congreso Regional," 12, 49. See also *Servicio Social* 11, no. 4 (October 1937), 229.

45. *Ceteche* (Antofagasta), second fortnight July 1938, 3, and 7 December 1939, 1. See also *La Crítica*, 13 May 1942, 1; 17 May 1942, 4, 5; and 18 May 1942, 4. On increasing worker influence within the CSO see the proposal in *CTCh*, 24 March 1943, 4.

46. *Ceteche* (Antofagasta), first fortnight December [1939?], 2.

47. El *Despertar Minero* (Sewell), 25 June 1939, 2, and 30 June 1939, 4; interview with Tomy Romeo, 4 June 1993.

48. *La Crítica*, 17 May 1942, 5. See also CTCh, cited in Illanes, "En el nombre," 352, and *Liberación* (Tomé), 20 May 1939, 2.

49. *La Crítica*, 12 May 1941, 8.

50. Allende, *La realidad médico-social*, 207; *La Crítica*, 9 November 1939, 3; *Vida Sana* (Valparaíso) 1, nos. 6–7 (October–November 1942): 6; *Vida Sana* (Temuco), second period, 1, no. 5 (May 1941): 5; *La Crítica*, 12 May 1941, 8.

51. Interview with Tegualda Monreal, 17 June 1993; interview with Tomy Romeo, 4 June 1993.

CHAPTER FIVE

1. *Servicio Social* 23, no. 3 (May–August 1949): 35, 39. See also Ponce Ponce, "Desavenencias conyugales," 86. On traditional notions of gender right see Stern, *Secret History of Gender*.

2. *Estadística Chilena* 18, no. 12 (December 1945): 542, and 23, no. 12 (December 1950): 601; Chile, Dirección General de Estadística, *Anuario estadístico año 1939*, 18; *Anuario estadístico año 1940*, 19; *Anuario estadístico año 1945*, 14; and *Anuario estadístico año 1950: Demografía y asistencia social*, 15. *Servicio Social* 23, no. 3 (May–August 1949): 38. Urbina Moya, "Proyecciones del servicio social," 108. We should be wary, however, about generalizations based on relatively small statistical shifts (Scott, *Gender and the Politics of History*, 167–77).

3. Compare Donzelot, *Policing of Families*, which occludes questions of agency and minimizes the effects of diverse modalities of state control.

4. *Vida Sana* (Valparaíso) 1, no. 2 (June 1942): 6.

5. Cañas Valenzuela, "Estudio de los problemas," 27–30. *Boletín del Ministerio de Salubridad* (October 1939): 31–32.

6. *Vida Sana* (Valparaíso) 2, no. 9 (January 1943): 3, 7. For a sample CSO survey see Orrego Navarro, "Estudio de los problemas económico-sociales."

7. *La Crítica*, 20 November 1939, 7. On the manipulation of statistics see Scott, *Gender and the Politics of History*, 113–38.

8. Allende, *La realidad médico-social*, 5. *Boletín Médico-Social de la Caja de Seguro Obligatorio* 11, nos. 117–19 (July–September 1944): 347. *Vida Sana* (Temuco) 1, no. 1 (November 1938): 1. See also *Boletín Médico-Social de la Caja de Seguro Obligatorio* 12, nos. 125–27 (March–May 1945): 139.

9. Chile, *Código Civil*, libro III. On civil law in Argentina, Chile, and Uruguay see Lavrin, *Women, Feminism, and Social Change*, chs. 6 and 7.

10. For statistics on arrests for abandonment of home see *Estadística Chilena* 23, no. 12 (December 1950): 720. On paternity legislation see Rioseco Tapia, "Situación de los hijos ilegítimos." The quotation is from *Boletín Médico-Social de la Caja de Seguro Obligatorio* 11, nos. 117–19 (July–September 1944): 349.

11. On the celibacy tax see *Boletín del Ministerio de Salubridad* (July 1939): 51–53. On the preventive medicine law see Pimentel Orellana, "La medicina preventiva." On the Caja de Habitación see Aqueveque Castro, "Experiencias obtenidas," 23–25, 37, and Paredes Quijada, "El servicio social frente a la legislación del trabajo," 39. For similar CSO housing policies see *Servicio Social* 9, no. 3 (July–September 1935): 191. On the need for a family wage see Allende, *La realidad médico-social*, 32–36.

12. On the benefits granted by the social security system see Meneses Zúñiga, "La ley 4.054"; Santana et al., "Algunos problemas sociales"; Weitzman Fliman, "La Caja de Seguro Obligatorio"; and Norambuena Lagarde, "El servicio social en la Caja de Seguro Obligatorio." State publications that explained eligibility for benefits include *Revista del Trabajo* 5, no. 8 (August 1935): 75; and *Vida Sana* (Valparaíso) 2, no. 9 (January 1943): 8; 2, no. 10 (February–March 1943): 8; and 2, nos. 11–12 (April–May 1943): 8. On worker efforts to expand benefits see *Boletín Sindical del Comité Regional del Partido Comunista*, September 1940, 1, 4; *Ceteche* (Antofagasta), 7 December 1939, 3; and *El Despertar* (Iquique), second period, 1 January 1953, 4, and 9 January 1953, 2.

13. Alvarez Pacheco, "El servicio social ante el problema de la madre soltera," 145–46. See also Urbina Moya, "Proyecciones del servicio social," 93–94, and *Servicio Social* 12, no. 4 (October 1938): 184.

14. Aqueveque Castro, "Experiencias obtenidas," 28; *Pampa* (January 1949): 7; *Servicio Social* 18, no. 2 (May–August 1944): 36.

15. Interviews with Tomy Romeo, 4 June 1993 and 15 June 1993.

16. *Revista Chilena de Higiene y Medicina Preventiva* 8, no. 3 (September 1946): 148–88.

17. *Vida Sana* (Temuco) 1, no. 1 (November 1938): 1. *Boletín Médico-Social de la Caja*

de Seguro Obligatorio 11, nos. 117–19 (July–September 1944): 347. Quotations from *El Obrero Municipal*, June–July 1944, 4, and *Vida Sana* (Temuco) 1, no. 1 (November 1938): 7.

18. Cañas Valenzuela, "Estudio de los problemas," 87.

19. *Servicio Social* 11, no. 3 (November 1937): 160–66. Ibid. 14, no. 2 (April–June 1940): 133, my emphasis.

20. *Servicio Social* 11, no. 3 (November 1937): 155–60.

21. Grenovich, "Rol del servicio social," 92–94.

22. Allende, *La realidad médico-social.* On the importance of this work see *Vida Sana* (Valparaíso) 1, nos. 6–7 (October–November 1942): 5, and *Barricada,* second fortnight July 1940, 4.

23. Allende, *La realidad médico-social,* 3, 196. For strikingly similar formulations see *Servicio Social* 12, no. 4 (October 1938): 151, and *Boletín Médico-Social de la Caja de Seguro Obligatorio* 13, no. 146 (December 1946): 727–31. Along the same lines see *Boletín del Ministerio de Salubridad* (July 1939): 39–53, and (March 1937): 14–17; and "Proyecto de salubridad integral enviado al Congreso Nacional," *Boletín Médico-Social de la Caja de Seguro Obligatorio* [8, nos. 79–82 (January–April 1941)?]: 369–70.

24. Allende, *La realidad médico-social.* On demographic concerns see Jensen, "Representations of Gender," 153–55, and Klaus, "Depopulation and Race Suicide," 188–89.

25. Arriagada Campos, "Acción del servicio social," 11. See also *Pampa* (January 1949): 7, and Alvarez Pacheco, "El servicio social ante el problema de la madre soltera," 68. For historical accounts that emphasize male mobility see Salazar, "La mujer de 'bajo pueblo,' " 99–103; Salazer, "Ser niño huacho"; and Klubock, "Sexualidad y proletarización," 66–68.

26. On masculine camaradería see *Servicio Social* 9, no. 4 (October–December 1935): 306; Cárcamo Lastra, "Servicio social en la manufactura de metales 'MADEMSA,' " 26; *Ceteche* (Antofagasta), second fortnight July 1938, 2; Klubock, "Sexualidad y proletarización," 75–76; and Klubock, *Contested Communities.* On "wild" versus "tame" forms of masculine deportment see Alonso, *Thread of Blood,* 79–84. Gutmann, *Meanings of Macho,* stresses men's uneven adherence to norms of proper masculinity and men's willingness to change in response to women's demands and feminism. In contrast to my account, which points to how state actions facilitated and promoted certain changes in men, Gutmann downplays the strength of state-enforced norms.

27. *Vida Sana* (Valparaíso) 2, no. 9 (January 1943): 6.

28. *Aurora de Chile* (7 October 1949): 15. See also *Vida Sana* (Valparaíso) 2, no. 9 (January 1943): 3.

29. See Chapter 1, and Klubock, *Contested Communities.* Though one cannot always trust elites to accurately portray subaltern motivations, welfare professionals clearly believed that masculine insubordination expressed a rejection of capitalist work norms.

30. *El Siglo,* 4 July 1943, 5; CTCh, October 1945, 3; *Vanguardia Hotelera,* second period, January 1938, 1; Klubock, *Contested Communities.*

31. Ortega Fuentes, "Acción de la lucha antivenérea," 58. Gabriel González Videla's

1946 campaign platform called for enhanced recreational programs (*Alianza Democrática*, 11 October 1946, 4).

32. *¿Qué Hubo?*, 1 August 1939, 30; *Acción Social*, no. 84 (December 1939): 3–4; no. 81 (September 1939): 1–4; and no. 109 (February 1942): 2–10; CTCh, second fortnight July 1939, 10. On the Hogar Pedro Aguirre Cerda see *La Voz de Conchalí*, second fortnight June 1947, 5, and *El Centinela*, 4 March 1944, n.p. On the Centro Valparaíso see *Vida Sana* (Valparaíso) 1, no. 8 (December 1942): 1, 4–6.

33. The quotation is from Chile, Dirección General de Informaciones y Cultura, "Recopilación," 202. *Acción Social*, no. 84 (December 1939): 3–4; *Servicio Social* 19, nos. 2–3 (September–December 1945): 31.

34. The first quotation is from Allende, *La realidad médico-social*, 122. *Vida Sana* (Valparaíso) 2, no. 10 (February–March 1943): 3, and 3, nos. 28–29 (September–October 1944): 1; *Boletín Médico-Social de la Caja de Seguro Obligatorio* 13, no. 140 (May 1946): 199. The second quotation is from *Boletín del Ministerio de Salubridad* (January 1940): 30.

35. *Vida Sana* (Valparaíso) 2, no. 10 (February–March 1943): 3. See also ibid. 2, no. 9 (January 1943): 3, and *La Crítica*, 14 September 1942, 3. The Mesa Alarcón story is in *Vida Sana* (Temuco), second period, 1, no. 6 (June 1941): 3.

36. Ponce Ponce, "Desavenencias conyugales," 11–16, 61.

37. Ibid., 64–69; Urbina Moya, "Proyecciones del servicio social," 60–65; Charney Venegas, "Sindicatos textiles," 67–68.

38. Schiappacasse Ferretti, "El problema económico de la madre soltera," 57–58. See also *Boletín Médico-Social de la Caja de Seguro Obligatorio* 13, no. 140 (May 1946): 199, and Vallejos González, "Organización de la oficina de servicio social en la Sección Arriendos," 27–28.

39. Seguel Morales, "Madre soltera," 50. The term "future mother" was used in *Servicio Social* 11, no. 3 (November 1937): 160, and *La Crítica*, 2 November 1939, 6.

40. The term "rebel mother" can be found in Norambuena Lagarde, "El servicio social en la Caja de Seguro Obligatorio," 24. On women's reticence toward marriage see Behar, *Translated Woman*; Tinsman, "Los patrones del hogar"; Lancaster, *Life Is Hard*; and Stern, *Secret History of Gender*.

41. *Vida Sana* (Valparaíso) 2, nos. 13–14 (June–July 1943): 5.

42. "Reglamento del servicio asistencial de la madre y el niño de la CSO," [c. 1936], in Díaz Delgado, "Protección de la maternidad"; *Acción Social*, no. 52 (August 1936): 1–2. *Vida Sana* (Temuco) 1, no. 5 (April 1939): 7, and 1, no. 1 (November 1938): 2; *Vida Sana* (Valparaíso) 1, no. 3 (July 1942): 4, 6, and 1, no. 4 (August 1942): 5; *La Crítica*, 2 November 1939, 6; *Servicio Social* 20, no. 1 (January–April 1946): 46; Peralta, "La atención materno-infantil," 53. On puericulture and motherhood see Lavrin, *Women, Feminism, and Social Change*, ch. 3.

43. *Vida Sana* (Valparaíso) 1, no. 3 (July 1942): 6. The quotation is reported in Pinto Ureta, "Estudio de las condiciones," 86–87. See also Soletic, "La mujer obrera y sus problemas," 37–44.

44. *Boletín de la Sociedad Chilena de Obstetricia y Ginecología* 3, no. 3 (April 1938): 185–87, 190–91; "Sinopsis estadística de los servicios de Beneficencia," cited in Ferrero Mate de Luna, "El problema materno-infantil ante la ley," 157. See also Alvarez Pacheco, "El servicio social ante el problema de la madre soltera," 101, 107. On abortion see Lavrin, *Women, Feminism, and Social Change,* 186–89.

45. On birth control see *Vida Sana* (Valparaíso) 1, no. 5 (September 1942): 8. On the legalization of abortion see *La Mujer Nueva,* February 1936, 1; *La Palabra* (Valdivia), 1 February 1936, 3; and *El Siglo* (Mulchén), 25 January 1935, 6. For justifications of abortion see also *Boletín del Ministerio de Salubridad* (May 1937): 11–12, and *Boletín de la Sociedad Chilena de Obstetricia y Ginecología* 3, no. 3 (April 1938): 184–205. On the risks to women posed by abortion see Peralta, "La atención materno-infantil," 24. On the risks abortions posed to mothers see Allende, *La realidad médico-social,* 86, and *Boletín de la Sociedad Chilena de Obstetricia y Ginecología* 3, no. 3 (April 1938): 189–91. On birth control and the movement for voluntary motherhood in the United States see Gordon, *Woman's Body, Woman's Right.*

46. *Revista Chilena de Higiene y Medicina Preventiva* 3, no. 3 (December 1940): 160–61. *Vida Sana* (Valparaíso) 1, no. 4 (August 1942): 8; Seguel Morales, "Madre soltera," 39; *Boletín del Ministerio de Salubridad* (May 1937): 11–12; but compare *Boletín del Ministerio de Salubridad* 1, no. 5 (September 1942): 8.

47. On prenatal allowances see *Rumbo* (November 1939): 48; and Salvador Allende, "Oficio del Señor Ministro de Salubridad," [16 November 1939], in Chile, Cámara de Diputados, 21 November 1939, 7a. sesión (sesiones extraordinarias, 1939, I, 423–24). On maternity benefits in general see Meneses Zúñiga, "La ley 4.054," and Weitzman Fliman, "La Caja de Seguro Obligatorio."

48. For a breakdown of the category "single mother" see, for example, Consejo de Defensa del Niño, *Memoria correspondiente al año 1941,* 116. On the poverty of single mothers see Arriagada Campos, "Acción del servicio social," 12, and Allende, *La realidad médico-social,* 75.

49. *Rumbo* (June 1940): 79; *Aurora de Chile* (5 June 1939): 17; Alvarez Pacheco, "El servicio social ante el problema de la madre soltera," 122, 132–33; *Servicio Social* 12, no. 4 (October 1938): 183, 192–93; *Vida Sana* (Valparaíso) 1, no. 4 (August 1942): 5–6; 1, nos. 6–7 (October–November 1942): 3; 2, no. 9 (January 1943): 6; and 2, nos. 20–21 (January–February 1944): 5. On domestic servants see *Servicio Social* 11, no. 3 (November 1937): 169, and *Boletín Médico-Social de la Caja de Seguro Obligatorio* 11, nos. 117–19 (July–September 1944): 351. The idea of setting up maternal refuges predated the popular fronts, yet before this period the Beneficencia's Casa de la Mujer was the only existing refuge. Calls for CSO-run maternal refuges are in *Acción Social,* no. 14 (March 1933): 33–34, and no. 32 (November 1934): 66–68; and *Boletín Médico-Social de la Caja de Seguro Obligatorio* 2, no. 22 (March 1936): 95.

50. For cases where social workers found employment for women as laundresses or domestic servants see Arriagada Campos, "Acción del servicio social," 31; *Servicio Social* 12, no. 4 (October 1938): 184–85; Norambuena Lagarde, "El servicio social en la

Caja de Seguro Obligatorio," 266; and Schiappacasse Ferretti, "El problema económico de la madre soltera," 50.

51. Cases of social workers helping women initiate legal proceedings for child support or convincing fathers to take up their financial responsibility can be found in *Servicio Social* 12, no. 4 (October 1938): 183–84, and Schiappacasse Ferretti, "El problema económico de la madre soltera," 53. Compare Arriagada Campos, "Acción del servicio social," 63.

52. Urbina Moya, "Proyecciones del servicio social," 107–8, 112–13.

53. For disapproval of female employment see Navarro Torres, "El aborto," 42, and *Servicio Social* 30, no. 2 (May–August 1956): 10, 28; but compare *Boletín Médico-Social de la Caja de Seguro Obligatorio* 11, nos. 117–19 (July–September 1944): 349–51. Compare my analysis to Jensen, "Representations of Gender"; Klaus, "Depopulation and Race Suicide"; and Michel, "Limits of Maternalism," 277–78. These works emphasize that the French state addressed the needs of working mothers, while the U.S. state did not. However, they overlook the ways in which the figure of the working mother could simultaneously be recognized or tolerated and labeled as deviant. For a comparative look at attitudes toward women's work in the Southern Cone of Latin America see Lavrin, *Women, Feminism, and Social Change*, 80–96.

54. *Servicio Social* 14, no. 1 (January–March 1940): 25. Allende, *La realidad médico-social*, 78–79. See also *Boletín Médico-Social de la Caja de Seguro Obligatorio* 11, nos. 117–19 (July–September 1944): 351, and 4, nos. 44–45 (February 1939): 23. Compare *Servicio Social* 14, no. 1 (January–March 1940): 27–28, which found that infant mortality and child death was notably lower among the children of fifty wage-earning women than among the offspring of fifty housewives.

55. Norambuena Lagarde, "El servicio social en la Caja de Seguro Obligatorio," 24, 26. See also Alvarez Pacheco, "El servicio social ante el problema de la madre soltera," 72; Orrego Navarro, "Estudio de los problemas económico-sociales"; and *Vida Sana* (Valparaíso) 3, nos. 42–43 (November–December [1945]): 3.

56. The quotations are from Orrego Navarro, "Estudio de los problemas económico-sociales," 45, and Norambuena Lagarde, "El servicio social en la Caja de Seguro Obligatorio," 26. See also *Aurora de Chile* (7 October 1939): 17, and Schiappacasse Ferretti, "El problema económico de la madre soltera," 30–31. Compare Santana et al., "Algunos problemas sociales," 10.

57. Alvarez Pacheco, "El servicio social ante el problema de la madre soltera," 107; *Boletín Médico-Social de la Caja de Seguro Obligatorio* 4, nos. 44–45 (February 1939): 12, 16; *Servicio Social* 14, no. 1 (January–March 1940): 9, and 12, no. 4 (October 1938): 174.

58. *Boletín de la Sociedad Chilena de Obstetricia y Ginecología* 3, no. 3 (April 1938): 200–205; *Servicio Social* 30, no. 2 (May–August 1956): 14; *Boletín Médico-Social de la Caja de Seguro Obligatorio* 4, nos. 44–45 (February 1939): 21. Compare *Servicio Social* 14, no. 1 (January–March 1940): 29.

59. A 1943 survey of 2,061 industrial and commercial establishments that employed 35,074 women and girls found that 7,897 women employees (22.5 percent)

were married with children; 2,688 (7.7 percent) were married without children; 2,658 (7.6 percent) were single with children; and 21,831 (62.2 percent) were single without children (*Revista del Trabajo* [1944?]: 35–36).

60. *Servicio Social* 12, no. 4 (October 1938): 188; Arriagada Campos, "Acción del servicio social," 108; Urbina Moya, "Proyecciones del servicio social," 85, 108; *Servicio Social* 30, no. 2 (May–August 1956): 9–12. *Servicio Social* 12, no. 4 (October 1938): 172, correlated young women's need to work, which led them to abandon their parents' homes prematurely, and pregnancy outside marriage.

61. *Servicio Social* 14, no. 1 (January–March 1940): 32. Orrego Navarro, "Estudio de los problemas económico-sociales," 19. Urbina Moya, "Proyecciones del servicio social," 88–90.

62. Urbina Moya, "Proyecciones del servicio social," 88–90, 108; *Servicio Social* 23, no. 3 (May–August 1949): 41–43.

63. The representation of women as essentially "pure" evoked the Virgin Mary. On how medical and scientific-rational thought reformulated religious themes see Poovey, *Uneven Developments*, ch. 2.

64. The quotation is from *Vida Sana* (Valparaíso) 1, no. 4 (August 1942): 8. Ibid., 1, no. 1 (May 1942): 8, and 2, no. 10 (February–March 1943): 3; *Vida Sana* (Temuco) 1, no. 1 (November 1938): 2, 7–8, and 1, no. 3 (February 1939): 2; Cárcamo Lastra, "Servicio social en la manufactura de metales 'MADEMSA,'" 36–37.

65. Allende, *La realidad médico-social*, 101–2.

66. Fuentealba Sepúlveda, "El servicio social ante las ciencias penales," 139; Navarro Torres, "El aborto," 13; *Boletín del Ministerio de Salubridad* (January 1940): 27–29.

67. *Vida Sana* (Valparaíso) 2, nos. 20–21 (January–February 1944): 7.

68. The quotation is from *Servicio Social* 12, no. 4 (October 1938): 169. See also Navarro Torres, "El aborto," 26; Alvarez Pacheco, "El servicio social ante el problema de la madre soltera," 153; *Boletín del Ministerio de Salubridad* (July 1939): 39–53; and Peralta, "La atención materno-infantil," 46.

69. *Servicio Social* 12, no. 4 (October 1938): 180–81. See also Norambuena Lagarde, "El servicio social en la Caja de Seguro Obligatorio," 19; Arriagada Campos, "Acción del servicio social," 30–33; Seguel Morales, "Madre soltera," 42–43, 59; Allende, *La realidad médico-social*, 103; and *Boletín del Ministerio de Salubridad* (July 1939): 39–53.

70. Fuentealba Sepúlveda, "El servicio social ante las ciencias penales," 141–45; Pacheco Escobar, "Prostitución en menores," 96–99, 106–13.

71. Grenovich, "Rol del servicio social," esp. 63; Ortega Fuentes, "Acción de la lucha antivenérea," 19. For state regulations regarding prostitution and sexually transmitted diseases see *Boletín Médico-Social de la Caja de Seguro Obligatorio* 9, nos. 93–95 (March–May 1942): 140, 194, 244–47. On measures elsewhere in Latin America see Guy, *Sex and Danger*, and Findlay, *Imposing Decency*.

72. *Vida Sana* (Valparaíso) 1, no. 5 (September 1942): 6; Ortega Fuentes, "Acción de la lucha antivenérea," 19, 41; *Boletín del Ministerio de Salubridad* (October 1939): 19–29; Fuentealba Sepúlveda, "El servicio social ante las ciencias penales," 139–43; *Vida Sana*

(Valparaíso) 1, no. 1 (May 1942): 7. Compare Guy, *Sex and Danger*, and Findlay, *Imposing Decency*, which focus on an earlier period and stress efforts to police prostitutes.

73. Chile, Cámara de Diputados, 8 November 1939, 2a. sesión (sesiones extraordinarias, 1939, I, 145).

74. The quotation is from *Vida Sana* (Valparaíso) 1, no. 4 (August 1942): 8. See also *Vida Sana* (Temuco) 1, no. 5 (April 1939): 3, and *Boletín del Ministerio de Salubridad* (January 1940): 27–29. Compare *Vida Sana* (Temuco) 1, no. 3 (February 1939): 3. The medical establishment was divided over proposed legislation that mandated premarital blood tests, obliged physicians to report patients who did not follow through on treatment, and criminalized sexual practices in which a syphilitic knowingly infected a sexual partner. On these measures see Chile, Cámara de Diputados, 8 November 1939, 2a. sesión (sesiones extraordinarias, 1939, I, 145); Dirección General de Sanidad, "Proyecto de reglamento sobre profilaxis de las enfermedades venéreas," in *Boletín Médico-Social de la Caja de Seguro Obligatorio* 9, nos. 93–95 (March–May 1942): 258–59, 261–62; "Bases para una campaña y legislación anti-venéreas," *Boletín Médico-Social de la Caja de Seguro Obligatorio* 6, no. 58 (March 1939): 141–43; and *La Crítica*, 14 November 1939, 3. For Allende's position as minister of health see *Boletín del Ministerio de Salubridad* (October 1939): 3–4. For plans to control venereal disease drafted before 1938 see *Boletín Médico-Social de la Caja de Seguro Obligatorio* 1, no. 11 (April 1935): 3–7, 21–22, and 2, no. 17 (October 1935): 10–15.

75. In 1938 in Tarapacá, for instance, the campaign distributed 2,500 posters, 3,500 postcards, 1,200 letters to employers, 2,500 illustrative sheets (*láminas*), and 15,500 posters and flyers. And during a fifteen-day campaign in Valparaíso in 1942, ninety informational meetings were held. See "Campaña antivenérea y defensa de la madre y el niño en la provincia de Tarapacá: Segunda memoria anual, enero a diciembre 1938, presentada por el Dr. Nicolás Taborga" (Iquique, 1939) in *Boletín Médico-Social de la Caja de Seguro Obligatorio* 6, nos. 60–61 (May–June 1939): 116–24; *Boletín Médico-Social de la Caja de Seguro Obligatorio* 9, nos. 93–95 (March–May 1942): n.p.; *Vida Sana* (Valparaíso) 1, no. 2 (June 1942): 8; *Ceteche* (Antofagasta), first fortnight December [1939?], 2; *Revista Chilena de Higiene y Medicina Preventiva* 1, nos. 2–3 (January–March 1937): 133.

76. Before penicillin was brought to Chile, around 1950, the treatment of syphilis was painful and lengthy, lasting between two and three years. It consisted of weekly injections of heavy metals, including arsenic, bismuth, and mercury. Residents of rural areas, who had to travel miles to reach health posts, were especially likely to abandon treatment. In the mid-1940s, a "massive" treatment for the disease promised to cure patients through five days of intravenous arsenic. However, the possible side effects were horrifying: nausea, vomiting, headaches, rashes, arm-aches, fever, convulsions, renal or liver failure, and anemia. On the treatment of syphilis see *Vida Sana* (Temuco) 1, no. 1 (November 1938): 5; *Vida Sana* (Valparaíso) 1, no. 5 (September 1942): 5; *Boletín Médico-Social de la Caja de Seguro Obligatorio* 9, nos. 93–95 (March–May 1942): 173–74; and *Revista Médica de Chile* 72, no. 6 (June 1944): 503. According to *Revista Médica*,

fewer than 30 percent of patients who initiated treatment were effectively cured. "Campaña antivenérea," 34, affirmed that around 44 percent of CSO syphilis patients in Tarapacá province had abandoned treatment. A Concepción social worker maintained that over 30 percent of patients abandoned treatment (Ortega Fuentes, "Acción de la lucha antivenérea," 36). In 1935, before massive education campaigns, a CSO document claimed that in a Santiago *consultorio* only 12.5 percent of syphilis patients were cured (*Boletín Médico-Social de la Caja de Seguro Obligatorio* 1, no. 11 [April 1935]: n.p.). For appeals to citizen collaboration see *Vida Sana* (Valparaíso) 1, nos. 6–7 (October–November 1942): 8, and *Vida Sana* (Temuco) 1, no. 5 (April 1939): 3.

77. *Ceteche* (Antofagasta), first fortnight December [1939?], 2; "Campaña antivenérea"; *Vida Sana* (Temuco) 1, no. 5 (April 1939): 4. On campaign cooperation committees see also *Boletín Médico-Social de la Caja de Seguro Obligatorio* 9, nos. 93–95 (March–May 1942): 240–41.

78. On the procedure for searching out *focos de contagio* and for summoning patients to appointments see *Boletín Médico-Social de la Caja de Seguro Obligatorio* 9, nos. 93–95 (March–May 1942): 241–44; *Revista Chilena de Higiene y Medicina Preventiva* 10, no. 3 (September 1948): 151–57; and *Vida Sana* (Valparaíso) 2, no. 10 (February–March 1943): 45. For cases in which patients were reported to Sanidad or threatened with this measure see Cañas Valenzuela, "Estudio de los problemas," 84–85; Norambuena Lagarde, "El servicio social en la Caja de Seguro Obligatorio," 30, 34–35; Grenovich, "Rol del servicio social," 48–49, 91; and Ortega Fuentes, "Acción de la lucha antivenérea," 39, 53, 59. But compare *Boletín Médico-Social de la Caja de Seguro Obligatorio* 11, nos. 117–19 (July–September 1944): 352, which suggested that patients should be encouraged to speak personally to those they had infected.

79. Norambuena Lagarde, "El servicio social en la Caja de Seguro Obligatorio," 34–35.

80. Ibid.

81. *Servicio Social* 12, no. 4 (October 1938): 155; Grenovich, "Rol del servicio social," 45, 55–56; *Vida Sana* (Valparaíso) 2, no. 10 (February–March 1943): 4–5.

82. *Vida Sana* (Valparaíso) 1, no. 5 (September 1942): 4–5, and 2, nos. 13–14 (June–July 1943): 4–5; *Vida Sana* (Temuco) 1, no. 1 (November 1938): 5, 7, 8; Grenovich, "Rol del servicio social," 58, tables 1, 5, 6, n.p.; *Revista Chilena de Higiene y Medicina Preventiva* 10, no. 3 (September 1948): 155, and 3, no. 3 (December 1940): 152; Mayorga Marcos, "Servicios coordinados," 49; Ortega Fuentes, "Acción de la lucha antivenérea," 19.

83. *Vida Sana* (Temuco) 1, no. 1 (November 1938): 7; *Vida Sana* (Valparaíso) 1, no. 1 (May 1942): 7; 1, no. 5 (September 1942): 6; and 2, no. 10 (February–March 1943): 3; *Boletín Médico-Social de la Caja de Seguro Obligatorio* 9, nos. 93–95 (March–May 1943): 144–48.

84. The term "repertoire of rule" is from Corrigan and Sayer, *Great Arch*, 4–5. On the "public" and "private" alliances that undergirded efforts to reform the family in France see Donzelot, *Policing of Families*.

85. Given my use in this chapter of historical records generated by state agents, the state's possible, or partial, construction of female compliance must be kept in mind.

86. Charney Venegas, "Sindicatos textiles," 76–95.

CHAPTER SIX

1. Guzmán, *La sangre y la esperanza*.

2. Ibid., 181.

3. Ibid., 176–80, 74–93.

4. Ibid., 98–99.

5. On this and other aspects of the literary "Generation of '38," see Teitelboim, *El oficio ciudadano*.

6. Interview with Elena Varela, 30 July 1993.

7. On the hegemonic character of the Chilean Left see Sabrovsky, *Hegemonía y racionalidad política*.

8. Interview with Blanca Flores and Edmundo Sepúlveda, 4 June 1993. Sepúlveda Leal, secretary-general of the POS and deputy for the party, later joined the Socialist Party. Flores's father was POS founder and Communist Party leader Carlos Flores.

9. Ibid.; Moulian and Torres Dujisin, "Concepción de la política." The continuities between bourgeois and proletarian morality described by Moulian and Torres Dujisin clearly became more pronounced during the popular-front era.

10. *AS*, no. 5, n.d., 5. Interview with Iris Figueroa, 5 April 1993. See also Muñoz, *Carbón*, 23.

11. *AS*, no. 3, n.d., 1. *Ahora* (Iquique), cited in *Obrero Textil*, 30 June 1937, 3–4. *Tribuna Juvenil*, July 1935, 3; *Chispa* (Iquique), second fortnight April 1939, n.p.

12. Sindicato Industrial Obrero Andes Copper Mining Co., "Pliego de peticiones"; *AS*, no. 3, n.d., 1; *Obrero Textil*, 30 June 1937, 3–4; quotation from Partido Socialista, "Reglamento nacional," 33.

13. Teitelboim, *Hijo del salitre*, 131–32. Moulian and Torres Dujisin, in "Concepción de la política," posit the emphasis on education and control as reflecting the artisanal roots of the Chilean labor movement.

14. *CTCh*, October 1945, 3. Ibid., July 1946, 5.

15. *El Obrero Municipal*, December 1936, 2. *Obrero Textil*, 4 December 1936, 3; *Ahora* (Iquique), cited in *El Obrero Textil*, 30 June 1937, 3–4; *Chispa* (Iquique), second fortnight April 1939, n.p.; *Obrero Municipal*, May 1939, 3.

16. Interview with Emperatriz Villarroel, 6 April 1993.

17. *El Progreso* (Curicó), 25 November 1944, 2; *Claridad*, 23 December 1937, 1; *La Crítica*, 14 September 1942, 3. Interview with Emperatriz Villarroel, 6 April 1993.

18. Allende, *La realidad médico-social*, 119. Partido Comunista, "Informes y resoluciones," 21.

19. *La Crítica*, 17 November 1939, 3. See also ibid., 28 October 1939, 2, and 26 Oc-

tober 1939, 1; El Despertar Minero (Sewell), second fortnight August 1943, 6; and Juventud en Marcha (Concepción), 24 April 1937, 2. The quotation from La Crítica is a virtual paraphrase of the decree that set up the Defensa de la Raza, published in Acción Social, no. 81 (September 1939): 1–4.

20. My appreciation of recreational groups comes from interview with Iris Figueroa, 5 April 1993; interview with Blanca Flores and Edmundo Sepúlveda, 4 June 1993; and interview with Irma Moreno, 14 June 1993.

21. Partido Socialista, "Reglamento nacional," 33. Teitelboim, Hijo del salitre, 145; Boizard, Cuatro retratos, 98, 110–11.

22. La Crítica, 6 May 1942, 7, and 26 October 1939, 10; Sindicato Industrial Obrero Andes Copper Mining Co., "Pliego de peticiones"; El Despertar Minero (Sewell), second fortnight August 1943, 6; Mundo Nuevo, third period, 1 March 1941, 6; Liberación (Tomé), 16 September 1939, 2; La Palabra Socialista (Valdivia), 15 July 1939, 4, and 18 November 1939, 6; quotation from Partido Comunista, "Informes y resoluciones," 22. For a discussion of an initial attempt to implement prohibition see Chile, Cámara de Diputados, 14 September 1938, 74a. sesión (sesiones ordinarias, 1938, III, 3421–22).

23. El Santiago Watt 3, nos. 38–39 (March–April 1946): 14; Partido Comunista, "Informes y resoluciones," 22; Partido Comunista, "¡Adelante!" 44; Sindicato Industrial Obrero Andes Copper Mining Co., "Pliego de peticiones." El Despertar Minero (Sewell), 30 April 1941, n.p.; quotation from CTCh, October 1945, 8. On drinking and the application of dry laws in El Teniente see Klubock, Contested Communities, 59–61, 122–23, 155–64.

24. Communist Youth organizing around sports coincided with the emerging popular-front orientation. See interview with Emperatriz Villarroel, 6 April 1993; Tribuna Juvenil, July 1935, 3; Rumbo (January 1940): 19; CTCh, October 1945, 8; and Barricada, third period, second fortnight October 1941, 4; quotation from AS, no. 5, n.d., 5. On employer-sponsored recreational activities in Brazil see Weinstein, For Social Peace, 235–39.

25. Interview with Roberto Quiroga, 24 August 1994. Interviews with Iris Figueroa, 5 April 1993 and 12 May 1993.

26. El Santiago Watt 3, nos. 38–39 (March–April 1946): 14; interview with Clara Velarde, 25 March 1993; interview with Emperatriz Villarroel, 6 April 1993. On the discrepancies between the pronouncements of Left organizations and working-class customs see Klubock, Contested Communities.

27. Servicio Social 9, no. 4 (October–December 1935): 306–7. Interview with Iris Figueroa, 5 April 1993; interview with Clara Velarde, 25 March 1993; interview with Graciela Trujillo, 20 April 1993.

28. Interview with Carmen Lazo, 21 April 1993. See also interview with Fresia Gravano, 4 April 1993.

29. Chispa (Iquique), second fortnight April 1939, n.p.; Tribuna Juvenil, July 1935, 3.

30. La Voz del Campo (Talca), 19 June 1937, 3; El Fideero, January 1944, 3; Partido

Comunista, "XI Congreso," 16; interview with Iris Figueroa, 5 April 1993; interview with Graciela Trujillo, 20 April 1993; interview with Clara Velarde, 25 March 1993.

31. Interviews with Carmen Lazo, 21 April 1993 and 15 July 1999. Interview with Iris Figueroa, 5 April 1993.

32. Interview with Violeta de la Cruz, 26 April 1993. Interview with Clara Velarde, 25 March 1993.

33. Interview with Iris Figueroa, 5 April 1993. Interview with Clara Velarde, 25 March 1993.

34. Interview with Iris Figueroa, 5 April 1993.

35. Muñoz, Carbón; quotation on 126–27.

36. Liberación (Tomé), 15 July 1939, 2; CTCh, June 1946, 14; La Voz del Gremio, first fortnight October 1943, 4; Obrero Textil, 4 August 1937, 1–4; quotation from Principios, no. 3 (September 1941): 23–25. Castro, Sewell, 72–75. For similar rhetoric among working-class activists see Findlay, "Free Love and Domesticity," and James, "Poetry, Factory Labour, and Female Sexuality."

37. For anticlerical views see El Pueblo (Talca), 30 March 1947, 1, and Combate, 29 July 1939, 2, 9.

38. Interview with Tomy Romeo, 4 June 1993. Interview with Carmen Lazo, 21 April 1993. Interview with Clara Velarde, 25 March 1993.

39. Interview with Tomy Romeo, 4 June 1993. Interview with Irma Moreno, 14 June 1993.

40. Interviews with Carmen Lazo, 21 April 1993 and 15 July 1999. Guerrero, "Por una Juventud Comunista," 17. Interview with Elena Pedraza, 23 April 1993. See also Corvalán, Algo de mi vida, 93–94.

41. Interview with Mercedes Fuentealba, 28 April 1993.

42. Navarro Torres, "El aborto," 39. Interview with Iris Figueroa, 5 April 1993; interview with Clara Velarde, 25 March 1993. Barricada, second fortnight October 1938, 6.

43. Tribuna, c. 1940, 3.

44. I am drawing here on Michel Foucault's rejection of the "repression thesis" as an explanation of sexual control and on his view of discipline as productive of social reality. See Foucault, History of Sexuality. For an account that stresses the resistant aspects of popular sexual practices see Findlay, Imposing Decency.

45. El Siglo, 20 April 1966, 4.

46. Tribuna, c. 1940, 3. See also La Crítica, 12 May 1942, 7, and Avance (Magallanes), 6 February 1944, 5.

47. Interview with Clara Velarde, 25 March 1993. Interview with Fresia Gravano, 4 April 1993. On male economic responsibilities see Claridad, 21 December 1937, 3; La Voz del Gremio, 11 September 1943, 3, 4; and Noticiario Sindical, August 1951, 12. Studies that explore the reasons for marital conflict include Stern, Secret History of Gender, and Tinsman, "Los patrones del hogar."

48. Principios, no. 3 (September 1941): 23–25. Alianza, first fortnight December

1936, 8. Memoirs, autobiographies, and biographies of prominent leftists include Lafferte, *Vida de un comunista*; Corvalán, *Algo de mi vida*, 17–19; Palestro Rojas, *Jornadas de lucha*; and *El Siglo*, 22 January 1956, 3, and 20 April, 1966, 4.

49. Interview with Fresia Gravano, 4 April 1993. Clara Velarde (interview, 25 March 1993) and Iris Figueroa (interview, 5 April 1993) insisted that, as upstanding men, their fathers did not hit their mothers. On domestic violence see also *El Despertar Minero* (Sewell), 1 August 1941, n.p. On the promiscuity of living quarters see, for example, *El Despertar Minero* (Sewell), 1 March 1941, n.p. Whether politically conscious wives or children were more aware than other women and children of a "right" not to be beaten is a question that merits more attention. On domestic violence in the United States see Gordon, "Right Not to Be Beaten." For a pioneering historical study of wife beating in Chile see Tinsman, "Los patrones del hogar."

50. Interview with Graciela Trujillo, 20 April 1993. *El Obrero Municipal*, December 1936, 2. Castro, *Sewell*, 72–75.

51. Interview with Irma Moreno, 14 June 1993. *El Campo*, second fortnight July 1943, 5. For an advice column see *Tribuna Juvenil*, 21 March 1936, 5.

52. Interview with Mercedes Fuentealba, 28 April 1993. See also interview with Mario González, 23 August 1994; *El Obrero Municipal*, September 1936, 2; May 1939, 3; and May–June 1944, 3; and *El Socialista* (Puerto Natales), 1 January 1935, 4.

53. Interview with Graciela Trujillo, 20 April 1993.

54. Ibid.; interview with Mario González, 23 August 1994; interview with Mercedes Fuentealba, 28 April 1993; interview with Clara Velarde, 25 March 1993.

55. Violeta de la Cruz (interview, 26 April 1993) reported that when she asked husbands to bring their wives to meetings they sometimes refused, saying their wives had to stay home with the children. De la Cruz's husband's own jealousy forced her to retreat from politics for a period.

56. Interview with Tomy Romeo, 4 June 1993. Interviews with Iris Figueroa, 5 April 1993 and 12 May 1993; interview with Graciela Trujillo, 20 April 1993; interview with Verónica Aguayo, 23 June 1988.

57. Interview with Elena Pedraza, 23 April 1993; interview with Iris Figueroa, 5 April 1993; interview with Emperatriz Villarroel, 6 April 1993; interview with Irma Moreno, 14 June 1993. Interview with Fresia Gravano, 4 April 1993; interview with María Mendoza, 1 April 1993. In Castro's *Sewell* (54–55, 102) women's desire to control their fertility was turned into a rejection of capitalism.

58. CTCh, 10 September 1943, 2; interview with Mercedes Fuentealba, 28 April 1993.

59. *Principios*, no. 6 (August–September 1951): 14, and no. 55 (January 1946): 12. See also *Bandera Roja*, third week July 1936, 3.

60. Interview with Mercedes Fuentealba, 28 April 1993. *El Surco* (La Ligua), 1 February 1941, n.p. *Obrero Textil*, 30 June 1937, 3. *Principios*, no. 33 (March 1944): 22, urged militants to put the cause before family.

61. Interview with Clara Velarde, 25 March 1993. Interview with Blanca Flores and Edmundo Sepúlveda, 4 June 1993.

62. Interview with Clara Velarde, 25 March 1993. Interview with Irma Moreno, 14 June 1993.

63. Interview with Clara Velarde, 25 March 1993. Interviews with Elena Pedraza, 23 April 1993 and 20 July 1999.

64. Partido Comunista, "¡Adelante!" 51.

65. Partido Comunista, "Estatutos," 7. *Chispa* (Iquique), second fortnight March 1939, 5. Corvalán, *Algo de mi vida*, 80.

66. *Principios*, no. 33 (March 1944): 26–27. Although the Socialist Party did not punish or correct deviant militants, its statutes demanded that before being admitted to the party a potential militant prove that he led "an honorable public and private life" (Partido Socialista, "Declaración de principios," 19–20).

67. Délano, *La base*. On the commission see Eduardo Labarca, *El Chile de Luis Corvalán*, 259. Party cells thus resembled in some ways the neighborhood committees used by revolutionary governments in Cuba and Nicaragua. On the Sandinista Defense Committees see Lancaster, *Life Is Hard*.

68. My reading of struggles for representation as manly disputes that distanced some men as well as most women from power owes much to Rose, "Respectable Men, Disorderly Others."

69. Mallol Pemjean, "La verdad," 21–23. For other internecine battles in which foes' lack of concern for family members was denounced see *Combate*, 19 April 1940, n.p., and Ibáñez, "Discurso pronunciado," 10.

70. *Tribuna Juvenil*, 21 March 1935, 4.

71. *CTCh*, June 1946, 1.

72. Ibid., 5.

73. *Principios*, no. 30 (June–August 1955): 20. See also ibid., no. 29 (May–June 1955): 13.

74. *Combate*, 11 March 1940, 2. Ibid., 23 September 1940, n.p. *CTCh*, June 1946, 1. *Combate*, 30 September 1939, n.p. See also *Tribuna* (Puerto Natales), 19 December 1940, 3. On similar rhetoric used by popular movements elsewhere see Findlay, "Free Love and Domesticity," and James, "Poetry, Factory Labour, and Female Sexuality."

75. Interviews with Irma Moreno, 14 June 1993 and 14 July 1999.

76. *CTCh*, July 1946, 6.

77. *El Obrero Municipal*, March 1944, 2.

78. Partido Comunista, "Problemas de organización," 3.

79. *AS*, n.d., n.p.

80. *Principios*, no. 19 (July 1953): 28.

81. *CTCh*, August 1946, 3. *La Voz del Cristalero*, 9 January 1945, 2. *Combate*, 11 March 1940, n.p. Partido Socialista, "Reglamento nacional," 32.

82. *El Despertar Minero* (Sewell), second fortnight October 1942, 4. See also *El Obrero Municipal*, April 1945, 6.

83. *Informaciones* (Illapel), second fortnight January 1946, 2.

84. On women strikers see interview with Mario González, 23 August 1994; interview with Roberto Quiroga, 24 August 1994; and interview with Graciela Trujillo,

20 April 1993. On the Beneficencia see *Noticiario Sindical*, 31 January 1949, 1, and CTCh, 1 May 1943, 4. For discussions of potentially disruptive feminine fringes of the labor movement see Scott, *Gender and the Politics of History*, 68–90, and Rose, "Respectable Men, Disorderly Others."

85. *Rumbo* (March 1940): 24.

86. On representation see Spivak, "Can the Subaltern Speak?"

87. On the dual, cultural and natural, bases of masculinity see Alonso, *Thread of Blood*, 79–84. Compare Scott, *Gender and the Politics of History*, 28–50. Although I agree with Scott that gender invokes natural differences to legitimate power, I argue that the discourse of progress and scientific-rational thought are potent sources of legitimation as well.

88. On "expansive" versus limiting forms of constructing hegemony see Mouffe, "Hegemony and New Political Subjects."

89. On the ways in which opposition and the existence of a referent of externality cement hegemony see Laclau and Mouffe, *Hegemony and Socialist Strategy*, esp. 122–34.

CHAPTER SEVEN

1. On Cora Cid see *Acción Social*, no. 78 (May 1939): 1. On Contreras see *Rumbo* (January 1940): 57–60. On Marchant see MEMCh Boletina, November–December 1946, APEC A1 9. On women's electoral effort in favor of Aguirre Cerda see Lenka Franulic's article in *Hoy* (n.d., c. 1938), APEC.

2. The sixty groups represented on Santiago's provincial FEChIF council in 1947 included the Association of University Women, Women's Medical Association (physicians), Association of University Nurses, University of Chile Law Center, Social Workers' Association, Teachers' Union of Chile, Professional Union of Midwives No. 1, an association of workers in the Dirección General del Trabajo, National Society of Teachers, Association of White-Collar Railway Workers of the Second Zone, associations of welfare workers from five different public girls' schools, and a handful of other groups made up of professional women. See FEChIF, *Boletín*, no. 4, September 1947, APEC A4 5, and no. 5, November 1947, APEC A4 9. See also *La Voz de los Empleados de Tarapacá* (Iquique), second fortnight August 1936, 2.

3. Social workers called for making their services obligatory in all factories and for measures to improve their salaries and ensure promotions (Segundo Congreso Nacional de Mujeres, APEC A1 13; *Servicio Social* 21, nos. 1–3 [January–December 1947]: 37–38). On the committee headed by Campusano see FEChIF, *Boletín*, no. 4, September 1947, APEC A4 5. On professionals' advocacy for women as expressed by Lacoste see newspaper clipping dated 24 October 1947, APEC A1 15. In the same vein see Plan de trabajo en sectores intelectuales, APEC A1 3. For the Saavedra quotation see *Mujeres Chilenas*, October 1947, 4.

4. On this measure see *La Crítica*, 8 November 1939, 7.

5. MEMCh *antología*, 37.

6. "El Movimiento pro Emancipación de las Mujeres de Chile en el décimo aniversario de su fundación," in MEMCh antología, 41–42; ibid., 37. FEChIF, Boletín, no. 4, September 1947, APEC A4 5.

7. FEChIF, Boletín, no. 5, November 1947, APEC A4 9. On women's organizing around community development see also Memoria presentada al Segundo Congreso Nacional del MEMCh, [1940], APEC A1 4, and Noticias (La Serena), 19 December 1943, 4.

8. Orientación (September 1948): 7.

9. On the appointment of Caffarena and Yávar see MEMCh antología, 25. Memoria presentada al Segundo Congreso Nacional del MEMCh, [1940], APEC A1 4. The interview with Caffarena is published in Eltit, "Elena Caffarena," 18–20.

10. Memoria anual del MEMCh Valparaíso, April 1947–1948, APEC A1 19; FEChIF, Boletín, no. 4, September 1947, APEC A4 5.

11. On MEMCh and FEChIF clinics see La Mujer Nueva, and FEChIF, Boletín, no. 4, September 1947, APEC A4 5. On day care see FEChIF, Boletín, no. 5, November 1947, APEC A4 9, and MEMCh Boletina, November–December 1946, APEC A1 9. On literacy, education, and its ability to augment citizen participation see Memoria presentada al Segundo Congreso Nacional del MEMCh, [1940], APEC A1 4; María M. de Castro and Olga Valencia, MEMCh, Campamento La Paloma, 13 September 1947, APEC A1 2 16; Orientación (October 1948): 2; Mujeres Chilenas, October 1947, 4; Conclusiones aprobadas en los foros verificados en celebración del día internacional de la mujer, 9–10 March [1949], APEC A1 1 5; and Elena Barreda and Olga Poblete de Espinoza to señor don Enrique Molina, minister of education, n.d., APEC A1 10.

12. MEMCh, Circular, no. 8, April 1948, and no. 9, July 1948, APEC A1 21; Eliana Bronfman to Olga Poblete, 15 March 1949, APEC A1 24; Memoria de las actividades desarrolladas por la Cooperativa de Edificación MEMCh Limitada desde el 8 de marzo de 1950 hasta el 22 de abril de 1951, APEC A1 31; Cuenta de abril de 1951 a abril de 1952, de la Cooperativa Población MEMCh, APEC A1 31; Eliana Bronfman and Victoria Miranda, Cooperativa de Edificación MEMCh Ltda., to señor vice presidente de la Sociedad Constructora de Establecimientos Educacionales, APEC A1 31; Memoria de las actividades desarrolladas por la Cooperativa de Edificación MEMCh Ltda. desde junio de 1955 a junio de 1956, APEC A1 31.

13. Servanda de Liberona, Elsa Orrego, Ana Liberona, and Custodia Moreno to Olga P. de Espinoza, Oficina Ricaventura, 6 February 1948, APEC A1 21.

14. Elvira Reyes de Lucero to Olga Poblete, Santiago, 30 May 1950, APEC A1 24. Olga Poblete de Espinoza to Gobinda Villalobos, Santiago, 30 March 1948, APEC A1 21. Servanda de Liberona, Elsa Orrego, Ana Liberona, and Custodia Moreno to Olga P. de Espinoza, Oficina Ricaventura, 6 February 1948, APEC A1 21. On Villalobos's participation in the FEChIF congress see Lista de memchistas que asistieron al Segundo Congreso Nacional de Mujeres de Santiago, APEC A1 13.

15. Servanda de Liberona, Elsa Orrego, Ana Liberona, and Custodia Moreno to Olga P. de Espinoza, Oficina Ricaventura, 6 February 1948, APEC A1 21.

16. For an extended discussion of these issues see Antezana-Pernet, "Mobilizing Women," chs. 4 and 5.

17. Memoria presentada al Segundo Congreso Nacional del MEMCh, [1940], APEC A1 4. For the quotation from Yávar see *Libertad* (Curicó), second week September 1938, 3. On maternalism see the introduction to Koven and Michel, eds., *Mothers of a New World*, 5; Gordon, *Pitied but Not Entitled*, esp. 55–56; Boris, "What about the Working"; and Allen, "Maternalism in German Feminist Movements." Compare Ladd-Taylor, "Toward Defining Maternalism."

18. On this aspect of the party system see Valenzuela, *Political Brokers*, ch. 8.

19. Carta del MEMCh a mujeres elegidas en elecciones municipales de abril de 1947, APEC A1 9; MEMCh, *Circular*, no. 4, August 1947, APEC A1 10; Posición del MEMCh frente a las elecciones municipales, c. April 1947, APEC A1 11.

20. Interview with Iris Figueroa, 12 May 1993.

21. Interview with Mercedes Fuentealba, 28 April 1993; interview with Graciela Trujillo, 20 April 1993.

22. CTCh, second fortnight July 1939, 2. *La Voz del Metalúrgico*, 6 November 1948, 7. See also *El Siglo*, 10 March 1943, 3; CTCh, 26 August 1939, 4, and July 1946, 6; *Informativo CTCh*, second period, second fortnight April 1949, 2; and "Movimiento pro Emancipación de las Mujeres de Chile" (n.p., c. 1945), APEC A1 6.

23. Boletín informativo de la comisión política de la FEChIF, APEC A4 6; Posición del MEMCh frente a las elecciones municipales, c. April 1947, APEC A1 11. See also *Orientación* (November 1948): 1, and MEMCh to Pedro Aguirre Cerda, 4 January 1941, quoted in "El MEMCh y el voto político" (n.p., 1948), APEC A3 10.

24. *Orientación* (November 1948): 2.

25. Amanda Labarca, *Feminismo contemporáneo*, 144.

26. Boletín informativo de la comisión política de la FEChIF, APEC A4 6.

27. MEMCh to Pedro Aguirre Cerda, 4 January 1941, quoted in "El MEMCh y el voto político" (n.p., 1948), APEC A3 10.

28. On education for campesinos see Elena Barreda and Olga Poblete de Espinoza to señor don Enrique Molina, minister of education, APEC A1 10, and MEMCh, *Circular*, no. 4, August 1947, APEC A1 10.

29. On opposition to electoral fraud see interview with Blanca Flores and Edmundo Sepúlveda, 4 June 1993; *Rumbo* (Tocopilla), first fortnight March 1937, 1; *Crónica* (Valdivia), 18 March 1944, 4; MEMCh, "¡Ud. quiere que su hijo sea un hombre honrado . . . !" APEC; *Mundo Nuevo*, third period, September 1946, 7; and *El Pueblo* (Talca), 30 March 1947, 1. On municipal elections see "Mujer: Puedes y debes influir en tu propio destino," APEC, and Memoria presentada al Segundo Congreso Nacional del MEMCh, [1940], APEC A1 4.

30. Aniceto Rodríguez in Partido Socialista, "Tareas para un buen militante," 20. Amanda Labarca, newspaper article, 11 June 1946, 3, APEC. See also *Consigna*, 1 May 1935, n.p.; *Claridad*, 28 December 1937, 3; *Frente Popular*, 2 September 1937, n.p.; "El MEMCh y el voto político" (n.p., 1948), APEC A3 10; and Boletín informativo de la comisión política de la FEChIF, APEC A4 6.

31. Acta no. 2, sesión de trabajo de la sexta comisión del Segundo Congreso Nacional de Mujeres, 18 September 1947, APEC A1 13.

32. Fundamentación de los considerandos y resoluciones presentados a la sesión plenaria del Segundo Congreso Nacional de Mujeres, 20 September 1947, APEC A1 13.

33. For an account of the closing session of the FEChIF congress see De la reunión del MEMCh del 23 de septiembre del 47, donde da cuenta de la clausura del Congreso FEChIF en Valparaíso, 1947, APEC A1 13. The quotations from González Videla come from this document. See also Gaviola et al., *Queremos votar*, 76.

34. On MEMCh's withdrawal from FEChIF see Olga Poblete and Elena Barreda to the president of FEChIF, Santiago, 20 April 1948, APEC.

35. Eltit, "Elena Caffarena."

36. Elena Caffarena to Conservador de Bienes Raíces, January 1949, in ibid., 23.

37. Amanda Labarca, *Feminismo contemporáneo*, 144; Elena Caffarena to the editor of the newspaper *Democracia*, August 1951, APEC A10 6.

CONCLUSION

1. Welfare state formation in Chile thus resembled that of Britain or France more than that of the United States. See Gordon, *Pitied but Not Entitled*; Skocpol, *Protecting Soldiers and Mothers*; and the essays in Gordon, ed., *Women, the State, and Welfare*; Bock and Thane, eds., *Maternity and Gender Policies*; and Koven and Michel, eds., *Mothers of a New World*.

2. See Introduction. This data says nothing about male wages per se, or about male wages as compared to those of women. It does suggest that for some workers material improvements may have been more substantial than previously thought.

3. In his study of El Teniente, Thomas Klubock ("Hombres y mujeres en El Te-niente") found that court cases dealing with domestic issues proliferated with the advent of the popular fronts.

4. Compare Collier and Collier, *Shaping the Political Arena*, and Bergquist, *Labor in Latin America*.

5. On the historiography of these cases see French, *Brazilian Workers' ABC*, introduction; James, *Resistance and Integration*, ch. 1; Joseph and Nugent, eds., *Everyday Forms of State Formation*, 2–23; and Rubin, *Decentering the Regime*, chs. 1 and 8.

6. French, *Brazilian Workers' ABC*; Middlebrook, *Paradox of Revolution*; James, *Resistance and Integration*, ch. 1. Compare Wolfe, *Working Women, Working Men*.

7. On the influence of the Left in Mexico see Carr, "Fate of the Vanguard."

8. Vaughan, *Cultural Politics in Revolution*. For similar approaches see Rubin, *Decentering the Regime*, and Nugent and Alonso, "Multiple Selective Traditions." Compare Becker, "Torching La Purísima," and Becker, *Setting the Virgin on Fire*.

9. Besse, *Restructuring Patriarchy*.

10. Ibid., ch. 7; quotation on 198; Lavrin, *Women, Feminism, and Social Change*; quotation on 359. On women's mobilizations around their particularities as women see Bouvard, *Revolutionizing Motherhood*; Jelin, ed., *Women and Social Change in Latin America*, 1–11,

184–207; Feijoo and Gogna, "Women in the Transition to Democracy"; and Alvarez, *Engendering Democracy*.

11. Vaughan, "Modernizing Patriarchy."

12. Stern, *Secret History of Gender*; quotation on 330.

13. Weinstein, "Unskilled Worker, Skilled Housewife," 85, 88.

14. On this issue see Fraser, *Unruly Practices*, 120–21.

BIBLIOGRAPHY

INTERVIEWS

All interviews were conducted in Santiago.
* indicates a pseudonym.
Aguayo, Verónica* (23 June 1988)
Chaigneau, Amalia (25 June 1993)
Chaigneau, Amalia, Olivia Piña, and Ester Atlagic (12 July 1993)
de la Cruz, Violeta (26 April 1993)
Figueroa, Iris (5 April 1993 and 12 May 1993)
Flores, Blanca, and Edmundo Sepúlveda (4 June 1993)
Fuentealba, Mercedes (28 April 1993)
González, Mario (23 August 1994)
Gravano, Fresia (4 April 1993)
Heredia, Pércival (7 May 1993)
Lazo, Carmen (21 April 1993 and 15 July 1999)
Mendoza, María (1 April 1993)
Monreal, Tegualda (17 June 1993)
Moreno, Irma (14 June 1993 and 14 July 1999)
Pedraza, Elena (23 April 1993, 28 May 1993, and 20 July 1999)
Quiñones, Aída (19 May 1993)
Quiroga, Roberto* (24 August 1994)
Romeo, Tomasa [Tomy] (4 June 1993, 15 June 1993, 15 July 1993, and 28 July 1999)
Trujillo, Graciela (20 April 1993)
Varela, Elena* (27 July 1993, 30 July 1993, and 27 July 1999)
Velarde, Clara (25 March 1993)
Villarroel, Emperatriz (6 April 1993)
Yávar, Elena (13 September 1993)

GOVERNMENT DOCUMENTS

Chile. "Censo de población, 1940." In *Estadística Chilena* 18, no. 6 (June 1945); 18, no. 12 (December 1945); 19, no. 9 (September 1946).
——. *Código civil.* Santiago, 1944.
——. *Código del trabajo.* Santiago, 1942.
Chile. Caja de Seguro Obligatorio. *Anuario estadístico año 1946.* Santiago, 1948.
——. *Anuario estadístico año 1947.* Santiago, 1949.
——. *Anuario estadístico año 1949.* Santiago, 1951.
Chile. Cámara de Diputados. Sesiones extraordinarias. Santiago, 1933–51.
——. Sesiones ordinarias. Santiago, 1933–39.
Chile. Dirección General de Informaciones y Cultura. "Recopilación de las disposiciones

legales y reglamentarias sobre los servicios que integran la Dirección General de Informaciones y Cultura." [Santiago?], 1943.

Chile. Dirección General de Estadística. *X Censo de la población* [1930]. Santiago, 1935.

——. *Anuario estadístico año 1935: Finanzas, bancos y cajas sociales.* Santiago, [1937?].

——. *Anuario estadístico año 1939: Demografía y asistencia social.* Santiago, [1941?].

——. *Anuario estadístico año 1940: Demografía y asistencia social.* Santiago, 1942.

——. *Anuario estadístico año 1945: Demografía y asistencia social.* Santiago, 1948.

——. *Anuario estadístico año 1950: Demografía y asistencia social.* Santiago, 1954.

——. *Anuario estadístico año 1950: Finanzas, bancos y cajas sociales.* Santiago, 1954.

Chile. Servicio Nacional de Estadística y Censos. *XII Censo general de población* [1952]. N.p., n.d.

Consejo de Defensa del Niño. *Memoria correspondiente al año 1941.* Santiago, 1944.

——. *Memoria correspondiente al bienio 1944–1945.* Santiago, n.d.

PAMPHLETS

Pamphlets are from the collections of the Biblioteca Nacional and the Biblioteca del Congreso, Santiago, Chile.

Allende, Salvador. "La contradicción de Chile" [IV Congreso Extraordinario del Partido Socialista, Valparaíso, 15 August 1943]. Santiago, n.d.

——. "El Partido Socialista proclama el 25 de octubre como fecha de reconquista." Santiago, 1943.

Contreras Labarca, Carlos. "Por la paz, por nuevas victorias del Frente Popular." Santiago, c. 1939.

Federación de la Juventud Socialista. "Reglamentos de la Federación de la Juventud Socialista." Santiago, 1946.

Fonseca, Ricardo. "Plan inmediato de gobierno del Partido Comunista." Santiago, 1946.

Guerrero, Víctor. "Por una Juventud Comunista de masas." Santiago, c. 1941.

Ibáñez, Bernardo. "Discurso pronunciado en el acto de inauguración de la Tercera Conferencia Nacional Industrial y Campesina CTCh." Santiago, 1946.

"Juntas de vigilancia y asociaciones de dueñas de casa. Organización y atribuciones." Santiago, 1947.

Mallol Pemjean, Mario. "La verdad sobre los dirigentes regionales de Iquique del Partido Socialista de Chile." [Iquique?], c. 1941.

Partido Comunista. "¡Adelante por el cumplimiento del programa del Frente Popular!: Sesión plenaria del Comité Central del Partido Comunista de Chile." Santiago, c. 1941.

——. "Estatutos del Partido Comunista de Chile aprobados por el XIII Congreso Nacional celebrado en 1946." N.p., n.d.

——. "Informes y resoluciones: Política parlamentaria; política municipal; cultura, prensa y propaganda." Santiago, 1940.

——. "XI Congreso del Partido Comunista de Chile." Santiago, c. 1940.

——. "Problemas de organización." Santiago, 1938.

Partido Socialista. "Congreso Extraordinario del Partido Socialista, Santiago, 7, 8, 9 de agosto de 1944." Santiago, c. 1944.

——. "IV Congreso Extraordinario del Partido Socialista realizado en Valparaíso en agosto de 1943." Santiago, 1943.

——. "Declaración de principios, estatutos, y reglamento orgánico del Partido Socialista de Chile." Santiago, 1947.

——. "La juventud en el Frente del Pueblo." Santiago, 1939.

——. "I Congreso Regional del Partido Socialista en la provincia de Tarapacá: Resoluciones adoptadas." Santiago, 1939.

——. "Reglamento nacional de defensa." Santiago, 1940.

——. "Tareas para un buen militante." Santiago, 1947.

——. "Una etapa de clarificación socialista." [IV Congreso General Extraordinario, August 1943, and Primer Pleno, January 1944]. Santiago, c. 1944.

Sindicato Industrial Obrero Andes Copper Mining Co. y Potrerillos Raylway [sic] Corp. "Pliego de peticiones presentado a los sres. gerentes y sub-gerentes generales." [Potrerillos], c. 1937.

THESES

Alvarez Pacheco, Graciela. "El servicio social ante el problema de la madre soltera." Memoria, Escuela de Servicio Social, Ministerio de Educación Pública, [Valparaíso?], 1944.

Aqueveque Castro, Eliana. "Experiencias obtenidas en práctica realizada en la Caja de Habitación de Concepción." Memoria, Escuela de Servicio Social, Universidad de Chile, Concepción, 1949.

Arriagada Campos, Delia. "Acción de servicio social en la Gota de Leche 'Almirante Villarroel' de Talcahuano." Memoria, Escuela de Servicio Social, Ministerio de Educación Pública, Concepción, 1947.

Cañas Valenzuela, Luz. "Estudio de los problemas que se presentan en la 'Sección Lactantes' del Consultorio No. 3 de la CSO." Memoria, Escuela de Servicio Social, Junta de Beneficencia, Santiago, 1941.

Cárcamo Lastra, Olga. "Servicio social en la manufactura de metales 'MADEMSA.' " Memoria, Escuela de Servicio Social, Ministerio de Educación Pública, Santiago, 1945.

Charney Venegas, Haydee. "Sindicatos textiles y sus relaciones con el servicio social." Memoria, Escuela de Servicio Social, Ministerio de Educación Pública, Concepción, 1947.

Chávez Guzmán, Marta Ena. "La mujer ante el derecho del trabajo." Memoria, Facultad de Ciencias Jurídicas y Sociales, Universidad de Chile, 1939.

Díaz Delgado, Albertina. "Protección de la maternidad de las asalariadas y seguro de maternidad." Memoria, Facultad de Ciencias Jurídicas y Sociales, Universidad de Chile, 1941.

Espinoza Muñoz, Zarina. "La Dirección de Auxilio Social y la labor desarrollada por la asistente social en los sectores Pila y Estación Central." Memoria, Escuela de Servicio Social, Ministerio de Educación Pública, Santiago, 1947.

Ferrero Mate de Luna, María. "El problema materno-infantil ante la ley." Memoria, Facultad de Ciencias Jurídicas y Sociales, Universidad de Chile, 1946.

Fuentealba Sepúlveda, Renato. "El servicio social ante las ciencias penales." Memoria, Facultad de Ciencias Jurídicas y Sociales, Universidad de Chile, 1942.

Grenovich, Paulina. "Rol del servicio social en el control de la sífilis: Experiencias epidemiológicas en la investigación de los contactos en el Hospital San Luis de Santiago." Memoria, Escuela de Servicio Social, Junta de Beneficencia, Santiago, 1944.

Lillo Hermosilla, Hilda. "Hogar Modelo Pedro Aguirre Cerda." Memoria, Escuela de Servicio Social, Universidad de Chile, [Santiago?], 1949.

Mallet Simonetti, Armando. "Asignaciones familiares." Memoria, Facultad de Ciencias Jurídicas y Sociales, Universidad de Chile, 1942.

Mayorga Marcos, Rosario. "Servicios coordinados frente a la lucha antivenérea (estudio realizado en el servicio social de la CSO de Temuco)." Memoria, Escuela de Servicio Social, Facultad de Ciencias Jurídicas y Sociales, Universidad de Chile, Temuco, 1952.

Mellado, Franklin. "Las asignaciones familiares." Memoria, Escuela de Derecho, Universidad de Concepción, 1958.

Meneses Zúñiga, Flora. "La ley 4.054 de seguro obligatorio de enfermedad, vejez e invalidez." Memoria, Facultad de Ciencias Jurídicas y Sociales, Universidad de Chile, 1936.

Mora Campos, María. "Protección a la familia obrera." Memoria, Facultad de Ciencias Jurídicas y Sociales, Universidad de Chile, 1944.

Navarro Torres, Rosa. "El aborto como problema social." Memoria, Escuela de Servicio Social, Ministerio de Educación Pública, Concepción, 1944.

Norambuena Lagarde, Isabel. "El servicio social en la Caja de Seguro Obligatorio." Memoria, Escuela de Servicio Social, Junta de Beneficencia, Santiago, 1943.

Orrego Navarro, Glasfira. "Estudio de los problemas económico-sociales presentados por 50 madres obreras y 50 madres dueñas de casa Centro San Eugenio CSO." Memoria, Escuela de Servicio Social, [Junta de Beneficencia?], Santiago, 1941.

Ortega Fuentes, Nora. "Acción de la lucha antivenérea en Concepción." Memoria, Escuela de Servicio Social, Ministerio de Educación Pública, Concepción, 1947.

Pacheco Escobar, Georgina. "Prostitución en menores." Memoria, Escuela de Servicio Social, Universidad de Chile, Valparaíso, 1948.

Paredes Quijada, Rolando. "El servicio social frente a la legislación del trabajo." Memoria, Facultad de Ciencias Jurídicas y Sociales, Universidad de Chile, 1945.

Peralta, Helga. "La atención materno-infantil en la Caja de Seguro Obligatorio." Memoria, Escuela de Servicio Social, Universidad de Chile, Santiago, 1951.

Pimentel Orellana, Manuel. "La medicina preventiva en sus aspectos económico y social." Memoria, Facultad de Ciencias Jurídicas y Sociales, Universidad de Chile, 1948.

Pinto Ureta, Margarita. "Estudio de las condiciones de vida de 100 familias atendidas en la Sociedad Gotas de Leche de Valparaíso." Memoria, Escuela de Servicio Social, [Universidad de Chile?], Valparaíso, 1951.

Ponce Ponce, Lucía. "Desavenencias conyugales en el hogar del obrero municipal." Memoria, Escuela de Servicio Social, Ministerio de Educación Pública, Santiago, 1945.

Rioseco Tapia, René. "Situación de los hijos ilegítimos y de la madre soltera ante la sociedad y la ley." Memoria, Facultad de Ciencias Jurídicas y Sociales, Universidad de Chile, 1938.

Schiappacasse Ferretti, Rina. "El problema económico de la madre soltera estudiado en el Centro de Defensa del Niño." Memoria, Escuela de Servicio Social, Ministerio de Educación Pública, Concepción, 1946.

Seguel Morales, Gudelia. "Madre soltera." Memoria, Escuela de Servicio Social, Ministerio de Educación Pública, Temuco, 1946.

Soletic, Milena. "La mujer obrera y sus problemas." Memoria, Escuela de Servicio Social, Ministerio de Educación Pública, Santiago, 1946.

Torres Romero, Lilia. "Condiciones de vida y de trabajo de los obreros de la Compañía Nacional de Tejidos 'El Salto.'" Memoria, Escuela de Servicio Social, Universidad de Chile, Santiago, 1950.

Urbina Moya, Blanca. "Proyecciones del servicio social en la industria 'Fábricas Textiles Caupolicán-Chiguayante' S.A." Memoria, Escuela de Servicio Social, [Universidad de Chile?], Concepción, 1948.

Urquieta Tognarelli, Margarita. "Problemas psico-sociales del obrero siderúrgico chileno." Memoria, Escuela de Servicio Social, Ministerio de Educación Pública, Santiago, 1946.

Bibliography 323

Valderrama, Luis. "El salario en nuestra legislación social." Memoria, Facultad de Ciencias Jurídicas y Sociales, Universidad de Chile, 1964.

Vallejos González, María. "Organización de la oficina de servicio social en la Sección Arriendos del Comisariato Departamental de Talcahuano." Memoria, Escuela de Servicio Social, Universidad de Chile, Concepción, 1951.

Villarroel Rojas, Carlos. "Aspectos fundamentales de la política de protección familiar obrera." Memoria, Facultad de Ciencias Jurídicas y Sociales, Universidad de Chile, 1936.

Weitzman Fliman, Raquel. "La Caja de Seguro Obligatorio." Memoria, Facultad de Ciencias Jurídicas y Sociales, Universidad de Chile, 1947.

Yanulaque Garrido, Raquel. "La Asociación de Dueñas de Casa." Memoria, Escuela de Servicio Social, Universidad de Chile, Santiago, 1950.

PUBLISHED PRIMARY SOURCES

Allende, Salvador. *La realidad médico-social chilena (síntesis)*. Santiago: n.p., 1939.

Boizard, Ricardo. *Cuatro retratos*. Santiago: n.p., 1950.

Castro, Baltazar. *Sewell*. Santiago: Editorial Cultura, 1946.

Corvalán, Luis. *Algo de mi vida*. Barcelona: Editorial Crítica, 1978.

Délano, Luis Enrique. *La base*. Santiago: Editora Austral, 1958.

Durand, Georgina. *Mis entrevistas*. Santiago: Editorial Tegualda, 1943.

Eltit, Diamela. "Elena Caffarena: El derecho a voz, el derecho a voto." México: Ediciones Casa de Chile en México, 1993.

Guzmán, Nicomedes. *La sangre y la esperanza*. Buenos Aires: Ediciones Siglo Veinte, 1947.

Labarca, Amanda. *Feminismo contemporáneo*. Santiago: Zig-Zag, 1947.

Labarca, Eduardo. *El Chile de Luis Corvalán: Una entrevista de 27 horas*. Barcelona: Editorial Fontamara, 1975.

Lafferte, Elías. *Vida de un comunista*. 2nd edition. Santiago: Editora Austral, 1971.

Millas, Orlando. *En los tiempos del Frente Popular*. Vol. 1 of *Memorias*. Santiago: CESOC, 1993.

MEMCh antología. N.p., c. 1983.

Muñoz, Diego. *Carbón*. Santiago: Editora Austral, 1953.

Palestro Rojas, Tito. *Jornadas de lucha y vida*. Santiago: América Latina Libros, 1989.

Santana, Inés, Amalia Vergara, Aída Figueroa, and Raquel Weitzman. "Algunos problemas sociales." Santiago: n.p., 1943.

Teitelboim, Volodia. *Hijo del salitre*. Santiago: Editora Austral, 1952.

———. *El oficio ciudadano*. Santiago: Editorial Nascimento, 1973.

Vergara, Marta. *Memorias de una mujer irreverente*. 1st. rev. ed. Santiago: Editora Nacional Gabriela Mistral, 1974.

NEWSPAPERS

All newspapers were published in Santiago unless otherwise indicated.

Acción Social

Acción Socialista

La Aguja

La Aguja (Valparaíso)

Ahora (Iquique)
Alianza
Alianza Democrática
Alianza Libertadora de la Juventud (Antofagasta)
AS
Avance (Magallanes)
Bandera Roja
Barricada
Boletín de la Confederación Regional de Aspirantes a Colonos de la Zona Devastada (Concepción)
Boletín Oficial del Comité Nacional pro Baja de las Subsistencias
Boletín Sindical del Comité Regional del Partido Comunista
Brecha
El Campo
El Centinela
Ceteche (Antofagasta)
Chispa (Iquique)
Claridad
Combate
Consigna
El Corraleño (Corral)
El Correo de Valdivia (Valdivia)
La Crítica
Crónica (Valdivia)
CTCh
CTCh (Antofagasta)
La Defensa
El Despertar Minero (Sewell)
El Fideero
Frente Popular
Frente Popular (Valparaíso)
El Grito del Obrero Agrícola
La Hora
Informaciones (Illapel)
Informativo CTCh
Julio Barrenechea (Temuco)
Juventud en Marcha (Concepción)
Liberación (Tomé)
Libertad (Curicó)
Machete (Tocopilla)
El Mensaje Obrero (Rancagua)
Mujeres Chilenas
La Mujer Nueva
Mundo Nuevo
La Nación
Noticiario Sindical
Noticias (La Serena)
El Obrero Gastronómico (Valparaíso)
El Obrero Municipal

Obrero Textil
El Organizador
La Palabra (Valdivia)
La Palabra Socialista (Valdivia)
Pedro Aguirre Cerda
El Popular (Antofagasta)
El Progreso (Arauco)
El Progreso (Curicó)
El Pueblo (Talca)
Rumbo (Tocopilla)
El Siglo
El Siglo (Mulchén)
Socialismo
El Socialista (Concepción)
El Socialista (Puerto Natales)
El Surco (La Ligua)
El Toro
Tribuna
Tribuna (Puerto Natales)
Tribuna Juvenil
Tribuna Textil
Unidad (María Elena)
Unidad Gráfica
Unificación (Tomé)
Vanguardia Hotelera
Vanguardia Socialista (Yungay)
Vida Sana (Temuco)
Vida Sana (Valparaíso)
La Voz de Conchalí
La Voz de la Mujer
La Voz de la Provincia (Valdivia)
La Voz del Campo (Talca)
La Voz del Cristalero
La Voz del Gremio
La Voz de los Empleados de Tarapacá (Iquique)

PERIODICALS

All periodicals were published in Santiago.
Acción Social
Aurora de Chile
Boletín del Ministerio de Salubridad, Previsión y Asistencia Social
Boletín de la Sociedad Chilena de Obstetricia y Ginecología
Boletín Médico-Social de la Caja de Seguro Obligatorio
El Chiflón
Estadística Chilena
Orientación

Pampa
Principios
¿Qué Hubo?
Revista Chilena de Higiene y Medicina Preventiva
Revista de Asistencia Social
Revista Médica de Chile
Revista del Trabajo
Rumbo
El Santiago Watt
Servicio Social
Tribuna Social
La Voz del Metalúrgico

SECONDARY SOURCES

Allen, Ann Taylor. "Maternalism in German Feminist Movements." Journal of Women's History 5, no. 2 (Fall 1993): 99–103.
Alonso, Ana María. "The Politics of Space, Time and Substance: State Formation, Nationalism, and Ethnicity." Annual Review of Anthropology 23 (1994): 379–405.
———. Thread of Blood: Colonialism, Revolution, and Gender on Mexico's Northern Frontier. Tucson: University of Arizona Press, 1995.
Alvarez, Sonia. Engendering Democracy in Brazil: Women's Movements in Transition Politics. Princeton: Princeton University Press, 1990.
Anderson, Benedict. Imagined Communities: Reflections on the Origin and Spread of Nationalism. London: Verso, 1983.
Angell, Alan. Politics and the Labour Movement in Chile. London: Oxford University Press, 1972.
Antezana-Pernet, Corinne. "El MEMCh en provincia: Movilización femenina y sus obstáculos, 1935–1942." In Disciplina y desacato: Construcción de identidad en Chile, siglos XIX y XX, edited by Lorena Godoy, Elizabeth Hutchison, Karin Rosemblatt, and M. Soledad Zárate, 287–329. Santiago: SUR/CEDEM, 1995.
———. "Mobilizing Women in the Popular Front Era: Feminism, Class, and Politics in the Movimiento Pro-Emancipación de la Mujer Chilena (MEMCh), 1935–1950." Ph.D. dissertation, University of California, Irvine, 1996.
Baron, Ava. "The Masculinization of Production: The Gendering of Work and Skill in U.S. Newspaper Printing, 1850–1920." In Gendered Domains: Rethinking Public and Private in Women's History, edited by Dorothy Helly and Susan Reversby, 277–88. Ithaca: Cornell University Press, 1992.
Barrera, Manuel. "Desarrollo económico y sindicalismo en Chile: 1938–1970." Santiago: Vector, working paper, 1979.
Barría Serón, Jorge. Los movimientos sociales en Chile desde 1910 hasta 1926. Santiago: Editorial Universitaria, 1960.
Becker, Marjorie. Setting the Virgin on Fire: Lázaro Cárdenas, Michoacán Peasants, and the Redemption of the Mexican Revolution. Berkeley: University of California Press, 1995.
———. "Torching La Purísima, Dancing at the Altar: The Construction of Revolutionary Hegemony in Michoacán, 1934–1940." In Everyday Forms of State Formation: Revolution and the Negotiation of Rule in Modern Mexico, edited by Gilbert Joseph and Daniel Nugent, 247–64. Durham: Duke University Press, 1994.

Behar, Ruth. *Translated Woman: Crossing the Border with Esperanza's Story.* Boston: Beacon Press, 1993.

Benhabib, Seyla, ed. *Democracy and Difference: Contesting the Boundaries of the Political.* Princeton: Princeton University Press, 1996.

Bergquist, Charles. *Labor in Latin America: Comparative Essays on Chile, Argentina, Venezuela, and Colombia.* Stanford: Stanford University Press, 1986.

Besse, Susan. *Restructuring Patriarchy: The Modernization of Gender Inequality in Brazil, 1914–1940.* Chapel Hill: University of North Carolina Press, 1996.

Bock, Gisela, and Pat Thane, eds. *Maternity and Gender Policies: Women and the Rise of the European Welfare States, 1880s–1950s.* New York: Routledge, 1991.

Borges, Dain. " 'Puffy, Ugly, Slothful and Inert': Degeneration in Brazilian Social Thought, 1880–1940." *Journal of Latin American Studies* 25, no. 2 (May 1993): 235–56.

Boris, Eileen. "What about the Working of the Working Mother?" *Journal of Women's History* 5, no. 2 (Fall 1993): 104–7.

Borón, Atilio. "La evolución del régimen electoral y sus efectos en la representación de los intereses populares: El caso de Chile." *Revista Latinoamericana de Ciencias Políticas*, no. 3 (1971): 395–431.

——. "Movilización política y crisis política en Chile (1920–1970)." *Aportes* 20 (April 1971): 41–69.

Bouvard, Marguerite Guzmán. *Revolutionizing Motherhood: The Mothers of the Plaza de Mayo.* Wilmington, Del.: Scholarly Resources, 1994.

Brading, David. "Manuel Gamio and Official Indigenismo in Mexico." *Bulletin of Latin American Research* 7, no. 1 (1988): 75–89.

Carr, Barry. "The Fate of the Vanguard under a Revolutionary State: Marxism's Contribution to the Construction of the Great Arch." In *Everyday Forms of State Formation: Revolution and the Negotiation of Rule in Modern Mexico*, edited by Gilbert Joseph and Daniel Nugent, 326–52. Durham: Duke University Press, 1994.

Carrière, Jean. "Landowners and the Rural Unionization Question in Chile: 1920–1948." *Boletín de Estudios Latinoamericanos y del Caribe* 22 (July 1977): 34–52.

Casanueva, Fernando, and Manuel Fernández. *El Partido Socialista y la lucha de clases en Chile.* Santiago: Quimantú, 1973.

Cavarozzi, Marcelo. "The Government and the Industrial Bourgeoisie in Chile: 1938–1964." Ph.D. dissertation, University of California, Berkeley, 1975.

Chakrabarty, Dipesh. "The Difference-Deferral of (A) Colonial Modernity: Public Debates on Domesticity in British Bengal." *History Workshop* 36 (Autumn 1993): 1–34.

——. "Postcoloniality and the Artifice of History: Who Speaks for the 'Indian' Pasts?" *Representations* 37 (Winter 1992): 1–26.

Chatterjee, Partha. *Nationalist Thought and the Colonial World: A Derivative Discourse.* London: Zed Books, 1986.

——. *The Nation and Its Fragments: Colonial and Postcolonial Histories.* Princeton: Princeton University Press, 1993.

Collier, Ruth Berins, and David Collier. *Shaping the Political Arena: Critical Junctures, the Labor Movement, and Regime Dynamics in Latin America.* Princeton: Princeton University Press, 1991.

Connell, Robert. *Gender and Power.* Stanford: Stanford University Press, 1987.

——. *Masculinities.* Stanford: Stanford University Press, 1995.

Cooper, Frederick. "Conflict and Connection: Rethinking African History." *American Historical Review* 99, no. 5 (December 1994): 1516–45.

Coronil, Fernando. "Listening to the Subaltern: The Poetics of Neocolonial States." *Poetics Today* 15, no. 4 (Winter 1994): 643–58.

Corrigan, Philip, and Derek Sayer. *The Great Arch: English State Formation as Cultural Revolution*. New York: Blackwell, 1985.

Cruz-Coke, Eduardo. *Historia electoral de Chile 1925–1973*. Santiago: Editorial Jurídica, 1984.

Daire, Alfonso. "La política del Partido Comunista desde la post-guerra a la Unidad Popular." In *El Partido Comunista en Chile*, compiled by Augusto Varas, 141–238. Santiago: CESOC/FLACSO, 1988.

de la Cadena, Marisol. "The Political Tensions of Representations and Misrepresentations: Intellectuals and Mestizas in Cuzco (1919–1990)." *Journal of Latin American Anthropology* 2, no. 1 (Fall 1996): 112–47.

——. "Silent Racism and Intellectual Superiority in Peru." *Bulletin of Latin American Research* 17, no. 2 (1998): 143–64.

Delaney, Carol. "Father State, Motherland, and the Birth of Modern Turkey." In *Naturalizing Power: Essays in Feminist Cultural Analysis*, edited by Sylvia Yanagisako and Carol Delaney, 177–99. New York: Routledge, 1995.

DeShazo, Peter. *Urban Workers and Labor Unions in Chile, 1902–1927*. Madison: University of Wisconsin Press, 1983.

Diccionario biográfico de Chile. 2nd–10th eds. Santiago: Empresa Periodística Chile, 1939–58.

Dietz, Mary. "Context Is All: Feminism and Theories of Citizenship." In *Dimensions of Radical Democracy*, edited by Chantal Mouffe, 63–85. London: Verso, 1992.

Donzelot, Jacques. *The Policing of Families*. New York: Pantheon Books, 1979.

Drake, Paul. *Socialism and Populism in Chile, 1932–1952*. Urbana: University of Illinois Press, 1978.

Elshtain, Jean Bethke. *Power Trips and Other Journeys: Essays in Feminism as Civic Discourse*. Madison: University of Wisconsin Press, 1990.

Espinoza, Vicente. *Para una historia de los pobres de la ciudad*. Santiago: SUR, 1988.

Faúndez, Julio. *Marxism and Democracy in Chile: From 1932 to the Fall of Allende*. New Haven: Yale University Press, 1988.

Feijoo, María del Carmen, and Mónica Gogna. "Women in the Transition to Democracy." In *Women and Social Change in Latin America*, edited by Elizabeth Jelin, 70–114. London: Zed Books, 1990.

Figueroa Ortiz, Enrique, and Carlos Sandoval Ambiado. *Carbón: Cien años de historia (1848–1960)*. Santiago: CEDAL, 1987.

Findlay, Eileen. "Free Love and Domesticity: Sexuality and the Shaping of Working-Class Feminism in Puerto Rico, 1900–1917." In *Identity and Struggle at the Margins of the Nation-State: The Laboring Peoples of Central America and the Hispanic Caribbean*, edited by Aviva Chomsky and Aldo Lauria-Santiago, 229–59. Durham: Duke University Press, 1998.

——. *Imposing Decency: The Politics of Sexuality and Race in Puerto Rico, 1870–1920*. Durham: Duke University Press, 1999.

Foucault, Michel. *The History of Sexuality*. Vol. 1. New York: Vintage Books, 1990.

——. *Power/Knowledge: Selected Interviews and Other Writings, 1972–1977*, edited by Colin Gordon. New York: Pantheon Books, 1980.

Fraser, Nancy. *Unruly Practices: Power, Discourse, and Gender in Contemporary Social Theory*. Minneapolis: University of Minnesota Press, 1989.

French, John D. *The Brazilian Workers' ABC: Class Conflict and Alliances in Modern São Paulo*. Chapel Hill: University of North Carolina Press, 1992.

French, John D., with Mary Lynn Pedersen Cluff. "Women and Working-Class Mobilization in Postwar São Paulo, 1945–1949." In *The Gendered Worlds of Latin American Women Workers: From the Household and Factory to the Union Hall and Ballot Box*, edited by John D. French and Daniel James, 176–207. Durham: Duke University Press, 1997.

Frías, Patricio, Magdalena Echeverría, Gonzalo Herrera, and Christian Larraín. *Organización sindical: Historia y proyecciones.* Vol. 3 of *Industria textil y del vestuario en Chile.* Santiago: Programa de Economía del Trabajo, 1987.

Furci, Carmelo. *The Chilean Communist Party and the Road to Socialism.* London: Zed Books, 1989.

Gálvez, Thelma, and Rosita Bravo. "Siete décadas de registro del trabajo femenino, 1854–1920." *Revista Estadística y Economía* (Santiago) 5 (December 1992): 1–52.

Gaviola, Edda, Ximena Jiles, Lorella Lopresti, and Claudia Rojas. *Queremos votar en las próximas elecciones: Historia del movimiento femenino chileno, 1913–1952.* Santiago: CEM, 1986.

Gilroy, Paul. *The Black Atlantic: Modernity and Double Consciousness.* Cambridge, Mass.: Harvard University Press, 1993.

———. *"There Ain't No Black in the Union Jack": The Cultural Politics of Race and Nation.* Chicago: University of Chicago Press, 1987.

Gómez, María Soledad. "Factores nacionales e internacionales de la política del Partido Comunista de Chile (1922–1952)." In *El Partido Comunista en Chile,* compiled by Augusto Varas, 65–140. Santiago: CESOC/FLACSO, 1988.

Góngora, Mario. *Ensayo histórico sobre la noción de Estado en Chile en los siglos XIX y XX.* 4th ed. Santiago: Editorial Universitaria, 1986.

González Miranda, Sergio. *Hombres y mujeres de la pampa: Tarapacá en el ciclo del salitre.* Iquique: Taller de Estudios Regionales, 1991.

Gordon, Linda. *Heroes of Their Own Lives: The Politics of Family Violence, Boston, 1880–1960.* New York: Penguin Books, 1988.

———. "New Feminist Scholarship." In *Women, the State, and Welfare,* edited by Linda Gordon, 9–35. Madison: University of Wisconsin Press, 1990.

———. *Pitied but Not Entitled: Single Mothers and the History of Welfare, 1890–1935.* New York: Free Press, 1994.

———. "A Right Not to Be Beaten: The Agency of Battered Women, 1880–1960." In *Gendered Domains: Rethinking Public and Private in Women's History,* edited by Dorothy Helly and Susan Reversby, 228–43. Ithaca: Cornell University Press, 1992.

———. *Woman's Body, Woman's Right: A Social History of Birth Control in America.* New York: Penguin Books, 1974.

———, ed. *Women, the State, and Welfare.* Madison: University of Wisconsin Press, 1990.

Gramsci, Antonio. *Selections from the Prison Notebooks.* Edited and translated by Quintin Hoare and Geoffrey Nowell Smith. London: International Publishers, 1971.

Guha, Ranajit. *Dominance without Hegemony: History and Power in Colonial India.* Cambridge, Mass.: Harvard University Press, 1997.

———, ed. *A Subaltern Studies Reader, 1986–1995.* Minneapolis: University of Minnesota Press, 1997.

Gutmann, Matthew. *The Meanings of Macho: Being a Man in Mexico City.* Berkeley: University of California Press, 1996.

Guy, Donna. *Sex and Danger in Buenos Aires: Prostitution, Family, and Nation in Argentina.* Lincoln: University of Nebraska Press, 1990.

Hahner, June. *Emancipating the Female Sex: The Struggle for Women's Rights in Brazil, 1850–1940.* Durham: Duke University Press, 1990.

Hartmann, Heidi. "Capitalism, Patriarchy, and Job Segregation by Sex." *Signs* 1, no. 1 (Spring 1976).

Heise González, Julio. *Ciento cincuenta años de evolución institucional.* Santiago: Editorial Andrés Bello, 1960.

Helg, Aline. "Race in Argentina and Cuba, 1880–1930: Theory, Policies, and Popular

Reaction." In *The Idea of Race in Latin America*, 1870–1940, edited by Richard Graham, 37–69. Austin: University of Texas Press, 1990.

Hughes, Thomas P. *American Genesis: A Century of Invention and Technological Enthusiasm*. New York: Viking, 1989.

Hutchison, Elizabeth. "El feminismo del movimiento obrero chileno: La emancipación de la mujer en la prensa obrera feminista, 1905–1908." *Proposiciones* (Santiago), no. 21 (1992): 50–64.

———. "Working Women of Santiago: Gender and Social Transformation in Urban Chile, 1887–1927." Ph.D. dissertation, University of California, Berkeley, 1995.

Illanes, María Angélica. "*En el nombre del pueblo, del estado y de la ciencia (. . .)*": Historia social de la salud pública, Chile 1880–1973*. Santiago: Colectivo de Atención Primaria, 1993.

———. "El proyecto comunal en Chile (fragmentos) 1810–1891." *Historia* (Santiago), no. 27 (1993): 213–329.

James, Daniel. "Poetry, Factory Labour, and Female Sexuality in Peronist Argentina." *Journal of Latin American Cultural Studies* 6, no. 2 (November 1997): 131–52.

———. *Resistance and Integration: Peronism and the Argentine Working Class, 1946–1976*. Cambridge: Cambridge University Press, 1988.

Jelin, Elizabeth, ed. *Women and Social Change in Latin America*. London: Zed Books, 1990.

Jensen, Jane. "Representations of Gender: Policies to 'Protect' Women Workers and Infants in France and the United States." In *Women, the State, and Welfare*, edited by Linda Gordon, 152–77. Madison: University of Wisconsin Press, 1990.

Jobet, Julio César. *El Partido Socialista de Chile*. 3rd ed. Santiago: Prensa Latinoamericana, 1971.

Joseph, Gilbert, and Daniel Nugent, eds. *Everyday Forms of State Formation: Revolution and the Negotiation of Rule in Modern Mexico*. Durham: Duke University Press, 1994.

Kaplan, Temma. "Female Consciousness and Collective Action: The Case of Barcelona, 1910–1918." *Signs* 7, no. 3 (Spring 1982): 545–66.

Kessler-Harris, Alice. "The Just Price, the Free Market, and the Value of Women." In *Gendered Domains: Rethinking Public and Private in Women's History*, edited by Dorothy Helly and Susan Reversby, 263–76. Ithaca: Cornell University Press, 1992.

Kirkwood, Julieta. *Ser política en Chile: Las feministas y los partidos*. Santiago: FLACSO, 1986.

Klaus, Alisa. "Depopulation and Race Suicide: Maternalism and Pronatalist Ideologies in France and the United States." In *Mothers of a New World: Maternalist Politics and the Origins of Welfare States*, edited by Seth Koven and Sonya Michel, 188–212. New York: Routledge, 1993.

Klubock, Thomas Miller. *Contested Communities: Class, Gender, and Politics in Chile's El Teniente Copper Mine, 1904–1951*. Durham: Duke University Press, 1998.

———. "Hombres y mujeres en El Teniente: La construcción de género y clase en la minería chilena del cobre, 1904–1951." In *Disciplina y desacato: Construcción de identidad en Chile, siglos XIX y XX*, edited by Lorena Godoy, Elizabeth Hutchison, Karin Rosemblatt, and M. Soledad Zárate, 223–53. Santiago: SUR/CEDEM, 1995.

———. "Sexualidad y proletarización en El Teniente." *Proposiciones* (Santiago), no. 21 (1992), 65–77.

Knight, Alan. "Racism, Revolution, and *Indigenismo*: Mexico, 1910–1940." In *The Idea of Race in Latin America*, 1870–1940, edited by Richard Graham, 71–113. Austin: University of Texas Press, 1990.

Koven, Seth, and Sonya Michel, eds. *Mothers of a New World: Maternalist Politics and the Origins of Welfare States*. New York: Routledge, 1993.

Laclau, Ernesto. *New Reflections on the Revolution of Our Time*. New York: Verso, 1990.

Laclau, Ernesto, and Chantal Mouffe. *Hegemony and Socialist Strategy: Towards a Radical Democratic Politics*. London: Verso, 1985.

Ladd-Taylor, Molly. "Toward Defining Maternalism in U.S. History." *Journal of Women's History* 5, no. 2 (Fall 1993): 110–13.

Lancaster, Roger. *Life Is Hard: Machismo, Danger, and the Intimacy of Power in Nicaragua*. Berkeley: University of California Press, 1992.

Landes, Joan. *Women and the Public Sphere in the Age of the French Revolution*. Ithaca: Cornell University Press, 1988.

Lavrin, Asunción. *Women, Feminism, and Social Change in Argentina, Chile, and Uruguay, 1890–1940*. Lincoln: University of Nebraska Press, 1995.

——. "Women, Labor, and the Left: Argentina and Chile, 1890–1925." *Journal of Women's History* 1, no. 2 (Fall 1989): 88–116.

Levenson-Estrada, Deborah. "The Loneliness of Working-Class Feminism: Women in the 'Male World' of Labor Unions, Guatemala City, 1970s." In *The Gendered Worlds of Latin American Women Workers: From the Household and Factory to the Union Hall and Ballot Box*, edited by John D. French and Daniel James, 208–31. Durham: Duke University Press, 1997.

Loveman, Brian. *Chile: The Legacy of Hispanic Capitalism*. New York: Oxford University Press, 1979.

——. "Political Participation and Rural Labor in Chile." In *Political Participation in Latin America*. Vol. 2 of *Politics and the Poor*, edited by Mitchell Seligson and John Boothe, 183–97. New York: Holmes and Meier, 1979.

McClintock, Anne, Aamir Mufti, and Ella Shohat, eds. *Dangerous Liaisons: Gender, Nation, and Postcolonial Perspectives*. Minneapolis: University of Minnesota Press, 1997.

Macías, Anna. *Against All Odds: The Feminist Movement in Mexico to 1940*. Westport, Conn.: Greenwood Press, 1982.

Mallon, Florencia. *Peasant and Nation: The Making of Postcolonial Mexico and Peru*. Berkeley: University of California Press, 1995.

——. "The Promise and Dilemma of Subaltern Studies: Perspectives from Latin American History." *American Historical Review* 99, no. 5 (December 1994): 1491–515.

Mandler, Peter, ed. *The Uses of Charity: The Poor on Relief in the Nineteenth-Century Metropolis*. Philadelphia: University of Pennsylvania Press, 1990.

Michel, Sonya. "The Limits of Maternalism: Policies toward American Wage-Earning Mothers during the Progressive Era." In *Mothers of a New World: Maternalist Politics and the Origins of Welfare States*, edited by Seth Koven and Sonya Michel, 277–320. New York: Routledge, 1993.

Middlebrook, Kevin. *The Paradox of Revolution: Labor, the State, and Authoritarianism in Mexico*. Baltimore: Johns Hopkins University Press, 1995.

Milkman, Ruth. "Gender and Trade Unionism in Historical Perspective." In *Women, Politics, and Change*, edited by Louise Tilly and Patricia Gurin, 87–107. New York: Russell Sage Foundation, 1990.

Molyneux, Maxine. "Mobilization without Emancipation? Women's Interests, the State, and Revolution in Nicaragua." *Feminist Studies* 11, no. 2 (Summer 1985): 227–54.

Morris, James. *Elites, Intellectuals, and Consensus: A Study of the Social Question and the Industrial Relations System in Chile*. Ithaca: Cornell University Press, 1966.

Mouffe, Chantal. "Hegemony and New Political Subjects: Toward a New Concept of Democracy." In *Marxism and the Interpretation of Culture*, edited by Cary Nelson and Lawrence Grossberg, 89–104. Urbana: University of Illinois Press, 1988.

——. *The Return of the Political*. London: Verso, 1993.

Moulian, Tomás. "Violencia, gradualismo y reformas en el desarrollo político chileno." In

Estudios sobre el sistema de partidos en Chile, by Adolfo Aldunate, Angel Flisfisch, and Tomás Moulian, 13–60. Santiago: FLACSO, 1985.

Moulian, Tomás, and Isabel Torres Dujisin, "Concepción de la política e ideal moral en la prensa obrera: 1919–1922." Santiago: FLACSO, Documento de Trabajo no. 336, 1987.

——. *Discusiones entre honorables: Las candidaturas presidenciales de la derecha,* 1938–1946. Santiago: FLACSO, n.d.

Muñoz Gomá, Oscar. *Chile y su industrialización: Pasado, crisis y opciones.* Santiago: CIEPLAN, 1986.

Norval, Aletta. "Letter to Ernesto." In *New Reflections on the Revolution of Our Time,* by Ernesto Laclau, 135–58. New York: Verso, 1990.

Nugent, Daniel, and Ana María Alonso. "Multiple Selective Traditions in Agrarian Reform and Agrarian Struggle: Popular Culture and State Formation in the Ejido of Namiquipa, Chihuahua." In *Everyday Forms of State Formation: Revolution and the Negotiation of Rule in Modern Mexico,* edited by Gilbert Joseph and Daniel Nugent, 209–46. Durham: Duke University Press, 1994.

Nunn, Frederick. *Chilean Politics, 1920–1931: The Honorable Mission of the Armed Forces.* Albuquerque: University of New Mexico Press, 1970.

O'Hanlon, Rosalind. "Recovering the Subject: *Subaltern Studies* and the Histories of Resistance in Colonial South Asia." *Modern Asian Studies* 22, no. 1 (February 1988): 189–224.

Ortega, Luis. "La industria del carbón entre 1840 y 1880." Santiago: Cuadernos de Humanidades, Universidad de Santiago, 1988.

——, ed. *La Guerra Civil de 1891: Cien años hoy.* Santiago: Universidad de Santiago, 1991.

Owensby, Brian. *Intimate Ironies: Modernity and the Making of Middle-Class Lives in Brazil.* Stanford: Stanford University Press, 1999.

Parker, Andrew, Mary Russo, Doris Sommer, and Patricia Yaeger. *Nationalisms and Sexualities.* New York: Routledge, 1989.

Parker, David S. *The Idea of the Middle Class: White-Collar Workers and Peruvian Society, 1900–1950.* University Park: Pennsylvania State University Press, 1998.

Pateman, Carole. *The Disorder of Women: Democracy, Feminism and Political Theory.* Stanford: Stanford University Press, 1989.

Pedersen, Susan. "Catholicism, Feminism, and the Politics of the Family during the Late Third Republic." In *Mothers of a New World: Maternalist Politics and the Origins of Welfare States,* edited by Seth Koven and Sonya Michel, 246–76. New York: Routledge, 1993.

Phillips, Anne. *Democracy and Difference.* University Park: Pennsylvania State University Press, 1993.

Pimstein, Abraham. "Algunas referencias históricas para el estudio de la medicina pública en Chile, desde la Conquista hasta la fusión de los servicios médico-sociales 1541–1952." *Cuadernos de Bibliotecología y Documentación,* no. 1. Santiago: Escuela de Bibliotecología, Universidad de Chile, 1970.

Pinto, Julio. *Trabajos y rebeldías en la pampa salitrera: El ciclo del salitre y la reconfiguración de las identidades populares* (1850–1900). Santiago: Universidad de Santiago, 1998.

Pinto Santa Cruz, Aníbal. *Chile: Un caso de desarrollo frustrado.* Santiago: Editorial Universitaria, 1962.

Pizarro, Crisóstomo. *La huelga obrera en Chile: 1890–1979.* Santiago: SUR, 1986.

Poblete, Olga. *Una mujer: Elena Caffarena.* Santiago: La Morada/Editorial Cuarto Propio, 1993.

Poovey, Mary. *Uneven Developments: The Ideological Work of Gender in Mid-Victorian England.* Chicago: University of Chicago Press, 1988.

Poulantzas, Nicos. *State, Power, Socialism.* London: Verso, 1980.

Prakash, Gyan. "Writing Post-Orientalist Histories of the Third World: Indian Historiography

Is Good to Think." In *Colonialism and Culture*, edited by Nicholas B. Dirks, 353–87. Ann Arbor: University of Michigan Press, 1992.

Ramírez Necochea, Hernán. *Origen y formación del Partido Comunista de Chile.* Santiago: Editora Austral, 1965.

Remmer, Karen. "The Timing, Pace and Sequence of Political Change in Chile." *Hispanic American Historical Review* 57, no. 2 (May 1977): 205–30.

Reyes Alvarez, Jaime. "Los presidentes radicales y su partido. Chile, 1938–1952." Santiago: Centro de Estudios Públicos, Documento de Trabajo no. 120, 1989.

Rojas Flores, Jorge. *La dictadura de Ibáñez y los sindicatos (1927–1931).* Santiago: Dirección de Bibliotecas, Archivos y Museos, 1993.

Rojas Flores, Jorge, Alfonso Murúa Olguín, and Gonzalo Rojas Flores. *Historia de los obreros de la construcción.* Santiago: Programa de Economía del Trabajo, 1993.

Romero, Luis Alberto. "Condiciones de vida de los sectores populares en Santiago de Chile, 1840–1895: Vivienda y salud." *Nueva Historia* (London) 3, no. 9 (1984): 3–86.

———. "Rotos y gañanes: Trabajadores no calificados en Santiago, 1850–1895." *Cuadernos de Historia* (Santiago), no. 8 (December 1988): 35–71.

Rose, Sonya. "Respectable Men, Disorderly Others: The Language of Gender and the Lancashire Weavers' Strike of 1878 in Britain." *Gender and History* 5, no. 3 (Autumn 1993): 382–97.

Roseberry, William. "Hegemony and the Language of Contention." In *Everyday Forms of State Formation: Revolution and the Negotiation of Rule in Modern Mexico*, edited by Gilbert Joseph and Daniel Nugent, 355–66. Durham: Duke University Press, 1994.

Rubin, Jeffrey W. *Decentering the Regime: Ethnicity, Radicalism, and Democracy in Juchitán, Mexico.* Durham: Duke University Press, 1997.

Sabrovsky, Eduardo. *Hegemonía y racionalidad política: Contribución a una teoría democrática del cambio.* Santiago: Ornitorrinco, 1989.

Safford, Frank. "Race, Integration, and Progress: Elite Attitudes and the Indian in Colombia, 1750–1870." *Hispanic American Historical Review* 71, no. 1 (February 1991): 1–33.

Salazar, Gabriel. "La mujer de 'bajo pueblo' en Chile: Bosquejo histórico." *Proposiciones* (Santiago), no. 21 (1992), 89–107.

———. "Ser niño huacho en la historia de Chile." *Proposiciones* (Santiago), no. 19 (1990): 55–83.

Sangari, Kumkum, and Sudesh Vaid, eds. *Recasting Women: Essays in Colonial History.* New Delhi: Kali for Women, 1989.

Sassoon, Anne Showstack, ed. *Women and the State: The Shifting Boundaries of Public and Private.* London: Unwin Hyman, 1987.

Scott, Joan. *Gender and the Politics of History.* New York: Columbia University Press, 1988.

———. *Only Paradoxes to Offer: French Feminists and the Rights of Man.* Cambridge, Mass.: Harvard University Press, 1996.

Scully, Timothy. *Rethinking the Center: Party Politics in Nineteenth- and Twentieth-Century Chile.* Stanford: Stanford University Press, 1992.

Sinha, Mrinalini. "Gender in the Critiques of Colonialism and Nationalism: Locating the 'Indian Woman.'" In *Feminism and History*, edited by Joan Scott, 477–504. New York: Oxford University Press, 1996.

Skocpol, Theda. *Protecting Soldiers and Mothers: The Political Origins of Social Policy in the United Sates.* Cambridge, Mass.: Harvard University Press, 1992.

Spivak, Gayatri. "Can the Subaltern Speak?" In *Marxism and the Interpretation of Culture*, edited by Cary Nelson and Lawrence Grossberg, 271–313. Urbana: University of Illinois Press, 1988.

Stepan, Nancy. *"The Hour of Eugenics": Race, Gender, and Nation in Latin America.* Ithaca: Cornell University Press, 1991.

Stern, Steve J. *The Secret History of Gender: Women, Men, and Power in Late Colonial Mexico.* Chapel Hill: University of North Carolina Press, 1995.

Stevenson, John Reese. *The Chilean Popular Front.* Westport, Conn.: Greenwood Press, 1942.

Stoler, Ann Laura. *Race and the Education of Desire: Foucault's History of Sexuality and the Colonial Order of Things.* Durham: Duke University Press, 1996.

Stoner, K. Lynn. *From the House to the Streets: The Cuban Woman's Movement for Legal Reform, 1898–1940.* Durham: Duke University Press, 1991.

Thane, Pat. "Women in the British Labour Party and the Construction of State Welfare, 1906–1939." In *Mothers of a New World: Maternalist Politics and the Origins of Welfare States,* edited by Seth Koven and Sonya Michel, 343–77. New York: Routledge, 1993.

Tinsman, Heidi. "Los patrones del hogar: Esposas golpeadas y control sexual en Chile rural, 1958–1988." In *Disciplina y desacato: Construcción de identidad en Chile, siglos XIX y XX,* edited by Lorena Godoy, Elizabeth Hutchison, Karin Rosemblatt, and M. Soledad Zárate, 111–46. Santiago: SUR / CEDEM, 1995.

Urzúa Valenzuela, Germán. *Historia política de Chile y su evolución electoral (desde 1810 a 1992).* Santiago: Editorial Jurídica, 1992.

Urzúa Valenzuela, Germán, and Anamaría García Barzelatto. *Diagnóstico de la burocracia chilena, 1818–1969.* Santiago: Editorial Jurídica, 1971.

Valdés, Teresa, Marisa Weinstein, Isabel Toledo, and Lilian Letelier. "Centros de madres 1973–1989: ¿Sólo disciplinamiento?" Santiago: FLACSO, Documento de Trabajo no. 416, 1989.

Valdés, Ximena, Sonia Montecino, Kirai de León, and Macarena Mark. *Historias testimoniales de mujeres del campo.* Santiago: CEM, 1983.

Valenzuela, Arturo. *The Breakdown of Democratic Regimes: Chile.* Baltimore: Johns Hopkins University Press, 1978.

——. *Political Brokers in Chile: Local Government in a Centralized Polity.* Durham: Duke University Press, 1977.

Valenzuela, Arturo, and Alexander Wilde. "Presidential Politics and the Decline of the Chilean Congress." In *Legislatures in Development,* edited by Ian Smith and Louis Musolf, 189–215. Durham: Duke University Press, 1979.

Varas, Augusto, comp. *El Partido Comunista en Chile.* Santiago: CESOC / FLACSO, 1988.

Vaughan, Mary Kay. *Cultural Politics in Revolution: Teachers, Peasants, and Schools in Mexico, 1930–1940.* Tucson: University of Arizona Press, 1997.

——. "Modernizing Patriarchy: State Policies and Rural Households in Mexico, 1930–1940." In *Hidden Histories of Gender and the State in Latin America,* edited by Elizabeth Dore and Maxine Molyneux, 194–214. Durham: Duke University Press, 2000.

Verba, Ericka. "The Círculo de Lectura [Ladies' Reading Circle] and the Club de Señoras [Ladies' Club] of Santiago, Chile: Middle- and Upper-Class Feminist Conversations (1915–1920)." *Journal of Women's History* 7, no. 3 (Fall 1995): 6–33.

Weinstein, Barbara. *For Social Peace in Brazil: Industrialists and the Remaking of the Working Class in São Paulo, 1920–1964.* Chapel Hill: University of North Carolina Press, 1996.

——. "Unskilled Worker, Skilled Housewife: Constructing the Working-Class Housewife in São Paulo, Brazil, 1900–1950." In *The Gendered Worlds of Latin American Women Workers: From the Household and Factory to the Union Hall and Ballot Box,* edited by John D. French and Daniel James, 72–99. Durham: Duke University Press, 1997.

White, Luise. "Separating the Men from the Boys: Constructions of Gender, Sexuality, and

Terrorism in Central Kenya, 1939–1958." *International Journal of African Historical Studies* 23, no. 1 (1990): 1–25.

Winn, Peter. *Weavers of Revolution: The Yarur Workers and Chile's Road to Socialism.* New York: Oxford University Press, 1986.

Wolfe, Joel. *Working Women, Working Men: São Paulo and the Rise of Brazil's Industrial Working Class.* Durham: Duke University Press, 1993.

Yanagisako, Sylvia, and Jane Collier. "Toward a Unified Analysis of Gender and Kinship." In *Gender and Kinship: Essays toward a Unified Analysis,* edited by Jane Collier and Sylvia Yanagisako, 14–50. Stanford: Stanford University Press, 1987.

Yanagisako, Sylvia, and Carol Delaney. "Naturalizing Power." In *Naturalizing Power: Essays in Feminist Cultural Analysis,* edited by Sylvia Yanagisako and Carol Delaney, 1–22. New York: Routledge, 1995.

Zeitlin, Maurice. *The Civil Wars in Chile.* Princeton: Princeton University Press, 1984.

Zimmerman, Eduardo A. "Racial Ideas and Social Reform: Argentina, 1890–1916." *Hispanic American Historical Review* 72, no. 1 (February 1992): 23–46.

INDEX

Abortion, 166, 168–69, 173, 213
Acción de Mujeres Socialistas (AMS, Socialist Women's Action), 98, 100
Agency, 3, 15, 259, 274; subaltern, 13, 18, 20; feminist, 19; of men, 23, 159–61, 165, 166, 174, 175, 180; working-class, 28, 190, 191, 238; of women, 167, 176–78, 205, 232
Aguirre, Juanita, 39
Aguirre Cerda, Pedro, 6, 27, 46, 49, 57, 62, 85, 86, 153
Alcohol consumption: MEMCh and, 106; state and, 150, 162–65, 181; women and, 165–67; Left and, 189, 190, 193–95, 196, 197, 221; Communist Party and, 218; in Brazil, 272. See also Vices, men's
Alessandri, Arturo, 30–31, 33
Alianza Democrática, 8
Allende, Salvador, 27–28, 37, 39, 40, 124, 129, 134–35, 153, 159–61, 172, 175, 178, 199
Alliances, 18–20; between elites and subaltern classes, 4, 94, 266–67, 269, 273–74; crosscutting of, 193, 227, 228, 274. See also Solidarity; Unity, working-class
AMS. See Acción de Mujeres Socialistas
Anti-Communism. See Repression: post-1947
Antifeminism, 22, 97, 101–4, 261
Anti-intellectualism, 22, 97, 108, 111, 112–13, 115, 120, 122, 260
Argentina, 266–67
Asociación de Dueñas de Casa (Housewives' Association), 119–20, 121, 232, 238, 259, 264
Association of University Women, 233
Astica, María, 86, 237–38
Autonomy, 117–19, 191–93, 207, 296 (n. 52); subaltern, 10, 18, 19–20, 227, 266–67, 274; individual, 11; of feminists, 19, 22, 96, 111–12, 114, 115, 122, 236, 262; of men, 68; of women, 150, 151, 167, 173–74, 271; of Left, 189–90, 196–99; of consumer move-

ment, 264. See also Disciplinary practices: subaltern reformulations of; Labor movement: militancy and autonomy of; Men: defiance of gendered norms; Women: defiance of gendered norms; Working class: militancy and autonomy of

Beneficencia (Beneficent Aid Society), 29, 126, 127, 129, 144–45, 146, 169
Berman, Natalio, 37, 134
Betting. See Vices, men's
Birth control, 169, 173, 213
Bourgeois-democratic revolution, 34, 40, 102–3, 104, 114, 261, 294 (nn. 18, 19)
Braden Copper Company. See El Teniente
Brazil, 266–67, 269–70, 272–73
Breast-feeding, 29, 81, 172
Bronfman, Eliana, 237–38, 240

Caffarena, Elena, 93, 95, 107, 122, 240, 261, 262; personal archive of, 20; on women's work, 80, 83–88; on day care, 82; founds MEMCh, 99–100; and popular-front politics, 101–2; resigns MEMCh, 111–13; on gender differences, 113–14, 250; returns to MEMCh, 116; eschews clientelism, 236–37; on democracy, 248–49
Caja de Seguro Obligatorio (CSO, Obligatory Insurance Fund), 125, 126, 132–35, 264; CTCh and, 7; creation of, 31; allies with workers, 62, 132, 263, 266; maternity subsidies and day care, 81, 82; and worker entitlement, 123–24, 256; expansion of, 126–27; workers support, 130, 144–45, 146; dissolution of, 147; educates workers, 153; benefits, and constitution of family, 154–55; and recreation, 163–64; and single mothers, 169–70; and venereal disease, 178, 179
Campesinos. See Countryside
Campusano, Julieta, 118, 234
Cañas, Luz, 151–52, 156, 157, 159
Capitalists: immorality of, 189–90, 203–4, 205, 207, 210, 256; Left blames for

78–79, 87–88, 89, 90–91, 140, 291 (n. 65); women's exclusion from, 64, 76–78, 81, 85
Labor movement, 64, 65, 186, 263–64; militancy and autonomy of, 5, 7–8, 60, 61, 264, 266; alliance of men and women workers in, 22, 77–78, 88–94, 260, 262; and Arturo Alessandri, 30; co-opted by Ibáñez, 31–32; and popular-front alliance, 50–51, 255–56; and family wage, 68, 70, 285 (n. 59); in Latin America, 267–68. See also Confederación de Trabajadores de Chile
Lacoste, Graciela, 234
Lafferte, Elías, 55, 106. See also Hijo del salitre
La Mujer Nueva (newspaper), 105. See also Movimiento pro Emancipación de la Mujer Chilena
La realidad médico-social chilena (Allende), 153, 159–61, 172, 175
La sangre y la esperanza (Guzmán), 74, 185–88, 190
Laundering. See Domestic service
Laws: labor and welfare, 29, 30, 31, 260, 263; minimum-wage, 35; family allowance, 60, 62, 64–65, 67, 70–71, 288 (n. 24); maternity, 80–82, 169; wage, discriminatory toward women, 84, 89–90; and constitution of family, 153–54; application of maternity, 289 (n. 42). See also Civil Code; Labor Code; Protective labor legislation; Wage: minimum
Lazo, Carmen, 54, 199, 200, 204, 205
Leadership, 16–18, 19–20, 122, 251, 266, 279 (n. 28); popular-front, 8–9, 40; within subaltern groups, 20; vanguardist, 56, 57, 254, 273, 274; of Left, 114, 188, 194, 215, 218–23, 224–26, 226–29, 255; of professionals, 151–52, 258; of Communist Party, 217–18; of MEMCh, 238; of women's movement, 240
Left: mediates between popular-front leaders and popular classes, 5–6, 7, 268; and ministerial posts, 15; pre-1938, 28, 189–90; conflict within, 34–35; and MEMCh, 95–97, 100–104; members of, employed by state, 124; and science, 128–29; and professionals, 187; and progress, 192; and recreation, 195–97; and women's sexual virtue, 198–207; and marriage, 208–12; divisions within, and morality, 218–23; hierarchy within,

224–25; and working-class constituents, 226–28; and popular-front leaders, 260. See also Bourgeois-democratic revolution; Socialist morality
Leftist: defined, 277 (n. 2)
Lesbianism, 103, 109
Ley de defensa de la democracia (law for the defense of democracy). See Repression: post-1947
Liga de Consumidores, 117–19
Literacy, 6, 57, 155–56, 157, 190, 242, 278 (n. 9)

Mallol Pemjean, Mario, 219–20
Mandujano, Graciela, 113, 116, 117, 118, 120, 236, 259
Marchant, María, 233
Markmann de González Videla, Rosa, 55, 119
Marriage, 150–54, 166, 171–72, 173, 174, 201–3, 208–12, 222, 260
Marxism, 11–12, 15
Masculinity, 162–67, 244–45, 254–57, 284 (n. 53), 285 (n. 2), 287 (n. 23); and work, 50, 52–54, 59–60, 94, 123–25, 162; housewives and, 72–73; and male sociability, 74, 151, 162, 196–99; and vice, 100, 150, 191; and sexuality, 175; Left and, 208–18; and divisions within Left, 218–23; and the state, 302 (n. 26); and working-class militancy and autonomy, 302 (n. 29)
Material rewards. See Incentives, material
Maternalism, 240
Maternal refuges, 169, 176, 235
Maternity benefits. See Laws: maternity; Laws: application of maternity
Medicalization, 47, 48, 128–29, 142, 151–52
Medicine, social. See Social medicine
MEMCh. See Movimiento pro Emancipación de la Mujer Chilena
Men: as breadwinners, 59–76 passim; and professionals, 142–45; responsibilities toward family, 149, 153–56, 171, 174–75, 185–87, 208–9, 212, 253, 271; defiance of gendered norms, 151, 159, 161–63, 173–74, 180–81, 183, 254, 257, 302 (nn. 26, 29); and alcohol, 165–66, 194–95; and Left, 211, 213–15, 219–20; authority within family, 231, 255; contributions to nation, 256;